PRESIDENTIAL COMMUNICATION AND NEWS MEDIA

How Do News Media Flatter Or Criticize The President?

대통령과 언론, 친구인가 적인가

이 책은 방일영문화재단의 지원을 받아 저술 · 출판되었습니다

PRESIDENTIAL
COMMUNICATION
AND NEWS MEDIA

How Do News Media Flatter Or Criticize The President?
대 통 령 과   언 론 , 친 구 인 가   적 인 가

Won Tai Seol · 설 원 태

nBook

TABLE OF CONTENTS

PREFACE

The author has been interested in American presidency from around 1995 while working as an international news reporter. Foreign news, and American affairs in particular, have intrigued the author. While working as a foreign news reporter, the author has been concerned with news from the United States. That led the author to focus on the U.S. presidents, whose power can move and shape America and the world. Part of the reasons for the author's interest in American presidency and American affairs might have been that the author's college and graduate major was English, to be specific, English education and that the author has been interested in international affairs. Foreign language majors normally have keen interest in the country of the language they studied.

The author's interest in American presidency led to reading books on that topic. The author has read books such as: *The American Presidency: Origins and Development, 1776-1993, 2nd Ed.* (1994, Milkis & Nelson); *The Presidency and the Political System, 4th Ed.* (1995, Nelson Ed.); *Presidential Leadership: Politics and Policy Making, 3rd Ed.* (1994, Edwards & Wayne); Ibid, 6th Ed. (2003); *The Press and the Presidency: From George Washington to Ronald Reagan* (1985, Tebbel & Watts); *Understanding the Presidency, 3rd Ed.* (2003, Pfiffner & Davidson); *Portraying the President: the White House and the News Media* (1981, Grossman & Kumar); *The White House World: Transitions, Organization, and Office*

Operation (2003, Kumar & Sullivan, Ed.); *Mass Media and American Politics* (2002, Graber); *The President and The Public* (1982, Graber); and *News: The Politics of Illusion, Third Ed.* (1996, Bennett), and so forth. Reading these books made the author more sensitive to functions of the U.S. presidents and presidential communication. Portions or all of these books deal with presidency and news media. As a journalist, the author came to think about linking presidency and news media. A decade of personal interest in this area led the author to study the topic of "presidential communication" and how journalists report on the presidency, that is, media's portrayal of the president.

While taking graduate courses in journalism at San Jose State University, California, U.S.A., from August 2002 to December 2003, the author wrote a Master of Science thesis titled *Presidential Image of George W. Bush as Depicted by the New York Times*. The author read various journalism books during this period. This book may be an extension of the master's thesis by including President Roh Moo Hyun's image as described by the *Kyunghyang Daily News*. This book is a combination of literature review of presidential communication theories and an analysis of newspaper coverage of George W. Bush as printed by the *New York Times* and that of Roh Moo Hyun as portrayed by the *Kyunghayng Daily News*. In a word, this is a book of presidential communication and journalism interacting with each other.

There are only limited number of books on Korean presidents in Korea. Books on presidential communication may be even fewer. Most of the books on Korean presidents are in the form of memoirs, writings by journalists or presidential assistants as observers. There are few systematic and scholarly studies on Korean presidents and fewer studies on presidential communication. Considering that presidents play a crucial role in the course of a country and that presidential communication can make or break the presidential politics and his policy implementation, studies of presidency and presidential communication need to be more active in Korea.

President Roh Moo Hyun (presidency, February 2003 to February 2008) has generated a slew of troubles with conservative newspapers of Korea since his inauguration. The author's wish is that Roh's and his successors' communication skills get more refined and sophisticated in order not to create unnecessary conflicts with the media. President George W. Bush has not been very satisfied with media coverage of the Iraq War since the second half of 2003. But he rarely vented his dissatisfaction with the news media. Instead, Bush's publicity team has made every effort to get better coverage from the media in other ways. The author is assured that presidents' mastering of communication skills and journalists' refined and profound reporting of the presidency can contribute to the stability and efficiency of presidential political processes. Under Roh government's rule, relations between Roh and conservative newspapers have been too rocky and will be so during the remainder of his term.

January 5, 2005
Won Tai Seol

CHAPTER **I**

Events that are congruent with media routines are more likely to be covered than discongruent events. News that is off the beaten path (e.g., not on the journalists' beat) may go unreported. Issues and events that don't include good film/video footage may not be included in television newscasts. A press conference held just before a newspaper's deadline is more likely to be included than one just after. Events that fit an organization's definition of news are more likely to be covered (Routines of Media Work 1: Shoemaker & Reese, 1996, p. 265).

WHY SHOULD WE
DISCUSS PRESIDENTIAL COVERAGE?

Overview of Book

This book discusses ongoing interactions between presidency and journalism. Presidents use a variety of strategies to get favorable coverage from news media; and journalists have their own unlimited ways of reporting on the presidents either positively or negatively. The two are constantly striving to set the public agenda by sending their respective messages to the public with a view to having the public on their side. One can safely say that the two are always competing or cooperating to take the initiative, to set the public agenda, and finally to define the situation of a country. Part of the balance sheet pertaining to this strife may be media's daily news coverage of the presidency.

This book on the one hand shows how dissatisfied American presidents have been with media coverage of them and how their dissatisfaction was misguided, what tactics or strategies they use to get pleasing coverage, how the two sides compete and cooperate to decide on stories, and how Bush's publicity machine operates. The book on the other hand presents how news media frame presidential stories, what the nature of White House beat is, and how news media cover the presidency positively or negatively. Theoretical discussion was largely drawn from literature on American presidency.

After discussion of presidential communication and media's story framing, this book embarks on actual research of presidential coverage of the *New York Times* and the *Kyunghyang Daily*

News. The same research methods were used for both newspapers. After analysis of the two newspapers, this book attempts to make a generalization as to how news media can portray the president positively or negatively.

This book examined presidential coverage of Geroge W. Bush as portrayed by the *New York Times* and then that of Roh Moo Hyun as portrayed by the *Kyunghyang Daily News* (The Kyunghyang Shinmun). At the time of this writing (July 2003 to December 2004), the presidency of Bush and that of Roh are an ongoing political phenomenon. Bush's first term of office was scheduled to terminate in January 2005 and Roh's term will end in February 2008. With President Bush's election victory in November 2, 2004, his second term will end in January 20, 2009.

First, this book analyzes President George W. Bush's imagery as portrayed by the *New York Times* during four crucial time spans in his presidency: Bush's inauguration in January of 2001; September 11 terrorist attacks in 2001; War against terrorism (or War against the Taliban regime in Afghanistan) in October 2001; and War against Iraq (or Second Persian Gulf War) in March 2003.

After a month of indecision about the outcome of the presidential election, President-elect Texas Governor George W. Bush did not have enough time to form his cabinet. Bush administration started weak, with no conspicuous mandate and with popular vote losing to his presidential contender Al Gore. The September 11 terrorist attacks on American soil marked a dividing line in the sense of national security or insecurity in American minds. The national infamy and psychological shocks experienced by Americans posed a serious challenge for President Bush. This nation needed a "national soother" and a "crisis leader" for the victims and Americans on the whole. The retaliatory war against the Taliban which followed the terrorist attacks meant that President Bush led the nation as a wartime leader. The war in Afghanistan increased in intensity gradually, first by bombing and then by sending in troops. The Second Persian Gulf War that started in March of 2003 was another opportunity for Mr. Bush to serve the nation as a wartime leader. Despite the pros and cons over the two wars against terrorism, it is undeniable that Mr. Bush led Americans through the two wars.

Generally speaking, strong national leadership is required during these critical periods, especially, during the wartime. The above four periods may be very crucial in Bush's presidency. The war against terrorism in Afghanistan and the war against Iraq were controversial, given the domestic and international opposition. Under these critical circumstances, how the New York Times depicted President Bush can be a matter of grave concern. Did it portray him in a favorable light, highlighting his national and international leadership role, and thus advancing his policy goals? Did this newspaper portray the Bush administration in a negative light by directly or indirectly criticizing him, by conveying messages of Bush's critics or political opponents? Next, this book analyzes President Roh Moo Hyun's imagery as portrayed by the *Kyunghyang Daily* during six crucial time spans in his presidency: Roh's inauguration in February 2003; Proposal of confidence vote in October 2003; Pre-impeachment; Impeachment resolution by the National Assembly in March 2004; General election on April 2004; Resumption of presidential function by the ruling of the Constitutional Court in May 2004. In such a short duration of time, Roh experienced fierce ups and downs in his presidency. In these crucial research periods, it may be worthwhile to look into news coverage of the presidency as portrayed by a major newspaper. How did this newspaper describe Roh in his first month? How did this newspaper report when Roh suddenly proposed confidence vote? How did this paper portray Roh just before he was impeached, after he was impeached, when Roh-backed Woori Party won the general election, and when he resumed his presidential functions? And how did this paper portray Roh positively or negatively in these research periods? This book seeks to answer these questions.

Why Is Presidential Coverage Significant?

People are exposed to presidential news almost daily. They know what the president says or does through media reports. News stories about George W. Bush, the 43rd President of the United States of America, are so pervasive that not only American people but also people worldwide are interested in the presidential coverage conveyed by the news media. The same may hold true for President Roh Moo Hyun. What Roh says or does, or even what he thinks about or he plans to do is conveyed through news media.

The pervasiveness of presidential news may be a reflection of the importance of the presidential news. Presidency scholars George C. Edwards and Steven J. Wayne (1994) presented several research findings to show that almost three-fourths of national government news focuses on the president. This may be either the result of the public's demand for presidential news or the result of the White House's aggressive publicity efforts to supply presidential news.

Presidential communication, emanating from the White House or the Blue House (or, Chung Wa Dae), is arguably the utmost political communication mediated through news media or non-news media. It can be said that in this mediation process journalists on the one hand and the president or the White House and Blue House publicity personnel on the other are continuously engaged in the wrangling over the newsworthiness of presidential coverage. The end product of these interactive processes are the news reports of the president, which may be either positive, neutral, or negative toward the president. In this vein, studying presidential image or presidential coverage conveyed by a news medium may mean analyzing the end result of interactions between journalists of a news organization and the White House or the Blue House publicity machine.

An understanding of presidential image in the media will equip consumers of presidential news with a better understanding of presidential politics and policy implementation. This understanding is all the more important, because policies made and implemented by the president can lead the whole country to a completely different destination. Understanding the mechanisms of the presidential image conveyed by the media will enable the public to look at the reverse side of the news stories. This means that news or image manipulation may be conducted by the White House or Blue House publicity officials. In a democratic society, building of public agenda and making policies can be achieved through political procedures along which mass media convey the presidential image, the manners in which the presidential image is received and processed by the public, and the ways in which the publics shape their opinions based on the media image of the president.

Many scholars and media practitioners say that the proportion of television news coverage is increasingly significant in domestic and international politics. Political scientist Doris A. Graber (2002) especially placed heavy emphasis on the importance of television in the modern political processes. She implied that television is perhaps more important than any major East Coast newspapers in America. However, it is undeniable that the *New York Times* is one of the major news media that play an important role in setting the political agenda in America. It should also be acknowledged that this newspaper largely reflects liberal voices in American society (Fallows, 1997; Graber, 2002).

The author will seek to analyze the presidential image conveyed by the *New York Times* for two reasons. First, this newspaper is one of the most influential Eastern news organizations, which report detailed movements of the American government. Second, *The New York Times* fairly frequently leads the tone of news coverage of certain events in American news media and sometimes in news media of the world. Political scientists Michael B. Grossman and Martha Joynt Kumar (1982) wrote that the *New York Times* purports to be the "newspaper of the record" as compared with other news media. They described this newspaper as:

The *New York Times* closely follows what a president does each day: the speeches he gives, the news conferences he holds, his business trips, ceremonies, and bill-signings. The *New York Times* is a newspaper of the record. Because of that emphasis, its stories record presidential events and actions in detail. They provide a complete treatment of what happened, who was involved, and what it means (Graber, 1982, pp. 105-08).

The present author realized that the *New York Times* frequently ran transcripts or excerpts of important presidential addresses or other important politicians. Considering the comparative importance of the *New York Times* news in the agenda-setting functions, analysis of this newspaper's coverage of the Bush presidency may be meaningful. It is also true that this newspaper was led to support U.S. government policy lines, that is, Bush's war on Iraq, as was shown by Ben Bagdikian (2004, p. 81-84).

President George W. Bush will be recorded in American history as the president who conducted the first war in the 21st century, even though the justifiability of the "war on terrorism" may need more discussion. While staging the war on Afghanistan and Iraq, Bush's presidency has transformed itself. He started as a weak president with little mandate (or, small *political capital*), but he was granted broad powers to wage the anti-terrorism war after September 11 attacks. It will be meaningful to examine how the *New York Times* portrayed Bush's presidency in this crucial modern era.

President Roh Moo Hyun won the election that few anticipated him to win. Roh professed that he would pursue reforms but he has met with systematic and persistent resistance within the administration and the establishment. Roh and his team were not mainstreamers heretofore. Continued scandals and investigation involving his aides and relatives decreased his popularity ever since his office-taking. His proposal of confidence vote and presidential impeachment by the Korean National Assembly created crisis situations for Roh. Newspaper coverage of Roh became polarized and broadcasters largely portrayed him favorably, while conservative newspapers such as *Chosun Ilbo* and *Donga Ilbo* described him in a negative light. During these critical periods of Roh presidency, it may be worthwhile to look into news coverage of him by a Korean newspaper, the *Kyunghyang Daily News*.

Presidential News Is Growing Important

Plenty of news stories about President George W. Bush's activities or President Roh Moo Hyun's are easily available today merely by accessing news stories online, watching television, or reading newspapers or newsmagazines. It is easy to turn to television sets or newspapers to learn about what President Bush or President Roh has said or done and about the public's reactions. Technological innovations such as electric printing press, cable television, satellite TV, the Internet, plus increasing literacy of people have made it easier for people of today to access mass-circulation newspapers or television news or non-news programs which carry a variety of presidential news.

But things have not always been this way. Before the Civil War (1861-65) in America, newspapers were generally small, heavily partisan, and limited in circulation. In the 20th century, a view of presidential leadership different from that of the founding era of more than 200 years ago began to emerge in America. The new outlook --- one in which the president advances his policy agenda through direct popular leadership --- developed both out of the perceived necessity of bold national leadership and out of the words and deeds of "strong" presidents. Dramatic changes were occurring in American politics and abroad. The expansion of American federal government's role during the Spanish-American War (1898) and World War I (1914-18) kindled support for and great interest in the activities of the government in Washington. The increased interest in national affairs was also caused by the renewed prominence of presidency following a long era of congressional ascendancy. Theodore Roosevelt (presidency, 1901-09) maintained that the president must act as a "steward" of the people. Roosevelt, who took an activist view of the presidency, exploited the new opportunities to reach the public provided by the mass-circulation press. Roosevelt used the White House as a "bully pulpit" to dramatize himself and the issues in which he was interested. He sought and gained extensive access to the press in order to forge a more personal relationship with the American people.

Ever since Theodore Roosevelt occupied the White House, news about the president has played an increasingly prominent role in the printed press, both in absolute terms and relative to coverage of Congress or the national government as a whole. Research on contemporary presidency has found that almost three-fourths of national government news focuses on the president (Edwards and Wayne, 1994, p. 137, p. 166).

In addition to the increase in the quantity of news, the number of reporters who cover the White House has increased. This may be closely correlated with the increase in presidential coverage. The White House press corps has grown, with much of the increase having taken place in recent decades. Political scientist John H. Kessel (2001) stated that about 1,700 persons hold White House credentials today. During Franklin D. Roosevelt's administration (presidency, 1933-45), the number of the reporters who covered the White House full-time and attended the press secretary's daily briefings (or, the "regulars") was 15 to 20, and decades later no more than 22. By the time of Gerald R. Ford administration (presidency, 1974-77), 60 reporters attended press secretary Ron Nessen's briefings, and roughly 100 regulars covered the Carter White House (presidency, 1977-81). The sheer number of the journalists makes the news briefings more formal, Kessel remarked. These days about 70 reporters and 15 photographers regularly cover the White House and crank out massive presidential stories and photos almost everyday (Kessel, 2001, pp. 57-58).

Given the high percentage of news coverage accorded the president, do presidents really matter to the news organizations?

Political scientists Timothy E. Cook and Lyn Ragsdale (1995) showed how important the presidential news can be to news media:

In recent decades, the White House has become more and more the central newsbeat in Washington, making the president the central protagonist not only of that beat, but perhaps of the entire national news --- especially of television news, in which the White House story commonly leads the broadcast. To a greater extent than any other political actors in the United States, presidents have reporters come to them rather than having to seek the reporters out. The media presume that, because of the president's centrality as head of state and head of government, virtually anything that presidents do could well be newsworthy. Indeed the president is probably the only political figure whose activities are followed 24 hours a day in the United States or in any other country which adopted the presidential system. One Washington bureau chief morbidly (but candidly) told the sociologist Herbert Gans that "they might cover the president expecting that he would die (Nelson, 1995, p. 306)."

Why Does Presidential Coverage Matter?

Political scientist Richard Neustadt (1960) emphasized the importance of persuasion as the source of presidential power. Neustadt noted that the challenge for activist presidents is to leverage their powers to persuade others to do what the president wants done. He argued that presidential power is "the power to persuade (Nelson, 1995, p. 302)." Presidential persuasion of today implies a very important aspect of presidential leadership. Presidents attempt to persuade other politicians by bargaining or domination (Kerbel, 1991). Presidents may also appeal directly to the people (or, "go public") for policy goals.

Considering these means of persuasion, mass media can be a convenient way to persuade the public. Nowadays, so many newspapers, major TV networks, and round-the-clock cable television stations cover the White House that the president can muster support from these mass media to pursue his policy goals. (How about the Blue House in Korea? The same may hold true.) Media, especially electronic media, have been important means for presidents to "go over the heads of opponents" to the public. As persuasion is one of the powerful ways to carry out governance, mass media have been a tool for them. Favorable *presidential coverage* (or, *presidential images*) cultivated through the mass media enables presidents to implement their policies more easily.

These days media's depiction of presidents plays a major role in determining whether the *presidential image* can be positive, neutral, or negative (in other words, favorable, neutral, or unfavorable). The level of support for the presidential policies relies heavily on the presidential images. While the presidential images conveyed by the newspapers and television may vary, it is undeniable that mass media play an active role in determining presidential images and thereby in influencing the success or failure of presidential politics and policies. Political scientist Doris A. Graber (2002) explained how and why media's images of the presidents are significant in the political arena of today:

> Media coverage is the lifeblood of politics because it shapes the *perceptions* (Seol's emphasis) that form the reality on which political action is based. Media do more than depict the political environment; they *are* (Graber's emphasis) the political environment. Because direct contact with political actors and situations is limited, *media images* (Seol's emphasis) define people and situations for nearly all participants in the political process. The quantity of such images is rising thanks to new technologies (Graber, 2002, p. 277).

Why do presidents care about the media's portrayal of them,

that is, their media images? Presidents need positive media images during election campaigns and their terms of office. Presidential candidates badly need media's positive depictions of them to win the election and then they need media to carry out their policies as presidents. After elections, the success of presidential policies; the length, vigor, and effectiveness, of a president's political life; and the general level of support for the political system depend heavily on presidential images that the media convey to the public. Making sure that these images are favorable, therefore, becomes a prime concern for presidents. Staffs of various presidents concur that the national media play a very significant role in the White House decision-making process and in the White House meetings. On the whole, the more time is spent discussing the media than any other institution, including Congress. All policies are developed and presented with media reactions in mind (Graber, 2002, pp. 277-78).

No matter how powerful a president may be, media coverage of him (or "presidential image of the media") is vital in shaping his public image, thus in making or breaking his policy making and policy implementation. Presidential coverage is all the more important because for most Americans, understanding the presidency occurs not primarily through textbooks but through the daily reporting and commentary of the media. Most people get to know the political world through the messages conveyed to them through the media. For that reason, presidents and their aides are profoundly concerned about what happens in the media. *Presidents understand that for the public, the media image of the president is reality* (Pfiffner and Davidson, 2003, p. 145).

An anecdote in which James Baker made a response to a question by an NBC correspondent sheds light on why the presidential image is so important and uncompromiseable. Baker was one of Ronald Reagan's (presidency, 1981-1989) top aides and later secretary of state in the Geroge H. W. Bush administration (presidency, 1989-1993). Baker was once asked as to why the president seemed so unwilling to compromise on a tough budget proposal he submitted to Congress. Baker replied that any show of compromise or weakness was undesirable because "everything is cast in terms of winning or losing" in the media. Thus the president could not back down no matter how unrealistic his position. To be seen as unrealistic was preferable to being perceived as a loser, because being perceived as a loser would make him a loser. While discussing the above-mentioned anecdote, political scientist W. Lance Bennett (1996) noted that "there is no political reality apart from news reality." News reality can be interpreted as meaning "news coverage or media images." Bennett wrote that "it is clear that controlling political images in the news is a primary goal of politics."

One campaign manager for an American presidential candidate said that "the media 'is' the campaign." This means that during campaign as well as in office media's image of a political actor plays a very important role. Baker's remarks and those of one campaign manager above imply that news reality or media image of the political actor is the ultimate goal of politics. In the same vein, positive presidential image conveyed by news media may be one of major goals of presidential politics.

Bennett argued that as far as politicians, presidents included, are concerned, their news images or news reality is more important than political reality. According to him, political actors create news reality through repeated use of political images. In view of their political uses, it is not surprising that images are of great concern to politicians. Failure to control the news is often equated with political failure. Bennett went so far as to say that "leaders who disillusion their followers live shorter political lives than leaders who learn to represent situations to their best political advantage (Bennett, 1996, p. 78-82)."

With the importance of presidential image in news media increasing, media's image of the president can make or break the presidential politics. Presidents arguably depend on the media's coverage of them to lead the country. This book will seek to find out how the *New York Times* portrayed President Bush during the four research periods in his presidency. The book will also try to discover how the *Kyunghyang Daily News* portrayed President Roh during the six time spans in his early presidency.

Before going into that, this book will discuss the ways in which the White House and news media interact and negotiate with each other to produce presidential news. The discussion section in Chapter II looks at strategies of presidential communication and media's tactics of story framing and then investigates how together the two sides produce presidential news. Although presidential publicity officials exert considerable control over media's coverage of the White House or Blue House, news media have their own framework to generate presidential images. News media can convey negative images of the president indirectly by conveying opposition or criticism from the people or political opponents. In this sense, *the totality of President Bush's images conveyed by the New York Times is definitely the end product of these complex and active interactions between the New York Times journalists on the one hand and the White House, the Bush administration, the American public, and the world community on the other. By the same token, the totality of President Roh's images conveyed by the Kyunghyang Daily is the end product of interactions between journalists of this newspaper on the one hand and the Blue House, the Roh administration, the Korean public, and the world community on the other.*

CHAPTER **II**

Events are more likely to be covered than issues. Journalists can more easily defend covering events than issues, which by definition are more ambiguous. Covering events is so common in journalism that covering events has itself become a routine (Routines of Media Work 2: Shoemaker & Reese, 1996, p. 266).

PRESIDENTIAL COMMUNICATION AND MEDIA'S STORY FRAMING

PRESIDENTIAL PERSPECTIVES

Presidential Discontent with Media Coverage of Them

In more than two centuries' history of American presidency, American presidents have always wanted the print media and recently the electronic media to portray them in a favorable light. (George Washington's presidency started in April 30, 1789.) But presidents have largely been dissatisfied with their images conveyed by the media. Presidents have had ample resources to manipulate the media to get pleasing coverage, whereas the media have resisted being manipulated. In the initial stages of the presidency in American history, presidents were troubled by extremely partisan newspapers. However, with the advent of the mass-circulation newspapers, the interaction of the two sides entered into a new era. The history of interaction between the media and the presidency can be described as that of attempts for presidents to manipulate and for media to resist manipulation. Political scientist Carolyn Smith (1990) described President Ronald Reagan's (presidency, 1981-89) discontent with the media as follows:

> Ronald Reagan turned to an aide at the end of a picture session. "Sons of bitches," he muttered, referring to the assembled reporters. News microphones inadvertently recorded the president's private aside because technicians had not finished disconnecting the sound system. Reporters turned to presidential spokesman Larry Speakes. He replied

that the president doesn't recall saying it --- he doesn't recall anybody else saying it. If he said anything, he said, "It's sunny, and you are rich (Smith, 1990, p. 1)."

This episode shows that even former president Reagan, with the nickname "Great Communicator" for his tactful manipulation of the media, was not content with the media's portrayal of him. The nickname was given to him, because he made great use of the media in publicizing his policies. Dissatisfaction with the media was not confined to actor-turned president Reagan.

Thomas Jefferson (presidency, 1801-09), the great defender of freedom of the press, was also dissatisfied with images of him conveyed by the press. When Jefferson became exasperated with the press as president, he complained that "even the least informed of the people have learned that nothing in a newspaper is to be believed." He said that newspapers, for the most part, presented only the caricature of disaffected minds and that the abuses of freedom of the press had been carried to a length never before known or borne by any civilized nation. These observations, it should be noted, came from the man who earlier had written that "were it left to me to decide whether we should have a government without newspapers or newspapers without government, I should not hesitate to prefer the latter (Edwards and Wayne, 1994, p. 138)."

While Jefferson's attitudes towards the press are certainly contradictory, considerations of the media environment at that time provides another context to understand his agonies. As W. Lance Bennett (1996) says, partisan reporting was prevalent in the early days of the American republic, including Jefferson's time. Bennett's remarks are meaningful to the extent that he discussed both pros and cons of partisan reporting, offering additional background explanations for presidential discontent with the press in the past:

In the early days of the American republic, the news was anything but objective. Most newspapers were either funded by, or otherwise sympathetic to, particular political parties, interests, or ideologies. Reporting involved the political interpretation of events. People bought a newspaper knowing what its political perspective was and knowing that political events would be filtered through that perspective. In many respects, this is a sensible way to approach the news. If one knows the biases of a reporter, it is possible to control for them in interpreting the account of events. Moreover, if reporting is explicitly politically oriented, different reporters can look at the same event from different points of view (Bennett, 1996, p. 147).

Former president Bill Clinton (presidency, 1993-2001) was no exception in expressing his discontentment with the media. While he was president-elect, Clinton said emphatically about the role of the media. According to Cook and Ragsdale (1996), Clinton said:

> I think the watchdog function is fine. But it's often carried to extremes in a search for headlines. And I am supposed to take these people seriously as our sole intermediaries to the voters of this country? Sure, they should do their watchdog function, but anyone who lets himself be interpreted to the American people through these intermediaries alone is nuts (Nelson, 1996, p. 297).

Presidential dissatisfaction with media coverage of them may be universal. President Roh frequently has vented dissatisfaction with conservative Korean newspapers' coverage of him. Roh said to diplomats in Seoul that they should not send reports to their home countries based only on the titles of Korean newspaper stories. He requested the diplomats assembled at the Blue House to inquire him, government employees, or the people before dispatching reports of Korean situation (*Kyunghyang Daily*, June 05, 2004, p. 2). This shows eloquently how Roh's deep distrust of Korean newspapers' coverage of him and his politics. The author has to add that Roh did not raise complaint about broadcasters' coverage of him. The three major Korean broadcasters such as KBS, MBC, and SBS, portrayed Roh in a very sympathetic light, thus ultimately inciting massive candle-light demonstrations in favor of Roh just after the impeachment resolution was passed at the National Assembly in March 2004 (*Chosun Ilbo; Donga Ilbo; Joongang Daily,* June 11, 2004, pp. 1-3).

Even Japan's Prime Minister Junichiro Koizumi expressed his hopes that political neutrality provision in Broadcasting Law needs to be deleted in order to get favorable coverage of him and his party (Liberal Democratic Party) members by establishing a pro-LDP channel. He thought that his party was severely criticized by broadcasters and did not enjoy friendly broadcaster coverage during Lower House election campaign period (*Kyunghyang,* July 21, 2004).

Presidential Coverage Was Positive: Grossman & Kumar Study

Was the presidential dissatisfaction with their media coverage grounded in hard facts? Contrary to the deep-rooted dissatisfaction of the American presidents with their media images, Michael Grossman and Martha Kumar (1981) showed in their research that American media portrayed their presidents in an unexpectedly favorable light. Grossman and Kumar conducted research on media portrayal of U.S. presidents by the *New York Times* and the weekly newsmagazine *Time* for 25 years from 1953 to 1978, and then CBS Evening News for 10 years from 1968 to 1978. The two scholars were surprised to find that the presidential images were unexpectedly favorable in all the three media. Their argument read:

When all White House stories in the *New York Times* and *Time* are considered for the 25-year period, one is struck by how favorable they are. Each organization presented two favorable stories about the White House for each that was

unfavorable. Because the aggregate number of CBS stories were tabulated from the ten-year period that includes six years of Vietnam and Watergate, the CBS figures are not comparable to figures for the two print sources, which were based on stories for 25 years. But comparison based on a year-by-year analysis shows CBS Evening News following the same trends as the other two sources
(Graber, 1982, p. 89).

In their research, the two scholars asked three coders to decide the tone of presidential news stories as positive, neutral, and negative, based on the overall impression that the stories gave them. The coders worked in pairs on each medium after having received a general instruction as to how to code the stories. Grossman and Kumar wrote that *in spite of the danger of the subjective nature of the coders' task* (Seol's emphasis), their responses were quite similar. The coders working on the *New York Times* had the same assessment findings on tone in 86% of the stories while the coders for *Time* agreed on 77% stories, and those for the CBS News in 87% of the stories.

Grossman and Kumar's table assembled tone assessments recorded by the two coders like "positive-positive," "positive-neutral," "neutral," "negative-neutral," and "negative-negative." In coding stories, "neutral" meant both of "neutral" assessments or balancing off of "positive" and "negative" assessment made by the two coders: that is, assessment "neutral" means "neutral-neutral", "positive-negative, or "negative-positive."

According to Grossman and Kumar's research, the number of presidential stories amounted to 2,550 for *Time,* to 5,270 for the *New York Times,* and to 922 for CBS Evening News. Grossman and Kumar showed their research results in the following table:

Table 1:

Tone of White House Stories in the New York Times,
Time, and CBS News

Tone of Story	N Y T (N=5,270)	Time (N=2,550)	CBS News (N=922)
Positive-positive(%)	39.5%	44.9%	31.6%
Positive-neutral "	9.2	15.1	6.9
Neutral "	24.1	11.8	22.9
Negative-neutral "	4.7	8.2	6.0
Negative-negative "	22.5	20.0	32.6

Source: Grossman & Kumar 1981, p. 256

According to Grossman and Kumar's survey, the number of presidential stories is calculated to amount to 210.8 stories (*New York Times*), 102 stories (*Time*), and 92.2 stories (CBS News) per year, respectively. This ultimately means that the *New York Times* printed 0.57 stories per day, *Time* carried 1.96 stories per week, and CBS News broadcast 0.25 stories per day (Seol's calculation, based on their figures).

What presidential events were depicted as positive or negative? Grossman and Kumar identified certain events that tended to be positive or negative. According to them, the categories of stories which tended to be rated as positive in tone included those that emphasized the president's leadership role, his activities as a family man, his desirable personal qualities, and almost every story that deemphasized conflict and criticism. For example, when President Carter (presidency, 1977-81) went to New York City in August 1978 to sign a bill bailing out the city, he was surrounded by appreciative politicians who made supportive comments. The ceremony and comments were reported in the press. This piece was coded "favorable." The categories of stories judged to be negative included those that emphasized things that were going wrong for the president, conflict and criticism, what the administration had failed to achieve, and people who were not supporting presidential policies. For example, a May 11, 1978, *New York Times* article headlined "ABA Chief Criticizes Carter's Attack on Lawyers" was coded negative (Graber, 1982, pp. 89-90).

What about presidential photos? Grossman and Kumar (1981) found that presidential photos were more favorable than stories. The two scholars assessed the White House photographs with the same methods. The proportion of positive pictures was much higher than that of positive presidential stories. The authors explained that the ability of the White House to mold photographers' routines makes it more likely that positive pictures of the president will appear. They stated that the pictures accompanying news stories are even more favorable than the stories. Most pictures of the president convey a positive image because they are taken in settings that are favorable to the president, e.g., presidents speaking at the Rose Garden, leaving or entering church, or being on vacation. Grossman and Kumar showed how negative presidential stories and positive photos are placed together regardless of positive or negative value:

> Even more favorable are the pictures that accompany news stories. There were almost no negative pictures in either the *New York Times* or *Time,* and there were only a few negative films on the CBS News. In contrast to the two print sources, whose pictures were overwhelmingly favorable in tone, the majority of the CBS film was relatively neutral. Pictures often are favorable even when they accompany an unfavorable story. A negative news story, such as a front-page article suggesting the failure of a diplomatic meeting, may be accompanied by a positive picture in which the president appears at a ceremony with a foreign leader. There were almost no negative pictures, such as one of a president frowning at a popular congress-

man or interest-group leader, in either the *New York Times* or *Time*, and there were only a few negative films on the CBS News (Grossman & Kumar, 1981, p. 256; Graber, 1982, p. 91).

Grossman and Kumar (1981) pointed out that pictures and stories often do not go hand in hand, especially when the stories are negative. According to them, pictures usually are favorable even when they accompany an unfavorable story. Articles about the relationship between the president and Congress, the president and members of his administration and White House staff members were generally among the most negative stories that appeared in the *New York Times* and *Time* throughout the 25-year period. In *Time*, the stories about relations between the president and Congress were favorable in less than 20% of the cases. In no subject area were stories favorable in more than 42% of the cases. Yet the majority of pictures accompanying the stories were favorable with only one exception (Graber, 1982, pp. 92-93).

With regard to the findings of Grossman and Kumar's research, Graber (1982) pointed out a weakness of their study in the capacity of the editor. She wrote:

> The authors' evaluations of media matters are based largely on quantitative comparisons, yet the significance of stories may hinge more strongly on their substance than on the frequency of appearance. For instance, negative stories frequently have much greater impact than their positive counterparts. Ten stories about the presidents' polish and suavity in handling foreign diplomats may pale into oblivion in the face of one story about a major faux pas. In that situation, is it fair to claim that the president has received coverage that is predominantly favorable? (Graber, 1982, p. 86)

In view of the strong impact of negative images, Graber's explanation sounds convincing to some extent, *even though it may be hard to calculate how many positive stories can offset the hurtful impact of one negative story* (Seol's comment). Graber pointed out that the mere fact that the presidential stories featured prominently in the media does not necessarily mean that they will be noticed or used by the public. Hence, the need to differentiate media images from media effects. This topic will be addressed afterwards.

Story Types and Temporal Patterns of Presidential Coverage

Grossman and Kumar (1981) stated that the White House story is a homogenized story. They argued that the three news media, the *New York Times, Time*, and CBS Evening News, showed strikingly similar patterns in the types of stories they write and the subjects they cover, as well as the overall tone of their coverage. *They noted that approximately 80% of their stories are similar* (Seol's emphasis).

Grossman and Kumar (1981) presented a breakdown of types of presidential stories of the *New York Times*: News 78.9%, Analysis 2.6%, Feature 3.1%, Editorial 7.1%, Column 4.9%, Text 3.4%. Their breakdown of presidential stories also showed a similarity in the subjects dealt with by the three media. Although there was a difference in the amount of coverage they gave to each subject, the same general categories of subjects were treated as important by the three news media. The categories shown by the *New York Times* were: Program and Policy 24.7%, Activity 30.5%, Personal 12.2%, Vice President 6.1%, Congress and administration 10.9%, Election 6.7%, Staff 2.7%, President and press 1.4%, and Watergate 4.7%. The category of "program and policy" includes domestic and foreign policy news as well as budget. "Personal" encompasses lifestyle news about the president and his family. Activity involves messages, meetings, appointments, and the like.

Are there any temporal trends in the presidential coverage as presidents proceed with their office? One of the most outstanding contributions Grossman and Kumar made in media research may be their discovery of coverage patterns of the White House. Grossman and Kumar (1981) stated that the continuing character of the coverage can be seen in two important fluctuations that appear in most administrations, that is, the number of stories and their tone. According to them, the largest number of stories and the largest number of favorable stories appear during the first year, meaning "honeymoon period". It is unusual for the tone to rise after that first year. There were six administrations in the 25-year span from 1953 to 1978. In all but two, those of Lyndon Johnson (presidency, 1963-69) and Richard Nixon (1969-74), there was a constant pattern in the number of White House stories appearing in all the news sources studied. The pattern has been that the largest number of stories appear during the first year of the administration, and the lowest number are found in the final year. The two researchers said:

> The first year of an administration has received the largest number of stories not because of the high level of activity but because newspeople believe that the public is keenly interested in learning about the new arrivals. They want to know what the president is like and what kind of people his family members are. They want to know what he intends to do during his time in office, even if he is not prepared to bring forth solid proposals in his first month in office. After the media think the public's interest in who the people in the administration has been satisfied, they turn toward articles on the President's actions. The number of stories declined in the second year, even though the administration might have been more active than it had been in its first year. If a president serves two terms, there probably would be a rise in coverage during his reelection campaign, as there was with President Eisenhower. Presidents tend to be more active and more visible during a campaign, and these activities give rise to an increased number media contacts with him. The final year of an

administration has represented a low point in the number of media for all presidents in the study except President Nixon and President Johnson in *the New York Times* (Grossman & Kumar, 1981, p. 261).

In respect of media coverage trends of presidential news, Graber (2002) said that "the relationship between the media and the chief executive often displays *three distinct phases* (Seol's emphasis)." According to Graber, there used to be a honeymoon period, a time of cooperation when the media conveyed the president's messages about organization of the new administration, appointment of new officials, and plans and proposals for new policies. At this early stage few policies and proposals traditionally are implemented, so there is little opportunity for adverse criticism. Presidents and their advisors, eager to get their stories across, make themselves readily available to the media and supply them with ample information.

Once the administration embarks on controversial programs and becomes vulnerable to criticism of its record, the honeymoon ends. This is happening earlier and more abruptly now than in the past. Controversies are attractive to the Washington press corps when they involve dramatic conflicts at the highest levels of government. They can be easily covered through interviews with Washington-based sources. The White House may retaliate by withholding news, by restricting presidential contacts with the press, and by increasing public relations activities.

If the rifts between media and the executive branch become exceptionally wide, there may be a third period in which both sides retreat from their mutually hostile behavior to take a more moderate stance. This phase frequently coincides with a reelection campaign, when newspeople try harder to provide impartial coverage, and presidents are more eager to keep newspeople happy (Graber, 2002, pp. 282-84).

In the Nixon administration, however, the pattern changed. Watergate shattered any normal patterns in press coverage of his administration, with tremendous increase in the number of presidential stories with negative images.

Bill Clinton (presidency, 1993-2001) is another example not fitting into their pattern. Clinton never had a honeymoon with the press. From the start, tension and conflict underlay the relationship. His first several months, for example, were marked by coverage that leaned toward the negative images. Clinton's bad first weeks, with the storm over his proposal to lift the ban on gay men and lesbians in the military, were followed by mini-scandals in May 1993 about the White House travel office and a $200 presidential haircut. This will be discussed in the Chapter IV.

Highly positive coverage returned with Clinton's trip to the G-7 (Group of Seven Industrialized Countries) summit and his tour of the flood-ravaged Midwest. Presenting these facts, Cook and Ragsdale (1995) argued that little evidence exists of either a honeymoon or consistently increasing antagonism. Cook and Ragsdale commented that "the relations between the president and the press seem to be variable, even volatile, perhaps so unpredictable as to be inexplicable (Nelson, 1995, p. 298)."

Political scientist Doris A. Graber (2002) argued that incumbent President George W. Bush (presidency, 2001-09) did not enjoy the honeymoon period, either. She wrote that "President Bush received far less attention from newspapers, newsmagazines, and network television news than either Clinton or the elder Bush had garnered. George W. Bush, as well as Bill Clinton, had his honeymoon spoiled by predominantly negative comments about his initial legislative programs." Graber (2002) observed that the Bush administration, which began in January of 2001, illustrates the shriveling of the honeymoon period (p. 283). These coverage trends show that the pattern Grossman and Kumar discovered does not necessarily hold water in recent years. As will be shown in Chapter IV, the *New York Times* reported that several of Bush's initial policy initiatives, which were purported to please the conservatives, met with direct opposition from parties concerned.

Presidential Tactics (1): Control and Manipulation

Researcher of presidential spin control John Anthony Maltese (1992) introduced an episode in which Mr. Dick Cheney, then Congressman and currently Vice President of the United States (vice presidency, 2001-09) emphasized the importance of "controlling media agenda." Maltese described his conversation with Cheney, who was scheduled to leave for the White House to work as secretary of defense in the President George H. W. Bush's administration (presidency, 1989-93). While discussing presidential press relations with Maltese, Cheney emphasized the importance of controlling the media agenda. This episode clearly shows that the cabinet-level officials have deeply-ingrained convictions that the administration should always control media agenda and obtain positive presidential images for various political interests:

> To have an effective presidency, Cheney reminded me, the White House must control the agenda. An essential element of that control, he explained, is the ability to maintain discipline within the administration itself. Any appearance of disunity among the president's ranks will be seized upon by the media as an opportunity for a story --- one that will undermine the president's agenda (Maltese, 1992, p. 1).

It may be quite natural that an official like Dick Cheney, who served as White House chief of staff for President Gerald R. Ford (presidency, 1974-77), stressed the importance of controlling the media agenda. This implies that the president as well as presidential chief of staff wants to always control the media's portrayal of the presidency in their favor. Enter Bush junior's administration with Dick Cheney as Vice President and George W. Bush, a president "equipped with demonstrated interest in control of communications" (Kumar's words). It is understandable why the Bush administration has *an unprecedentedly tightly-knit communications operations* (Seol's emphasis). (But there occurred an identity leak of a covert CIA agent at the Bush administration to damage Bush opponents. Seol's comment.) To achieve media agenda, the White House has varied offices to control presidential images: Office of Communications for long-term presidential image making; Office of Telecommunications Policy for overall presidential influence on broadcast stations' programming by policy coordination; Office of Media Relations to influence local press; Press Office for day-to-day presidential image making by offering daily press conferences and other press-related activities, and so forth. Television advisors were also recruited for improved presidential images on television. In a word, "the history of the media and presidential relations can be called that of media manipulation to obtain favorable presidential images" (Kessel, 2001).

Edwards and Wayne (1994) stated that the White House's relations with the media occupy a substantial portion of the time of a large number of aides. *About one third of the high-level White House staff is directly involved in media relations* (Seol's emphasis) and a policy of one type or another, and most staff members are involved at some time in influencing the media's portrayal of the president. The person in the White House who most often deals directly with the press is the president's press secretary. Probably the central function of press secretaries is to serve as conduits of information from the White House to the press. Press secretaries also serve as conduits from the press to the president. They must sometimes explain the needs of the press to the president.

Since the time of William Loeb Jr., Theodore Roosevelt's (presidency, 1901-09) press secretary, the White House has attempted to coordinate executive branch news. Presidents have assigned aides to clear the appointments of departmental public affairs officials, to keep in touch with the officials to learn what news is forthcoming from the departments, and to meet with them to explain the president's policy views and to try to prevent conflicting statements from emanating from the White House and other units of the executive branch.

Coordinating the news from the White House itself has also

been a presidential goal. Presidents have sometimes monitored and attempted to limit the press contacts of White House aides, who have annoyed their bosses by using media for their own purposes. Recent administrations have also made efforts to coordinate publicity functions within the White House, attempting to present the news in the most favorable light, such as preventing two major stories from breaking on the same day, smothering bad news with more positive news, and timing announcements for maximum effect.

With respect to presidential efforts to control and manipulate media agenda, Graber (1997) elaborated on how the presidents utilize "control tactics" to get favorable images. She noted that the White House uses mostly three communication strategies (pp. 281-83).

Win favor. Presidents or presidential aides may woo reporters by offering good story material as well as occasional scoops that may bring distinction to individual reporters. They may try to cultivate reporters' friendships by being accessible, by treating them with respect, and by arranging for their creature comforts. To keep reporters in line, presidents may threaten them directly or obliquely with withdrawal of privileges. These may include accommodations in the presidential plane, special interviews, or answers to their questions during news conferences. Presidents may also publicly condemn individual reporters or their organizations for undesirable reporting.

Shape the news flow. Presidents may try to guide the flow of news by the thrust of their commentary and by controlling contacts with the press. For example, when publicity about illegal transfers of arms to Nicaragua had damaged President Reagan's administration, Reagan managed to divert media attention from the affair by sponsoring a popular Economic Bill of Rights. Presidents periodically restrict their contacts with the media largely to picture sessions to avoid questions about embarrassing failures. Presidents may space out releases so that there is a steady, manageable flow of news. If they want emphasis on a particular story, they may withhold competing news that breaks simultaneously. Sometimes a barrage of news is released or even created to distract attention from sensitive developments. To control news flows and ensure that the administration speaks with a single voice, presidents may prohibit their staffs from publicly disagreeing with their policies on pain of dismissal.

Orchestrate coverage. Ways of arranging activities to create favorable presidential image are limitless. They include creating newsworthy events, heightening suspense through news black-outs prior to major pronouncements, and staging public cere-monies as media spectacles at times when there are few compet-ing events. Political successes may be coupled with political failures in hopes that publicity for success will draw attention away from the failure.

These are only part of the tactics that presidents utilize to obtain favorable coverage. Presidents have their own internal news values that journalists can almost never ignore. Presidents have unlimited resources to control the media. In this regard, Cook and Ragsdale (1995) depicted *how helpless journalists can be* (Seol's emphasis) in the face of the powerful onslaughts of presidential communication tactics:

> Because of their near-automatic news value, presidents, more than other sources, can dictate the terms of access. Consequently, reporters can easily end up as virtual prison-ers in the all but hermetically sealed White House press-room, reluctant to roam far from their connection to fame and fortune in the news business. Instead of encouraging innovation and enterprise, the White House breeds anxiety among reporters about missing the story that everyone else is chasing (Nelson, 1995, p. 306).

Another perspective of looking at presidential news control was provided by political scientist W. Lance Bennett (1996). In terms of controlling news to get the message across, Bennett discussed three types of news control: i) Fully controlled news situations; ii) Partially controlled news situations; and iii) Uncontrolled news situations (Bennett, 1996, pp. 90-100).

Fully controlled news situations: Fully controlled media presentations are often called "pseudo-events (Daniel Boorstin's term)." Pseudo-events disguise actual political circumstances with realistic representations designed to create politically useful images. A pseudo-event uses careful stage setting, scripting, and acting to create convincing images that often have little to do with underlying reality of the situation. By incorporating fragments of an actual situation into a standardized presentation, a pseudo-event tempts the imagination to fill in the blanks and build a complete understanding out of fragmentary facts. In a well-fashioned pseudo-event, the script, the action, and the setting make enough reference to known properties of the situation to make it difficult to distinguish between what is real and what is merely realistic. A well-conceived event has such strong story lines that it becomes hard for reporters to find alternative news angles. Even when truly significant spontaneous occurrences find their way by accident into a carefully staged performance, the overall theme of the performance is often strong enough to downplay the spontaneous elements in the plots of resulting news stories.

To cite an example, in 1970 Richard Nixon shared his Thanksgiving dinner with a group of wounded Vietnam veterans. The event served the dual purpose of counteracting his image as a cold person and promoting support for his new interest in the human side of the war. After the dinner, an enterprising reporter interviewed soldiers who sat at Nixon's table. Although this reporter discovered a bombshell news that Nixon had made a daring attempt to rescue American prisoners, the reporter and his editors at *The Washington Post* decided to lead the story with the "President spends Thanksgiving with the troops" angle. Nixon's disclosure was buried in later paragraphs of the article.

Partially controlled news situations: Some political situations are not easy to control and they sometimes have an element of spontaneity. For example, press conferences can be controlled insofar as choice of time, place, and opening remarks, but they always contain some risk of unexpected or hostile questions from the press. In other cases, an official may be surprised by an issue and asked to comment, even though he or she is unprepared to do so. Sometimes the most effective means of operating in a hard to control situation is to hide in the background and release information through an anonymous news leak. Leaks are useful for delivering messages in many unstable situations. Information leaked to a reporter may receive more attention than it deserves and other news outlets may pick it up. Officials can also sound public opinion by leaking. Timing is important in leaking.

When in 1982 Reagan's budget showed a gross departure from his earlier promises, his media staff evidently decided to leak for the purpose of alleviating damage on Reagan. The budget director leaked the budget on Friday by "forgetting" his copy in a congressional hearing room following a high-level congressional briefing. Normally, the budget is delivered to the press on a Friday with a strict embargo not to publish any stories about it until the president has delivered his budget message to Congress and the nation on Monday. The story that would have dominated Monday's headlines was scattered across the less visible weekend news channels. When asked about the apparent leak, White House communication director Divid Gergen denied it and explained that the embargo stamp had been omitted "accidentally" from the budget books taken to the briefing.

Uncontrolled news situations: Few things strike more fear in the heart of a politician than a news story that has gotten out of control. Sometimes control of a story is lost because the underlying reality of a situation is simply too big to hide, as was the case with Lyndon Johnson's increasingly empty assurances that the United States was winning the war in Vietnam. In some cases, former insiders blow the cover on a story, as happened when John Dean delivered his damaging Watergate testimony against Richard Nixon or when Daniel Ellsberg leaked secret government documents about Vietnam. A classic case in point was Gerald Ford's blunder during a presidential debate when he claimed there was no Soviet domination in Eastern Europe.

While there is no magic formula for turning out-of-control situations into fully controlled public relations bonanza, there are important news management techniques that politicians ignore only at their peril. Presidents not only experience more media pressure than most politicians, but they also have more resources to manage the press. Thus it is not surprising that the most sophisticated methods for news control have emerged from presidential press operations. As research by John Anthony Maltese shows, the White House press operation has grown phenomenally both in size and sophistication during the half century from Truman to Clinton.

One the whole, the prevailing definition of presidential news allows a president to make news virtually whenever he wants to do so. Over the past two decades, attention to the president has increased, and 25% of all domestic national news now concerns presidents or presidential candidates (Entman, 1990, p. 155). In terms of presidents' intention to control news media, Edwards and Wayne (2003) provided an apt argument:

> No matter who is in the White House or who does the reporting, presidents and the press always struggle for dominance. Presidents are inherently policy advocates and want to be able to *define a situation and receive favorable coverage* (Seol's emphais). They will naturally assess the press in terms of how it aids or hinders their goals. The press, on the other hand, has the responsibility for presenting and assessing what is really going on. Although the press may fail in its efforts, it will assess itself on those criteria. Presidents want to control the amount and timing of information about their administrations, while the press wants all the information that exists without delay. As long as their goals are different, presidents and the press are likely to be adversaries (p. 155).

Presidential Tactics (2):
Negotiation and Cooperation

While the presidential control and manipulation tactics to get favorable media image is being carried out, the process of negotiation and cooperation between the White House and journalists proceeds. Political scientists Timothy Cook and Lyn Ragsdale (1995) explained how the negotiation is conducted between the president and the press. The two scholars brought to light how the two sides can be simultaneously *interdependent and independent* (Seol's emphasis) vis-a-vis the other side:

> Presidents and the news media rely heavily on one another to do their jobs. Presidents need the news media to get their message out, to set the political agenda, to create favorable public moods, and to pressure otherwise recalcitrant political actors. Similarly, the news media use presidents as central protagonists around whom they can organize their daily production of news. The top news story is typically a presidential story; the top domestic newsbeat is at the White House (Nelson, 1995, pp. 297-330).

These remarks reflect the day-to-day practices of the interaction between the presidents and the media. There is a constant negotiation evolving about the importance and interest in presidential news. Cook and Ragsdale noted that presidents designate importance in three ways. First, they select issues or ignore them for presidential involvement. Second, they can stage events that will draw attention to particular issues and concerns. Third, they can choose the venues for involvement with the media.

But the two sides can also be independent of each other in various aspects. The president and the press act independently of each other in pursuit of their own fundamentally different interests. Cook and Ragsdale (1995) commented on their independence:

Amid this mutual reliance, however, presidents and journalists are also independent of one another. The interests of presidents and the press, although intertwined, are fundamentally different. Presidents, like all politicians, want to get their information to the public and to other politicians in a form that is as favorable as possible to their own interests. But reporters, partly because of their commitment to serving their audiences, partly because of their commitment to balance and neutrality, and partly because of their professional aspirations, are not willing to be *unwitting adjuncts* to the White House. The result is what we call an ongoing *negotiation of newsworthiness* within the White House, within the news media, and between the two regarding which of the thousands of things that presidents, their families, and their advisors do in a given day will become news (Nelson, 1995, p. 299).

Cook and Ragsdale showed what can become news of the day. It can be safely said that there is an ongoing process of negotiation of newsworthiness between the president and the media. This negotiation involves what gets covered, who gets asked about a story, and how and for how long the story is covered. It is a negotiation that evolves between the White House and the press, as the stories rise, develop, and fall; as alternative sources speak out or clam up; and as presidential and journalistic strategies change during the course of a president's term and from one president's term to another's. What is newsworthy one day may be old news the next. What is good news coverage for one president may be critical news coverage for another.

Cook and Ragsdale argued that there are four phases of negotiation between the two sides: negotiation of process, negotiation of content, negotiation of valence, and negotiation of results. In terms of negotiation of news content, they indicated that importance and interest in news content are divergent between the two sides:

News, it is often said, is supposed to be both important

and interesting. The president has the greatest control in ascertaining importance, but the news media are more influential in designating interest. The division of labor was best captured by a plaque that appeared on the desk of Reagan's chief White House spokesperson, Larry Speakes: "You don't tell us how to stage the news, and we won't tell you how to cover it." Although jocular, Speakes' plaque reveals the area that each side is presumed to dominate --- and suggests that the news from the White House is a co-production (Nelson, 1997, p. 309).

This is an illustration of the negotiation of news content, which represents description of the president. This also shows how independently the media and the White House can operate. Does one party get the upper hand over the other in their relationships? The presidents and the media seem to be on an equal footing. Cook and Ragsdale drew a conclusion about the relationship of the president and the media as follows:

Although each side relies on the other in the negotiation of newsworthiness, neither dominates. The presidency and the news media are independent institutions that command important and unique resources. Journalists worry about maintaining access to powerful sources such as the president, but only if such access leads to a product that their superiors --- who, after all, pay their salaries --- will assess favorably. The two sides need to provide stories that maximize both the production values of vividness and clarity and the journalistic norms of balance and neutrality. Reporters, moreover, derive satisfaction and self-esteem from their professional autonomy. Any indication that they are mere press agents, or "flacks," for the president would lead to a loss of prestige within the profession (Nelson, 1995, pp. 308-09).

Even if presidents can restrict reporters' access and focus them on some topics, the news media still have the final say about the ultimate product --- by raising certain issues, interjecting doubts, questioning motives, and seeking out critical sources for balance. Hence, the Fourth Estate, even though the media are constantly exposed to the risks of being controlled and manipulated by the presidency. In this way, negotiation and cooperation will continue between the White House and the journalists over the presidential images.

Presidential Tactics (3):
Cooperation and Intimidation

Sometimes cooperative relationships between the two sides turn into intimidation (Bennett, 1996, pp. 100-106). Most newsmakers strive to maintain cooperative relations with the press by scheduling press conferences and issuing releases at times convenient for making deadlines; offering scoops and exclusive interviews to friendly reporters; and even wining and dining the press eager to bask in the limelight of the famous and powerful.

Oftentimes simple courtesies can pay big dividends in terms of controlling the timing, content, and amount of coverage. For example, shortly after Ronald Reagan became president, he attended a major North-South economic summit conference in Mexico. The conference was sure to receive a great deal of press coverage because it was Reagan's first major diplomatic venture outside the country and because it was an important forum for defining the nature of the debt crisis that threatened all the countries in the Western Hemisphere. Although a huge press entourage accompanied Reagan on his trip, few of those reporters ventured beyond the comfortable American compound to find out how other countries viewed their own problems. According to one observer, Secretary of State Alexander Haig promised the press to "feed as often as possible" and the Reagan administration kept his promise. Many American journalists' accounts of what happened at the conference came straight from that official source. Some members of the White House press spent an entire week without meeting a single foreign delegate.

Cooperation with the media extends beyond the care and feeding of reporters to the scheduling of major news events so they don't conflict with entertainment programming that generate ratings and revenues for the TV networks. Times have changed since the golden days of broadcasting, when a political broadcast gave prestige to a network and saved the production costs of live programs.

Now the problem of media access is a much more delicate economic matter resolved for the most part by running political messages during the regularly allocated news slots on the broadcast networks. Politicians' attempts to communicate with the American public at other times can cost a network upward of $200,000 for every 30-second commercial spot it loses when a political broadcast preempts an entertainment program. Failure to cooperate with these corporate economic realities could cool political relations with the media. For example, David Gergen said that he had never called TV networks to do a speech on Tuesday night at 8 o'clock without first asking what's on the air that night.

To the extent that a spirit of cooperation is established, it is easier for the press strategists who work for newsmakers to feed the messages of the day to the press. The art of message management was never carried to a higher form than during the Reagan years in the White House. Having established a largely cooperative relationship with the press, the Reagan administration concentrated on the content, salience, and credibility of its messages.

Even in the most cooperative and harmonious press relations, however, some clouds will surely appear. When cooperation fails, intimidation of the press is the next step for news control. On several occasions, for example, the Reagan administration chose to intimidate the media, and it paid off.

In one incident, a speech by President reagan on U.S.-Soviet relations and national defense was the kickoff for the annual administration propaganda campaign to increase the already sizable military budget. Gaining support for such increases during a time of budget crisis and international instability meant generating fearful images of a hostile Soviet enemy. Such images were routinely delivered without comment by the press to the American people. On the evening of February 26, 1986, however, ABC News broke with tradition and did something different. Following the president's speech and a reply from the Democrats, ABC host David Brinkley was left with more time than originally scheduled for a brief interview with Vladimir Posner, a correspondent for Radio Moscow. A short question-and-answer session with the Russian might have gone unnoticed, but when Reagan finished his speech early, Brinlkey had to fill the remaining 8 minutes before the start of TV drama Dynasty. Brinkley let Posner fill the time with Soviet positions on the arms race and reactions to Reagan military policies.

It may have seemed to ABC at the time that the American people would benefit from hearing the "enemy" speak directly, but the network had another reaction from the White House. The next morning, ABC News received a scathing letter from White House director of communication Patrick J. Buchanan, who compared ABC's decision to the BBC's putting on a Nazi following a Churchill speech. Within a few hours, ABC News executive Richard Wald issued a statement admitting that the network had made a mistake, and ABC News president Roone Arledge sent President Reagan a telegram of personal apology.

In another example, Bill Kovach and Tom Rosenstiel (1999, pp. 43-50) showed how presidential aides intimidated journalists in the context that the two authors tried to explain how powerful sources grew. Kovach and Rosenstiel noted that the growing leverage over the press by sources and the more news outlets seeking for sources have given sources what some observers see as a new arrogance. President Ronald Reagan's (presidency, 1981-89) Press Secretary Marlin Fitzwater, for instance, said: "You see a picture of the White House that I don't recognize. You see a White House that intimidates, that attacks the press, that threatens them with putting them out of business and never talking to them and never giving interviews and withholding stories. And you see a media reacting to it, allowing themselves in many cases to be intimidated in ways I never really thought was possible." The two authors went on:

Fitzwater may be right about intimidation, but the practice began well before Clinton's White House tenure. Fitzwater's predecessor, Reagan White House spokesman Larry Speakes, employed similar bullying tactics. He would denounce reporters who had criticized or challenged him and threaten to put them "out of business," which meant he would no longer answer the phone calls or talk to them. He would even do this in public to intimidate other reporters. NBC News correspondent Chris Wallace was frozen out for years. Fitzwater himself, while he didn't employ intimidation, was hardly unsophisticated in the Bush and Reagan White Houses in the art of massaging and manipulating the press. Like Mike McCurry, Clinton's press secretary, he was far more genial about it (Kovach & Rosenstiel, 1999, pp. 45-46).

Presidential Tactics (4): News Management

Professor of University of Washington W. Lance Bennett (1996, pp. 96-100) noted that "managing the media has become an essential part of successful governing and politics." Increasingly, this is true for all levels of politics from city hall to the White House. Although the basic methods can work much the same at all levels, nowhere is the news-making game played with more intensity and for higher stakes than in the White House. In the case of the president, the sheer growth of the news media in the last half of this century requires considerable daily management.

When President Harry S. Truman (presidency, 1945-53) ordered atomic bombs to be dropped on Japan in 1945, he personally broke the news to a White House press corps that numbered 25 reporters. Bill Clinton arrived in Washington to find that more than 1,700 reporters cover the White House, and a total of 2,800 people including television producers, technicians and other crew members are allowed to pass through the press entrance of the president's residence. It is hard to imagine any politician interacting with such a crowd in the absence of considerable staging, planning and scripting. And so the White House press operations have grown along with, and sometimes ahead of, the press corps.

Richard Nixon (presidency, 1969-74) created the White House Office of Communications with the aim of controlling the flow of information out of the entire executive branch and "going over the heads of the press" to communicate directly with the people. These goals were disrupted when the Watergate affair and a series of congressional investigations aroused a press pack that followed a trail of scandal that led eventually to the Oval Office.

Elected on a promise to restore trust in government, Jimmy Carter (presidency, 1977-81) neglected news management with a possibly foolish determination to run a White House that was open to the press. With plot assists from a struggling economy, opponents in Congress, and an embarrassing 444 days of news about Americans being held hostage in Iran, the media helped the voters send Carter out of Washington with unpopularity levels approaching those suffered by Richard Nixon in the polls. It was not until the Reagan presidency that the White House Office of Communications was fully developed into the well-oiled public relations machine that helped turn Reagan into the "Great Communicator."

The Reagan press management plan was so effective that the chief image maker, Richard Wirthlin, was crowned Advertising Man of the Year in 1989. He did not receive his industry's top award for his creative work for General Foods or Mattel Toys, but for his accomplishments as director of consumer research for Ronald Reagan. Another measure of the success of the Reagan press program is that even when the press attempted to be critical, the efforts seldom produced results. The so-called "teflon" coating provided by the Reagan publicity team seemed to protect the president from the press.

It is clear that George H. W. Bush's (presidency, 1989-93) White House did not set out to manage the media as completely as the communications group did it during the Reagan era. CBS News White House correspondent Lesley Stahl could be heard complaining about the "night and day" difference. Another reporter said, "That's not an impeachable offense yet but it does raise some interesting questions. Not least for the White House press corps, which seems to be looking back on the slick, well-packaged Reagan presidency with a touch of nostalgia."

Despite George H. W. Bush's decision to spend less time managing the press, the media criticism became too much to tolerate, and the White House soon brought back the media team that got him elected. For example, former public relations executive Sig Rogich, who had produced several Bush campaign commercials in 1988, came to the White House as Special Assistant to the President for Activities and Initiatives (i.e., chief image maker). Rogich was rewarded for helping to restore the Bush image by being named ambassador to Iceland. In 1992 Bush once again forgot the lessons of news and image management, and Mr. Rogich was recalled from Iceland to produce Bush campaign commercials. However, Rogich and the other image doctors arrived too late. The Bush media management team was far too disorganized during the 1992 campaign to save the president's image or his reelection.

News management became an early preoccupation of the Clinton political organization. Indeed, it had to be, considering the attacks on his draft record and his sex life during the 1992 campaign. Yet Clinton flirted dangerously with ignoring the press, sometimes trying to circumvent the news altogether. When the press became too concerned with Clinton's personal problems, the candidate went directly to the people through appearances on 60 Minutes, MTV, various talk shows, and specially produced electronic town hall programs that created the illusion of intimacy with audiences. When his media image improved, the Clinton news team staged events like the direct-to-the-voter bus tours that sparked considerable positive coverage from the press. Even after the election victory, Clinton apparently continued to seethe about the personal press attacks he had suffered during the campaign. Convinced that as president Clinton would go over the heads of the news media, the Clinton team closed off the hallway between the press room and the White House press and kept the presidential press pack at a distance. The results were devastating. Clinton became the object of massive journalistic criticism, prompting him to complain that his honeymoon with the press was too short. The *Washington Post* editorial page editor Meg Green wrote that she had never seen an administration "pronounced dead" so early.

At last Clinton brought David Gergen, former White House communication director under Reagan, on board to manage his press operations. When Gergen was allowed to implement a variety of press management techniques, there was visible improvement in Clinton's news control. However, Clinton's continuing personal frictions with the press corps did not make Gergen's job easy, and he was never given the freedom to run the Clinton press operation that he had been granted under Reagan. This reluctance to give full reign to the "Sultan of Spin" (as Gergen was dubbed by journalists) remains puzzling in light of a report that the communication style Clinton most admired was that of Ronald Reagan.

Given the power of the well-managed media, few politicians at any level of government today can afford to ignore the techniques of public relations (or, strategic communications, in Jarol B. Manheim's words). For political scientist Manheim, Clinton's decision to hire David Gergen is typical of the "strategic communication" process that dominates politics today. As a result of the technologies of strategic communications (polling, market research, news and image management), the political process is not just a record of events, it is an event in and of itself--an integral part of the political process linking politicians and people in the struggle for government power. Therefore, appreciating the link between power and communication requires abandoning any idea that the news is somehow on the outside of politics looking in (Bennett, 1996, p. 3).

Although few play the game as well as or as willingly as the Reagan White House did, practically no one seems willing to dismiss media management as unnecessary. Even reporters confess at times that their jobs are made easier when politicians deliver a prepackaged product to them in plenty of time to meet their deadlines.

Publicity Machine of President George W. Bush

Presidency scholar Martha Joynt Kumar (2003) wrote that "President George W. Bush has a demonstrated interest in communications and, in case of the war on terrorism, just what the challenges are in getting people to understand the issues and the urgency of response." According to her, Mr. Bush assembled White House officials and emphasized the importance of communications in fighting terrorism. Shortly after September 11th attacks, White House assistants sent some documents to Camp David for Bush to sign. These documents were purported to freeze financial assets suspected of sponsoring terrorism. Mr. Bush was furious. He wanted a signing ceremony to show that it was the first action to fight terrorism. Mr. Bush said, "Why am I just signing this document and is Treasury Secretary Paul O'Neill announcing this tomorrow? This is the first strike in this new war against terror. It's not with a missile. It's with a stroke of a pen." The communications operation put together a Rose Garden signing ceremony for the following morning. Head of Office of Communications Dan Bartlett said that Mr. Bush spotted the opportunities that his staff did not (Kumar's interview with Bartlett on May 22, 2002, in Washington D.C.).

As the first president to come into office with a master's degree in business administration (MBA) and with decades of experience in business management, President George W. Bush employed management principles when he organized his administration. According to presidential personnel director and deputy chief of staff Clay Johnson and presidential senior adviser Karl Rove, Bush's management style goes back to management analyst Peter Drucker. Rove fleshed out Mr. Bush's core principles: i) Set the goal; ii) Bring the staff together and provide them with clear direction on how they should accomplish the stated goals, including methods and philosophy; and iii) Define limits within which individual staff members may operate.

In the communications area, the direction of the president's goals and results orientation can be summarized in the words of one of those assigned to carry out their plans. *At the heart of their communications operation is a management precept that President George W. Bush "makes news on his terms"* (Seol's emphasis). This was an observation made by Jim Wilkinson, the Director for Planning in the Office of Communications (Kumar's interview with Wilkinson on July 3rd, 2002, in Washington D.C.). Making news on the president's terms requires an organization focused on planning and getting ahead of events. Good communication requires well-prepared organization supporting the president's own communications abilities.

The communications strategies of the Bush administration appear to be based on political strategist Mary Matalin's ideas. According to Kumar, Matalin does not differentiate between communications in campaigning and governing. "Communication has to be clear, it has to be repetitive, it has to be coherent, it can't be internally or intellectually inconsistent. In addition, you have to have a receptive zone," Matalin said. "You have got to make people want to hear what you're saying. It has to have relevance. So you have different tactics for different places. Hitting all those zones requires a well tuned organization" (Kumar's interview with Matalin on Oct. 3rd, 2002, in Washington D.C.). These principles of organization are just as important to the structure of the communications operations as they are to the functioning of the White House staff. Kumar (2003) explained that there are three levels of communications operations in the Bush White House: Strategy, Operations, and Implementation.

(1) Strategy Level: People and Instruments

The organizational structure Mr. Bush and his advisers developed to translate strategies into operations contains a group of four basic White House units with additional resources for those at the strategic level. The existing communications units found in the last three administrations are tied together through those at the strategic level. Karen Hughes, former Counselor to the President and currently an outside adviser in regular contact with those at the White House (that is, as of March of 2003 and afterwards, Seol's note), had the communications portfolio coordinating planning with Karl Rove, Senior Adviser to the President.

The offices with the operations and implementation responsibilities are the Office of Communications, the Press Office, the Office of Media Affairs, and the Speechwriting Unit. All four units handle tasks associated with publicity operations no matter who is president. Organizations that vary from one administration to another are the supervisory arrangements for the units. The Office of Strategic Initiatives and the other offices in the grouping of political outreach units headed by Karl Rove, is a resource for the communication operation. Like Hughes operation, Rove's office coordinates preexisting units dealing with political and interest group relations, including the Office of Political Affairs, the Office of Intergovernmental Affairs, and the Office of Public Liaison. Between them, Hughes and Rove cover White House relations with nongovernmental groups and institutions. Both of the chief strategists are involved in the process of identifying goals and having them adopted.

A basic planning tool for the Bush communications team is the message of the day. They want to make certain not to overload the circuits with competing messages. "The idea is to give the press one thing to cover," said a White House staff member during a background interview. "You are going to get the President's word once a day, so if they are running a story, they have to use his words. And if they only get those words, it seems simple. That's why Karen is so good at breaking it down to the most simplistic terms (Kumar, 2003)." In circulating message of the day, the Bush administration is no different from the several previous ones (Seol's comment).

(2) The Operations Level: Carrying Strategy into Messages and Appearances

President Bush established an organization that retained the four basic elements of the publicity structure found in most administrations since that of Richard Nixon (presidency, 1969-1974). These offices are Press Office, the Office of Communications, the Office of Media Affairs, and the Speechwriting Unit. The number of people on staff in the four offices is fairly similar in the Bush and Clinton White Houses. The Bush people had a total of 43 people in 2001, while the Clinton people had 39 in 1998. The difference lies in the emphasis of each. The Bush White House favors the long-range planning operations and puts their resources there. Following are publicity offices of the Bush White House and their functions:

Press Office: Daily Operations. As it has traditionally done, the Press Office is focused on the daily operation. The Press Secretary plays little role in the overall communications strategies because of the daily emphasis of his office and the volume of work he deals with each day. Press Secretary Ari Fleischer (in office from January 2001 to July, 2003) explained, "The Press Office is much more operational and much more implementational." The Press Office is the place where daily press relations are handled and where plans developed elsewhere for daily coverage are carried out. Mr. Scott McClellan, Fleischer's deputy, took over the post of Press Secretary on July 15th, 2003 (*The New York Times*, August 12, 2003, A14).

Office of Communications: Events Management and Integration with Other Institutions. This office is responsible for creating the focus of the day, organizing the planning up to four months out, and coordinating with White House and administration personnel. Dan Bartlett, who heads the office also handles an assessment of how their work was received. While this office is the unit where events are internally planned and executed, it is also the place where they find out how they are doing and develop strategies in response to what they are discovering.

Office of Media Affairs: Local and Specialty Press. This office deals with the regional and local press. Specialty press, such as Hispanic, Polish, and African-American news organizations, as well as radio, is taken care of through this office. In addition, the website is managed. In the Bush administration, this office is particularly geared towards the follow-up for presidential events. When he goes on the road following a speech, for example, this office handles the local press.

Speechwriting Unit: The Words. President Bush came into the White House with a preexisting set of expectations on the part of those used to dealing with presidents. News organizations, government officials at every level, and interest groups counting themselves as important to the president's policy interests, all had expectations of hearing from the president in response to their interests. In their individual ways, each sector preferred to hear publicly from the president, rather than those of surrogates whether they were cabinet secretaries or the press secretary. The communications operation created and provided support for approximately 650 annual public appearances President Bush had in 2001 and then in 2002. In 2001, Mr. Bush had 136 question and answer sessions with reporters and another 19 news conferences. For all these sessions, the communications operation, especially the speechwriting unit, has an enormous load of work. The unit has gone from 10 to 12 staff members from 2001 to 2002.

Coalition Information Centers and Office of Global Communications: Communicating Abroad. The Bush White House added units to focus their communications operations on a world-wide market. They did so with the Coalition Information Centers created after the September 11th attacks and aimed at responding to the publicity attacks against the United States. in Afghanistan and in Muslim countries where Americans were under attack. Tucker Eskew, who headed the

Office of Media Affairs at the time of the September attacks, moved to London to coordinate publicity with Alastair Campbell, spokesperson for Prime Minister Tony Blair. The idea was to have an offensive and defensive operation where the American government and its allies could act within the same news cycle as the opponents, most especially the Taliban. This information battle was assessed successful afterwards.

A more formal and broader effort to combat an unfavorable U.S. image created the Office of Global Communications, a unit established in the White House in July, 2002, and then through an executive order in January, 2003. Eskew, who heads that office, said that "It's going to be strategic and thematic and proactive. It's going to coordinate among agencies to try to take the President's construct, his framework for communications, and integrate it to what we are already doing." If there is something good that is communications-related and if it deserves to be on the President's schedule or agenda, this office will help elevate it to that level. The office is part of the White House, which indicates the office's importance to Mr. Bush (Kumar, 2003).

The Office of Strategic Initiatives: The most important secondary operation. This office is under the direction of Senior Adviser Karl Rove. His operation maintains liaison with state officials through Political Affairs, and with interest groups through the Office of Public Liaison. With his contacts outside of the White House, he can get a read on the effectiveness of their communications and guidance on where they need to focus their attention with their publicity for the president. This office serves as an echo chamber. An important aspect of Rove's operation is to listen to how they are doing as well as to get information out to those the president and his staff want to reach. This is two-way communication.

(3) The Implementation Level: "Winning the Picture"

Because presidential events are very often covered live on television from beginning to end by cable, the potential resonance of each word means that a great deal of attention must be placed on taking advantage of the opportunity to get the president's message across to the public. Karl Rove described the importance of creating pictures that can communicate the message. Rove observed that "in the post-1980 era, we all owe it to Michael Deaver." According to Rove, Deaver said, "Turn off the sound of the television and that's how people are going to decide whether you won the day or lost the day, the quality of the picture. That's what they are going to get the message by, with the sound entirely off." While discussing the importance of pictures, Rove said:

There is a reason why that old saw, a picture is worth a thousand words, how we look, how we sound, and how we project is important. So winning the picture is important and having a president with the right kind of people to drive and hone the emphasis of the message, to be seen in a positive, warm, and strong way. The fact that they are on their best day is important. As in earlier administrations, most especially those of Presidents Reagan and Clinton, White House communications operations focus heavily on getting the picture right (Kumar's interview with Karl Rove).

(4) Control of Departmental Publicity Operations: Root Causes of Success for the Bush Communications Team

Kumar (2003) wrote that "an innovation of President Bush and his team is the successful control they exercise over publicity officers in the departments. While earlier administrations have paid attention to departmental public affairs units, they were not as successful as the Bush administration in controlling the appointment of officials there, coordinating policy themes, and making use of departmental resources." The Bush White House established control over those positions when they came into office.

White House Chief of Staff Andrew Card explained: "I make

sure our communications team is not just a team in the White House. It is a communications team for the Executive Branch of government. Our legal team is a legal team for the government." The move to control the release of information by departments is part of a larger effort to control relations of the departments with their outside world. Card explained the type of coordination devices they use to make certain people in the White House and those in the departments understand one another. "There is a call every morning with the communications teams from all of the cabinet agencies. And I know Josh Bolten keeps in touch with their policy wonk types and White House Counsel Al Gonzales with the lawyers and so White House liaison people are very important too (Kumar's interview with Card)."

Kumar noted that controlling departmental public affairs offices allows the president and his staff to avoid the problem many previous administrations have faced with such units focusing their attention on the departmental secretary and his or her goals rather than those of the president. Victoria Clarke (or, Torrie Clarke), who was the public affairs officer at the Pentagon during the Second Gulf War worked in the campaign for George W. Bush and worked earlier for his father as well. (Clarke quit her job of Assistant Secretary of the Department of Defense several moths after major phases of the Iraq War ended. She was in charge of the "embedded journalism" policy for war coverage, Seol's note.) As the Bush administration began, Mindy Tucker, who worked the Florida shift after the November election, was placed at the Justice Department in the public affairs operation. By having people with demonstrated loyalty to Mr. Bush and with a history of knowing the campaign, Mr. Bush and his staff avoid situations where the departmental spokesperson focuses on his or her attention on the cabinet officer to the detriment of the president. When President Carter was in office, he had trouble with Secretary of Health, Education, and Welfare Joseph Califano, who often would move in his own direction without consulting with the White House staff on initiatives he was taking, such as his campaign against tobacco usage.

From time to time, newspaper articles appear containing anonymous White House sources pointing out a cabinet member who appears to have strayed too far from his or her own original portfolio. On February 15th, 2003, a Washington Post article "A Star with Too Many Points? Critics Fear Candid Rumsfeld Impeded Iraq Coalition" was an anonymous warning from the White House to a cabinet member. In the story about Defense Secretary Donald Rumsfeld and his impact on the administration's foreign policy efforts, an anonymous White House official observed, "Sometimes the stalking horse gets a little far out in front of the parade." Such criticism usually served to rein in the administration official singled out for the White House criticism.

Note: This section is mostly indebted to Professor Marth Joynt Kumar's paper entitled "Communications Operations in the White House of President George W. Bush: Making News on His Terms" (2003). Professor Kumar of Department of Political Science at Towson University, Towson, Maryland, sent this paper to the author via email on July 7, 2003. She is also Director of White House 2001 Project. The author guessed that she completed writing this paper around the spring of 2003.

Presidential Techniques for Projecting Positive Images

The fact that the George W. Bush administration has adopted a management approach in its governance, and in communications operation in particular, does not necessarily mean that the White House staff view the White House as a company and Mr. Bush as their CEO. White House Deputy Chief of Staff Clay Johnson, who has a great deal of private sector experience, disabused of that notion. Clay said, "For me, one of the biggest differences is that I hear people describe *the purpose of the White House as to maximize the value of the president's time and voice. The president's time is an incredible asset* (Seol's emphasis). I guarantee you no company defines their headquarters' role as maximizing the value of their chairman's time and voice." The Bush White House is clearly one in which communication is valued throughout the organization with a structure to make optimal use of the president's time and voice (Kumar, 2003).

To maximize the president's time and voice, White House officials use a variety of techniques to project a positive image of the president. An incumbent president uses his numerous advantages to obtain favorable coverage in the media. The large, well-organized and well-financed White House staff makes elaborate and extensive preparations for the president's appearances at press conferences, public addresses, and ceremonies. It sets the ground rules and picks the locations for appearances by him or other White House officials. Although administrations differ considerably in their attitudes towards news organizations, they use the advantages of incumbency in similar ways to project their version of the president's personal qualities, leadership skills, and policy preferences. Each administration attempts to develop a positive image of the president by focusing the attention of the media on the man and his family. Each presents the president as a vigorous and capable leader. Each emphasizes that the president is an advocate of policies and a political philosophy that reemphasize traditional values while directing the country toward a better future. Grossman and Kumar (1981) described some techniques employed by White House officials to project a positive image of the president: i) Projecting personal qualities; ii) Projecting leadership qualities; iii) Projecting policy; and iv) Making the best use of news conferences. In all these four processes, news organizations play an active role in projecting the president's character and achievements to the public. They often collaborate by presenting a favorable image to the public, especially at the beginning of an administration when many journalists are fascinated by the president's personal habits and are willing to present an uncritical picture of his vision of how he will build the "good society." Grossman and Kumar noted that "an important part in all these attempts is the manner in which news organizations collaborate with or resist White House efforts to exploit the president's advantages (Grossman and Kumar, 1981, pp. 226-27)."

(1) Projecting Personal Qualities

A Man of the People: The White House tries to project an image of the president as a man of the people, even though he is a celebrity with a retinue of aides and attendants whose every activity is followed by the mass media. Presidents' aides make complicated arrangements and engage in a great deal of promotional activity in this effort *to portray the president as an average citizen* (in Grossman and Kumar's words) and *to induce the media to do that* (Seol's idea). In the Carter administration, for example, the president arranged to visit small towns such as Clinton, Massachusetts, and Salinas, California, where he stayed with local families before appearing at nationally televised town meetings. On television and in photos, the president was shown sitting at the breakfast table with his hosts. Later he was seen answering townspeople's questions in a setting that emphasized the participatory and homespun nature of the event. But the preparations for these visits were anything but casual (Grossman and Kumar, 1981, pp. 228-29).

The Family Man: Since the public wants an admirable model of family life, White House officials invariably present the president as the nation's ideal husband, parent, and grandparent. Warm family portraits taken by photographers on the White House staff are available to the media. Photographers who work for news organizations are given opportunities to film the president with his children, grandchildren, and parents. Animals, especially dogs, are also part of the Chief Executive's public domestic life. Theodore Roosevelt's menagerie even included a turkey.

Projecting the President through the First Lady: The president's wife plays an important role in projecting the image of the administration. The most typical role of the first lady is representing the president at cultural, charitable, and fashionable events. Although some first ladies --- Eleanor Roosevelt, for example --- have followed independent agendas and acquired their own followings, in most cases there has been an attempt to find a symbolic connection between the first lady's activities and those of her husband. Some first ladies become the president's alter ego for those segments of the public that sympathize with his politics but find his personality unattractive. Ford administration officials allowed Betty Ford to display her flair for life and express tolerant social attitudes because her husband was widely viewed as stodgy and conservative. On occasion a president tries to distract the media from his problems by emphasizing the first lady's attractive qualities as she performs these activities. John F. Kennedy (presidency, 1961-63) used his wife in this way in 1961 when his diplomatic meetings with European leaders failed to achieve either real or symbolic achievements. Kennedy undoubtedly was quite happy to describe his role, as he did, as that of the "man who accompanied Jacqueline Kennedy to Paris."

Using the Children: The president's children, like his wife, often present a difficult target for his enemies to hit and an attractive subject for the media to cover. Like the first lady, the children are thus used as surrogates when it might be difficult or inconvenient for the president to appear. For example, President Ford's son Jack stood in for his father on several occasions during the 1976 presidential campaign. News organizations are interested in the romantic activities of the young adults in the president's family and the play activities of his small children. The weddings of the daughters of Lyndon Johnson (presidency, 1963-69) and Richard Nixon (presidency, 1969-74) were given extensive media attention. During John Kennedy's term (1961-63), his children were a continuing subject of newspaper and magazine stories.

Media Collaboration: News organizations usually are willing partners in White House efforts to publicize the personal life of the president and members of his family. Because his personal qualities are easier to portray than the complex policy developments of his administration, editors have a larger appetite for family stories than for articles about, for example, governmental reorganization or natural gas deregulation. The desire of news organizations to obtain exclusive personal glimpses of the first family leads to opportunities for considerable manipulation by the White House. Because some reporters know their editors or producers will reward them for exclusive stories featuring the president's personal life, they *may* (Seol's emphasis) exchange favorable coverage of the president in the policy for access to him and his family (Grossman and Kumar, 1981, pp. 231-32).

(2) Projecting Leadership Qualities

White House officials want the media to portray the president as a decisive commander who is well regarded by political chiefs in America and other nations. When they suggest how he should respond to a crisis, implement a decision, or engage in diplomatic meetings, they consider how a particular course of action will "play" in the media. On many occasions, publicity benefits weigh heavily in the decision-making process. Former White House officials admit that publicity considerations are not neglected when a president decides to send in the marines, fire an unruly and unpopular subordinate, do something to demonstrate that he is an expert who is respected by the nation's intellectuals, or meet with other national leaders.

Appearing Decisive: Military Leadership and Firing Contrary Subordinates. Military decision-making provides great opportunities for a president to win the respect of the media and the approval of large segments of the public. Most recent presidents have benefited from the public perception that they were decisive military leaders: Franklin D. Roosevelt and Harry S. Truman during World War II, Truman and Dwight D. Eisenhower in Korea, Eisenhower in Lebanon, John F. Kennedy in Cuba, Lyndon B. Johnson and Richard Nixon in Vietnam, and Gerald Ford in the Mayaguez incident with Cambodia after the Vietnam War. Presidents often recognize their need to be regarded as decisive by potential adversaries and military allies.

Three presidents who served between 1965 and 1975, as well as their staffs and supporters, vowed that the United States would not be viewed as a helpless, pitiful giant during their terms. Their desire to be portrayed as decisive military leaders by media critics also played an important part in their decisions to use military force (Grossman and Kumar, 1981, pp. 232-33).

A president also hopes to appear strong and decisive when he fires a subordinate who challenges his authority. The decision to remove a subordinate is usually taken because the president and his advisers feel that it is necessary for the president to reaffirm his image as a strong leader. For example, President Ford (presidency, 1974-77) told a news conference that his decisions to remove Henry Kissinger from his White House post and James Schlesinger from the Defense Department were made because he desired his "team" in positions of authority. After Kissinger and Schlesinger left office, several aides admitted that they had hoped that the president's announcement would show that he and not the powerful Washington figures held over from the Nixon administration, was in charge.

Appearing to be in Command: The President as Expert and Effective Intellectual. One way to make the president appear to be in command is to portray him as knowledgeable about the problems of the government and the nation. President Kennedy's performances at presidential press conferences are acknowledged to have been prime exhibitions of this quality. Kennedy responded to reporters' questions with detailed information that he seemed to have at his fingertips. This expertise was well rehearsed. Kennedy, like his successors, had the assistance of a staff that was able to predict a majority of the questions and to provide him with the appropriate answers. The White House creates special situations for the president to display his expertise. This was the case when President Ford answered reporters' questions at a special briefing on the budget in January of 1976. Since the budget is a vast, complicated document covering a large number of government activities, the president's ability to field a wide range of questions served to rebut the notion that he lacked intellectual capacity. This, in fact, was the intention of his advisers.

Although presidents are advised to avoid forming too close an identification with the intelligentsia, most recent incumbents have recognized that their ability to mix well with intellectuals adds to their images as leaders who can cope with major problems they must confront. Presidents have appointed economists, political scientists, historians, and sociologists to prominent positions in their administrations. Contacts with writers, philosophers, and artists are also thought to be important to show that the president is capable of the deep understanding of issues that these intellectuals regard as their special achievement.

Being Recognized as an International Leader: The Value and Problems of Foreign Travel. Meetings between the president and foreign leaders are excellent opportunities for White House officials to portray the president as the embodiment of the national interest. During trips abroad and receptions in Washington, the president participates in impressive ceremonies that are reported by the media, but the actual negotiating sessions are closed. Thus correspondents usually have to accept the version given to them by government briefing officers. In Washington, reporters may be able to get around the blackout because, with so many people in Congress or the bureaucracy informed, someone is likely to talk. In a foreign setting, however, it is difficult for reporters to verify officially released information by checking with independent sources. Stories obtained from "leaks" by members of the president's entourage are likely to be self-serving versions planted by the administration. Finally, the "results" of the meeting often consist of a communique that is difficult for reporters to assess on the spot. In these circumstances, favorable publicity is a reward White House officials expect to obtain from their relations with reporters on presidential trips. Television is their primary target because it shows off the president in a glamorous or exotic setting.

However, the ever-larger press entourages that have followed presidents since Eisenhower's 1959 world swing have created problems for the White House. Foreign trips no longer provide automatic favorable coverage a president once could expect. Many news organizations send specialists on the host countries in addition to the reporters who describe the ceremonial activities. These specialists often provide a perspective different from the official version. Nevertheless, foreign travel remains an excellent presidential vehicle for displaying his leadership qualities. Most of the stories that appear on television or in print are straightforward accounts of the planned events of the trip that reflect favorably on what the president is doing. Further, there are many legitimate opportunities for trips that fill a useful diplomatic purpose and also contribute to the president's standing in the polls (Grossman and Kumar, 1981, pp. 235-38).

(3) Projecting Policymaker's Images

Liberal, conservative, and "pragmatic" presidents all use similar formats and forums to project their programs to the public. Often the forum becomes more important than any particular message to be communicated through it. The president may address a joint session of Congress or the opening of the United Nations; he may speak to a meeting of one of the numerous associations that offer him standing invitations; and he may address the nation on radio and television. In 1918 Woodrow Wilson (presidency, 1913-21) resurrected the practice of turning the president's constitutional obligation to "give to the Congress Information of the State of the Union" into a full-dress, personally delivered exhortation to adopt his legislative programs. Subsequently, it has been expected that the State of the Union address will be an occasion for the president to lay major policy proposals before the public. The White House staff wants the media to emphasize those portions of the speech concerning what the president believes to be the central concerns of his administration. In order to insure that they understand what the president means, reporters generally are given copies several hours before the address is delivered. Aides brief reporters and answer their questions on the substance and style of the speech.

In addition, the president uses the symbols and ceremonies of his office to associate himself with particular causes or programs. Presidents use ceremonies to demonstrate their policy commitments because they are usually telegenic, easy to stage at the White House, and invariably receive coverage on the evening news. Presidents also hold public bill-signing ceremonies; they welcome important domestic or foreign leaders associated with particular policies to the White House; they have their staff arrange conferences on subjects the administration wishes to sponsor; and they call for briefings and conferences at which the president or an aide attempts to enunciate policies.

(4) Utilizing News Conferences

The news conference is most important to news organizations because it is an event in which they are important public players. A presidential appearance almost always is a source of news, but it does not necessarily provide information. Although news conferences have been held in many different settings and have been governed by varying ground rules, *control seldom has passed out of the hands of the White House* (Seol's emphasis). Reporters usually receive the information the White House plans to give them. A closer look indicates that news conferences always have favored the president.

Press conferences of Franklin D. Roosevelt (presidency, 1933-45) have been described as informal events at which the president and reporters exchanged important information and good-natured banter. According to a sentimental version of the history of the relations between the president and reporters, this permissive and fruitful atmosphere soured when everything was placed on the record, and ended with the introduction of the live television news conference. The decision to allow in the cameras reflected White House concern that reporters might be filtering the message the president was trying to get to the public. *The televised press conference created a theater in which the president calls upon reporters to play their supporting roles to enhance his starring performance* (Seol's emphasis).

The contemporary press conference often is viewed as an open forum where reporters raise questions that concern the interests of the public. Reporters are not limited by constraints like the requirement that existed from 1921 to 1933 that they submit questions in advance. They are not restricted in the use of information that the president declares to be on background, off the record, or subject to review, as was the case before 1961. The absence of constraints, however, has not prevented presidents from maintaining control. The president decides when to hold a conference, how much notice reporters will be given, who will ask the questions, and what the answers will be. The president has a number of ways to set its tone and control what happens. He may begin the conference with an opening statement in which he announces a decision, appointment, or proposal that may become the basis for a number of reporters' questions. *Thus the ad hoc character of the conference is an illusion* (Seol's emphasis).

Presidents usually receive a thorough preparation for their news conferences. Probable questions are prepared by the staff along with suggested answers. For example, James Hagerty introduced briefing books during the Eisenhower administration in order to gather information from departments and agencies about the issues that might be raised by reporters. Sometimes presidents ask their aides to plant questions when they want to make statements on certain topics. Planting questions was a common technique during the early years of the public press conference. During the Eisenhower administration, reporters knew that the president called on those whose questions had been cleared in advance by Press Secretary Hagerty. The practice of using planted questions continued throughout the 1960s. Lyndon Johnson in particular thoroughly approved of the practice. Planting questions was such a standard practice during the Eisenhower administration that some foreign diplomats operated on the assumption that every question could be a planted one (Grossman and Kumar, 1981, pp. 241-49).

MEDIA PERSPECTIVES

Media's Framing of Presidential Images

(1) America's Imperial Media: "Frame the Presidents!"

Regardless of how much power the presidents can exert to manipulate media's presidential portrayal, the media have *some leverage* (Seol's emphasis) against the president. Political scientist Robert M. Entman (1990) described how powerful media can be while reporting on the presidents in his article "The Imperial Media" (DiClerico, 1990, pp. 154-67). Entman argued that the media complicate the task of presidential leadership by equating press interests with the public interest, by dissolving the distinction between public and private leadership, by focusing excessive attention on disputes within the executive branch, and by imposing contradictory expectations on the president. Entman explained how the media framed presidential images:

> Media practices thrust the president into the news. Presidential management of the media is often compatible with journalists' needs. But in choosing and defining political news stories, journalists look for powerful cast of characters, for conflict or controversy between its members, and for potential personal impact on audiences (DiClerico, 1990, p. 155).

Moreover, journalists frame their stories based on their own news value system. Entman noted that the processes that journalists use to frame the presidential news stories are fourfold. These processes of framing presidential news may provide grounds for presidential dissatisfaction with their images in the media:

i) Personalization: the neglect of historical or structural explanations by concentrating on individuals whose deliberate choices cause events

ii) Source standardization: the use of the same group of informants on the beat

iii) Dramatization: the depiction of interactions of news personalities so as to generate audience interest, pity, fear, and catharsis

iv) Surrogate representation: the enforcement of government responsive- ness to the public by pressing politicians to explain candidly their actions, motivations, and plans (DiClerico, 1990)

Although hindered by president's control over much newsworthy information and constrained by conventional definitions of news, reporters and their editors nonetheless have considerable autonomy, especially in seeking out news that can be narrated as drama unfolding. In the journalists' eyes, drama lies in stories of presidential involvement in domestic conflict and in history-making ventures, usually overseas. Drama is magnified when the outcomes are either highly uncertain or likely to mark a major change (Entman, 1990, pp. 155-56). In recent decades, journalists have taken a more aggressively critical stance toward the presidency since the perceived presidential betrayals of Vietnam and Watergate.

(2) Presidential News Selection: "Important or Interesting?"

News media have their own editorial policy in evaluating the value of presidential news. In the newsroom, there is ongoing conflict over selection between important and interesting presidential news. Cook and Ragsdale (1995) discussed the media definitions of "interesting" presidential stories. They argued that:

> Although the president can designate importance, the media have an advantage in indicating what is interesting. Reporters must "sell" their stories to superiors, who decide both how much to "budget" for a story (paragraphs in print, minutes and seconds in broadcast), and what will go into the news and where. Lacking specific indicators of what the audience wants to read or see, and doubtful, in any case, of the audience's ability to know what is of most value, reporters rely on seat-of-the-pants journalistic standards of interest (Nelson, 1995, pp. 310-12).

This observation is closely related to the arguments offered by Pamela J. Shoemaker and Stephen D. Reese (1996) that messages are conveyed through the filters of individual factors, media routines, organizational influences, and ideological influences. Following line of argument proposed by Shoemaker and Reese, presidential news may be viewed as any of the presidential messages that passed through four filters mentioned above. This also may be part of the selection processes for presidential news.

Argument by sociologist Herbert J. Gans (1979) about "enduring values" is also relevant here. Gans extracted eight clusters of enduring values from decades of scrutiny of American news media. His idea was that these eight clusters were a picture of American society the media thought it ought to be. See the following enduring value clusters:

i) Ethnocentrism: American news values its own nation above all others.

ii) Altruistic democracy: American democracy should be based on public interest and service.

iii) Responsible capitalism: An optimistic faith that, in the good society, businessmen and women will compete with each other in order to create increased prosperity for all.

iv) Small-town pastoralism: Emphasis on rural and anti-industrial values, viewing cities as problematic, inflicted with crime and fiscal insolvency.

v) Individualism: Emphasis on freedom of the individual, heroic acts of individuals.

vi) Moderatism: Discouragement of excess or extremism. Extreme behavior was criticized.

vii) Order: Social disorder discouraged.

viii) Leadership: Emphasis on competent leaders, as shapers of national changes. President is viewed as the foremost leader and ultimate protector of order in America. The president is the nation's moral leader, representative of the national values, and the agent of the national will (Gans, 1979).

Drawing from Gans' criteria of news values, Cook and Ragsdale put forward two sets of considerations for the journalists to rely on for presidential news selection:

i) News must correspond to what Gans calls "product considerations" or what others term "production values." Journalists for all media presume that the more timely, clear-cut, easily described, vivid, colorful, and visualizable something is, the more newsworthy it is.

ii) Reporters pay attention to cultural standards of what makes a "good story." Reporters return to what Gans has called the "enduring values" of the news, most overtly displayed in feature stories that celebrate "rugged individualism, mourn the passage of rural and small-town traditions, and discover altruistic leaders" in American life (Nelson, 1995, p. 311).

In this regard, Cook and Ragsdale added that reporters also rely on yesterday's news frequently. They said that "reporters determine the good stories of today based on the past stories."

(3) Categories of Presidential Activities and Presidential News

Political scientists George C. Edwards III and Stephen J.

Wayne (1994) discussed presidency in terms of seven areas of presidential activities. These seven categories may in turn shape the categories of presidential news, which will convey presidential images:

i) *The president and the public*: president who is interacting with public and how he is viewed by the public

ii) *The president's office*: how he behaves in the White House as chief executive and interacts with vice president

iii) *Presidential decision making (policymaking)*: how he comes to a decision; This category includes arenas such as domestic, foreign, and defense policy making.

iv) *Personalized presidency*: how he is portrayed as a human being

v) *The president and the executive branch*: how he leads the executive branch

vi) *The president and Congress*: how he prosecutes presidential duties vis-a-vis the Congress

vii) The president and the judiciary: how he prosecutes presidential duties vis-a-vis the judiciary

(4) Four Frames of Presidential News and Presidential Images

Are there categories of presidential news? And how can the presidential images be categorized? This issue was addressed previously, but this discussion offers an additional dimension. Cook and Ragsdale (1995) said that in all of the presidential stories, journalists and presidents alike depict an image of *a particular kind of protagonist* (Seol's emphasis). This concept can be interpreted to be "an ideal of presidential image." Their discussion of the presidential image is well-organized and noteworthy:

> The presidential narratives stem from an image of the president as the one person in charge of the government, speaking with a clear, lone voice. In this view, the president is the *nation's principal problem solver*, the one who identifies the nation's most pressing issues and offers solutions.

In times of crisis, presidents single-handedly protect the nation. They symbolize the nation and embody its moral and patriotic values. Thus, when journalists express concern about a president's "drift," "lack of focus," "indecision," "muddle," and "inconsistency," they are implicitly endorsing the single executive image about how presidents should act --- decisively, clearly, and with determination (Nelson, 1995, pp. 312-13).

This may be the widely held image or the expected role of the presidency that people have with the president. Cook and Ragsdale discussed four categories of "presidential narratives" (or presidential stories) which emanate from the *single executive image*, which means the single presidential image. They presented the four familiar presidential stories as following:

The story of the president as a problem solver: The story of the president as a domestic problem solver has become a familiar one. Since Theodore Roosevelt (presidency, 1901-09) first introduced the Square Deal and Woodrow Wilson (presidency, 1913-21) followed suit with the New Freedom, presidents have offered packages of legislative proposals designed to cure the most pressing ills of the nation. Some presidents have obligingly made the story more interesting by giving these proposals names --- the New Deal (Franklin D. Roosevelt, presidency 1933-45), the Fair Deal (Harry S. Truman, presidency 1945-53), the New Frontier (John F. Kennedy, presidency 1961-63), and the Great Society (Lyndon B. Johnson, presidency 1963-69). The story typically begins at the time of the first State of the Union message, during which the president lays out the problems of the country and promises to fix them. The story is then revisited off and on during the next weeks, months, and years, as the president succeeds or fails in Congress, in the executive branch, and in the public eye. The news story almost always ends the same way --- with some degree of disappointment that the president did not accomplish all that he set out to achieve.

The story of the president as an international leader: The story depicts the president as the world leader whose decisions keep the free world free or make the oppressed world free. In the story, the president acts boldly, dramatically, with a sense of crisis, and alone. Even when the secretaries of defense and state, the national security adviser, members of the Joint Chiefs of Staff, and the director of the Central Intelligence Agency are intimately involved in the decisions, the "single executive image" held by newspeople casts the president as the solitary decision maker, leading the forces of good against the forces of evil. During the Cold War, the story was of presidents fighting the red menace of communism. Since the collapse of the Soviet Union, presidents now fight other tyrants and dictators. For example, the story pictured former president George H. W. Bush (presidency, 1989-93) as representing the forces of democracy against the "butcher of Bagdad," the former Iraqi leader Saddam Hussein who was deposed from presidency and captured in 2003 during the Second Gulf War. The story ends on an upbeat note with the president successfully protecting the nation's and the world's best interests.

The story of the president as a representative of the people: Presidents are also part of a story about the American people in which the president articulates the American dream, American reinvigoration, and American success. In the story, the president acts as national cheerleader, boosting the collective morale of the country. The story is about presidents who match the values, aspirations, even the very lives of their fellow citizens. Thus, the story captures presidents in their ceremonial roles: lighting Christmas trees, laying wreaths at the tombs of war dead, visiting devastated disaster areas, and congratulating victorious athletes and returning astronauts. It also reveals presidents as ordinary people who enjoy vacation, develop illnesses, and have wayward siblings. This narrative, which resembles the timeless human interest stories that fill out a newspaper or close a television broadcast, is a continuing story and has no real ending. The ceremonial and ordinary-person aspects of the presidential story capture press attention throughout presidents' terms, even when their popularity is low and news coverage is negative.

The story of the president's mistakes: This story depicts the president as having committed a major public, political, or policy gaffe. At worst, presidents are presented as villains or, more ambiguously, as naive fools. The story takes two twists. In the first, the president does something that backfires in the world, in Congress, or in public opinion. So, for example, there is the story of Jimmy Carter's ill-fated helicopter rescue attempt of the American hostages in Iran. Former president George H. W. Bush's broken promise of "no new taxes" and Gerald Ford's pardon of Richard Nixon are additional examples. In another story line, the president acts illegally, appears to lie, says things publicly that contradict other reports about an event, or denies being aware of the apparently questionable actions of aides. In each instance, the president acts in a way that is contrary to the single executive image. One of the dominant stories during the Vietnam War was about President Johnson's "credibility gap." Johnson was routinely criticized for claiming ignorance about various efforts that intensified the American involvement in the war, many of which he had expressly ordered and each of which the press exposed in extensive daily war coverage (Nelson, 1997, pp. 312-14).

In sum, the four categories of "presidential narratives" tell the public, the press, and the president what to expect and when to expect it during the course of a presidential term. These stories often effectively establish boundaries to the negotiation of newsworthiness between the White House and the media. They provide a set number of story lines that journalists are likely to pursue. What is newsworthy depends on whether the event fits within one or more of the narratives. If the president does something outside the frames of presidential stories or acts in ways that the story frames do not acknowledge, journalists are less likely to be cooperative in getting the president's message out. In particular, *if the president cannot convincingly present himself as the problem solver, international leader, or representative of the people, the media can simply turn to the fourth available story frame of the presidential mistakes and errors* (Seol's emphasis).

(5) Superficiality and Triviality of Presidential Coverage

Edwards and Wayne (1994) addressed the issue of superficiality and triviality in presidential images. According to them, early in the 20th century Woodrow Wilson complained that most reporters were interested in the personal and trivial rather than in principles or policies. The authors argued that things have not changed much in the ensuing generations. In a background briefing in 1979 President Carter complained to reporters:

> I would really like for you all as people who relay Washington events to the world to take a look at the substantive questions I have to face as a president and quit dealing almost exclusively with personalities (Edwards and Wayne, 1994, p. 153).

Edwards and Wayne stated that media coverage of national news today is characterized by brevity and simplicity. Editors do not want to bore or confuse their viewers, listeners, or readers. Edwards and Wayne addressed the superficiality of presidential news as follows:

> One of the causes of the superficial coverage of the presidency is the demands of news organizations for information that is new and different, personal and intimate, revealing and unexpected. According to the White House correspondent for a major news chain: It's a lot easier for me to get 'my stories' into several newspapers in the chain with a story about Amy, President Carter's daughter, than with a story about an important policy decision. ABC White House correspondent Sam Donaldson once commented in much the same vein. He said that "A clip of convalescent Reagan waving from his window at some circus elephants is going to push an analytical piece about tax cuts off the air every time (Edwards and Wayne, 1994, p. 156-57)."

Edwards and Wayne explained that given the emphasis on the short run and the demand for details of the president's activities, reporters face continual deadlines. There is little time for reflection, analysis, or comprehensive coverage. One Washington bureau chief of *Newsweek* once said that "The worst thing in the world that could happen to you is for the President of the United States to choke on a piece of meat, and for you not to be there." This journalist said that when former President George H. W. Bush vomited at a state dinner in Japan, television networks had a field day, running the tape of the president's illness again and again.

A related factor contributing to the superficiality and triviality of the presidential news is the great deal of money and personnel needed to cover presidents, including following them around the globe on official business and on vacations. Because of this investment and because of the public's interest in the presidents, reporters must come up with something every day.

In addition, there are more than organizational imperatives at work. Reporters' backgrounds and personal interests also underlie the trivialization of the news. When they talk to each other about politics, they emphasize the superficial aspects --- who will be elected, what bills will pass, what personalities the principal actors have, and who has power. The typical White House reporter lacks special background on the presidency. Moreover, the White House press frequently lacks policy expertise relevant to understanding the issues with which the president deals. Thus, its focus on politics and personalities rather than on issues is not surprising (Edwards and Wayne, 1994, pp. 156-57).

Stories of George W. Bush fainting while eating pretzel and coming up with a bruise on his face may be an example of superficial coverage in a sense. Stories of presidential pets may be additional examples.

The story of President Roh Moo Hyun, whose voice became stronger, may be a third example (*Kyunghyang*, June 22, 2004). The story said that Roh's voice grew more powerful after he survived the impeachment resolution and the general election. The story was based on a scholar's analysis of voice quality of Roh.

Media Adversarialism as Ritual

Bennett (1996, pp. 149-152) noted that media's adversarial role may remain superficial. He said that media's adversarialism may be ritualistic. If the media were truly adversarial in their dealings with politicians, they would face a serious dilemma. The news could end up discrediting the institutions and values on which it depends for credibility. If officials and their positions were routinely attacked or held suspect by journalists, the media would have no source of official acknowledgements. To a remarkable degree, the illusion of news objectivity is maintained by the narrow range of perspectives admitted into the news and by the heavy reliance on official views to certify those perspectives as credible and valid.

It is equally true that the news would lose its image of objectivity if reporters openly catered to the propaganda interests of public officials and government institutions. If both genuine adversarialism and its complete absence would undermine the illusion of news objectivity, then there is an obvious implication: *Any observable adversarial behavior on the part of the press should reveal itself more as a posture of antagonism than as a no-holds-barred approach to the content of the news. A ritualistic posture of antagonism between press and government creates the appearance of mutual independence without throwing open the content of the news to the serious coverage of a broad range of political perspectives. Such ritualistic posturing dramatizes the myths of a free press and an open government* (Seol's emphasis).

As evidence of ritualistic adversarialism of the press, Bennett (1996) presented C. Jack Orr's study of the presidential press conference. Analyzing data from a sample of Kennedy, Johnson, and Nixon press conferences, Orr found that the proportion of hostile or critical questions was virtually constant across presidents, conferences, issue categories, and political contexts. Not only did the incidence of confrontational questions fall into a routine pattern, but nearly all hostile questions were personal in nature. Many of those personal questions signaled clear deference to office and institution. Moreover, questions that could have been phrased as strong political attacks generally instead contained open invitations to the president to redefine the issue or dismiss the entire question. Based on these patterns, Orr concluded that the adversarial postures of press and president create a dramatic image of journalistic aggressiveness while communicating a subtle message of institutional deference.

In an age in which personal image and public approval are important elements of political power, politicians may try to avoid even ritualistic skirmishes with the press pack. It is no accident that fewer press conferences have been held in recent decades, indicating that presidents prefer to deliver their messages to the public in more controlled settings. With news organizations increasingly keying on the most personal and dramatic aspects of politicians' lives, stepping in front of the pack can prove challenging to a president. For example, George H. W. Bush stepped to the podium with a world leader to announce the results of important talks (part of the politician's ritual) only to be asked about whether he had had a love affair a few years earlier. When Bill Clinton introduced Supreme Court nominee Ruth Bader Ginsberg to the press, the opening question from the press pack challenged the president's political motives for her appointment and so angered Clinton that he lectured the journalists on their common decency.

Broad ritualistic elements have also been observed in the reporting of less routine events such as scandals and crises. Such investigative reporting has been a hallmark of adversarial journalism. Despite the claims of journalists to the contrary, a number of observers have argued that crises and scandals have become routine news events, complete with standard reporting formulas. For example, in their analysis of news coverage of improprieties in Carter presidential aide Bert Lance's banking business, Altheide and Snow concluded that the scandal was cast quickly into standard reporting formulas. These formulas were not only instrumental in creating the scandal but also obscured indications of the actual political significance and magnitude of the incident. The coverage damaged Carter personally, yet connections between the scandal and its actual impact on office and state were assiduously avoided. The overall impression from the intense media investigation was one of dramatic confrontation between press and establishment.

The Nature of White House Beat: Depressing or Encouraging?

Grossman and Kumar (1981, pp. 181-205) presented a description of the nature of the White House as a newsbeat. Although the description was given more than two decades ago, the overall impression of the beat may still be valid today. According to them, the atmosphere in the White House provides a life support system rich in the ingredients that enhance a journalist's status but thin in elements that encourage high-enterprise reporting. Editors and producers provide space or time for the prominent display of a reporter's stories about the public presidency. But in order to cover the Chief Executive's activities, correspondents allow officials to herd them to briefings, ceremonies, and conferences where they are fed a diet of statements, releases, and rehearsed answers. Those who try to get information independently must wait for an escort before they can visit West Wing offices. Reporters who are not satisfied with the sustenance provided at scheduled media events find that officials who dispense information privately usually dictate the terms for its use and consumption. "There is no place where a correspondent can be more easily led than at the White House," commented James Naughton of the *New York Times*. "It is the nature of the beat."

Reporters congregate in the briefing room and the adjoining press areas at the center of the public White House, where they hope to get a sense of what is going on inside the private areas. What they get are echoes of their own thoughts rather than cross-currents of information flowing among White House officials. "The press room is hermetically sealed," remarked *National Journal* correspondent Dom Bonafede, who rarely mixed with other reporters there. "The mood in the White House press room is a mood the press itself creates." Barriers limiting unscheduled and informal movements by reporters affect their ability to cover the President. "I might as well be in Silver Spring (city of central Maryland mear Washington D.C., Seol's note)," Andrew Glass of the Cox Newspapers commented while standing at his desk---which was located only a few corridors away from where the president and most of the senior White House staff were sitting or standing at theirs. "You have no idea of what they're really doing. The only time you see them on the job is in a situation stage-managed by them."

Not surprisingly, reporters emphasize the frustrations rather than the benefits of their assignment. They suggest how difficult it is for them to get away from the pack when their organizations require them to follow all the other reporters attending the president. Another concern they share is that the range of technical stories involved in White House coverage is too great for a generalist reporter. Others complain that restrictions imposed by the staff allow the White House to shape their stories. Most comments reflected these negative concerns. "You can be manipulated so easily because you can't find them," Curtis Wilkie of the *Boston Globe* said in explanation of why, despite its prestige for a political reporter, he did not want the assignment. "It is very easy to get isolated here," Bob Schieffer of CBS News reflected. "I can see how you can have an imperial presidency." This makes a good contrast with Cook and Ragsdale's foregoing observation that "the top domestic newsbeat is the White House."

According to Grossman and Kumar (1981), only a few reporters responded positively to the assignment. Dennis Farney of the *Wall Street Journal* found satisfaction because "you were covering something that was demonstrably important and significant." At the same time Farney admitted that he felt "a pervasive anxiety, a fear that someone has something that I should have had. Reporters admitted that, despite their knowledge that they were being used, they often produced the stories the White House wanted. Peter Lisagor of the *Chicago Daily News* suggested that the White House can shape the news because news organizations place pressures on reporters that leave them vulnerable. He argued, "Anyone who says they're not being manipulated is lying to you."

Characteristics of White House Reporters

At the beginning of the 1980s the majority of White House regulars appeared to be between thirty-five and forty-five years old, according to Grossman and Kumar (1981, pp. 182-83). A small crowd of veteran reporters were further into the middle age, and John Osborne of the *New Republic* was the only regular who had passed seventy. Editors apparently realize that the physical strains of the job---the toll that the long hours extract from a reporter's energies---require the stamina and good health that usually accompany the earlier portions of life. The *New York Times*'s Martin Tolchin, a man much younger than Osborne, once said, "It is an extremely hard, demanding job. I fell asleep at 9:30 in my chair last week. I am exhausted. It is physically hard. I've increased my jogging just to stay in shape for those damn trips. It is a physically, intellectually, and socially demanding job."

Perhaps because of the constant physical effort, only a few correspondents spend many years as White House reporters. In contrast, when Timothy Crouse observed the White House regulars for his book *The Boys on the Bus* in 1972, he found a crowd of veteran correspondents who treated the assignment as a "sinecure" "one more quiet men's club," and "a slow death." By the middle of the 1970s, however, members of the prewar generation whose activities might have merited these caustic comments had passed from the scene. The senior White House correspondents in 1980 did not fit Crouse's description. For example, Frank Cormier of the Associated Press and Helen Thomas of the United Press International were well-regarded and vigorous correspondents.

Many younger reporters regard the job as a way station to higher professional positions and leave the White House assignment after two or three years. "The White House is a big ticket ... an institutional ticket," David Halberstam of the *New York Times* commented. "The guy who goes to the White House goes on to some bigger job within the newspaper." *New York Times* correspondents Tom Wicker and Max Franker became *Times* editors, while James Naughton left to take a position as a national editor of the *Philadelphia Inquirer*. Hugh Sidey left the White House beat to become chief of *Time*'s Washington bureau. According to Dennis Farney of the *Wall Street Journal*, his paper views the White House "as a place where you bring in someone you want to test---you give it to a younger reporter. The most prestigious reporters are on the Hill."

Can Generalists Cover the President Better?

Although some reporters had covered specialized areas such as economics or defense before they were assigned to the White House, most were generalists with a broad background as political correspondents (Grossmand and Kumar, 1981, pp. 183-84). With the notable exceptions of Dom Bonafede of the National Journal and John Osborne of the New Republic, reporters did not regard the presidency itself as an area about which it was necessary to acquire specialized knowledge and information. Even those with expertise in some specific areas---economic problems or urban affairs, for example---did not have a background in issues involving domestic policies, international relations, and defense. This has consequences. "A guy who really understands diplomatic affairs is usually an absolute dunce on domestic affairs and vice versa," Martin Tolchin of the *New York Times* suggested. As a result, White House correspondents skim the substance of many issues to focus politics or personalities. The specialists at the White House report on technical issues, but the reporters may neglect the organization's angle because they are unfamiliar with the administration.

Some reporters maintain that generalists have the right preparation for the White House beat. "There is no difference between covering the White House and covering the county courthouse, as far as I can see," one reporter said. "I have done them all." Other reporters claim that as explainers of the news, their job is to provide what Herbert Gans referred to in *Deciding What's News* as a "mirror image" of reality. These correspondents believe that technical stories are not their responsibility. They are explainers. For them, reporting is a reflection of the thing reported. Bob Schieffer of the CBS News described himself as an explainer and maintained that his job as a network correspondent was to report "what it was that was said today and what does it mean." A correspondent should gather the facts, then try to present them in a context that makes sense to the viewer or reader. Thus, Schieffer said, when he arrived at the White House as Ford took over from Nixon, "there was the muffin story, and you you do that kind of story because Ford didn't do anything. The he did something, he pardoned Nixon."

This section reminds one of the superficiality and triviality of presidential news discussed earlier. White House stories cannot but tend to become superficial, because most of the White House beat reporters are not equipped with specialized knowledge, because news editors do not want them to file complex issue stories, and because the beat reporters must crank out stories on a daily basis (Seol's comment).

Presidential Coverage as Products of Rules and Routines

Although Grossman and Kumar (1981) described how the reporters accessed sources in the White House more than two decades ago, it is still worthwhile to note how reporters managed to get information under firm rules of the White House beat. According to them, the first rule of the 1980s was that access to the president and the White House staff be controlled by the administration. At times this power was exercised firmly, as it was during the Eisenhower administration, when the Press Office was the only real source of information for most reporters. On other occasions, as in Kennedy, Ford, and Carter administrations, officials were usually accessible. The fact that White House officials retain this control led some reporters to describe themselves as *prisoners* (Seol's emphasis). "This is why most people don't like the White House once they get there," James Naughton remarked, "They are captives of the system." Even in "open" administrations, White House correspondents cannot drop by an aide's office as they could if they were covering the House or Senate. As a result, reporters develop sources, whom they meet outside the White House. Offering lunch in one of Washington's better restaurants was a technique used by reporters from news organizations with generous expense accounts.

A second rule was that the White House can specify what reporters may or may not attribute to a particular official. Although many press conferences had been on the record for many years, background briefings and interviews are used extensively by the president and other officials. When White House staff members give interviews, they usually want to talk "on background," meaning that they will not be named in the story. Officials want the protection from direct interrogation that background gives them, but they also fear that if their name appears too frequently in the media, the president, others on the staff, reporters will think they seek publicity for themselves. These rules remind one of the presidential control of news discussed earlier.

In the meantime, the routines involved in coverage of the public presidency make some reporters part of a conveyor belt system transmitting information from the White House to the media. Some correspondents complain that they are props in shows staged by the White House. They suggested that getting the daily story from the White House is a form of stenographic reporting in which correspondents transcribe what officials say. Another frequent complaint is that because the White House forces all reporters to follow similar routines, the result is "pack journalism"--a derogatory term implying that reporters present the same story in the same way because they think and act alike.

In addition to routines organized by the White House, reporters follow routines originating in the values of the profession. These also lead to similar behavior by many correspondents. For example, news means to look for what is new. "Our leads might all be the same because we are all looking for the new element," suggested James Deakin of the St. Louis Post-Dispatch. "There isn't all that much that is new, so if there is only one new thing, then we will lead with it." A second rule is "don't get scooped." This means a reporter can't afford to let a story get past him. A third rule is that conflicts and personalities make news. A fourth, that readers and viewers are interested in the politics of an issue rather than its technical aspects. Each of these routines leads reporters to trudge over the same ground that their colleagues are covering. It places most reporters in a defensive position and explains why there is so little investigative reporting at the White House. Peter Lisagor asserted, "The White House is the last place the Watergate story would have broken."

Presidential Images Contrasted with Other Concepts

This book examines presidential images (or, presidential coverage) as represented the *New York Times* and the *Kyunghyang Daily*: How these two newspapers portrayed President George W. Bush and President Roh Moo Hyun respectively. The author thinks that there are other concepts that need to be differentiated from "presidential images."

(1) Presidential News Stories vs. Presidential Photographs

The definitions of the word "image" provided by the Webster dictionary (Webster's II: New College Dictionary, 1995) are varied. Among them are: i) The idea of someone or something that is held by the public; ii) The character projected by someone or something to the public, especially by the mass media; iii) A reputation; and iv) A mental picture of something unreal or not present, and so on. An "image" can be defined as "a mental image of something or somebody." Therefore, "presidential image" may be operationally defined for this book as "the overall mental picture or impression that mass media project to the public in the form of stories or photographs."

Scholarly literature such as Grossman and Kumar's (1981) Portraying the President: The White House and the News Media discussed images of the White House in the media, but they did not give a clear definition of the presidential image. The definition of presidential image is closely linked to the scope of presidential stories. In this undefined situation, the two authors evaluated portrayal of the president ("tone of the White House stories," in the authors' words) as being positive (favorable), neutral, or negative (unfavorable).

Very often verbal images of the president and visual images of him may differ, as the two argued previously. The discrepancy in verbal and visual images can be discovered occasionally. Graber (2002) illustrated how this happened in three news media:

> The similarities between print and broadcast media in their patterns of coverage do not mean that various media organizations project identical images of public officials. For example, when a local newspaper, an elite newspaper, or network television covered two items --- a proposal by President Ronald Reagan to cut taxes and the president's 1984 trip to Europe --- three different sets of images emerged from the stories. The Durham Morning Herald, a local paper from North Carolina with limited resources for

independent news analysis, presented accounts drawn largely from the wire services. These stories featured the themes, ideas, and perspectives provided by the White House and cast the president and the events into a favorable light. The elite New York Times also reported the White House version of events, but subjected the White House reports to critical analysis. This created a much less rosy impression of the state of affairs. The CBS Evening News presented a more mixed picture. Verbal images were predominantly negative, but visual images, based on presidentially controlled photo opportunities, were highly favorable. Audiences for these three news sources thus were informed about the same events, but the tint of the interpretative lenses varied (Graber, 2002, p. 275)."

Graber's explanation showed that news stories and news photos may not necessarily go together. Images as depicted through presidential news stories and presidential photos may not be identical. However, the strength of visual images should never be ignored. Hence, the need to content-analyze the presidential stories together with presidential photos. And the relative importance of presidential stories vis-a-vis that of presidential photos varies depending on whether the media is a newspaper or television.

(2) Presidential Media Images vs. Political Reality

Media image and political reality may not go together. Graber (1982) offered a definition of the notion of image as "subjective projections and perceptions of reality, which rarely reflect it with total accuracy." She raised the possibility of differences between media image and reality. According to her argument, television made people aware that politics is largely a drama acted out before public audiences. It made them realize that images deserve to be investigated because of, rather than in spite of, the fact that they often diverge from reality in a major way. She presented a representative example of the discrepancy between the two:

> Is it wise to study images when reality could be studied instead? The answer is a resounding "yes." Images are reality, even when they grossly distort what is actually happening. People's perceptions are the reality on which they base their actions. In fact, perceptions may be more important than the "real facts," if the real facts remain unknown. President Nixon was reelected in 1972 with a landslide majority of votes because his image remained largely untainted by the Watergate burglary, which had occurred several months earlier. Even after the reality became fully known and understood, the public abandoned its favorable image only reluctantly (Graber, 1982, pp. 15-16).

It is also true that presidential images can be affected by things that are beyond the reach of the president's press relations. According to Rozell (2003), Ford's presidential press secretary Ron Nessen claimed that "no White House can do much about a president's image." In his view, if the economy is sound and people feel secure about their future, the president does not need much stage managing or a crafty media strategy to look good. If the economy falters and people are anxious about the future, however, the president's image suffers, no matter how articulate he may be or how much he glad-handles the press. Carter press secretary Jody Powell, responding to criticism that Carter's common-man symbolism was at the heart of the administration's image problem, stated that "a president might look good in blue jeans if it is going well and not so good if things are bad." Nessen and Powell are certainly correct to argue that forces larger that presidential press relations (e.g., the inevitable swings of the economy) significantly influence the public's perception of a president's leadership acumen, but the ways in which the public views those larger forces and the adequacy of the president's responses largely are determined by the media (Pfiffner and Davidson, 2003, p. 143).

(3) Presidential Media Images vs. Effects on Audiences

Arguably, presidential coverage performed by a news organization may have effects on the public. But this book confines its scope to the presidential images of Bush and Roh as conveyed by the *New York Times* and the *Kyunghyang Daily* but does not touch on its effects. Media scholars differentiate media contents from "media effects" in that the effects presuppose changes of attitude or perception on the part of audiences. Audiences can accept media contents selectively, thus lowering the power of media effects. They may show three kinds of reactions: i) Convert their existing perceptions; ii) Change their perceptions in a minor way; or iii) Reinforce their existing perception (McQuail, 2000, p. 423).

However, it still remains elusive how presidential coverage can affect the public's attitude to the president. Political scientist Cliff Zukin argued that the strongest effect of the media is reinforcement of the existing attitudes and opinions. In this vein, Graber said that "Most media stories are promptly forgotten. Stories that become part of an individual's fund of knowledge tend to reinforce existing beliefs and feelings. Acquisition of new knowledge or changes in attitude are the exception rather than the rule" (Edwards and Wayne, 2003, p.177). Although the public may selectively receive the impact from the news media, it is true that media's presidential coverage can build the public agenda. The presidents want to define the situation, and news media may follow their lead under certain circumstances.

(4) Presidential Images vs. Public Relations

Presidential images can be shaped by active public relations activity, which may be part of White House media manipulation. Rozell (2003) said that Franklin D. Roosevelt was a superb manager of news and adept at direct popular leadership. Although reporters at that time did not exhibit the same skepticism of official Washington that is customary today, FDR captivated reporters and used them with great effect to promote the

White House slant on events by sheer force of his personality and media savvy. For press conferences, reporters abided by White House rules that today would be dismissed as unacceptable: the president determined what information was on-background, off-the-record, or not-for-attribution. Reporters who did not follow the president's rules could be cut off from access to the White House. He requested that reporters who asked what he considered to be foolish questions wear a figurative dunce cap. FDR also made a point of flattering reporters by using their first names, soliciting their advice on matters of state, and even inviting some to the White House to join the Roosevelts' small, family dinners. Newspapers strictly abided by the White House rule that FDR, who was disabled from polio, not be photographed in a wheelchair or when being carried by his aides. When FDR fell down face-forward in the mud just before he was to deliver his 1936 nomination speech at Philadelphia's Franklin Field, no photographs were taken, and no one reported the mishap. James E. Pollard wrote some 50 years ago that "here was an administration with a concept of public relations far beyond that of any predecessor. Much of the early success of the New Deal was undoubtedly due to the constant steady flow of organized information from the White House and to the fact that most of the working correspondents were on the side of Mr. Roosevelt. He played their game and very often they were inclined to play his (Pfiffner and Davidson, 2003, p. 137)."

Ronald Reagan proved that it was still possible for modern presidents to win the battle of imagery with the media. Reagan, a former movie actor, came to the White House with a unique set of skills conducive to image-crafting. His administration gave high priority to the public relations aspects of the presidency. To a large extent, the president's daily activities were driven by the needs of the news media. Both he and his press relations staffers understood well the relationship between positive coverage and moving forward a policy agenda. White House Communications Director at the time David Gergen said that "we molded a communications strategy around a legislative strategy. We very carefully thought through what were the legislative goals we were trying to achieve and then formulated a communications strategy which supported them." During crucial periods of his tenure, Reagan was able to sustain enough public support to pressure Congress into approving his agenda and politically protect himself from the kinds of scandals and investigations that surely would have crippled other presidencies (Pfiffner and Davidson, 2003, p. 141).

Summary of Discussion and Research Questions

Political scientists argue that favorable presidential image is indispensable for presidents to implement their policy goals. Apart from discussion of the effects of favorable image on the constituents, favorable presidential image is arguably all the more crucial in times of national crisis or when strong national leadership is required.

Traditionally, most American presidents have been discontented with the media's portrayal of them. That is why presidents have continuously made efforts to control and manipulate the media's presidential news and thus to get a positive presidential image. Although presidents have overwhelming power in the game of getting the favorable presidential image, the media have their own independent power in framing the images of the presidency. Presidents can use a variety of media tactics to get positive coverage: they control, cooperate, negotiate, manipulate, and sometimes intimidate. The can also mobilize a variety of techniques.

A newspaper can convey the presidential image in the form of straight news, analysis, feature, editorial, column, text, and photos. The news accounts may cover presidential behaviors in the areas of program and policy, ceremonial activity, personal acts, relations with vice president, interactions with Congress and administration, election, interactions with staff, and relations with the media. Patterns of presidential coverage may change over time.

Presidential stories may cover such areas as i) The president and the public; ii) The president interacting with vice president; iii) Presidential decision making (policymaking) in arenas such as domestic, foreign, and defense policy making; iv) Personalized presidents as human beings; v) The leader of the executive branch; iv) The president and Congress; and vii) The president and the judiciary.

Media have tried to satisfy as large an audience as possible by framing presidential stories and ignoring pressures or demands from the presidency. The stories that are printed or aired are the end results that passed their product considerations.

A familiar image of the presidency propounded by Cook and Ragsdale (1997) may be part of the results produced by these complicated interactional processes. The two scholars argued that journalists and presidents alike have an idea of a particular kind of protagonist, which means "an ideal of presidential image." They stated that this single executive image of the presidency led to the four popularly held presidential images, which have been repeatedly conveyed and established by the mass media:

i) The story of the president as problem solver,
ii) The story of president as international leader,
iii) The story of president as representative of the people, and
iv) The story of the president's mistakes.

This book will examine and categorize media images of President W. Bush as conveyed by the *New York Times* and those of President Roh Moo Hyun as portrayed by the *Kyunghyang Daily*. This book will also try to generalize when and how the news media criticize and flatter the president based on case studies and expert theories.

The research will proceed along the theoretical lines described in this chapter during four critical time spans for Bush and six time spans for Roh. Although various theoretical frameworks presented in this chapter may overlap to some extent, these willbe examined and refined while research proceeds.

Simultaneously, this research will attempt to find out categories of presidential images not discussed by previous researchers, if any. This research will also examine the following four questions:

(1) Was there a "honeymoon period" between the New York Times and President Geroge W. Bush and between the Kyunghyang Daily and Roh Moo Hyun in the initial weeks of their presidency?

(2) Was the ratio of positive coverage higher than that of negative coverage for the two presidents? What was the percentage of the two and what do these figures stand for?

(3) The newspaper might have spotlighted President Bush as the leader dealing with a national crisis after September 11, and as the wartime leader during Afghanistan War and Persian Gulf War II. How did the New York Times do it? And what does this mean? In the case of President Roh, the Kyunghyang might have focused on the reformer's image. How did this newspaper achieve this?

(4) Was there superficial coverage of Mr. Bush and Mr. Roh?

Note: Chapter II was largely based on American presidency and news media. Cases and theories of Korean presidency will be added when the author comes up with relevant information.

CHAPTER **III**

The closer an event is to the media organization's definition of newsworthiness, the more likely it is to be covered. News organizations value consistency in their coverage over time (Routines of Media Work 3: Shoemaker & Reese, 1996, p. 266).

HOW SHALL WE ANALYZE PRESIDENTIAL COVERAGE?

One discussed mechanisms of presidential communication and journalistic story framing in Chapter II. The end product of interaction between the two sides is news coverage of the president. It is high time to do the fieldwork by examining the actual stories or photos of news media. This book chose two newspapers for analysis: the *New York Times* and the *Kyunghyang Daily News*. Time spans for analysis and means of evaluating stories or photos is discussed in this chapter. This is a preparatory step for analysis of presidential coverage of the two newspapers.

Time Periods for Research

The New York Times

The time spans for this research ranged from President Bush's inauguration on January 20th, 2001 to May 1st, 2003, on which day President Bush declared that "major combat operations in Iraq have ended." Bush said that the battle was "one victory in a war on terror that began on September 11th, 2001, and still goes on." This implies that Mr. Bush put great emphasis on U.S. wars on terrorism (*New York Times*, May 2, 2003, A1; *San Jose*

Mercury News, May 2, 2003, A1; *Wall Street Journal*, May 2, 2003, A1). His first term of office ended and his second term began in January, 2005.

This book probed how Mr. Bush was portrayed in the following four critical time spans in his presidency. The duration of about one month for each time periods may appear somewhat arbitrary, but the following four time periods are critically significant in Bush's presidency.

Period I: From January 20, 2001 to February 19, 2001 (*New York Times*, From 01-21-01 to 02-20-01): Bush's inauguration and jubilation.

Period II: From September 11, 2001 to October 6, 2001 (*New York Times*, From 09-12-01 to 10-07-01): September 11th terrorist attacks and the period of American national grief and consolation for Americans.

Phase III: From October 7, 2001 to November 6, 2001 (*New York Times*, From 10-08-01 to 11-07-01): War against the Taliban regime in Afghanistan, Beginning of anti-terrorism war. (June 13, 2002: Interim leader Karzai takes over power in Afghanistan, Seol's note.)

Period IV: From March 18, 2003 to May 1, 2003 (*New York Times*, From 03-19-03 to 05-02-03): The Second Persian Gulf War.

(January 29, 2002; *New York Times* 01-30-02, Wed): Bush's second State of the Union address. Some remarks about Afghan War.

(January 28, 2003; *New York Times* 01-29-03, Wed): Bush's third State of the Union address. Some remarks and forewarning about War in Iraq (or, Second Gulf War).

The Kyunghyang Daily News (The Kyunghyang Shinmun)

In the case of the *Kyunghyang Daily's* portrayal of President Roh Moo Hyun, the author demarcated six time spans.

Period I: From February 25, 2003 to March 24, 2003 (*Kyunghyang Daily*, From 02-26-03 to 03-25-03): Roh's inauguration.

Period II: From October 10, 2003 to November 9, 2003 (*Kyunghyang Daily*, From 10-11-03 to 11-10-03): Roh's proposal of confidence vote.

Period III: From February 27, 2004 to March 11, 2004 (*Kyunghyang Daily*, From 02-28-03 to 03-12-04): Pre-Impeachment, development leading to Roh's impeachment.

Period IV: From March 12, 2004 to April 14, 2004 (*Kyunghyang Daily*, From 03-03-03 to 04-15-03): Roh impeached. Impeachment resolution at the National Assembly.

Period V: From April 15, 2004 to May 13, 2004 (*Kyunghyang Daily*, From 04-16-04 to 05-14-04): General Election. Roh-backed Woori Party won the election.

Period VI: From May 14, 2004 to May 28, 2004 (*Kyunghyang Daily*, From 05-15-04 to 05-29-04): Resumption of Presidential Function. Roh regained his presidential office and began presidential duties.

Scope and Definition of Presidential Stories and Photos

In evaluating Bush coverage by the *New York Times*, this book will examine stories that carry "Mr. Bush" in major sections such as National, International, Business Day, World Business, Local Edition, and Weekend (WK). But sections such as Sports, Arts and Entertainment, Television, and Book Review were excluded. Stories on the front page and the penultimate page of section A were given heavier weight in discussing Bush stories, because stories placed here are regarded as more important.

Story types of President Bush that will be examined in this book consists of straight news, analyses, columns, editorials, and photos. The researcher content-analyzed these five types of presidential stories and photos.

In the case of the *Kyunghyang Daily*, stories printed on the main section will be examined. The scope of Roh stories and Roh photos will be similar to those standards applied to Bush's.

What news stories or photos constitute presidential coverage that conveys the images of President George W. Bush or President Roh Moo Hyun? Demarcating the scope of coverage which leads to depiction of presidential image can be the starting line for this research.

In the case of "Bush photos," it may be relatively simple. Photos that contain Bush's face, or his profile, or even his back may be regarded as Bush photos. But it still leaves the question unanswered whether the pictures that contained anti-war protesters who decried Mr. Bush about his war policy against Iraq in 2003 can be included in the Bush photos. In this book, these photos will be included in the Bush photos.

In the case of "Roh photos," the same standards will be applied. Stories of people's massive demonstration in support of Roh will be counted as positive to Roh.

When it comes to "Bush stories" that can affect Bush's images, it becomes more difficult to define. Grossman and Kumar's (1982) characterization of presidential news seems deceptively simple (Seol's comment):

> The White House story is the president: who he is, what he does, and what his programs, actions, and goals are. White House media coverage reflects the public president. The president is the most important continuing story the media deal with; he is of interest even when he is not active (Graber, 1982, pp. 101-02).

Following Grossman and Kumar's line of argument, Bush stories may be regarded as those stories that White House correspondents write about Mr. Bush, his actions, or his words. The stories may portray Bush favorably or unfavorably. But according to Grossman and Kumar's (1981) argument, White House reporters are less likely to produce stories that the White House finds offensive than are journalists who write signed opinion columns and editorials, *because White House reporters need continuing frank discussion with White House officials if they are to get important background information* (Seol' emphasis).

This issue will be addressed in Chapters IV and V.

In addition, Bush's image may also be affected by stories that do not cover the White House but write about the effects or reactions of White House's or Bush administration's policy borne upon the public. *The scope of news stories or photos that can affect the presidential image either positively or negatively should thus be broadened* (Seol's idea). Straight stories that carry criticisms uttered by Bush's political opponents or critical columns written by columnists or experts of specific policy areas can surely affect the presidential image negatively. Should these stories be included in the Bush story? This book included these stories in the "Bush stories" category and evaluated them as affecting Bush's image.

When it comes to various expressions such as "America" or "the United States," which may be a totality of representation symbolized by the president of the United States, the dividing line gets even fuzzier. Must these be included in the Bush stories? If the news stories were about massive protests inside and outside of America against the "The Second Gulf War", should they be seen as negative presidential coverage, although no express reference to the Bush presidency is found in the stories? Should the opposition of Germany and France against the U.S. war on Iraq also be counted into the negative coverage of Bush presidency? Admittedly, these news stories may affect the overall image of President Bush indirectly, given that he is the ultimate decision maker on war policy in the capacity of head of executive branch and commander-in-chief of American forces.

This book defined the scope of "Bush coverage" as inclusively as possible to assess the overall Bush's image printed on the pages of the *New York Times* during the four time spans for the research. In this vein, explicit expressions that clearly referred to President George W. Bush or Bush administration were naturally included in the Bush stories. Expressions such as "Bush," "Mr. Bush," "President Bush", "Bush administration," "Bush team," "Bush aides", "The White House," or "the president" that appear in the title, subtitle, or story paragraphs were also included in the "Bush stories." Stories that are clearly linked to

Bush image were included in the Bush coverage, even when the stories did not have the expressions shown above.

The following are characterizations of "Bush stories" that this book regarded as affecting Bush's image in the *New York Times*:

1) Stories that have "Mr. Bush" in the title or subtitle: Yes. These should be naturally regarded as Bush stories. In these stories, Mr. Bush in the title or subtitle clearly tells that the stories discuss Mr. Bush. Ordinarily, these stories have "Mr. Bush" within the story paragraphs.

2) Stories that do not have "Mr. Bush" in the title or subtitle, but have them within the paragraphs: Yes. These may not be problematic, either. In this case, stories that depict "Mr. Bush" explicitly within the story paragraphs will qualify as Bush stories. In 1) and 2), "Bush" ordinarily serves as the subject of a sentence.

3) Stories that depict Bush as an object of criticism or praise: Yes. When "Mr. Bush" does not appear in the title or subtitle, stories that depict Mr. Bush or his policy as an object to be praised or criticized by others will also be classified as Bush stories. Naturally, these stories affect the image of Mr. Bush favorably or unfavorably. They normally may have an explicit expression(s) "Mr. Bush" within the story paragraphs.

4) Stories that use Mr. Bush merely as a point of reference: No.

Even when the title (subtitle) does not mention Mr. Bush, stories may also address "Mr. Bush," but in a very remote manner within the story paragraphs. These stories discuss other main topics apart from Mr. Bush. These will *not* be included in the Bush stories.

5) Stories that have "Mr. Bush" neither in the title nor in the subtitle nor within the story paragraphs: Yes or No. These are problematic. If stories reflect the stream of current presidential affairs or policies, they were included. In case of antiwar demonstrations, even though the stories or the photos (or captions) did not include "Mr. Bush," these stories or photos were included in Bush stories if they were judged to affect Bush image indirectly to some extent.

Note: Almost the same criteria will be applied in sorting out and analyzing "Roh stories" in the *Kyunghyang Daily*.

Qualitative and Quantitative Analysis of Presidential Coverage

The author will evaluate stories and photos qualitatively, if they were judged to be affecting the images of President Bush or President Roh. A list of evaluations on each day's issue of the *New York Times* and the *Kyunghyang Daily* will be made as shown below.

First, the overall tone or impression of the presidential story will be examined. Fairly frequently the titles say whether the coverage is positive or negative. Certain adjectives, nouns, verbs, or phrases that represent the whole image or tone of the presidential story will be considered to evaluate the images of stories or photos. But this research has adopted a "holistic approach" in evaluating the presidential coverage of Bush or Roh.

Second, the stories were evaluated and classified into five groups. "Five-stage positive to negative scale" (Seol's idea) will be adopted based on the overall impression and analysis of the words or sentences used in the news stories or pictures. The evaluating words will be operationally defined as shown below. This measurement (or, coding of stories) will be performed as a kind of applied Likert-scale measurement.

The researcher made fours lists of "Bush's Images" depicted by the *New York Times* based on four time periods. The list for each phase was made up of the following factors:

1) Date and day of the week of the Bush story.
Ex: 03-18-03 (Tue)

2) Serial number of the day's Bush story, the page of the story and its place within the page, and on what subsequent page(s)

the story continued were also indicated. These factors indicate how much importance the *New York Times* attaches to the particular news stories or photos. If a story was printed "above the horizontal half-line," it was marked 1; if "under the horizontal half-line," marked 2, thus appearing in the shape of A1-1 or A10-2 (Seol's idea).

If a story occupies the space above the horizontal half-line of each page, then it is regarded as more important than the story under the half-line. When a story starting on top of a page occupied a long vertical column space on the a page, then it was marked "1", because its title was placed above the half-line. When there were a Bush story and relevant Bush photo together, then the one that takes higher place was reckoned.
Ex: 01-21-01, Sun, #1/ A1-1+A14+A16

3) Title, subtitle and other representative sentence(s) were shown. Next, the name of the reporter was shown after a slash. Titles and subtitles were put on the list. Reporter's name was also indicated.

Ex: 03-18-03, #2, Tue, A1-1+A14, "A New Doctrine of War; In Age of Unseen Enemies, President Says, Waiting for Opponent to Attack Is Suicide" by David Sanger

4) Types of stories and existence of photos were indicated. Five-step coding (+2, +1, 0, -1, -2) of the story (or photo) was marked.

Ex: Str (straight news) +Pho, +2
"Bush Gives 48 Hours, and Vows to Act" (03-18-03, Tue, #1, Str+Pho, A1-1+A14+A15, +2) by Richard W. Stevenson

5) Remarks, including reasons for evaluation.
Ex: Flattery or Direct criticism.

Afterwards, the list of each day's coding underwent a statistical treatment such as how many stories were positive or negative, how many very negative stories appeared on the front page, and so forth.

Note: Same methods will be adopted to analyze stories and photos of President Roh printed on the *Kyunghyang Daily*.

Operational Definition of Five-Step Coding Scale

Grossman and Kumar (1981) provided definitions of positive, neutral, and negative coverage. In the content analysis of the presidential coverage, Grossman and Kumar requested two coders to evaluate the general tone of the *New York Times* presidential stories. Based on the results by the two coders, Grossman and Kumar concluded that presidential coverage was unexpectedly favorable. They used "three-stage evaluation" using the terms: *favorable, neutral, and unfavorable*. Then they combined the results of the two coders into five-step measurement as was shown in Chapter II:

Positive-positive,
Positive-neutral,
Neutral (Neutral-Neutral, Positive-negative, or Negative-positive),
Negative-neutral, and
Negative-negative.

Grossman and Kumar's (1981) characterization of favorable, neutral, and unfavorable (or positive, neutral, and negative) coding read as follows:

1) Positive: Stories rated "positive" in tone included those that emphasized the president's leadership role, his activities as a family man, his desirable personal qualities, and almost every story that deemphasized conflict and criticism.

2) Neutral: "Neutral" stories contain contents that both coders found to be neutral and those that contain positive and negative elements which tend to balance each other off.

3) Negative: "Negative" stories included those that emphasized things that were going wrong for the president, conflict and criticism, what the administration had failed to accomplish, and who wasn't supporting the presidential policies.

This research drew on their coding methods but used five-step evaluation words based on the intensity of phrasing or wording (Seol's idea):

Very positive (+2),
Positive (+1),
Neutral (0),
Negative (-1),
Very negative (-2).

In addition, the characterization of neutral coverage was not clear in Grossman and Kumar' s study. Their definition "Contents that both coders found to be neutral" does not seem to provide any substantial criteria. In this study, the present author tried to provide more characteristics of positive, neutral, and negative coding in addition to Grossman and Kumar' s definitions:

(1) *Positive*: The author added to positive grouping the stories that described President Bush's activities or speech in (great) detail, depicted what he wants to do or say in the future, and even what he thinks of doing and plans to do. Stories that describe the president with some emotion or in an intimate manner were also grouped under this category.

(2) *Neutral*: A bland description of Bush's behavior, which is not clear whether positive or negative. And a story having both positive and negative descriptions in itself. Some dry descriptions of presidential activities were thought to be really neutral, but the researcher included some of these stories in the positive

grouping, because from the publicity officials' viewpoint these can be positive coverage, which may be journalistically objective.

(3) *Negative*: The author added to this grouping the stories that criticized the president. Critical editorials or columns were classified as negative. Stories that convey people's opposition to the president belong here.

There may be some nouns, verbs, adjectives, phrases, or sentences which manifestly denote positive or negative images. Words or descriptors used for positive or negative coverage will be examined as the content analysis proceeds. Words such as "declare, pledge, vow, and caring" can represent very positive images.

Grossman and Kumar (1982) admitted that their content analysis did not provide a definitive portrait of media coverage of the presidency. It may be a bit more difficult to evaluate presidential stories to be clearly positive, neutral, or negative, especially when presidential coverage is interpreted to be more inclusive as in this book (Seol's idea).

If media's presidential image is confined to the White House stories filed by White House correspondents alone, the number of the presidential stories may be much less, and analysis of the stories may be simpler. The number of presidential stories counted in Grossman and Kumar study reached 5,270 for 25 years. This means that the coders assessed 210 stories on the *New York Times* for one year, that is, *merely 0.57 story per day* (Seol's calculation and emphasis). One factor that made Grossman and Kumar's (1981) study appear plausible was the high correlation (86%, 77%, 87%) between the two coders' assessments.

The author coded a total of 575 stories from 134 days' issues of the *New York Times*, that is, *4.29 stories per day*. The number of stories that were judged to affect the image of President Bush (i.e., the number of stories grouped based on the "Scope of Bush Stories and Bush Photos") amounted to 160 (inauguration period), 124 (September 11th period), 138 (Afghan War period), and 153 (Iraq War period), respectively. Content analysis of the *New York Times* stories (all kinds of stories and photos included) was conducted by coding them recorded on microfilm from June, 2003 to September, 2003.

It should also be noted that the operational definition of positive, neutral, and negative image differs from the ordinary use of the words, because perception of the presidential images can vary depending on the audience's standpoint. To cite an example, Bush's 48-hour ultimatum to Saddam Hussein on "*New York Times*, 03-18-03, #1, A1-1" was assessed very positive (+2), considering that he exerted a decisive wartime leadership. But this piece must have had a very negative impact on Middle Easterners. Hence, the need to differentiate media image and media effect on the audience, as was discussed perviously.

Graber (1982) noted that the impact of adverse coverage is felt more bitterly. Her argument is convincing to some extent. However, considering that how many positive images can offset how many negative images is not yet proven, this research simply counted the number of positive, neutral, and negative stories and performed some statistical treatment about positive or negative images of Bush stories and photos.

Note: Same methods will be used to analyze and code stories of President Roh on the *Kyunghyang Daily*.

Earl Babbie's Advice on Content Analysis

Social research expert and Professor of Chapman University Earl Babbie (2001) discussed the concept of "manifest content" and "latent content" in conducting content analysis. Babbie argued that content analysis of the question "how erotic is a novel?" can be measured by counting words like "love, hug, kiss, and caress." He said that this kind of "manifest content" analysis would have the advantage of ease and reliability in coding and that this would let the reader of the research report know precisely how eroticism was measured (Babbie, 2001, p.

310). However, this method would have a disadvantage in terms of validity. Because the erotic novel conveys a richer and deeper meaning than the number of times the word "love" was used. Babbie's solution to this question was an alternative method: coding latent content, which measures underlying meanings. In the previous example, the coder might read an entire novel or a sample of paragraphs or pages and make an overall assessment of how erotic the novel was.

Grossman and Kumar (1981) did not give detailed instructions to the three coders to have them measure the overall impressions of the presidential stories. Their approach may have been a combination of analysis of manifest content and latent content. Babbie's comment on latent content read:

> Clearly, this second method (analysis of latent content) appears better designed for tapping the underlying meaning of communications, but its advantage comes at a cost to reliability and specificity. Especially if *more than one person* (Seol's emphais) is coding the novel, somewhat different definitions or standards may be employed. A passage one coder regards as erotic may not seem erotic to another. Even if you do all the coding yourself, there is no guarantee that your definitions and standards will remain constant throughout the enterprise. Moreover, the reader of your research report will likely be uncertain about the definitions you've employed (Babbie, 2001, p. 310).

Babbie's solution to this problem was to use both methods: analysis of both manifest and latent content. He wrote that "wherever possible, the best solution to this dilemma is to use both methods. It may not necessarily be the absolute solution, but it may be a tolerable solution." Following Babbie's argument, the adoption of quantitative and qualitative analysis and then triangulation of both may be one solution to decrease subjectivity of this research. The method of combining both "manifest content" analysis and "latent content" analysis may be applicable to the content analysis of news stories lke this research.

Triangulation for Comprehensive Interpretation

For a comprehensive interpretation of the research findings, triangulation of qualitative and quantitative analysis will be performed. Research findings from qualitative and quantitative analysis will be combined to extract meanings from them. Comparison with previous research or other scholarly work will also be provided. By combining both qualitative and quantitative analysis, the research could be more comprehensive.

Note: Same research methods will be applied to analysis of the *Kyunghyang Daily*, wherever possible. Research methods discussed in this chapter will be put into practice in the following two chapters.

CHAPTER **IV**

The more journalists cover an event, the more similar their coverage will be. "Pack journalism" results in sharing of ideas and confirmation of news judgments and the observation of other journalists. Editors tend to question coverage that is different from that of other news organizations (Routines of Media Work 4: Shoemaker & Reese, 1996, p. 266).

THE NEW YORK TIMES AND GEORGE WALKER BUSH

This chapter is a finding from fieldwork research on the stories and photos of American President George Walker Bush (presidency, 2001-09) during his first term as conveyed by the *New York Times*. Analysis of presidential images portrayed by this newspaper was conducted based on discussion and methods in the previous two chapters. Presidential images conveyed by this newspaper but not discussed in the foregoing chapters are discussed here under other groupings. One will discover how diverse and limitless the portrayals of presidential images can be, both positively and negatively. The portrayals of presidential images appear to be results of human literary creativity and imaginative power.

Qualitative Analysis: How did the Newspaper Portray Bush?

Period I. Bush's Inauguration and One Month in Office

This is analysis of the *New York Times* coverage of President Bush from the issue of January 21, 2001 to that of February 20, 2001. Presidential inauguration is a national celebration.

Although there was a heated dispute over the results of the election, most of the Americans followed the decision of the U.S. Supreme Court that ruled that Bush was the winner. The *New York Times* stories conveyed or might have led this climate and congratulated George W. Bush as the legitimately-elected president. After the inauguration there ensued cabinet appointments, policy announcements such as education and overseas abortion policy, and Bush's initiatives of funding religious organizations in assisting the underprivileged. Some policies were opposed by relevant organizations affected by them, and this was reflected on the pages of this newspaper.

The New York Times conveyed a climate of jubilation, reported personnel appointments and policy announcements, and described Mr. Bush as an international and military leader. With the passage of one week in the Bush presidency, the newspaper ran a spate of stories that assessed the transition as being "smooth and without much fuss."

Positive Coverage

(1) Perfectly Positive Image: Inauguration, Jubilation, Successful Transition, and Appointments

The block-type headline "BUSH TAKING OFFICE, CALLS FOR CIVILITY, COMPASSION AND 'NATION OF CHARACTER' " that spanned the whole width of the newspaper, signaled the beginning of a term of the new president. This straight story subtitled "UNITY IS A THEME; In Inaugural Speech, He Asks Citizens to Seek 'a Common Good' "(01-21-01, #1, A1-1+A14+A16, +2) conveyed what Mr. Bush said in his inaugural speech and described the inauguration. (The notations in the parentheses denote date of issue, serial number of the story on the day, page and place within the page of the story, positive-negative coding, in the order.) Read how the first story on this day was written and grasp the message it tried to convey. In this story, Mr. Bush is the president and a "national unifier":

George Walker Bush was sworn in as the 43rd president of the United States today and, in an Inaugural Address that sought to unify the nation after one of the most disputed elections in its history, asked Americans to match "a commitment to principle with a concern for civility" (Para 1).

Mr. Bush used that last word again and again as he sounded a call for a common national purpose that transcended political divisions and partisan tempers (Paragraph 2).

Mr. Bush *pledged to dedicate himself to that ideal* and, his voice and words as muted in their way as the grey scene around him, spoke of unity and duty and responsibility (Paragraph 4).

"I ask you to be citizens," Mr. Bush said. "Citizens, not spectators. Citizens, not subjects. Responsible citizens, building communities of service and a nation of character (Paragraph 5).

The news analysis on this day's issue titled "Tradition and Legitimacy; A Nation's Old Rituals Begin to Dissolve Lingering Clouds of a Bitter Election Battle" (01-21-01, #2, A1-1+A16, +2) granted legitimacy to Bush's presidency:

Inevitably, a question mark hung over George W. Bush as he raised his right hand in the chill, damp air of the capital today, and swore to "preserve, protect and defend the Constitution of the United States." But *at that very moment, through that very act, the president started to dispel the challenges to his legitimacy* (Paragraph 1).

But *the debate* (about his legitimacy as president, Seol's note) *is likely to grow softer as the nation grows accustomed to pictures of Mr. Bush speaking from the Oval Office, boarding Air Force One, accompanied everywhere he goes by the strains of "Ruffles and Flourishes" and "Hail to the Chief"* (Paragraph 5).

On this day's issue, a straight story linking Mr. Bush and his father offered a more emotional flavor to the scene of joy. The story titled "Proud Father and Son Bask in History's Glow" (01-21-01, #3, A1-1+A17, +2) discussed "crying over joy":

> In the days leading up to the inauguration *they talked about crying*. Both son and father worried that they would go overboard with it, that a little telegenic mistiness might turn into something soggier (Paragraph 1).
>
> President-to-be George W. Bush said that he would not look too long or hard at his dad, lest the floodgates open. *Former President George Bush joked that he had written his doctor to ask if he could "prescribe anything to dry up tears"* (Paragraph 2).
>
> But the Bushes were also experiencing something more intimate and nuanced, *a peak moment of shared triumph in a father-son drama that could easily have turned out another way* (Paragraph 7).

The three foregoing stories depicted Mr. Bush as the president, granted legitimacy to him, and described him as the joyful victor of the presidential election.

The next day, a straight story about Bush's first day in office appeared. The story "On First Day, Bush Settles Into a Refitted Oval Office; He Greets Public After Touring New Home" (01-22-01, #1, A1-1+A12, +2) depicted Mr. Bush's first day at the White House. There was no important message from him, but the front page this story occupies reflects that presidential stories can be important even without significant political messages. (The movement of the Bushes to the White House itself can convey a very important political message, Seol's comment.) The story said that the president "slept pretty well" at the White House on his first night.

At the end of the first week of Bush presidency, the *New York Times* assessed the transition to be successful. A spate of related stories about Bush's "smooth start" appeared. Seven stories discussed Bush's smooth initial days in office.

The title of the story "BUSH'S TRANSITION LARGELY A SUCCESS, ALL SIDES SUGGEST; Careful Planning Seen; Analysts Find a Few Missteps but Note a Deft Touch in Dealing With Congress" (01-28-01, #1, A1-1+A14, +2) eloquently says what this piece is about. The message is easily grasped:

As President Bush completes his first week in office, prominent Republicans and even many Democrats agree that *he has presided over one of the most orderly and politically nimble White House transitions in at least 20 years* (Paragraph 1).

If the first days offer any clue, they say, *Mr. Bush may avoid the kind of stumbles* that disrupted the early days of past presidents and hobbled them as they tried to turn their campaign promises into action (Paragraph 2).

Independent academics and analysts as well as politicians in both parties said *Mr. Bush had carefully calibrated his legislative offering* this week by introducing his education package in a way that made it palatable to many Democrats, even as he reassured conservatives by moving to prohibit federal aid to groups that counsel on abortion overseas (Paragraph 3).

They said that Mr. Bush displayed a deft touch in stroking lawmakers, and that *his aides have been surprisingly responsive to members of Congress at a time when previous administrations would still be skirmishing over office space* (Paragraph 4).

And next, the editorial "Mr. Bush's Smooth Start" (02-04-01, Sun, #2, WK16, +1) said that "Democrats in Washington admit to being impressed by the new president's charm offensive" (Para 1). A follow-up editorial "Smart Start on Defense Budgeting" (02-07-01, #3, A18-1, +2) conveyed a similar tone.

A column titled "White House Memo: Presidency Takes Shape With No Fuss, No Sweat" (02-10-01, Sat, #1, A1-1+ A12, +2) provided additional flavor to the stories of successful transition. This added a human and intimate touch to the description:

Every new chief executive inhabits the role in a distinctive way, and *George W. Bush is establishing a no-fuss, no sweat, "look-Ma-no hands" presidency*, his exertions ever measured, his outlook always mirthful (Paragraph 7).

If Bill Clinton's trademark expression was the quarter-bitten lower lip, a deliberate signal of empathy, *Mr. Bush's is the impish grin, a deliberate signal of confidence and good cheer*. He revels in unpretentiousness, and he seems wholly undaunted by his new responsibilities (Paragraph 8).

In this vein, the editorial "Between Two Eras" (02-11-01, Sun, #1, WK16-1, +2) said that "a president who entered office with a shaky mandate is performing above expectations" (Paragraph 1). This editorial also said that *"Mr. Bush takes the presidency seriously"* (Paragraph 2).

One week later, a feature story "Shadow President; This Episode of 'The Clintons' Makes Bush the Star" (02-18-01, Sun, #5, WK4, +1) said that "Mr. Bush's first weeks in office have passed with very little critical examination in the news media, and the Democrats have been unable to challenge him effectively" (Paragraph 6).

A feature story on the same day titled "Week in Review; Entanglements; A New View of Where America Fits in the World; For Bush, taking charge of events means not getting overextended" (02-18-01, #7, WK1 + WK14, +1) conveyed a similar message.

In this regard, political scientist Pfiffner (2003) concurred. He noted that "President George W. Bush's transition into office was one of the shortest, but most efficiently run in recent times. He evaluated:

> Because of the growth of the size and scope of the national government, transitions since 1970s have been elaborately planned and bureaucratized. There never seems to be enough time to fully prepare to take over the government. Yet because of the delay in the administrative outcome of the 2000 election, the incoming Bush administration had

five fewer weeks for officially preparing to take office, about half as much time as other administrations. *Surprisingly, under the circumstances, they accomplished the major tasks of the transitions* (Seol's emphasis) --- designating a White House staff, naming a cabinet, and laying the groundwork for their initial policy agenda --- with dispatch (Pfiffner and Davidson, 2003, p. 454).

This made a good contrast with stories of his predecessor Bill Clinton. In January, 1993, the images that the *New York Times* drew about then-President Clinton looked totally different. The titles of the following five stories explain themselves:

"Joint Chiefs Fighting Clinton Plan To Allow Homosexuals in Military" (01-23-93, A1-1+A10, Straight);
"Clinton Concedes He Erred on Baird Nomination; Aides Say He Continues to Seek a Woman for Attorney General" (01-23-93, A1-1+A9, Straight);
"Early Damage Control" (01-23-93, A1-1+A9, Analysis);
"Challenges From a Headstrong Public; Rebuking the Powerful On Baird and Gay Ban" (01-29-93, A1-1+A12, Analysis); and
"CLINTON ACCEPTS DELAY IN LIFTING MILITARY GAY BAN; BOW TO OPPONENTS; President Tells Pentagon to Draft Order for Him to Sign in 6 Months" (01-30-93, A1-1+A8, Straight).

(2) The Image of a National Leader, Conciliator or Unifier

The incoming president Geroge W. Bush had to reunite the divided electorate and rally support for him. He emphasized unity of the country in his inaugural address (01-21-01, #1, A1-1) and the *New York Times* analysis (01-21-01, #2, A1-1) seemed to grant legitimacy to him as discussed above. The following stories can be grouped here under this subcategory.

The straight story "Bush, the Conciliator, Meets With Democrats" (02-03-01, Sat, #1, A10-1, +2) conveyed the image of a "national conciliator" after fierce election disputes:

> President Bush *ventured into enemy territory* today, meeting with Senate Democrats to outline his hopes for his first year in office (Paragraph 1).
> Later in the day, in a speech to Republican members of Congress at a retreat in Williamsburg, Va., he *vowed to make the case for deep tax* cuts "over and over again" until Americans were convinced that his plan would help the middle class and act as a remedy for economic slowdown (Paragraph 2).

The seven stories below falls under this grouping. These stories conveyed Bush's image as a national leader, unifier, and conciliator in various ways:

"Transcript of inaugural address: President; 'I Ask You to Be Citizen' (01-21-01, #7, A14-2 + A15-2, +2);
"THE SPEECH; In His Inauguration Address, Bush Lingers on a Promise to Care" (01-21-01, #8, A16-2, +2);
"A Vision of Unity" (01-21-01, #14, Ed, WK16-1, +1);
"Bush to Attend Democratic Caucuses; But President Restates Stance on Issues That Separate the Parties; Agreeing to a move intended to shift a partisan tone" (01-27-01, #1, A11-1, +1);
"Bush, in Outreach Bid, Meets Black Caucus" (02-01-01, #2, A1-2 + A18, +1);
"With Conciliatory Gestures, Bush Reaches Out in Reprise of Successful Clinton Tactic" (02-02-01, #5, A17-2, +1); and
"A Day of Remembrance in Oklahoma City; Bush dedicates Museum at Site of Oklahoma City Bombing" (02-20-01, #2, A1-1 photo + A12 story, +2).

(3) The Image of a Policymaker

During the initial days in office, presidents usually announce a number of "ambitious" policies to transform the country to a better place to live in. Some are approved and some face public opposition. The news media at first convey what the presidents announce and then they report reactions from the people affected by the policies either positively or negatively. Sometimes government agencies can support the president's policy agenda, thus portraying Bush favorably. The following 16 stories are part of Bush stories as a policymaker:

"BUSH ACTS TO HALT OVERSEAS SPENDING TIED TO ABORTION; Reverses Clinton Policy; Action on 28th Anniversary of Roe v. Wade Limits the Use of Family Planning Aid" (01-23-01, #1, A1-1+ A14+ A16, +1);

"Education Plan By Bush Shows New Consensus" (01-23-01, #2, A1-1 + A14, +1);

"THE TAX CUT PLAN: Bush's Proposal to Cut Taxes Is Swiftly Introduced in Senate" (01-23-01, #5, A15-2, +1);

"IN POLICY CHANGE, GREENSPAN BACKS A BROAD TAX CUT; White House Is Pleased; Guarded Endorsement by Fed Chief, Who Says Vigilance Is Needed on Deficits" (01-26-01, #1, A1-1 +C1, +1);

"THE NEW ADMINISTRATION: Early Acts and Last-Minute Moves; THE ABORTION ISSUE; Opponents of Abortion Cheer New Administration" (01-23-01, #7, A16-1, +1);

"Bush Pushes Ambitious Education Plan; Would Use U.S. Aid to Force Schools to Meet Standards" (01-24-01, #1, A1-1+ A14, +2);

"Bush Education Plan Could Have Big Impact Locally; bonus money for improvements by poor students" (01-24-01, #7, B8-1, +1);

"In First Radio Addresses, Bush Softens on School Vouchers" (01-28-01, #3, A14-1, +1);

"NEW BUSH OFFICE SEEKS CLOSER TIES TO CHURCH GROUPS; Academic To Lead Effort; Plan will Seek the Integration of Private Organizations With Social Programs" (01-29-01, #1, A1-1+ A20, +1);

"President Offers Plan to Promote Oil Exploration; Uses California Crisis to Sell Energy Policy" (01-30-01, #1, A1-1+ A20, +2);

"Bush Fleshes Out Details of Proposal to Expand Aid to Religious Organizations" (01-31-01, #6, A15-1, +1);

"Bush Plans Small Rise for Pentagon Pending Review, Aides Say" (02-01-01, #5, A17-1, +1);

"Bush Wants Tax Cut Sooner To Aid Economy This Year" (02-05-01, #4, A12-1, +1);

"BUSH TO PROPOSE MAKING A TAX CUT EFFECTIVE IN 2001; Plan Moved Up By A Year" (02-06-01, #1, A1-1+ A16, +1);

"BUSH IN FIRST STEP TO SHRINK ARSENAL OF U.S. WARHEADS; To Order Defense Review" (02-09-01, #1, A1-1 + A10, +2); and

"BUSH DETAILS PLAN TO FOCUS MILITARY ON NEW WEAPONRY; A Break With The Orthodoxy" (02-14-01, #1, A1-1 + A26, +2).

As shown above, the president's policy areas are limitless. The above-mentioned stories may be descriptions of the president's policymaking activities in an objective manner (neutral, 0) by the journalists. But from the perspective of the White House public affairs (or, public relations) officials, these stories may be products of their publicity activities and thus can be assessed positive coverage (+2 or +1).

(4) The Image of a Decisive Military Leader

During this inauguration period, presidential image as military leader was not salient. However, when Mr. Bush approved U.S. jet attacks on Iraqi "No Fly" zone, the *New York Times* spotlighted Bush's role (or image) as the commander-in-chief (or, military leader). The following five stories fall under this subgroup.

The front page straight story titled "U.S. AND BRITISH JETS STRIKE AIR-DEFENSE CENTERS IN IRAQ; Provocation Cited; Bush Approves Attacks Beyond 'No Fly' Zone" (02-17-01, #1, A1-1+ A4, +1) conveyed the image of a military leader. This story said that "air attacks against radar stations and air defense command centers ... were what Bush called a necessary response to Iraqi provocation" (Para 1).

Then, a relevant news analysis said that "Mr. Bush declared his leadership." The analysis "The World Stage, Act I; First Act For Bush, Declaring Leadership" (02-17-01, #2, A1-1+ A4, +1) justified and highlighted Bush's military action:

> On the first four days of what President Bush designated "national security week," he promised troops in Georgia a pay raise, visited NATO outpost ... (Paragraph 1).
> *He consented to the Pentagon's request to bomb Iraq,* ... to make the statement that Mr. Bush, not yet a month into his presidency, had arrived on the world stage, that despite his inexperience there, he was a player (Paragraph 3).

The related excerpt was carried with the title "In the President's Words on the Bombing; 'It's a Routine Mission' " (02-17-01, #4, A4-2, +2).

The relevant editorial "Air Strikes in Iraq" (02-17-01, #5, A16-1, +1) said that "Yesterday's attack was justified as a response to intensified targeting of allied planes patrolling the 'no-fly' zone."

And a column titled "No Choice But To Strike; To contain Iraq, expect more air strikes" (02-17-01, #7, A17, +1) justified the attack.

(5) The Image of a Person in Charge: Making Appointments

The *New York Times* ran a spate of appointments stories, conveying the image of Mr. Bush as the person in charge. But the appointment of Ashcroft was controversial. The following 10 stories are part of appointment stories falling under this subcategory:

"Bush Appoints Powell's Son To Lead F.C.C." (01-23-01, #11, C1-1 +C2, +1);

"Senate Confirms Nominees For E.P.A. and Interior Posts" (01-31-01, #7, A15-2, +1); and

"Bush's Choice Seen Winning Trade Position" (01-31-01, #8, A15-2, +1).

However, when it comes to Bush's nomination of Ashcroft as attorney general, the *New York Times* ran a mix of stories. The editorial "Opposing the Ashcroft Nomination" (01-23-01, #9, A20-1, -2) offered direct opposition to Bush's nomination:

> Given this newspaper's long history of defending civil liberties, reproductive freedom, gay rights and racial justice, we cannot endorse Mr. Ashcroft as an appropriate candidate to lead a department charged with providing justice for all Americans (Last paragraph).

With the passage of time, Ashcroft nomination was accepted, and this newspaper ran a story on Congressional confirmation of him. The following shows how the stories evolved:

"SENATE COMMITTEE BACKS BUSH CHOICE FOR JUSTICE DEPT; Ashcroft Vote Is 10 to 8; Heated Debate on Nomination Begins on Floor, With Vote Likely Later This Week" (01-31-01, #1, A1-1 + A14, +2);

"By Resisting Ashcroft, Democrats Send a Signal; This nomination appears clinched. The fight is over future ones" (01-31-01, W, #3, A14-1, -2);

"Excerpts From Remarks by Hatch and Schumer on Ashcroft's Nomination" (01-31-01, #4, A14-2, -2);

"ASHCROFT DEBATE SHOWS DEEP RIFTS; Democrats Deliver a Message, but Confirmation Is Likely" (02-01-01, #1, A1-1+A20, -1);

"SEANTE CONFIRMS ASHCROFT AS ATTORNEY GENERAL, 58-42, CLOSING FIVE-WEEK BATTLE; Victory for Bush; But Tally of Democrats Hints at New Fights Over Court Picks" (02-02-01, #1, A1-1 + A16, +2); and

"EDITORIAL OBSERVER; How George W. Bush Can Reach

Black Voters; John Ashcroft makes racial detente much more difficult" (02-03-01, #2, A12-2, -2).

(6) The Image of an International Leader

During this period only a few stories appeared under this category. Bush's scheduled meeting with Mexican President Vicente Fox was a major story.

A straight story "Bush and Fox Hope Nations Will Become Better Amigos" (01-31-01, #2, A8-1, +1) portrayed Bush in a positive light:

> Presidents Bush and Vicente Fox will meet on Feb. 16 at Mr. Fox's ranch (Paragraph 2).
> "Our common border is no longer a line that divides us, but ..."(Paragraph 3).

The following are other news stories which convey the image of Bush as an international leader:

"BUSH DUE TO VISIT MEXICO TO DISCUSS OBTAINING ENERGY; Plan Faces Big Obstacles; President's Vision of Shared Resources Would Be Costly and Legally Challenging" (02-13-01, #1, A1-1+ A10, +1);
"U.S. and Mexico to Open Talks On Freer Migration for Workers; Bush Signaling New Focus on Immigration Issues" (02-16-01, #1, A1-1 + A8, +1);
"BUSH GIVES MEXICO BACKING ON DRIVE AGAINST NARCOTICS; Annual Review At Issue; President Signals Support for Effort to End a Ritual That Carries Sanction Threat" (02-17-01, #3, A1-1 + A8, +1); and
"Canada Determined to Be First Neighbor to Bush" (02-05-01, #2, A7-1, +1).

(7) Personal Qualities: Intimate and Favorable Coverage

There appeared five personal quality stories which described

Mr. Bush in an intimate and favorable light.

A story titled "INAUGURAL DIARY; Great Political Theater With a Touch of Pomp" (01-21-01, #5, A13-1, +2) described the inaugural dance together with an advance photo on the front page, in which the First Couple danced:

> The sense that American political life resembles a Robert Altman movie has rarely been more vivid than during the parade celebrating George W. Bush's inauguration. In the glare of television lights, the blue and white presidential reviewing stand looked as insubstantial as a stage set. *The leader of the free world, his family and company saluted and waved from behind a barrier of bulletproof plastic, looking tiny as toys* (Paragraph 1).

And a feature story titled "The Nation; Oval Office; Room With a Hue" (01-28-01, Sun, #5, WK16-1, +1) gave additional flavor:

> If presidential choices in decor were really any measure of judgment, then the country would have good reason for alarm ... (Paragraph 1).
> George W. Bush promptly redecorated the Oval Office, replacing Bill Clinton's festive rug-sofa combo with more sober tones reminiscent of the Reagan years (Photo caption).

A column titled "Political Notebook: Back Home In Crawford And Having A Texas Ball" (02-19-01, #1, A13-1, +1) described "a belated inaugural ball staged for President Bush near his 1,600-acre ranch."

The foregoing stories are intimate, soft, and favorable to Bush and his family. The following two stories were already discussed:

"Proud Father and Son Bask in History's Glow" (01-21-01, #3) and

"On First Day, Bush Settles Into a Refitted Oval Office" (01-22-01, #1).

Negative Coverage

During this jubilant one-month period, there appeared only a limited number of negative (-2, -1) stories. The *New York Times* buried one harsh story deep inside, which described people protesting against Bush taking office. In the words of protestors, Bush was a thief of the presidency. Other negative stories were concerned with public's opposition to Bush's new policies. The following eight stories are examples of negative coverage.

The story titled "THE DEMONSTRATIONS: Protesters in the Thousands Sound Off in the Capital" (01-21-01, #9, A17-1, -2) may be interpreted to be direct opposition to Bush's taking presidenial office. Surprisingly to the author, Bush was described as a thief of presidency and an egg was thrown at him:

> As President Bush's limousine passed, many waved signs proclaiming "Hail to the Thief." Others carried American flags with corporate logos replacing the 50 stars. An egg was thrown at the president's car (Paragraph 4).

The above story may be a representative example of striking a balance between positive and negative stories. At any rate, it is true that this story reflects part of the people's voice. But this story was buried deep inside. Therefore, the main focus of coverage rested on the positive aspect, that is, congratulating Bush.

An editorial titled "Faith-Based Services" (01-30-01, #6, A22-1, -2) criticized Bush's policy agenda as dangerous:

> Mr. Bush's ambitious proposal to channel federal funds to "faith-based" groups to serve social needs is a potentially dangerous erosion of the constitutionally shielded boundary between church and state (Paragraph 1).

The story titled "A Bush Aide Faults Plan to Repeal Estate Tax" (02-10-01, Sat, #4, A10-1, -2) provided a salient example of controversy within the White House. The story was about "rebellion from within." The *New York Times* carried this story on the national edition but crossed it out in the late edition. It seemed such a sensitive and disruptive story!

A straight story titled "Bush Team Under Attack on Emissions Talks" (02-16-01, #3, A12-1, -2) was a direct attack on Bush team's environmental policy:

> Critics, who include industry executives and some environmental lobbyists, say the administration is betraying a lack of urgency. "Damage is being done right now," said a Washington lobbyist for foreign oil exporters ... (Paragraph 5).

A story titled "Critics Seek To Overturn Abortion Rule; Oppose Bush Limits On Aid Sent Abroad; An old policy, newly reinstated, rekindles an old debate" (02-16-01, #4, A12-1, -2) was direct opposition to Bush's abortion policy abroad:

> A bipartisan group of lawmakers mounted a drive in the House and Senate today to overturn the new Bush administration policy on international family planning assistance, which they argue is counter- productive and cruel (Paragraph 1).

A straight story titled "2 Moderate Republicans Oppose Bush Tax Plan as Democrats Offer Their Own; Criticism from two sides raises questions about how deep reductions might be" (02-16-01, #6, A16-1, -2) offered attacks on Bush's tax policy.

A column titled "A Deadly Global Gag Rule; Bush's abortion policy will cost lives overseas" (01-27-01, #4, A15-1, Op-Ed) again faulted Bush's abortion policy abroad.

And a story "Questions Raised On New Bush Plan To End Estate Tax" (01-29-01, Mon, #2, A1-2 + A21, -2) attacked Bush's tax policy on the front page, thus having greater impact.

As shown above, negative stories are mostly concerned with Bush's policies. Attackers are columnists, people affected adversely by the policies, or interest groups opposed to the policies.

Neutral Coverage

Advice to Bush, stories made up of positive and negative parts together in one story, or prediction of his future courses mostly constituted neutral (0) coverage. Read the following four stories.

"A Cliche-Free First 100 Days; Bush must serve sound ideals --- conservative ones" (Column, 01-21-01, #15, WK17-1, 0) was assessed neutral because it did not depict him either in a positive or a negative light. This column gave him advice.

A straight story titled "Bush to Focus on a Favorite Project; Helping Religious Groups Help the Needy; A vigorous debate over church and state is expected" (01-26-01, #2, A17-1, 0) showed a mix of positive and negative coverage, thus evaluated neutral (0).

A straight story "BUSH PROPOSES AID ON MEDICARE; Many in Congress See Need to Rework Program Instead" (01-30-01, #2, A1-1 + A18, 0) is another example of mixing positive and negative contents.

A column titled "Essay: Question Time; Can Bush handle the tough ones?" (02-15-01, #4, A31-1, Op-Ed, 0) raised questions about Bush's future, thus was assessed neutral. This story might have aroused readers' interest.

Period II. September 11 Attacks and Bush's Decision to Retaliate

This is analysis of the *New York Times* coverage of President Bush from the issue of September 12, 2001 to that of October 07, 2001. September 11 terrorist attacks on America in 2001 had a tremendous impact on the American political arena as well as on the international society. This made a great turning point in American diplomacy and in Bush's presidency. The whole world was "artificially" reorganized by Mr. Bush into terrorist bloc on the one hand and anti-terrorist bloc led by America on the other. The *New York Times* stories portrayed President Bush as a national as well as an international leader on the counter-terrorism battlefront. The newspaper also shed light on his role as a "national soother" and then as a "crisis leader," which was hardly witnessed previously. Mr. Bush rallied support for this war on the Taliban regime, but he decided to act largely alone without much assistance from foreign countries. In this process, there occurred controversy among Bush aides over the scope of retaliation against Afghanistan.

Positive Coverage

(1) The Image of a Crisis Leader or Military Leader

The banner headlines on the September 12, 2001 issue of the New York Times showed the shocks Americans experienced at the sight of the surprise attacks. Stories conveyed and described the magnitude of shocks Americans received.

The first story about the attacks was titled "U.S. ATTACKED; HIJACKED JETS DESTROY TWIN TOWERS AND HIT PENTAGON IN DAY OF TERROR; President Vows to Exact Punishment for 'Evil'+ A14, Bush Commits U.S. to Hunt Down Both Terrorists and Their Supporters" (09-12-01, Wed, #1, A1-1+ A14, +2) conveyed the shocks, Bush's somber mood, and his determination to revenge:

> Hijackers rammed jetliners into each of New York's World Trade Center towers yesterday, toppling both in a hellish storm of ash, glass, smoke and leaping victims, while a third jetliner crashed into the Pentagon in Virginia.

There was no official count, but *President Bush said thousands had perished*, and in the immediate aftermath the calamity was already being ranked the worst and most audacious terror attack in American history (Paragraph 1).

The attacks seemed carefully coordinated. The hijacked planes were all en route to California, and therefore gorged with fuel, ... (Paragraph 2).

President Bush, facing his first major crisis in office, vowed that the United States would hunt down and punish those responsible for the "evil, despicable acts of terror" which, he said, took thousands of American lives. He said the United States would make no distinction between those who carried out the hijackings and those who harbored and supported them (Paragraph 16).

"These acts of mass murder were intended to frighten our nation into chaos and retreat, but they have failed," a somber president told the nation in an address from the Oval Office shortly after 8:30 p.m. (Paragraph 17).

"The search is under way for those who are behind these evil acts," Mr. Bush said. "We will make no distinction between the terrorists who committed these acts and those who harbor them" (Paragraph 18).

A relevant story titled "A Somber Bush Says Terrorism Cannot Prevail" (09-12-01, #2, A1-2+ A4, +2) delivered his solemn message of retaliation and his efforts to calm the nation:

President Bush *vowed tonight to retaliate against those responsible* for today's attacks on New York and Washington, declaring that he would "make no distinction between the terrorists who committed these acts and those who harbor them." "These acts of mass murder were intended to frighten our nation into chaos and retreat, but they have failed," the president said in his first speech to the nation from the Oval Office. "Our country is strong. Terrorist acts can shake the foundation of our biggest buildings, but they cannot touch the foundation of America

(Paragraph 1)."

His brief speech this evening came after a day of trauma that seems destined to define his presidency. *Seeking to at once calm the nation and declare his determination to exact retribution, he told a country numbed by repeated scenes of carnage that "these acts shattered steel, but they cannot dent the steel of American resolve* (Paragraph 2)."

This story demonstrated an unshaken, strong national leadership of Mr. Bush at the sight of the unheard-of national crisis on the American soil. Mr. Bush also showed his deep faith in the American system.

The straight story "AFTER THE ATTACKS; Washington's Responses; THE PRESIDENT; Bush Labels Aerial Terrorist Attacks 'Acts of War' " (09-13-01, #2, A15-1, +2) conveyed Bush's message that he defined terrorist attacks as acts of war:

President Bush *declared today that the attacks on the World Trade Center and the Pentagon were "acts of war."* He spent much of the day trying to rally an international coalition for what would become a massive military response --- once the enemy was identified (Paragraph 1).

The story titled "BUSH AND TOP AIDES PROCLAIM POLICY OF 'ENDING' STATES THAT BACK TERROR; LOCAL AIRPORTS SHUT AFTER AN ARREST; President to Visit New York --- bin Laden Singled Out" (09-14-01, Fri, #1, A1-1 + A18, +2) depicted Bush as vowing a comprehensive campaign:

The Bush administration today singled out Osama bin Laden, the Islamic militant who operates from Afghanistan, as a prime suspect in Tuesday's catastrophic terror attacks and *vowed a comprehensive military campaign* to demolish terrorist networks and topple regimes that harbor them (Paragraph 1).

A related news analysis under the title "No Middle Ground

Exists In War Against Terrorism" (09-14-01, #2, A1-1 + A4, +2) explained Bush's policy lines imposing a stark choice on other countries:

Sketching in the outline of an aggressive new American foreign policy, the Bush administration today gave the nations of the world a stark choice: stand with us against terrorism or face the certain prospect of death and destruction (Paragraph 1).

One of the representative examples of military leadership may be the story about Bush ordering the military to get ready. The straight story titled "BUSH TELLS THE MILITARY TO 'GET READY'; BROADER SPY POWERS GAINING SUPPORT; Long Battle Seen; 'We're at War,' He Says --- Support in Poll for Armed Response" (09-16-01, Sun, #1, A1-1 + A5 + A6, +2) conveyed Bush's resolve to wage a war:

President Bush told American military today to get ready for a long war against terrorism, and vowed to "do what it takes to win (Paragraph 1)."
In a brief appearance with his senior advisers at Camp David, where they met to plan the new offensive, Mr. Bush said point-blank: "We're at war. There's been an act of war declared upon America by terrorists, and we will respond accordingly (Paragraph 2)."
"My message is for everybody who wears the uniform to get ready," Mr. Bush said (Paragraph 3).

A straight story titled "BUSH ORDERS HEAVY BOMBERS NEAR AFGHANS; DEMANDS BIN LADEN NOW, NOT NEGOTIATIONS; Deploys Warships; President Is Addressing Congress Tonight to Lay Out His Aims" (09-20-01, #1, A1-1 + B6, +2) forewarned an impending war decision:

President Bush ordered heavy bombers and other aircraft to within easy striking distance of Afghanistan and insisted that its ruling Taliban turn over Osama bin Laden and other suspected leaders of a terrorist organization believed to be behind last week's attacks in New York and Washington (Paragraph 1).

The story titled "BUSH PLEDGES ATTACK ON AFGHANISTAN UNLESS IT SURRENDERS BIN LADEN NOW; HE CREATES CABINET POST FOR SECURITY; Bar Talks, Saying Hosts Will Share the Terrorists' Fate" (09-21-01, #1, A1-1 +B4, +2) showed Bush's resoluteness and forcefulness:

President Bush demanded tonight that Afghanistan's leaders immediately deliver Osama bin Laden and his network and close down every terrorist camp in the country or face military attack by the United States (Paragraph 1).

"These demands are not open to negotiation or discussion," the president said in an address to a joint meeting of Congress (Paragraph 2).

The story titled "BUSH SAYS 'TIME IS RUNNING OUT'; U.S. PLANS TO ACT LARGELY ALONE; Rumsfeld Returns; Administration Says It Has Enough Backing for Long Campaign" (10-07-01, #1, A1-1 + B5, +2) sounded like an ultimatum. This story offered the image of a strong military leader and conveyed the urgency of the situation:

Working with the fluid coalitions of friendly countries whose tasks are still undefined, President Bush warned the Taliban government of Afghanistan today that "full warning has been given, and time is running out" (Paragraph 1).

With the advent of September 11 attacks, Bush's presidency has taken a totally new direction. The story titled "In Four Days, a National Crisis Changes Bush's Presidency" (09-16-01, #2, A1-2 + A19, +2) shed light on the transformation of Bush presidency:

In the course of the next four days, George W. Bush was transformed into a president at the helm of the White House, and a nation, in crisis (Paragraph 5).

By this morning with downtown Washington locked down by the military, *he was conducting a war council* at Camp David and *demanding that countries around the world, starting with the Arab world, declare whether they were allies in the war on terrorism* (Paragraph 6).

He seemed *far steadier* than he had in the week. He told the cabinet what he had seen in New York, calling the scene "the signs of the first battle of war." ... (Penultimate Paragraph).

"This is a great nation, we're kind and peaceful," Mr. Bush said. "But they have stirred up the might of the American people, and we're going to get them" (Last Paragraph).

(Connected with this, the *New York Times* carried a front story to this effect again on Jan 1, 2002. The story titled "Taking Command in Crisis, Bush Wields New Powers" said that Bush himself signed an order freezing the assets in the United States, which were suspected of having Islamic terrorist linkage. He did it himself instead of letting Treasury Secretary Paul H. O'Neill announce the measure to reinforce the message that Mr. Bush would direct the war against terrorism on many fronts. This point was addressed in the section Publicity Machine of George W. Bush.)

A story titled "THE PRESIDENT; In This Crisis, Bush Is Writing His Own Script" (09-19-01, #6, B11-2, +2) said that expressions like "want him dead or alive," "evil-doers," and "smoke them out and get them running" are things of Bush's own making. This was an intimate, personal, and soft story written by Elisabth Bumiller, White House correspondent.

A column titled "WHITE HOUSE MEMO: For President, a Mission and a Role in History + B2, Role Finds Bush Onstage, Waiting; Shoulders that once shrugged now broaden with weighty resolve" (09-22-01, #3, A1-1 + B2, +2) conveyed a very important message that emphasized the purpose of the Bush administration:

"*This* (war on terrorism, Seol's note)," Mr. Bush told them, "*is the purpose of this administration*" (Paragraph 4).

One of the president's close acquaintances outside the White House said Mr. Bush clearly feels *he has encountered his reason of being*, a conviction informed and shaped by the president's own strain of Christianity (Paragraph 8).

Retrospectively speaking, this story forecast the future course of the Bush administration (Seol's comment). "His sense of purpose of his administration and his encountering of his reason of being" became the foundation of his policy of war on terrorism, which became a buzzword since September 11 attacks. The following four stories fall under this subgroup:

"U.S. PUTS AFGHAN STRIKE AHEAD OF FULL PLAN; BUSH REWARDING PAKISTAN FOR ITS SUPPORT; Focus On Bin Laden; Officials Say Course of War on Terrorism Is Still to be Decided" (09-22-01, #1, A1-1 + B4, +1) forewarned an imminent retaliation.

"PRESIDENT SAYS U.S. IS 'IN HOT PURSUIT' OF TERROR GROUP; A Guerrilla War; Allied Units Reportedly Entered Afghanistan --- No U.S. Word" (09-29-01, #1, A1-1 + B4, +2) said that the U.S. embarked on the pursuit of terror groups but did not confirm the report.

"Bush Approves Covert Aid for Taliban Foes; $100 Million to Help Refugees Is Also Set" (10-01-01, #1, A1-1 + B2, +2) was related to this development.

"Bin Laden Is Wanted in Attacks, 'Dead or Alive,' President Says" (09-18-01, #1, A1-1 + B4, +2) portrayed Bush as the punisher.

(2) The Image of a National Soother

Just after the crisis period after September 11 attacks, Bush acted the national soother who solaced victims and visited attacked sites.

The image of national soother was provided by the story "BUSH LEADS PRAYER, VISITS AID CREWS; CONGRESS BACKS USE OF ARMED FORCES; A Day of Mourning; President, in New York Offers Resolute Vows Atop the Rubble" (09-15-01, #1, A1-1 + A6, +2).

When Mr. Bush visited New York City, his image as the national conciliator was highlighted. A column titled "WHITE HOUSE MEMO: Two Strangers, Bush and New York City, Meet and Embrace in Calamity's Wake" (09-15-01, #4, A6-2, +2) said that "rescue workers cheered the president when he shook hands with Mr. Giuliani and Mr. Pataki, Democrats of New York City, which was 'a foreign place' for Republican Bush."

(3) Personal Qualities and First Family

While Mr. Bush's image as a crisis leader or military leader represented resoluteness, the *New York Times* ran soft stories of the First Family. Soother's role may also be played by the First Lady.

The story titled "THE FORMER PRESIDENT; Juggling Being a Father to a Son and a President" (09-14-01, #4, A18-2, +1) depicted the burden of the presidency during the crisis by borrowing words of Bush's father:

He is a former president but also a father, and he commingled those roles today, speaking protectively of his son while also *reflecting on the burden of confronting a global challenge from the loneliness of the Oval Office* (Paragraph 1).

"I talk quite regularly to our son," the 41st president said affectionately of the 43rd president. "I've been doing that since he was a little kid (Paragraph 2)."

A story titled "The Pennsylvania Crash; 44 Victims Are

Remembered and Lauded; The first lady and a governor join the victims' families" (09-18-01, #4, B11-2, +1) conveyed Laura Bush's image as a national soother. This story also carried a photo of Laura Bush and Gov. Tom Ridge of Pennsylvania:

> Some 240 relatives had traveled here from all over the country. Mrs. Bush, who arrived from Washington, told them that while America shared in their grief, and that of all the other victims in last week's terrorist attacks, the burden was greatest for the surviving relatives (Paragraph 7).
>
> "America is learning the names, but you know the people," she said at the service. "And you are the ones they thought of in the last moments of life. You're the ones they called, and prayed to see again. You are the ones they loved" (Paragraph 8).

The story titled "THE FIRST LADY: Mrs. Bush Introduces Concert For Families; Music Meant to Soothe at Kennedy Center" (09-25-01, #6, B7-1, +1) conveyed a similar image:

> Adding high culture to *her increasingly public role as a grief counselor for the nation*, Laura Bush tonight inaugurated a Kennedy Center concert of opera, jazz and folk music that was organized to raise money for the families of those who died in the attacks on September 11 (Paragraph 1).
>
> Some relatives of the victims were in the audience, ready to listen to the music that Mrs. Bush called "the speech of the angels," and they gave her a loud, long round of applause (Paragraph 2).
>
> Mrs. Bush quickly cut it off with a no-nonsense chop of her hand (Paragraph 3).
>
> "I'm the one who should be applauding all of you," she said from the stage of the concert hall (Paragraph 4).

(4) Other Stories That Depict Bush Positively

Stories that described other events can sometimes affect Bush favorably. Read the following three stories:

"THE RESOLUTION; Measure Backing Bush's Use of Force Is as Broad as a Declaration of War, Experts Say; Congress walks a fine line of showing unity and retaining power" (09-18-01, #3, B7-2, +1) shows that Congressional resolution backing Bush's proposition affects him favorably.

"WASHINGTON RESPONSE; Congress Joins In Support Of President" (09-21-01, #8, B6-1, +2) is a follow-up to the above.

"Bush 'Is My Commander,' Gore Declares in Call for Unity; Urging support for the president in an effort to seek justice, not revenge" (09-30-01, Sun, #1, A29-1, +2) also belongs here.

Negative Coverage

The *New York Times* did not run many negative stories. This period was such a time of crisis that the situation did not allow for room for criticism. But columnist William Safire criticized Mr. Bush for not having come back to the Washington area just after the attacks. The column titled "Essay; New Day of Infamy; The questions we must answer" (09-12-01, #5, A27, Op-Ed, -2) said:

> But the Secret Service took full charge of President Bush, who was in Florida, running him secretly around the country making a nervous tape. Even in the first horrified moments, this was never seen a nuclear attack by a foreign power. *Bush should have insisted on coming right back to the Washington area, broadcasting --- live and calm --- from some secure facility not far from the White House* (Paragraph 14).
>
> In the president's absence from the city, Vice President Dick Cheney hurried to the Situation Room. No Haigian "I'm in charge" was needed, but an earlier and more visible

sense of steadiness would have helped. Despite the evacuation of executive and Congressional offices, Defense Secretary Donald Rumsfeld visited his wounded Pentagon troops and Condoleeza Rice, the national security adviser, remained in place (Paragraph 15).

In an apparent response to this, a straight story appeared on the front page the next day under the title "Aides Say Bush Was One Target Of Hijacked Jet" (09-13-01, #1, A1-2 + A16, +1). This piece said that "there was hard evidence that Bush was a target of terrorists."

In a counter-argument, Safire again wrote a follow-up column titled "Essay; Inside The Bunker; The view from the 'President's Emergency Operations Center' " (09-13-01, #7, A27-2, Op-Ed, -2):

The most worrisome aspect of these revelations has to do with the credibility of the "Air Force One is next" message. It is described clearly as a treat, not a friendly warning --- but if so, why would the terrorists send the message? More to the point, how did they get the code-word information and transponder know-how that established their *mala fides*? (Penultimate Paragraph).

"Bush Advisers Split on Scope of Retaliation" (09-20-01, #2, A1-1 + B5, -2) revealed disarray in front of the enemy. This was a rare piece of negative coverage on the front page:

The Bush administration is struggling with its first high-level quarrels over the scope and timing of its military response to last week's attack on the United States (Paragraph 1).

Some senior administration officials, led by Paul Wolfowitz earliest and broadest military campaign (Paragraph 2).

In response to these efforts, Secretary of State Colin L. Powell take the time to prepare the diplomatic groundwork for American military action (Paragraph 5).

This visible split within the administration was soon resolved with a follow-up story titled "From Many Voices Advising Bush, One War Strategy; A Bush team often at odds before September 11 has since coalesced" (09-23-01, Sun, #3, A1-1 + B2, +2).

"SAFETY AND LIBERTY; Senate Democrat Opposes White House's Antiterrorism Plan and Proposes Alternative; Concerns that citizens' rights might be curtailed unnecessarily" (09-20-01, #5, B6-2, -2) was additional criticism to Bush's harsh counter-terrorism policy.

In this respect, the story "Lawmakers Tap Brakes on Bush's Hurtling Anti-terrorism Measure" (09-25-01, #5, B7-1, -2) was additional opposing voice to Bush.

A news analysis titled "Issue Now; Does U.S. Have a Plan?" (09-27-01, #3, A1-1, -2) was a rare front page criticism to Bush's war plan. This piece said that "The rhetoric was rousing, but what form of military action to take appears to be an increasingly awkward issue (Paragraph 3).

A column titled "New Fears, New Alliances" (10-02-01, #1, A24-1, -2) carried a harsh criticism to the effect that "without any systematic analysis, without the usual process of review among government departments, the United States has adopted an entirely new foreign policy (Paragraph 1)."

Neutral Coverage

Predictions, explanatory stories, and columns offering advice fell under this grouping. The following four stories are examples:

"Awaiting the Aftershocks; Washington and Nation Plunge Into Fight With Enemy Hard to Identify and Punish" (09-12-01, #4, A1-2 + A24, 0) was a prediction and explanation about the situation. This piece said that "For Mr. Bush the attacks constitute a threat and an opportunity."

"A New War And Its Scale" (09-17-01, #2, A1-2 + A3, 0) was another explanatory piece.

The editorial titled "Nation-Building in Afghanistan" (09-27-01, #4, A20-2, 0) was advice to Buch as to what he should do in Afghanistan.

"MILITARY CALLED JUST ONE ELEMENT IN WAR ON TERROR; Briefing for Nato; Skepticism Among Allies --- Some Want to See bin Laden Evidence" (09-27-01, #1, A1-1 + B2, 0) was a mix of positive and negative contents.

Period III. War in Afghanistan

This is analysis of the *New York Times* coverage of President Bush from the issue of October 8, 2001 to that of November 07, 2001. News coverage during this period showed forceful military leadership of Mr. Bush, who made efforts to garner international cooperation. But he was forced to act largely alone and was hated by portions of Arabs. He showed some international leadership. In the war efforts, President Bush was supported by Democrats but was criticized by part of intellectuals. Although this war was retaliatory in nature, opposition to it was not negligible. During this period the image of Mr. Bush as a decisive military leader was more salient. This period was differentiated from Period II, considering that military attacks on Afghanistan started.

Positive Coverage

(1) The Image of a Decisive Military Leader

The straight story titled "U.S. AND BRITAIN STRIKE

AFGHANISTAN, AIMING AT BASES AND TERRORIST CAMPS; BUSH WARNS 'TALIBAN WILL PAY A PRICE'; Bomb and Missile Attacks --- Bin Laden Issues Threat" (10-08-01, Mon, #1, A1-1 + B3, +2) marked the start of the real retaliatory war. This piece showed Bush's strong military leadership:

Striking at night from aircraft carriers and distant bases, the United States and Britain launched a powerful barrage of cruise missiles and long-range bombers against Afghanistan today to try to destroy the terrorist training camps of Osama bin Laden's Qaeda network and the Taliban government that has protected it (Paragraph 1).

"On my orders, the United States military has begun strikes," President Bush said in a televised statement from the White House at 1 p.m., just more than an hour after the first explosions were reported in Kabul, the Afghan capital (Paragraph 2).

"These carefully targeted actions are designed to disrupt the use of Afghanistan as a terrorist base of operations and to attack the military capability of the Taliban regime," Mr. Bush said (Paragraph 3).

A related story titled "THE PLANNING; Quietly, Carefully, President Worked Toward a Decision on Attack -- Aid Combination" (10-08 01, #6, B6-1, +2) was a supplementary piece to the above story. This piece made a good contrast with the above-mentioned column "New Fears, New Alliances," (10-02-01, A25-1) which denounced lack of systematic analysis before adopting a new foreign policy.

"THE PLANNING; A Look Behind the Scenes, From White House Aides" (10-09-01, #1, B7-1, +2) described the scenes where Mr. Bush decided upon military strikes. This was a detailed and intimate description of the things that happened in the White House situation room, as narrated by the aides:

On Friday (Oct. 5th, Seol's note) morning in the White House situation room President Bush turned to General

Richard B. Meyers, the chairman of the Joint Chiefs of Staff, and asked, "Dick, is Tommy Franks ready to go?" He was referring to the crusty Army general who commands the American military in the Middle East and South Asia, and who was rapidly assembling forces for the coming war in Afghanistan (Paragraph 1).

Assured that General Franks was prepared to strike, the president said, "All right, then we are ready to go," according to the first detailed account of the past few days provided by senior White House officials (Paragraph 2).

"In One Month, A Presidency Is Transformed; A Leader With No Time For the Plans of Sept. 10" (10-11-01, #3, B1-1 + B11, +1) conveyed an image of "decisive Bush." This straight story described how Bush has transformed in a month (Bush's transformation was already discussed in Period II):

Inside and outside the White House, friends and advisers who once complained that the president had trouble getting his bearings when faced with a panoply of issues now assert that *he is focused as never before* (Paragraph 5).

"He appears different up close," said Senator Charles E. Schumer of New York, a Democrat who has found himself in a new, warm relationship with Mr. Bush. "He has a resolve, he has a confidence. He still has the same way of putting people at ease but you can see that this is somebody who is in the process of rising to the occasion (Paragraph 6).

Mr. Bush's ratings are at historic highs, greater than even those of his father after the Persian Gulf War. ... (Paragraph 7).

"BUSH OFFERS TALIBAN '2ND CHANCE' TO YIELD; SAYS HE'D WELCOME U.N. IN NATION-BUILDING; FBI ISSUES ALERT ON SIGNS OF NEW TERROR; 'Just Bring Him In'; President Hints He Will Halt War if bin Laden Is Handed Over" (10-12-01, #1, A1-1+ B5, +2) showed Bush's powerful leadership in chasing bin Laden and in asking for the role of the United Nations in the reconstruction of Afghanistan.

"PRESIDENT REJECTS OFFER BY TALIBAN FOR NEGOTIATIONS; Demands Surrender of bin Laden --- U.S. Bombs Fall in Kabul" (10-15-01, #1, A1-1 + B2, +2) by Elisabeth Bumiller is a follow-up story.

The editorial "Mr. Bush's New Gravitas" (10-12-01, #5, A24-1, +2) offered a eulogy to Mr. Bush. Bush became a different man:

> *The George W. Bush who addressed the nation at a prime-time news conference yesterday appeared to be a different man* from the one who was just barely elected president last year, or even the man who led the country a month ago. He seemed more confident, determined and sure of his purpose and was in full command of the complete array of political and military challenges that he faces in the wake of the terrible terrorist attacks of Sept. 11. It was for the most part a reassuring performance that gave comfort to an uneasy nation (Paragraph 1).

"MEDIA WATCH; To Reassure World, Bush Flies Confidently and Forcefully Without a Net" (10-12-01, #7, B5-1, +2) is another piece praising Bush's confident leadership.

"Bush's War Troika Seeking Blend of Military and Civilian Decision-Making; An old issue of how much oversight to impose on field commanders" (10-24-01, #3, B1-1 + B2, +2) gave additional flavor to Bush's wartime leadership.

"THE WHITE HOUSE; Bush Plans Speeches With Coherent, Unified Message; The president moves to counter the stumbles in war-related information" (11-02-01, #6, B7-1, +1) showed how much emphasis Bush put on communications in his war on terror:

> President Bush is planning several major speeches next week to counteract what some administration officials say has been a muddled effort to project a coherent, convincing

message to Americans about the war in Afghanistan and their safety at home (Paragraph 1).

Mr. Bush's speeches and appearances, one administration official said, was the first element in a new strategy of simplifying the messages that have come in a cascade of at times uncoordinated briefings from the White House, the Pentagon, the State Department and other government agencies (Paragraph 2).

At the same time, American and British officials have set up shop in the Indian Treaty Room of the Old Executive Office Building, *preparing a daily message to be broadcast around the world about the goals of the war on terrorism* --- and to reply to Taliban contentions of bombs gone awry, planes shot down and villages destroyed (Paragraph 3).

"For a President at War, Refuge at Camp David" (11-05-01, #1, A1-2 + B6, +1) was an intimate and favorable description of how Mr. Bush conducts the war on terrorism:

The plan had been to spend nearly every weekend at the Texas ranch, with the White House serving as a kind of Monday-to-midday-Friday pied-a-terre away from what was really home. *But then came Sept. 11, when George W. Bush was transformed into a wartime president who could no longer be seen fishing for long weekends in Crawford* while sending Americans to fight in Afghanistan (Paragraph 1).

As a result, Mr. Bush is spending more time than he ever imagined at Camp David, the presidential retreat in the Catoctin Mountains of Maryland that was born in another wartime, 1942, when Franklin D. Roosevelt picked it as an antidote to the stresses of the White House and named it Shangri-La (Paragraph 2).

It was at Camp David, Mr. Bush said, that the military campaign in Afghanistan was "first born" with his decision made on a Saturday morning, Oct. 6, to order the first wave of B-2 bombers from Missouri to their Afghan targets

(Paragraph 5).

"A president can never get away from his job," said the current President Bush, "but Camp David is set up for a president to both work and relax" (Last Paragraph).

And Bush's photo captioned "AND HERE'S THE PITCH; President Bush threw the ceremonial first pitch last night at Yankee Stadium just before Game 3 of the World Series" (10-31-01, #1, A1-1, +2) was meant to symbolize that Americans returned to the normal life after September 11 attacks.

(2) The Image of an International Leader

President Bush's summit meetings with President Jiang Zemin of China and President Vladimir Putin of Russia were instances of president's international leadership. Mr. Bush garnered support from them in fighting terrorism.

The photo captioned "First Meeting for Bush and Jiang; Mr. Bush emphasized his intention to press forward with the American fight against terrorism" (10-19-01, #1, A1-1) and the related straight story titled "THE PRESIDENT; Bush Meets China's Leader and Emphasizes Need to Fight Terrorism Together; Trying for detente, despite Republican distrust of China's military buildup" (10-19-01, #1-1, B4, +2) described Bush's efforts to gain China's cooperation:

President Bush and President Jiang Zemin of China met for the first time here this morning and emerged with Mr. Bush declaring that China had agreed to "cooperate with intelligence matters and interdict the financing" of major terrorist groups (Paragraph 1).

A follow-up story titled "BUSH MEETS JIANG; Citing Support for War, President Plays Down Contentious Issues" (10-20-01, #1, A1-1 + B4, +2) reported that he won support from Jiang:

President Bush said here today that "support is near unanimous" among Pacific Rim nations for both the military strikes in Afghanistan and the broader war he has declared against terrorism (Paragraph 1).

In another story, "Putin Sees Pact With U.S. On Revising ABM Treaty; Would Let Bush Proceed on Missile Shield" (10-22-01, #1, A1-1 + A8, +1) sounded like another success for Bush.

(3) Presidential Image Making through First Lady

Laura Bush's photo appeared with a title and a caption: A Special Storytime; Laura Bush read 'Grandfather's Journey' by Allen Say to 18 kindergarteners in Newark yesterday (10-17-01, #3, D5-2, +1). The first lady's visit was part of Teach for America Week 2001. Teach for America recruits college graduates to teach in schools in poor neighborhoods. Mrs. Bush, a former teacher, also gave a geography lesson and hugged the 5-year olds.

(4) Other Stories That Depict Bush Positively

The story "Rome Journal; A Bush Admirer Longs to Join America's A-List; A plan for a pro-American rally in Rome riles both right and left" (10-20-01, #2, A4-1, +2) provided a favorable image of Bush.

And the story titled "Bush Winning Gore Backers' High Praises; Foreign Policy Choices Seen as Ideal for Crises; Many Democrats are having a quiet change of heart on the president" (10-20-01, #5, B1-1 + B6, +2) is another example.

Negative Coverage

(1) Stories and Columns Conveying Opposition to Bush's War Plan

Bush's war plan met with a variety of opposition in and out of America. Some columns reminded Americans of the Vietnam quagmire and some said that guns won't win the Afghan war.

A column titled "A Military Quagmire Remembered; Afghanistan as Vietnam; Worries that sending ground troops would lead to a long war" (10-31-01, #5, B1-1 + B3, -1) sounded like a warning by reminding the readers of Vietnam:

> Like an unwelcome specter from an unhappy past, the ominous word *"quagmire" has begun to haunt conversations among government officials and students of foreign policy*, both here and abroad (Paragraph 1).
>
> *Could Afghanistan become another Vietnam*? Is the United States facing another stalemate on the other side of the world? ... (Paragraph 2).
>
> Strategically, the United States could benefit in Afghanistan from the Taliban's unpopularity with many Afghans, but American bombs falling on civilian targets will not win Afghan "hearts and minds" (Third from last Paragraph).

Another column titled "Guns Won't Win the Afghan War; Only diplomacy and covert action can oust Al Qaeda" (Column, 11-04-01, #7, WK13, Op-Ed, -1) argued:

> Neither the current bombing campaign nor the deployment of American ground forces to Afghanistan offers good military options for dealings with the Taliban and Al Qaeda. A better approach would emphasize ground-level diplomacy, with open wallets, among Pashtun leaders in central and southern Afghanistan, the fullest use of Pakistani intelligence and influence ... (Paragraph 1).

A story titled "U.S. Appears to Be Losing Public Relations War So Far" (10-28-01, #3, B8-1, -1) gave a warning:

> The Bush administration has belatedly deployed its forces

for a propaganda to win over the Arab public. But the campaign, intended to convince doubters that the American attacks on Afghanistan are justified and its Middle East policy is evenhanded, has so far proved ineffectual (Paragraph 1).

Thousands of words from American officials, it appears, have proved no match for the last week's news, which produced a barrage of pictures of wounded Afghan children and of Israeli tanks rolling into Palestine villages (Paragraph 2).

A story titled "PROTESTS; In Streets of Pakistani Cities, Cries of 'Death to America!'; 'Bush is a dog! Israel is a dog! Russia is a dog!' a group chants" (10-09-01, #3, B9, -1) provided a different view of Bush:

Quetta's day of protests began with a student rally organized by Jamat-e-Ulema-e-Islam, the militant religious party whose leader was placed under house arrest on Sunday. Muhammad Noor, another of the party's leaders, told the crowd, "If there is no peace in Afghanistan, there will be no peace anywhere in the world." The response came in unison: "Death to America!" and "Stop the strikes!" (Paragraph 23).

A story titled "Survey Shows Doubts Stirring On Terror War" (10-30-01, #1, A1-1 + B6, -1) represented doubts about the war in the form of a survey.

"THE CONTINENT; Public Apprehension Felt In Europe Over the Goals Of Afghanistan Bombings" (11-01-01, #6, B2, -1) reflected Europeans' view of the Afghan War.

"More and More, Other Countries See the War as Solely America's" (11-04-01, #3, B1-1 + B2, -1) provided a sobering view of the war.

(2) Other Stories That Depict Bush Negatively

The editorial "Half a Commander in Chief" (11-05-01, #2, A16-1, -1) criticized that Mr. Bush could not control domestic affairs, because he concentrated his energies solely on war in Afghanistan and not on domestic affairs:

> America seems to be governed by two presidents. The George W. Bush who is commander in chief has been keeping the country united at a time when the war in Afghanistan has run into problems. But *the George W. Bush running domestic policy is an entirely different person*, less a leader than a narrowly focused politician. If America is to fight terrorism within its own borders and conquer the economic recession, the commander in chief is going to have to take control at home, too (Paragraph 1).

"White House Memo: Home Front Is a Minefield For President" (10-25-01, #1, A1-1 +B8, -2) carried a similar tone.

A column titled "Abroad at Home: Mr. Bush's New World; His foreign policy turned upside down" (10-13-01, #1, A23-1, Op-Ed, -2) was additional criticism against Bush's abrupt about-face in foreign policy. The columnist argued that "Demonizing China as a potential enemy has disappeared with the need to enlist Beijing in the alliance against terrorism (Paragraph 4)."

A straight story titled "Bush Is Said to Scale Back His Religion-Based Initiative; But He Hopes to Push for Full Bill Next Year" (10-14-01, #2, A18-1, -1) showed that Bush retracted from his previous policy after having faced opposition.

Another story titled "G.O.P. Not Relying on Aid From Bush in '02 Elections; His Popularity May Not Translate Into Votes; Will the president's desire to appear bipartisan cost his party support?" (11-04-01, #2, A28-1, -1) was coded negative in that this story detracted from the political value that Bush possesses.

Neutral Coverage

"POLITICAL MEMO: On Home Front, Bush Seeks to Avoid His Father's Fate" (10-09-01, #2, B7-2, 0) was coded neutral (0). It was neither positive nor negative.

"Charities: Bush Voices Pride in Aid, But Groups List Hurdles" (10-17-01, #1, B3-1, 0) was a mix of positive and negative sentences, and thus was coded neutral.

The editorial "The War Has Just Begun" (10-27-01, #1, A18-1, 0) was a bland piece of writing, neither praise nor criticism.

"THE DEBATE: Guaging the Use of Ground Troops and the Scale of the Afghan War" (Column, 11-04-01, #5, B3-1, 0) was explanatory in nature, thus was coded neutral.

Period IV. War in Iraq

This is analysis of the *New York Times* coverage of President Bush from the issue of March 19, 2003 to that of May 02, 2003. The presidential image of this period can be characterized as a decisive wartime (or, military) leadership. *The New York Times* conspicuously portrayed Mr. Bush as a wartime leader in various ways. Broadly speaking, the *New York Times* highlighted Bush's wartime leadership in a sophisticated and balanced manner, reflecting opposing voices from inside and outside of America. Presidential news appeared at crucial moments to provide meanings to certain critical turning points. Perhaps Mr. Bush might have made timely statements for news coverage.

This newspaper portrayed Mr. Bush as a resolute wartime leader, provided authenticity and justification to his "pre-emptive strike" logic, and described war successes as expressed by Mr. Bush. This newspaper also conveyed human and intimate aspects of Mr. Bush in conducting the war. The cream of positive coverage may be the highlighting of media control policy (i.e., embedded journalism) on the battlefield to get favorable

war coverage. Arguably, America's war on Iraq officially started on March 17, 2003 (*New York Times*, May 18, 2003), with
President Bush's address to the nation (i.e., an ultimatum)
"giving Saddam Hussein 48 hours to leave Iraq." Military phase
of this war ended on May 1, 2003 with Bush's declaration, and
America's war on Iraq ended "on paper" with the transfer of
sovereignty to Iraqi interim government on June 28, 2004.

One needs to note that America's war on Iraq has been contemplated for years. To produce evidence for this, Bush pledged
repeatedly to disarm Iraq, regarding the country as a serious
threat to America in his State of the Union address (*New York
Times*, January 29, 2003). Mr. Bush called Iraq, Iran, and North
Korea "an Axis of Evil" in the State of the Union address, while
emphasizing "Secure America is top priority" (*New York Times*,
January 30, 2002).

Positive Coverage

(1) The Image of a Military Leader

The top story on the March 18, 2003, issue of the *New York
Times* had a full-width headline "Bush Gives Hussein 48 Hours,
and Vows to Act; Ready to Attack; Diplomatic Effort *Ends*
(Seol's emphasis) --- Terror Alert Level Is Raised for U.S." (03-
18-03, #1, A1-1 + A15 + A14, transcript, +2). The story conveyed the image of a forceful military leader:

> President Bush tonight gave Saddam Hussein 48 hours to
> go into exile or face attack from the United States and a
> handful of allies (Paragraph 1).
>
> In an address to the nation from the White House, made
> hours after he *abandoned* attempts to forge a united diplo-
> matic front against Iraq, *Mr. Bush made clear that hostili-
> ties could begin as soon as his two-day ultimatum* expires,
> perhaps sooner if Mr. Hussein openly spurns the demand

from the United States that (Paragraph 2).

For the president, the speech marked *a failed end* to six months of diplomacy intended to convince skeptical allies like France and (Paragraph 4).

Having unable to get the United Nations behind him, Mr. Bush now faces a war with *only Britain* providing substantial military support and many other nations --- as well as a portion of domestic public opinion --- *condemning him* for what they have called *a rush to war* (Paragraph 5).

As the italicized parts within the story show, the account itself appears to be quite balanced, conveying Bush's message and representing opposition to the war. But the headline carried a very stern message and it was strongly-worded; "time limit of 48 hours" and the phrases *vow to act* and *ready to attack* give a strong impact. The subtitle "Diplomatic Effort *Ends*" instead of "*Fails*" was favorable to Bush. The overall appraisal was very positive (+2) to Bush's image. This piece represented a strong military leadership.

Connected to this, the front-page news analysis (03-18-03, #2, A1-1+ A14, +2) titled "A New Doctrine for War; In Age of Unseen Enemies, President Says, Waiting for Opponent to Attack 'Is Suicide' " justified Bush's decision on war by providing theoretical backing, i.e., the pre-emptive strike logic, thus was assessed to be very positive (+2):

His argument for deposing Saddam Hussein boiled down to one precept. *In an age of unseen enemies who make no formal declarations of war, waiting to act after America's foes "have struck first is not self-defense, it is suicide* (Paragraph 2)."

President Bush thus turned America's first new national security strategy in 50 years --- the doctrine of pre-emptive military action against potential enemies amassing weapons of mass destruction --- into the rationale for America's latest war (Paragraph 3).

It is an aggressive view of America's duty that Mr. Bush never discussed during his presidential campaign, Yet he began to embrace that strategy within months of entering the Oval Office, and it became his fierce passion after Sept. 11, 2001.(Paragraph 4).

"Bush's Speech on Iraq; 'Saddam Hussein and His Sons Must Leave'; A transcript of President Bush's speech as recorded by *the New York Times*" (03-18-03, #5, A14-2, +2) was appraised very positive (+2), because the transcript conveyed verbatim what Bush had said, neither edited nor interpreted.

According to Maltese (2003), presidents like to appeal directly to the nation (or, "go public") and the transcript may be a means of direct appeal (Pfiffner and Davidson, 2003, pp. 146-58).

A column "Good Reasons for Going Around the U.N.; The war might be illegal, but it could still be legitimate" (03-18-03, Tue, #11, A33-1, Op-Ed, +1) additionally justified Bush's war decision and his going around the U.N.:

By giving up on the Security Council, the Bush administration has started on a course that could be called "illegal but legitimate," a course that could end up, paradoxically, winning United Nations approval for a military campaign in Iraq --- though only after an invasion (Paragraph 2).

The relevant history here is from Kosovo. In 1999, the United States, expecting a Russian veto of military intervention to stop Serbian attacks on ethnic Albanians in Kosovo, sidestepped the United Nations completely and sought authorization for the use of force within NATO itself (Paragraph 3).

"The President's Day; Just Another Day, Except for Its Conclusion" (A14-1, +1) described how calmly Bush came to the war decision.

A straight story "BUSH ORDERS START OF WAR ON IRAQ; MISSILES APPARENTLY MISS HUSSEIN; President Warns of Difficulty --- Airstrikes on Baghdad" (03-20-03, #1,

A1+A20, +2) conveyed presidential image of a strong wartime leader:

> President Bush ordered the start of a war against Iraq on Wednesday night and American forces poised on the country's southern border and at sea began strikes to disarm the country, including an apparently unsuccessful attempt to kill Saddam Hussein (Paragraph 1).
>
> Mr. Bush addressed the nation from the Oval Office at 10:15 pm (Paragraph 2).
>
> He added, "These are opening stages of what will be a broad and concerted campaign" (Paragraph 3).

A story tracing the roots of pre-emptive strike against Iraq appeared. The story "Pre-emption; Idea with a Lineage Whose Time Has Come" (03-23-03, Sun, #2, B1-2, +2) was a follow-up to the above analysis (03-18-03, #2, A14). This analysis explained that Republican conservatives such as Donald Rumsfeld and Paul Wolfowitz pushed the preemption strategy to President Bush.

The straight story titled "Bush Warns That the War in Iraq May Last Longer Than Expected" (03-23-03, #3, B10-1, +2) was meant to prepare Americans' psychology for a longer-than-expected war:

> President Bush gathered his war council at Camp David this morning, while warning that the war in Iraq "could be longer and more difficult than some have predicted (Paragraph 1)."
>
> Mr. Bush's caution reflected a concern that the relatively quick progress made by forces moving through southern Iraq could create expectations of a quick victory (Paragraph 2).

This story was brought up again the next day in the form of an analysis "Lowering Expectations; As Iraqi Resistance Stiffens, Bush Moves To Prepare U.S. Public for a Harder War" (03-24-

03, Mon, #1, A1-2 + B2, +2):

> Like a coach seeking psychological advantage, President Bush pressed an effort today to temper public anticipation of an early, relatively painless victory in the fighting in Iraq (Paragraph 1).
> "It is evident that it's going to take a while to achieve our objective," the President said on the White House lawn after returning from Camp David (Paragraph 2).

This topic was brought up for the third time in the form of a straight news, but the story appeared on the inside page, reflecting that this was not a new story.

The story "Commander in Chief; Bush Pleased by Progress, Tries to Lower Expectations" (03-24-03, Mon, #2, B12-2, +2) said that Mr. Bush delivered the same message at the White House, not at Camp David as previously.

A strong war message was delivered when Mr. Bush met with British Prime Minister Tony Blair. Leaders of America and Great Britain vowed to finish off Saddam Hussein's regime. The story "War to Keep Going Until Regime Ends, Bush and Blair Say" (03-28-03, #1, A1-2+B13, +2) read:

> President Bush and Prime Minister Tony Blair of Britain stood side by side at Camp David today, defending the progress of the war in Iraq and *in their vow to finish off Saddam Hussein regime no matter how long and trying the battles ahead* (Paragraph 1).
> Mr. Bush said *the war would last "however long it takes to win*," and that the coalition led by American and British forces was advancing day by day, in steady progress (Paragraph 2).

A straight story appeared on the front page with a headline: "WHITE HOUSE SAYS WAR IS 'ON TRACK'; SHOW OF SUPPORT; Bush Assails Hussein --- Syria and Iran Warned Not to Interfere" (03-29-03, Sat, #1, A1-1+B11, +2). This piece said that the war is on track, a positive image to Bush.

President Bush stated that Saddam's government does not exist as a result of military attacks. The story titled "BUSH SAYS REGIME IN IRAQ IS NO MORE; SYRIA IS PENALIZED; Cutting an Oil Pipeline; U.S. Is Also Pressing Iran as It Tries to Reshape Region With a New Democracy" (04-16-03, Wed, #2, A1-1 + B3, +2) is an additional example:

> President Bush *declared* today that "the regime of Saddam Hussein is no more," and his administration used America's rapid success in overthrowing the Iraqi leader to put new pressure on Iran and Syria, neighbors of the newly occupied nation (Paragraph 1).

The second Persian Gulf War *seemed to end* (Seol's emphasis) when Bush declared victory on May 1st, 2003. The straight news titled "Bush Declares 'One Victory in a War on Terror'; He Says Military Phase in Iraq Has Ended" (05-02-03, Fri, #1, A1-1 + A 16, +2) showed that Mr. Bush was a leader of the victor country and that he ended the war successfully by this declaration:

> *President Bush declared tonight that the military phase of the battle to topple Saddam Hussein's government was "one victory" in a war on terror that began on Sept. 11th, 2001,* and still goes on (Paragraph 1).
>
> Speaking from the deck of the aircraft carrier Abraham Lincoln before thousands of uniformed sailors and aviators as the ship approached San Diego Harbor, he argued that by vanquishing Mr. Hussein's government, he had removed "an ally of Al Qaeda," and he vowed to continue to search for banned weapons in Iraq (Paragraph 2).

(2) The Image of an International Leader

A story titled "Japanese Prime Minister Supports U.S. On Iraq Stance" (*New York Times*, 03-19-03, #4, A20-2, +1) was assessed to be positive (+1) to Bush's image as an international leader. The story said that "In the face of strong and growing opposition, Japan's Premier Junichiro Koizumi expressed strong support for the United States' ultimatum to President Saddam Hussein of Iraq (Paragraph 1)."

Bush's visit to Belfast was depicted in a very favorable light on three consecutive days. Before Mr. Bush went to Belfast a story appeared with a title "Bush Visit Is Viewed as Hopeful Sign for Ulster Impasse' (04-07-03, Mon, #1, A2-2, +2).

The next day, a follow-up story appeared on the front page under the title "BUSH MEETS BLAIR; Conference in Belfast Over Role of U.N. in Iraq After the War" (04-08-03, Tue, #1, A1-1 + B9, +1). This piece said that the two leaders "turned their attention to planning for a post-war Iraq, seeking to bridge their differences over how much of a role to give the United Nations in rebuilding the country and putting together a new government."

An editorial on this day titled "After the War" (04-08-03, #2, A22-1, +2) said that "Though more fighting lies ahead before the government of Saddam Hussein is crushed, Mr. Bush and Mr. Blair *wisely decided* (Seol's emphasis) to get together yesterday in Northern Ireland to start making decisions about the future of Iraq" (Paragraph 2).

This topic was rehashed in the form of an analysis titled "After the Conflict; Bush's Next Role; Mediator in Disputes Over Running Postwar Iraq; Two more battles; The United States vs. Europe, and State vs. Defense" (04-08-03, #3, B9-2, 0). This piece discussed the future role of Mr. Bush over Iraq in a dry style, and thus was assessed neutral.

A favorable analysis appeared concerning Bush's message. The analysis "Bush's War Message; Strong and Clear" (04-09-03, Wed, #1, A1-2 + B6, +2) put a flattering spin on the story:

At least for the moment, the political planets seem to be sliding into alignment for President Bush, and he looked and sounded as if he knew it when he appeared in Belfast, Northern Ireland, for a news conference with Prime

Minister Tony Blair of Britain (Paragraph 1).

Mr. Bush was *self-assured, blunt-spoken and aggressive.* For once, *the English language seemed his ally* rather than his worst enemy. He betrayed not the slightest doubt about the decisions he has made on the war in Iraq so far or the ones he faces (Paragraph 2).

A related straight story appeared on the same day under the title "Bush Sees Aid Role of U.N. as Limited In Rebuilding Iraq" (04-09-03, #2, A1-2 + B7, +1). This piece said that "President Bush pledged to grant the United Nation a 'vital role' in postwar Iraq, but defined that principally as providing food, medicine and aid (Paragraph 1)."

Another straight story followed under the title "Bush Pledges to Help as Ulster Nears a Junction in Peace Path" (04-09-03, #3, A4-2, +1) by Warren Hoge in Hillsborough. This story said that "President Bush gave the Northern Ireland peace effort *a push at a timely moment.*"

A front-page straight story appeared under the title "BUSH URGING U.N. TO LIFT SANCTIONS IMPOSED ON IRAQ; 12 Years of Trade Curbs; Oil Money Seen as Paying for Rebuilding, but Plan Could Reignite Council Feud" (04-17-03, #1, A1-1+ B36, +2) fell under this subgroup.

The same topic reappeared two days later under the title "Bush Plans to Ask U.N. to Lift Penalties Against Iraq in Phases; Oil-for-Food Program Would Continue" (04-19-03, Sat, #1, A1-1 + B6, +2).

(3) Personal Qualities: Intimate Coverage

The New York Times carried fairly many stories revealing personal qualities or conveying intimate and soft aspects of the president. These stories might have softened the harsh images of the wartime leader or might have been intended to show that war is conducted by human beings with human emotions.

"TV Watch; Soft Words That Convey a Hard Line" (03-18-03, #9, A18-2, +2) approached "blind flattery" and sounded like quite subjective. Read how the story was written:

> President Bush's final warning to Saddam Hussein was to "get out of Dodge," but his tone was less hard-nosed sheriff than Mr. Rogers gently urging a child to put down the loaded pistol (Paragraph 1).
> For months, Mr. Bush has appeared *unwaveringly confident* about his showdown with Mr. Hussein. Viewers know he is convinced. Last night, with war approaching, Mr. Bush tried to be convincing (Paragraph 2).

This piece was followed by another story "Days of Waiting and Wondering Ends with Word from President" (03-20-03, #2, A1-2 + A20, +2). This story described very favorably the way President Bush delivered the speech:

> President Bush picked up a copy of the speech in which he would *tell the world* that he had launched military strikes to topple Saddam Hussein. He gave *a little shake of his fist*, according to a person who saw the scene on a television monitor (Paragraph 1).
> Two hours later, Mr. Bush sat down in the Oval Office behind what is known the *"Resolute" desk*, which was donated to the United States (Paragraph 8).

At the height of the war, a straight story described how much Mr. Bush was involved in this war. The story titled "President, No Matter Where, Keeps Battlefield Close" (03-30-03, Sun, #2, B1-1+ B11, +2) highlighted Bush's serious involvement in this war:

> George W. Bush was standing three feet from his television screen in his cabin at Camp David last weekend, *absorbed in every detail of the news from Iraq*, when a correspondent came on to report that the president of the United States, according to White House officials, was not glued to TV (Paragraph 1).

Mr. Bush started laughing, said his close friend Ronald Betts, who was with the president at the time (Paragraph 2).

"He is just totally immersed," Mr. Betts said in an interview. Mr. Betts said that he and Mr. Bush talked of little else but the war over the last two days at Camp David last weekend, and that the president regularly turned in to the cable channels for updates on Iraq. When Mr. Bush saw something that concerned him, Mr. Betts said, he picked up the phone to tell Condoleeza Rice, his national security adviser who was at nearby cabin to look into it (Paragraph 3).

A week and a half into the invasion of Iraq, friends and administration officials say the president has emerged as *an engrossed commander in chief, who is far more gripped by daily battlefield developments than his father was in the first Persian Gulf War* (Paragraph 4).

This piece may be an extremely detailed portrayal of the president's acts in conducting a war from the journalist's viewpoint, but it sounded like a "disguised" flattery to the president. It is also soft in nature.

A column with soft touches about Mr. Bush appeared in the form of a reporter's column under the title "White House Letter: Another President Bush Watches on the Sidelines" (04-07-03, #3, B2-1, +2). This column, printed together with the photograph of former President Bush, described how the "41st" president (Bush senior) provided the "43rd" with the psychological assistance in this war:

> So far, Mr. Bush's only public comments about the war have been *totally in support of his son*, even when he is asked why this White House failed to build the kind of international coalition that he did in support of the first gulf war. The situation was different then, Mr. Bush says, because the objective of driving the Iraqis from Kuwait was much clearer (Paragraph 11).

One photograph of Mr. Bush visiting wounded soldiers appeared on the front page. The photo (04-12-03, Sat, #1, A1-1, +2) was assessed to be very positive. The caption of this photo did not indicate whether the photo was related to any story, but a relevant story titled "THE PRESIDENT; Bush Says Hussein Is Out, But War Is Not Yet Over; The president handed out 13 Purple Hearts" (04-12-03, #5, B9-1, +1) was printed inside. The caption that preceded the story read:

SOLDIER'S HONOR; Visiting troops wounded in Iraq, President Bush gave a Purple Heart yesterday to Army Sgt. First Class Thomas Douglas, with his wife, Donna, at Water Reed Army Medical Center in Washington.

A story about an emotional scene watched from inside the White House appeared. This straight story titled "How 3 Weeks of War in Iraq Looked From the Oval Office" (04-14-03, Mon, #1, A1-2 + B11, +2) described the scene in which Bush came to his decision on the war against Iraq, while Mr. Powell supported him psychologically:

Then the administration's warrior-turned-diplomat, Secretary of State Colin Powell, *reached out to touch the president's hand*. It was *a gesture of support*, but it was born, perhaps, of an understanding that the risks ahead were beyond the president's experience (Paragraph 3).

Two more favorable columns revealing Bush's human aspects ensued. The one under the title "WHITE HOUSE MEMO: Bush Shows Looser Side in an Interview" (04-26-03, Sat, #1, A13-1, +2) read:

Even when President Bush was in the middle of a meeting during the most critical moment of the war in Iraq, White House staff members would fetch him whenever the black-is-white Iraqi information minister, Muhammed Said al-Sahhaf appeared on television. Mr. Bush, it turns out, was a big fan (Paragraph 1).

Another column "White House Letter: Playing It Straight at an Odd Washington Ritual; An annual dinner that reflects the tone of the capital has a subdued air" (04-28-03, Mon, #1, A18-1, +2) described the scene where the White House correspondents dinner was held. The reporter wrote:

Saturday night's dinner for 2,500 in the Washington Hilton's cave-like ballroom, was presided over by a solemn President Bush, who was one of the presidents to make remarks from the dais that were intentionally not funny (Paragraph 2).
"He wasn't in the mood for frivolity," Mr. Deans said. *The main thing on his mind was the war* (Penultimate paragraph)."

In this story, Mr. Bush was frequently referred to. He was not in the mood for humor. This piece, directly and indirectly, described Bush's state of mind in a favorable light. The message was that Bush was always thinking about the war on Iraq.

(4) War Reports Affecting Mr. Bush Favorably

An analysis of the battlefield success gave Bush favorable coverage. The news analysis "Dash to Baghdad Leaves Debate in Dust; Military Successes Give Bush a Boost" (04-05-03, Sat, #1, A1-1, +2) described Bush in a very positive light:

No less remarkable has been the transformation of the political atmosphere at home and, to a lesser degree, abroad. The dramatic, lightning-like thrust of the tanks and Bradley fighting vehicles, their way eased by the devastating application of air power to the Republican Guard, has taken the political heat off President Bush and his hardnosed Pentagon boss (Paragraph 2).
The burgeoning debate over the size of the American

force in Iraq has been tamped down (Paragraph 3).

As the war hurtled toward American "victory" (although, as of November 2003, final victory seems to be still elusive, Seol's comment), the battlefield successes combined with Bush's high spirits. A straight story appeared under the title "U.S. FORCES TAKE CONTROL IN BAGHDAD; BUSH ELATED; Bush Tunes In And Sees Iraqis In Celebration" (04-10-03, Thur, #1, A1-2+B10, +2) presented this situation:

> An elated President Bush watched celebrating Iraqis drag a statue of Saddam Hussein through Baghdad today as Vice President Dick Cheney and Defense Secretary Donald H. Rumsfeld, barely disguised their glee and their disdain for critics of the Pentagon battle plan (Paragraph 1).
> Although the official word from the White House was that there would be no gloating and that the battles were not yet over, Mr. Cheney and Mr. Rumsfeld seemed to treat cautionary notes about hubris as so much political politeness (Paragraph 2).

A straight story about a poll finding that Americans see a clear victory conveyed a very favorable image of Mr. Bush. The story was titled "Americans See Clear Victory in Iraq, Poll Finds; Baghdad's fall has fortified Bush's political standing" (04-15-03, Tue, #1, B1-2 + B10, +2).

A follow-up straight story "POLITICAL STRATEGY; Bush to Use Ratings in War to Sell Proposed Tax Cut; A president determined not to relive the experiences of his father; With Americans uneasy over economy, Bush begins a new battle" (04-15-03, #2, B10-1, +2) gave an explanation of Bush's future political plans in a favorable light.

(5) Other Reports Affecting Mr. Bush Favorably

A story titled "Congress; Both Parties Close Ranks Behind the President" (03-18-03, #6, A14-1, +2) was assessed to be very positive to Bush (+2), because Bush's speech received unconditional support from the Congress.

An unexpected boon from the above was a piece titled "Steep Losses Are Narrowed After Bush and Blair Speak" (03-28-03, Fri, #5, C6-1, +1). The piece concerning stock prices began by mentioning Bush and Blair:

> Stocks rebounded from early decline yesterday, erasing most of the losses, after President Bush and Prime Minister Tony Blair defended the pace of war against Iraq (Paragraph 1).

One of the most favorable story appeared under the title "THE ADMINISTRATION; Even Critics of War Say the White House Spun It With Skill; A battlefield narrative that worked at home, if not everywhere" (04-20-03, Sun, #1, B14-1, +2). This piece detailed how the White House publicity officers devised ways to get a favorable spin and how journalists *collaborated* with them. This seemed an insider's story and a very favorable piece to Bush:

> The second Persian Gulf War was not only a runaway victory for the United States military, but for another aggressive force that fired off round-the-clock verbal communications operation (Paragraph 1).
>
> That is the assessment of the Bush administration's wartime public relations campaign by both its supporters and critics, who say the spin operation was extraordinarily successful in shaping a positive battlefield narrative, at least for American audiences (Paragraph 2).

This story traced the success at home to three major factors. First was the repeated use of phrases that critics branded propaganda, such as "coalition forces" and "death squads," that became part of the accepted language of war. Second was the powerful cinema verite journalism (or, "embedded journalism" policy by the Pentagon, Seol's comment) of reporters and photographers, whose words and pictures humanized the American soldiers they were with. Third was the message discipline of the White House that plotted appearances by top officials on a daily "communication grid," ensuring that in the first half of the day there was a news briefing by an administration official every two hours, and that everyone was saying more or less the same thing (Paragraph 3+Paragraph 4).

According to this story, Dan Bartlett, the White House communications director, began to use "death squads" to refer to the "fedayeen," which literally means "dying for a noble cause." Bartlett was quoted as saying that "It's not a positive thing they were doing." Bush administration officials used the term "regime change" as a euphemism for "the overthrow of Saddam Hussein." Bush regularly referred to Hussein's troops as "thugs." The most blatant use of loaded language was the term "coalition forces" to describe "what was principally a coalition of only two armies, with help from small numbers of Scud-hunting Australian commandos in western Iraq ."

The Bush administration's embedded journalism policy was based on an agreement between the Pentagon and the media. It was a give-and-take. The Pentagon got its word out on its military might --- "shock and awe" was the well-worn phrase on every anchor's lips, while the television news was well fed by the dramatic video footing (*Wall Street Journal,* March 24, 2003, A13).

Negative Coverage

(1) Bush's War Decision Criticized

The *New York Times* ran fairly many stories which deal with opposition to war. This newspaper ran three negative stories on March 18, 2003 alone. An editorial lambasted the decision on war; a column expressed profound doubts about the war decision; and a straight story addressed an antiwar resolution.

The editorial titled "War in the Ruins of Diplomacy" (03-18-03, #10, A32-1, -2) offered a direct criticism of Bush's war decision:

This war crowns a period of *terrible diplomatic failure, Washington's worst in at least a generation*. The Bush administration now presides over unprecedented American military might. What it risks is not America's power, but an essential part of its glory (Paragraph 5).

At a time when America most needs the world to see its actions in the best possible light, they will probably be seen in the worst. This result was neither foreordained nor inevitable (Last paragraph).

The column titled "Things to Come; Is this war only the beginning?" (03-18-03, #12, A33-1, -2) was additional attack on Bush's war plan:

What frightens me is the aftermath --- and I'm not just talking about the problems of postwar occupation. I'm worried about what will happen beyond Iraq --- in the world at large, and here at home (Paragraph 2).

The members of the Bush team don't seem bothered by the enormous ill will they have generated in the rest of the world. They seem to believe that other countries will change their minds once they see cheering Iraqis welcome our troops, or that our bombs will shock and awe the Iraqis (Paragraph 3).

The straight story "Dissent; A Mere 2 Votes Are Cast, but an Antiwar Resolution Jolts a Rural Township" (03-18-03, #8, A17-2, -1) datelined *Aaronsburg, Pa., Mar 12* said that "the antiwar resolution adopted *last fall* divided a rural town and that it was used as a propaganda by a Swedish television." This piece was regarded as a show of efforts to strike a balance, considering that the story dispatched on Mar 12 about an occurrence of last fall was printed.

When Mr. Bush issued an ultimatum to Hussein, several European leaders expressed worries. The front story titled "World Reaction; A Worried World Shows Discord, With France and Germany Leading Criticism of Bush" (03-19-03, Wed, #2, A1-2 + A15, -2) was evaluated very negative (-2), because the piece conveyed direct opposition to Bush's act on the front page.

Columnist Thomas L. Friedman faulted Bush's war decision. The column titled "D-Day; Making the best of a bad heart" (03-19-03, A29-1, -2) read:

> President Bush is fond of cowboy imagery, so here is an image that comes to mind (Paragraph 1).
>
> *President Bush has failed to build that (internationally cooperative) framework before going to war.* Though the Bush team came to office with Iraq project in mind, it has pursued a narrow, ideological and bullying foreign policy that has alienated so many people that by the time it wanted to rustle up a posse for an Iraq war, too many nations were suspicious of its motives (Paragraph 4).

A straight story titled "Threats and Responses: United Nations; Critics Say U.S. Lacks Legal Basis for Attack" (03-20-03, A19-1, -2) offered a direct attack on Bush's war decision:

> Diplomats who had failed for the last two months to argue on a unified approach to the Iraqi crisis ... offering angry post-mortems on the *diplomatic debacle* and arguing that the planned American-led invasion to disarm Iraq and oust Saddam Hussein *had no basis in international law* (Seol's emphasis) (Paragraph 1).

A straight story titled "Senator Deplores Attack on Iraq" (03-20-03, A20-2, -1) by the *New York Times* (no name of the reporter was given) was assessed negative (-1), because the story was short and placed in the lower part of the page. This story carried no photo of the senator, reflecting that the newspaper did not highlight this piece. But the tone of the story was very strong:

> Mr. Byrd, a Democrat first elected in 1958, said the Bush administration had made the world a more dangerous place by flaunting the nation's superpower status and asserting a new doctrine of pre-emption without international sanction (Paragraph 2).
> "Today I weep for my country," Mr. Byrd said, in his latest floor speech against the war (Paragraph 3).

The three foregoing stories and the story about Senator Byrd's objection to pre-emptive doctrine provided a good contrast with Japanese Premier's support of the war (03-19-03, #4, +1) and the column "Good Reasons for Going Around the U.N." (03-18-03, #11, +1) as discussed in the positive coverage section.

However, when American missiles were launched against Baghdad, the critical tone of the editorials became milder. The tone of the editorial itself became a little "strange." The editorial "The War Begins" (03-20-03, A32-1, -1) appeared permissive of the war:

> There is no strategic exit in the offing, as there was when the coalition forces stopped well short of Baghdad in 1991, There is no sense of international coalescence, a mission that bound disparate nations together (Paragraph 2).
> Our job here is not as transcendently clear as the soldiers' job. *Now that the first strikes have begun, even those who vehemently opposed this war will find themselves in a strange position of hoping for just what the president they have opposed is himself is hoping for: a quick, conclusive resolution fought as bloodlessly as possible.* People who have supported Mr. Bush all along may feel tempted to try to silence those who voice dissent. It will be necessary to remind them that we are in this fight to bring freedom of speech to Iraq, not to smother it back home (Paragraph 3)
> Whether they felt the idea of war in Iraq was a bad one

from the beginning, or --- like us --- they felt it should be undertaken only with broad international support, the yearning (Paragraph 4).

(In comparison, the editorial of the *Washington Post* titled "First Strike," 03-20-03, A28, appeared to support the war, and a lead column of the *Wall Street Journal* titled "A War That Will Bolster Bush", 03-20-03, A19, clearly supported Bush. When the Bush administration failed to discover the evidence of the weapons of mass destruction, the editorial of the *New York Times*, 09-26-03, A24-1, revealed a sense of having been betrayed. The editorial titled "The Failure to Find Weapons" said that "although this page did not support the war in Iraq, it never quarreled with one of the basic premises.")

The story about the Senate's reduction of Bush's tax plan was appraised very negative (-2). The straight news on the front page titled "Senate Votes to Reduce Bush's Tax Plan" (03-26-03, A1-2, -2) read that "Capitalizing on the concerns about the costs of war in Iraq, Senate Democrats won a vote to reduce President Bush's proposed tax cut by half, *a rare political defeat for a wartime president* (Paragraph 1).

A relevant news analysis accompanied the straight story. The analysis titled "How the President's $726 Billion Plan Was Cut in Half" (03-26-03, A12-2, -2) stated that "In a form of political jujitsu, Democrats employed the *growing unease about the war's effect on a shaky economy* to reduce the president's $726 billion tax cut proposal by half."

The analysis titled "Bush Peril: Shifting Sand and Fickle Opinion" (03-30-03, Sun, #1, A1-1 + B11, -2) by R. W. Apple Jr. was assessed very negative (-2), in that this appeared exceptionally on the front page. This piece was direct attack on Mr. Bush:

With every passing day, it is more evident that the failure to obtain permission from Turkey for American troops to cross its territory and open a northern front constituted a diplomatic debacle. With every passing day, it is more evident that the allies made two gross military misjudgments in concluding that coalition forces could safely bypass Basra and Nasiriya and that Shiite Muslims in southern Iraq would rise up against Saddam Hussein (Paragraph 4).

Deep doubts about the war were voiced within the Washington Beltway. The straight story "The Mood: As a Quick Victory Grows Less Likely, Doubts Are Quietly Voiced in Washington" (03-30-03, Sun, #3, B10-2, -2) by David Sanger described disarray on the battlefront inside Washington:

> After ten days of watching smart bombs, sandstorms and stiff resistance from the Iraqi regime, a capital that usually embraces the president in wartime is beginning to show fissures (Paragraph 1).
> Few have openly split with the president, or the decisions so far. But one does not have to scratch deep to hear the doubts (Paragraph 2).
> There are the Central Intelligence Agency analysts, quietly complaining that their warnings that Saddam Hussein government might not crack like peanut brittle were dismissed. There are ex-generals on nightly television, expressing unease about a plan (Paragraph 3).

There ensued five negative (-1) stories on the same page (B14) of the March 30th, 2003 issue of the newspaper. These all reported antiwar protests under the big title "A Nation at War: Coverage of the Conflict." These stories were assessed to be collectively offering unfavorable images of President Bush:

"The Opposition: Thousands Join in Boston to Demand End of War: 'This is not the United States I want to be associated with' ";
"Marches: In New York and New Jersey, Hundreds Join as Antiwar Protests Continue";
"Demonstrations: French Rallies Against War Shift Focus to Israel"; and

"Protesters: Decades Later, 60's Icons Still Live by Their Message" and
"In Ithaca, A Voice of Dissent."

But the climate seemed to be reversed by a story that partly rebutted the foregoing stories. A story titled "Bush Defends Progress of War and Is Cheered;Privately, Republicans Fret Over Uncertainties" (04-01-03, Tue, #1, B1-1+ B3, +1) read:

> President Bush mounted a vigorous defense of the progress made in the war against Iraq, seeking to rebut concerns in the military and nervousness within his own party about how the conflict is going and how it was planned (Paragraph 1).
> Some Republicans in Washington were clearly jittery about the course and conduct of the war (Paragraph 5).

This piece is a mixture of positive and negative coverage, but the weight was put on the positive, therefore was assessed to be (+1). The appropriate arrangement of these negative and positive stories seemed part of the efforts to maintain balance or objectivity in coverage or this may be a reflection of the complicated realities where pros and cons coexist (Seol's interpretation).
A columnist took issue with the manner Mr. Bush saluted the soldiers. The column "A Senseless Salute; It's a mistake for presidents to act like soldiers" (04-19-03, #2, A19-1, -2) said:

> This gesture is of course quite wrong: such a salute has always required the wearing of a uniform. But there is more to this than a decline in military manners. (Paragraph 2).

Two stories faulted the reconstruction contracts that went to Bechtel, which is closely linked to the Washington insiders.
The editorial titled "And the Winner Is Bechtel" (04-19-03, Sat, A12-1) argued that "The Bush administration should work hard to dispel that mistaken notion and should bend over back-

ward to avoid reinforcing it (Paragraph 1)."

And columnist Bob Herbert lambasted war pushers in his column titled "What Is It Good For?; The war pushers turn out to be the profit takers" (04-21-03, A23-1, -2). This implies that Bush's mention about weapons of mass destruction and Iraqi democracy might have been pretexts to assist those profit seekers.

(2) Other Stories That Affect Bush Negatively

Bush's asylum policy was criticized. The straight story titled "Immigration: New Asylum Policy Comes Under Fire" (03-19-03, A22-1, -2) was coded to be very negative, because "the Bush administration's decision to begin detaining asylum seekers from Iraq and 33 other countries where Al Qaeda groups operated *met with harsh criticism* from civil liberties groups and immigration lawyers" (Paragraph 1).

"Bush Orders a 3-Year Delay in Opening Secret Documents" (03-26-03, #4, A15-2, -1) was assessed to be negative.

And the relevant editorial "Secrecy: The Bush Byword" (3-28-03, #3, A16-2, -2) was assessed to be a harsh criticism.

Neutral Coverage

A straight story "Wait Over, Americans Voice A Mix of Relief and Anxiety" (03-18-03, #3, A1-2 + A17, 0) was a mix of positive and negative reports at the sight of the war decision.

"An Overview; March 17, 2003; Diplomatic Impasse, a U.S. Ultimatum to Iraq, and Civilian Fears" (03-18-03, #7, A14-2, 0) was a dry description of the day's events, thus was assessed neutral (0).

The straight news titled "U.S. BOMBS RAVAGE TARGETS IN BAGHDAD; WAVES OF TROOPS SWEEPING SOUTH IRAQ; Support for Bush Surges At Home, But Split Remains;

Poll Indicates Deep Partisan Differences Over President and Handling of War" (03-20-03, Sat, A1-1 + B10, 0) was coded neutral (0). This piece was a combination of very positive (+2) and very negative (-2) coverage:

American support for President Bush's policy in Iraq has surged now that the war began, but there are deep partisan divisions in the nation's view of the conflict, according to the latest *New York Times/ CBS* News Poll (Paragraph 1).

The poll found that 70 percent of Americans approved of Mr. Bush's handling of Iraq, an increase of 19 points in 10 days (Paragraph 2).

"White House Memo: Delaying Talk About Cost of War; Different theories about why a costly conflict has had no price tag attached" (03-23-03, Sun, A24-1, 0) provided bland explanations. The column could have criticized Mr. Bush, but the piece simply gave reasons for Bush's behavior and did not justify him, thus was assessed neutral (0):

They said that setting out the big price tag for the war and its immediate aftermath would complicate if not doom the White House's efforts to push through Congress a budget that makes room for Mr. Bush's latest round of tax cuts (Paragraph 4).

An analysis "After the Conflict: Bush's Next Role; Two more battles: The United States vs. Europe, and State vs. Defense" (04-08-03, B9-2, 0) discussed Bush's future role in postwar Iraq and was rated neutral (0). The piece was neither positive nor negative; it was explanatory.

Sometimes columns written by journalists or contributors make policy suggestions to the president. Do the suggestions affect the presidential image? Not quite. The column "Weighing the Price of Rebuilding; $20 billion a year, and oil revenues won't help much" (04-12-03, A13-1, 0) belonged here:

President Bush should continue and expand his efforts to

explain the rationale for postwar American engagement in Iraq and to describe the extent of the required commitment (Paragraph 2).

Prediction of Bush's future course of action constituted neutral coverage. The piece titled "War Dividend: Looking for Domestic Gains From the Success Abroad; Can the president's strong hand help pass unpopular policies?" (04-13-03, Sun, WK3-2, 0) was assessed to be neutral.

In this vein, the analysis titled "Bush's Next Test: A Soft Economy and a Tax Cut Plan Loom Above Re-election Campaign; Applying lessons from the first Bush presidency" (04-17-03, A22-1, 0) belonged here.

A column giving advice to the president was also rated neutral (0). The column titled "Dear President Bush: Tips for running Iraq from one who knows" (04-30-03, A27-1, 0) by Thomas L. Friedman provided advice to Bush, and was assessed to be neutral.

Quantitative Analysis: How Favorable was the Newspaper to Bush?

The number of total stories for each period and their breakdown of coding based on the qualitative analysis is shown in the following table. Quantitative analysis of news content below shows the proportions of positive and negative contents. The table below also shows the trend of coverage.

Table 2:

Tone of *New York Times* Coverage of President George
W. Bush During Four Times Periods of his Presidency

Period Tone	Inauguration n=106	Sept. 11 n=124	Afghan War n=138	Iraq War n=153
Very Positive	17.5%	31.4%	12.3%	27.4%
Positive	45.0	39.5	50.5	28.1
Neutral	17.5	8.9	13.7	14.5
Negative	11.3	11.3	22.5	18.9
Very Positive	8.7	8.9	1.5	11.1

$X^2 = (12, N=575) = 46.221, p<.001$
The differences were statistically significant beyond .001 level
of chi square. Therefore, occurrences were not accidental.

Period I (Inauguration): Data were collected from the *New
York Times* for 31 days, ranging from January 21, 2001 to
February 20, 2001.

Period II (September 11 attacks): Data were collected from the
New York Times for 27 days, ranging from September 12, 2001
to October 7, 2001.

Period III (War in Afghanistan): Data were collected from the
New York Times for 30 days, ranging from October 08, 2001 to
November 07, 2001.

Period IV (War in Iraq): Data were collected from the *New
York Times* for 46 days, ranging from March 18, 2003 to May
02, 2003.

It was calculated that the *New York Times* carried 4.29 stories
daily that can affect President Bush's image during the four

research periods. This makes a remarkable contrast with 0.57 stories per day printed by the *New York Times* in Grossman and Kumar's study.

As the above table shows, very positive (+2) coverage of Bush soared from his inauguration to September 11 (31.4%), declined during the Afghanistan War, and increased again during the Second Gulf War (27.4%). This reflects that the *New York Times* highlighted Bush's role as a crisis leader (September 11) and that the Afghanistan War was gradually expanded. This shows that in Afghan War there were less reports of Bush's decisive military leadership than during the Second Gulf War. In Second Gulf War, Mr. Bush frequently issued strongly-worded statements and the *New York Times* conveyed his messages verbatim, thus highlighting his military leadership. The trend in overall positive coverage (+2 and +1) shows that it started from 62.5%, increased to 70.9%, declined to 62.3%, which is Period I level, and to the lowest 55.5%.

The trend of overall negative coverage (-2 and -1) shows that while it stayed at the same 20% level during Period I (20.0%) and Period II (20.2%), it increased to 24.0% during Period III, and to remarkably high 30.0% during Period IV. This means that the *New York Times* conveyed the increasing antiwar sentiments in Period III and Period IV. If the ratios of positive coverage (+2, +1) and those of negative coverage (-2, -1) are combined, the trend of *New York Times* tone becomes more comprehensive. In Iraq War, this newspaper highlighted Bush's wartime leadership and simultaneously conveyed popular voices opposing the Iraq War, striking a sophisticated balance.

Triangulation: Comprehensive Interpretation of Research Findings

Period I. Bush's Inauguration

Presidential inauguration is a national celebration. Although there was a heated dispute over the results of the election, most Americans followed the decision of the U.S. Supreme Court that candidate Bush was the winner. The stories of the *New York Times* conveyed or might have led this climate and congratulated George W. Bush as the legitimately-elected president. After the inauguration there ensued cabinet appointments, policy announcements such as education policy, and Bush's initiatives of funding religious organizations which help the underprivileged. The *New York Times* conveyed a climate of jubilation, described personnel appointments and presidential policymaking, and showed Bush's international and military leadership. With the passage of one week in Bush presidency, the newspaper ran a spate of stories that assessed the transition as being smooth and without much fuss.

The percentage of positive coverage (62.5%; +2 and +1) reflects that the *New York Times* profusely shed light on the positive aspect of the newly sworn-in president in a jubilant climate of the nation and of his attempts to rally the country towards harmony after the agonizingly disputatious indecision. The overall ratio of positive coverage (positive-positive and positive-neutral) for 25 years was 48.7%, as was previously shown in Grossman and Kumar's study.

As was discussed above, the *New York Times* conveyed Mr. Bush's images as a national unifier, a conciliator, a policymaker at the initial weeks, a military leader against Iraq, a person in charge in appointing cabinet members and other federal positions, or an international leader who widened the scope of international cooperation. In addition, a very favorable light was shed on Mr. Bush himself and his family. The assessment of the newspaper and presidency scholars was "successful transition," considering such a short period for preparations.

There was only one very negative (-2) front-page story titled "Questions Raised On New Bush Plan To End Estate Tax"(01-29-01, A1-2). In this respect, this research finding differs from Graber's argument that Bush did not enjoy honeymoon period, as was discussed in Chapter II.

The list of very negative and very positive stories from Period I to Period IV will be attached in Appendices section.

Period II. September 11 Attacks

September 11 terrorist attacks on American soil in 2001 had a tremendous impact on the American political arena as well as on the international society. This made a great turning point in American foreign policy and in Bush's presidency. The whole world was "artificially and abruptly" reorganized by Mr. Bush into terrorist bloc on the one hand and anti-terrorist bloc led by America on the other. During this period, the *New York Times* stories portrayed President Bush as a national as well as an international leader on the counter-terrorism battlefront. The newspaper also shed light on his role as a national soother and as a crisis leader, which was hardly witnessed previously. First Lady Laura Bush played the role of surrogate national soother. Mr. Bush rallied support for this war on the Taliban regime, but he decided to act largely alone. In this process, there occurred controversy among Bush aides over the scope of retaliation against Afghanistan.

During this period, the percentage of positive coverage rose to 70.9%, signifying that Mr. Bush played the role of a crisis leader and a national soother. The *New York Times* conveyed the newly transformed presidential image. He gained support from the Congress allowing him to take broad retaliatory measures as well as drastic domestic security measures.

The fact that the percentage of positive coverage (70.9%) rose higher than during Period I implies that this newspaper followed Bush's lead or conveyed his messages verbatim. In this way, President Bush set the national agenda. In reality, Bush's job approval jumped from 51 percent in the September 7-10 Gallup poll to 86 percent on September 14-15 (Pfiffner & Davidson, 2003). The soaring of Bush's ratings may be correlated with the rise of positive coverage by the media (Seol's comment).

There appeared four very negative (-2) "front-page stories" during this period:

"World Leaders List Conditions On Cooperation; World Leaders List Terms to Join U.S. in Coalition, and Press Multilateralism" (09-19-01, A1-1);

"Bush Advisers Split on Scope of Retaliation" (09-20-01, A1-1);

"Issue Now, Does U.S. Have a Plan?" (09-27-01, A1-1); and

"Bush Law-Enforcement Plan Troubles Both Right and Left" (09-28- 01, A1-1).

Period III. War in Afghanistan

News coverage during this period showed more forceful military leadership of Mr. Bush, who made efforts to garner international cooperation on the anti-terrorism battlefront. He met Chinese leader Jiang Zemin to get support for his war on terror, but he failed to get wide support from other foreign countries. He was hated by large portions of Arabs. In the war efforts, President Bush was supported by Democrats but was criticized by part of intellectuals for his drastic security measures. Although this war was retaliatory in nature, opposition to it was not negligible. During this period, the image of Mr. Bush as a decisive military leader was rather salient. But as the war in Afghanistan was rather gradual (ground troops were sent in after bombing), news reports were relatively less urgent and less dramatic. The fact that the percentage of positive coverage (62.8%) was low and the percentage of negative coverage

(24.0%) was a bit higher implies that the retaliatory war was gradual and met with some opposition. This period was differentiated from Period II, considering that military attacks on Afghanistan started.

Only one very negative (-2) story appeared on the front page, which was titled "White House Memo: Home Front Is a Minefield For President" (10-25-01, A1-1).

Period IV. War in Iraq

The presidential image of this period can be characterized mostly as a decisive wartime leader. The war was performed dramatically in Iraq in a "shock and awe" fashion during the period of one month and a half. (The battle on the ground continued even after sovereignty was transferred to Iraq in June 28, 2004.) This war differed in nature from war in Afghanistan in intensity. The *New York Times* portrayed Mr. Bush as "a resolute" wartime leader. Simultaneously, this newspaper described the anti-war sentiments in and outside of America. The reports by the U.N. correspondent (03-20-03) and the London correspondent (03-19-03) offered a direct attack that this war was not legal. This newspaper seemed to grant legitimacy to the war by printing an analysis of pre-emptive strike logic on the front page.

How did the *New York Times* portray Mr. Bush as a wartime leader? Generally speaking, this newspaper highlighted Bush's wartime leadership in a sophisticated and balanced manner, conveying Bush's message verbatim while reflecting opposing voices from inside and outside of America. Presidential news appeared at crucial moments to provide meanings to certain critical turning points. For this effect, Mr. Bush might have made timely statements.

The *New York Times* portrayed Mr. Bush as a resolute national leader, provided authenticity and justification to pre-emptive strike logic, and described war successes as expressed by Mr.

Bush. The newspaper also conveyed "human and intimate aspects" of Mr. Bush in conducting the war. A series of Elisabeth Bumiller's reports during this period were very strong on this aspect. (See "Projection of Personal Qualities" section in Period IV of this chapter.) The cream of positive coverage may be the highlighting of media control policy (or "embedded journalism") on the battlefield to get favorable war coverage. The fact that the percentage of positive coverage was low (55.5%) and the percentage of negative coverage was high (30.0%) implies that this war was controversial to that extent. There appeared five very negative (-2) stories on the front page in this period:

"A Worried World Shows Discord, With France and Germany Leading Criticism of Bush" (03-19-03, A1-2);

"Senate Votes to Reduce Bush's Tax Plan" (03-26-03, A1-2);

"Bush Peril; Shifting Sand and Fickle Opinion" (03-30-03, A1-1);

"Senate Vote Could Sharply Reduce Bush Tax Cut" (04-12-03, A1-2);

and "IN A CONCESSION, BUSH LOWERS GOAL OF TAX CUT PLAN; Proposing $550 billion; White House Talks Tough, but the Final Deal May Well be Closer to $350 billion" (04-16-03, A1-1).

Research Questions Revisited and Research Findings

Returning to the four research questions raised at the end of Chapter II, the figures show the answers. First, about the honeymoon? This research found that the *New York Times* alloted 62.5% of their stories and photos to positive coverage (+2 and +1) of President Bush, whereas 20.0% was alloted to negative coverage (-2 and -1) during Period I. Roughly speaking, this means that President Bush enjoyed his honeymoon for one month after his inauguration.

Second, about the ratio of positive and negative coverage? The total number of the positive coverage for the four time periods was calculated to be 359 stories out of 575, or 62.4%. That of negative was 136 stories, or 23.7%. This means that the *New York Times* carried 2.64 positive (+2, +1) stories per one negative (-2, -1) story. This is the ratio of positive/negative coverage with which the *New York Times* depicted President Bush. Might these figures be satisfactory to Mr. Bush? Very probably, no. Because *President Bush wants to "make news on his terms"* as was discussed in the "Bush's Publicity Machine" section.

Third, What was the presidential image of Bush as conveyed by this newspaper? As was shown above, the *New York Times* spotlighted President Bush as the crisis leader after September 11, and as the wartime leader during Afghanistan War and Iraq War. The ratio of very positive coverage soared to 31.4% during Period II, the highest out of the four periods. This means that the *New York Times* highlighted Bush's role as a crisis leader. The ratio of very positive coverage of Period IV (27.4%) was higher than that of Period III (12.3%). This implies that the *New York Times* carried Bush's words verbatim during Period IV, allowing him to "set the public agenda." But the overall ratio of positive coverage shows that positive coverage of Bush during Period IV (55.5%) declined from that of Period III (62.3%), meaning that antiwar sentiment was conveyed by this newspaper. The increase of overall negative coverage from 24.0% in Period III to 30.0% in Period IV additionally corroborates this trend, thus striking a "sophisticated balance."

Fourth, was there superficial or trivial coverage of Mr. Bush? Some instances of intimate and soft coverage might belong here. But as the *New York Times* stories said, Mr. Bush "took his presidency seriously." There was very little superficial or trivial coverage of Mr. Bush.

(One of the exceptions might be the *New York Times'* front page report, photo on A1 and story on A18, on January 15, 2002, which discussed Mr. Bush's recovery after fainting while eating pretzel. But this piece can be a serious report depending on which aspect the public chooses to look at. The photo showed Bush with a bruise on his left cheek.)

As will be shown in the list in the Appendix section, the number of very negative (-2) stories that appeared on the front page amounted to 11 stories (25%). This reflects that 33 stories (75%) out of all 44 that directly attacked or opposed Bush's policies were buried on the inside pages. It is undeniable that the *New York Times* carried opposing voices from inside and outside of the Bush administration and in and out of America. However, these stories did not form the mainstream of the ongoing events. Just imagine that this newspaper ran on the front page a straight story that says that the war on Iraq lacks legal basis (03-20-03, #4, A19-1, Str, "Threats and Responses; United Nations; Critics Say U.S. Lacks Legal Basis for Attack" by Felicity Barringer). The negative impact on President Bush might have been much greater than when it was printed on page 19. The result is that this newspaper reflected the mainstream of the news (or followed the agenda set by the president), while conveying opposing voices in part.

Is there any correlation between story types and positive/negative coverage? The fact that 21 reports out of the whole 44 very negative stories are straight stories reflects that this newspaper made efforts to be objective by taking the form of straight stories. The fact that the number of news analysis by the reporters amounted to four while that of Op-Ed columns reached nine implies that outside columnists are freer to criticize Bush's policies.

The following table shows how the story types and negative/positive images are correlated. The table also shows that Bush stories on the Editorial and Op-Ed pages tend to be more negative than positive.

Table 3:
Story Types and Positive /Negative Coverage Story

Story type	Straight	Analysis	Editorial	Op-Ed	Column	Others	Sum
Very neg (-2)	21 (48%)	4 (9%)	7 (16%)	9 (21%)	0	3 (6%)	44 (100%)
Very pos (+2)	83 (66%)	7 (6%)	4 (3%)	3 (3%)	3 (2%)	26 (21%)	126 (100%)

Who wrote the largest number of very negative (-2) or very positive (+2) stories? Editorial writers collectively wrote the largest number of very negative stories; 6 editorials. But writers of Op-Ed columns were diverse. Reporter Rosenbaum wrote 3 very negative stories; Bumiller, Sanger, Apple, and Toner wrote 2 stories apiece. This shows that there is no main attackers or critics of Mr. Bush. The distribution of attackers are dispersed and not concentrated.

Then, who wrote the largest number of very positive (+2) stories? The statistics shows that Sanger wrote 25 stories; Bumiller 18; Stevenson 8; Bruni and Apple 6 apiece. Therefore, these two reporters are very likely to be White House correspondents!! Their stories tell that they are covering the White House. Their stories show very clearly that they are in a position to write intimate and detailed stories about President Bush.

As the "List of Very Positive Stories" at the Appendix A shows, Sanger's stories tend to be hard, whereas those of Bumiller tend to be both hard and soft. Bumiller seems to be stronger than Sanger in writing soft, intimate, and positive descriptions of the president, thus reflecting that she benefits from close and intimate cooperation with White House aides.

During the same four time periods, Sanger and Bumiller wrote only two very negative (-2) stories. The two reporters wrote together "White House Memo: Home Front Is a Minefield For President" (10-25-01, A1-1+B8, -2). This story said that "the administration's response to the spreading threat of anthrax has been ragged and confused." Sanger wrote the story "The Mood: As a Quick Victory Grows Less Likely, Doubts Are Quietly Voiced in Washington" (03-30-03, B10-2, -2). Bumiller wrote the story "IN A CONCESSION, BUSH LOWERS GOAL OF TAX CUT PLAN" (04-16-03, A1-1+A14, -2).

The number of very positive (+2) stories that appeared on the front page was 61 stories out of the total 126 very positive stories, or 48.4%. This implies that the front page stories during these four time periods conveyed rather verbatim and did not edit what the president said, described what he did as such, or justified his logic.

The ratio of very negative (-2) stories to very positive (+2) stories on the front page was calculated to be 11 to 61, that is, 18.03%. This implies that the *New York Times* mostly followed Bush's lead in setting the public agenda during the four research periods.

Altogether, these figures show that during the four critical periods, the *New York Times* might not have played the agenda-setting role but rather might have followed President Bush's lead in this function. During the first month of inauguration, this newspaper might have voluntarily highlighted Bush's bright side, while conveying opposing voices in part. But during the remaining three critical periods, this newspaper might have been forced to follow President Bush's lead, allowing him to define the situations. The situations were critical to that extent.

This research has confined its scope to the four time periods. The demarcation lines were drawn based on President Bush's definition of the situation and the reports of the *New York Times*. But the follow-up developments in late September 2003 implied that Mr. Bush has begun to lose his strong power to "define the situation" vis-a-vis the *New York Times*. As of late September, 2003, almost five months after the declaration of victory against Iraq on May 1st, with no clear foreseeable exit from the chaotic situation in Iraq and with everyday casualties of American soldiers reported, the *New York Times* began to negate Bush's power to define the situation. This newspaper began to set its own agenda that differ from those of Mr. Bush. The following titles show how this newspaper began to set its own agenda:

"2 U.S. Fronts: Quick Wars, but Bloody Peace" (09-19-03, A1-1+A10, Str);

"Medals for His Valor, Ashes for His Wife" (09-23-03, A1-2+A12, Str);

"Bush, at U.N.. Defends Policy Over Iraq, Tense Opening Day at World Gathering" (09-24-03, A1-1+A10, Str);

"An Audience Unmoved (by Bush's U.N. Address)" (09-24-03, A1-1+A11, Analysis); and

"DRAFT REPORT SAID TO CITE NO SUCCESS IN IRAQ ARMS HUNT, 4-Month Search by U.S., No Illicit Weapons Found, but Officials Describe Evidence of Suspicious Material" (09-25-03, A1-1+A10).

These stories and other ensuing ones may need to be analyzed to see how they would affect Bush's image. These stories may become negative signs that ultimately may affect his reelection bid in November 2004. Additionally, the *New York Times* editorial titled "The Failure to Find Iraqi Weapons" (09-26-03, A24-1, -2) highlighted the crumbling of basic premises of the war on Iraq in which this newspaper had confidence.

CHAPTER V

The more journalists read or view each others' stories, the more similar is their subsequent coverage of an event or issue. Journalists often read or view each others' stories, at least partially looking for confirmation that their own decisions have been correct (Routines of Media Work 5: Shoemaker & Reese, 1996, p. 266).

THE KYUNGHYANG DAILY NEWS AND ROH MOO HYUN

For content analysis of a Korean newspaper, which is published in Korean in Seoul and distributed nationwide in Korea, the same research methods discussed in chapter III were applied. Six time periods were selected for data analysis from President Roh Moo Hyun's term of office (February 2003 to February 2008). The periods for research were mainly from his first and second year as president. As of July 2004, Mr. Roh's presidency has still three and a half years more to go. But the following six time periods appear to mark important turning points for him, although arbitrarily selected by the author. Research results may be a bit subjective but this research is still worthwhile, because it is analysis of coverage of President Roh in itself and it can further serve as a foundation for comparison between the *New York Times* and this Korean newspaper. Qualitative analysis, quantitative analysis, and then triangulation will be conducted in this order. Data were collected from the *Kyunghynag Daily News* (Kyunghyang Shinmun), a Korean daily published in Seoul and distributed nationwide.

Qualitative Analysis:
How did the Newspaper Portray Roh?

Period I. Roh's Inauguration and
One Month in Office

This is analysis of the *Kyunghyang Daily News* coverage of President Roh from the issue of February 26, 2003 to March 25, 2003. This period was largely composed of coverage of Roh Moo Hyun's inauguration and one month in office; his low-key celebration, his new style as a leader, his transition with mixed evaluations, and his policy announcements.

The overall tone of coverage during this period can be characterized as welcoming a new reform-minded President Roh Moo Hyun. While Mr. Roh tried to carry out reforms, he was faced with opposition or, to some degree, rebellion to his reforms but he showed his decisiveness in personnel reforms. The new government showed many things that were unprecedented, putting an overall atmosphere of reform drives. However, it should be pointed out that Mr. Roh met with scandals involving his relatives and aides from the very early days in his presidency. This tarnished his image as a reformer.

According to the newspaper's coverage, President Roh Moo Hyun took office in a low-key celebration, mindful of the tragic accident in Busan, which occurred just before the inauguration. The newspaper showed that Mr. Roh was busy receiving foreign dignitaries even on the very first day of his presidency. After he was sworn in, Mr. Roh extended his hands for reconciliation, considering that he did not receive the overwhelming proportions of the votes. He lacked the mandate from the electorate just as President Geroge W. Bush did. He ordered his cabinet to draw a future policy line, which was compared with that of Mr. Bush, who gave instructions to carry out a policy. Mr. Roh showed little image of a policymaker during this period.

Mr. Roh intended to implement personnel reform in the

Prosecution Office, which aroused prosecutors to rebel against him. Faced with this, Mr. Roh declared that he could not trust high-ranking prosecutors. The chief prosecutor resigned, clearing a way for Mr. Roh to carry out personnel reforms. Before this, Mr. Roh announced that a new Minister of Justice would be a woman lawyer in her forties, which is very exceptional in the Ministry of Justice and the Prosecution Office that would be affected by her nomination.

Mr. Roh's new style of breaking away from the traditional may be closely linked to his reform drives. But personal qualities are another area to examine a president. He showed up at the cabinet meeting ahead of the schedule, waiting for other members of the cabinet to enter the conference room, which is untraditional. His style could be described as anti-authoritarianism. He was also portrayed as a hard worker who handled lots of events.

Criticism against Mr. Roh came from opposition parties and officials such as prosecutors. Sometimes irregularities of his relatives turned into a scandal. The disharmony between elderly and young presidential aides was additional pieces of negative coverage of the president, which was not found in the Bush administration during the first one month period. Internal fights within the Minju Party, where the president originated also caused damage to Mr. Roh. Only one story was printed about the First Lady: that was about her role at the Blue House as a monitor of activities of presidential relatives. There was one story that decreased the joy of inauguration.

Positive Coverage

(1) Low-Key Inauguration, Mood of Changes, and Transition with Mixed Evaluations

The banner headline on page one of February 26th of the newspaper marked the beginning of a new government led by

Mr. Roh. The headlines condensed what President Roh delivered in his inaugural address: "Let's Build Peace and Prosperity on the Korean Peninsula; Roh Mu Hyun, 16th President Takes Office; Stepping Stones for National Integration; Roh Presents Three National Objectives; Roh Views Co-Prosperity in East Asia and Appeals for People's Participation (02-26-03, #1, p.1, +2)." This straight story summarized what Mr. Roh spoke during the inauguration. The style of the story is serious, grave and dry, and without much embellishment. Read what he said:

> President Roh Moo Hyun had the swearing-in ceremony in the Hall of National Assembly on 25th and said that "we should change the Korean Peninsula, the last bastion of the Cold War, into a peace zone that beams signals of peace towards the world and we also should build a community of co-prosperity in East Asia, thereby developing a community of peace (Paragraph 1)."
> President Roh pronounced in his inaugural address titled "Towards an Age of Peace, Prosperity, and Take-Off" that "We are the who can work miracles when united. Let's participate in this great path to creating a new history of peace, prosperity, and take-off (Paragraph 2)."

He pledged to pursue educational reform, decentralization, technological innovation, and harmony between management and labor while tending more to alienated people and creating a warm society (Last Paragraph). The first story about Roh's taking office had one headline and two subheadlines. These headlines mostly showed what this story was about. This story conveyed in abstract what Mr. Roh said, and was coded +2.

A follow-up analysis titled "Roh Takes Office; The Period of Violations and Privilege Is Gone; What His Address Implies For The Government" (02-26-03, #3, p.3, +2) provided a favorable interpretation based on his address. The story went: "President Roh presented on the 25th in his address a blueprint of his administration for his 'participatory government.'(Paragraph 1)

A description of the ceremony was carried under the title

"Inauguration; Focused on Piety Among Harmony of Tradition and Modernity"(02-26-03, #4, p.3, +1) that the occasion was "pious and modest," considering the subway tragedy that occurred recently in Daegu City.

The serial feature story numbered 2 provided a more favorable analysis of the transition of the government. The title went: "Launch of Participatory Government 2; Changes in Leading Power Group; Conspicuous Rise of 'New Stream' Political Geography Varies" (02-26-03, #5, p. 3, +2). The story began with "The faces of the participatory government are young. They are reformists. They formerly belonged to the non-main-streams rather than to the mainstreams, the periphery rather than to the center."

The whole of page seven was used for several photos of celebration and stories about reactions from abroad. The title was in a fanfare mood: "Long March for Reform and Integration Started; Photos and Foreign Reactions" (02-26-03, #13, p. 7, +1). Reaction from the United States dispatched by Washington correspondent said that "Mr. Roh's Radical Tendency May Cause Relations to Worsen," and so the whole page was evaluated +1.

When the first week passed by, the newspaper carried a story evaluating Mr. Roh's transition. On March 3rd, this newspaper printed a story titled "The Anti-Authoritarian Blue House Nearer to the People; One Week of Roh Presidency Brings Mood of Changes; Conference Hall's Seating Is Rearranged Parallel as that of the White House; Aides' Meeting Conducted as a Discussion; Direct Explanation Will be Offered to the People" (03-03-03, #3, p. 3, +2). This piece eulogized the new style brought about by Mr. Roh "in an objective way." Examine how the story went:

March the 3rd marks the first week of Roh's presidency. Even with this short duration, a strong wind of changes blows in the Blue House. This wind is summarized as 'anti-authoritarianism' and 'openness (Paragraph 1).'
From Hierarchical to Horizontal: Mr. Roh altered the

seating arrangement of aides. He changed the seating arrangement from the dynastic one, in which the president sits in the middle and aides sit in order of rank, to an American-style parallel seating arrangement (Paragraph 2).

One official at the Blue House said that this rearrangement was purported to let the president and his aides agonize and discuss in ensemble at the same level seeing each other (Paragraph 3).

The above story, which seems to be an analysis, described seating arrangement and praised the democratic climate of the new president. This needs to be compared with coverage of the *New York Times* marking the first week of Mr. Bush's presidency. A spate of the *New York Times* stories (analysis, editorial, column, feature story) emphasized a "smooth transition" as assessed by both Republicans and Democrats, sometimes citing experts. In comparison, this newspaper focused on changes shown by the new president, implying that these changes made for a turn for the better. This piece appears to be superficial in that it did not discuss whether Roh's new seating arrangement made the conferences any more effective. This change may not be substantial in performing presidential functions. See stories about Bush's first week in office for comparison.

When one month passed by since Roh presidency started, this newspaper printed three stories evaluating one-month performance by Roh. The editorial on page two was a mixture of positive and negative sentences. The editorial titled "One Month Performance of Mr. Roh's: Changes and Tribulations" (03-25-03, #2, p. 2, 0). This piece touched on "lots of messages brought forth by Mr. Roh through personnel recruitment and policy proposals." This editorial also talked about "positive signs such as reform drives and a kind of arrogance."

A second story on March 25th was also coded neutral (0). This analysis discussed positive and negative sides of a new president under the title "One Month of Roh's Presidency: New Politics Brings Some Expectations While Cross-Currents of Reform Create Some Worries; Untraditional Recruitment

Receives Applause But Roh Hesitates About Chaebol Reform Because of Economic Difficulties" (03-25-03, #4, p. 8, 0). The analysis read:

> Overall, one month of Mr. Roh's presidency was a period of tribulations during which his motivations were well-intended, but he met with actual resistance, which is never negligible. (Paragraph 1).
> Minister of Culture Lee Changdong, would-be incarnation of President Roh created an uproar by trying to enforce a new 'reporters' guidelines,' which allegedly purported to improve the reporting methods (Last Paragraph).

However, as will be discussed later, a column by the newspaper's editorializer wrote a scathing criticism (-2) about Roh's one-month performance.

When compared with the inauguration coverage of President Bush, President Roh's inauguration was low-key. The political culture in Korea may be that the President should not show excessive jubilation on his victory. Even considering the tragedy that occurred in Daegu City before the inauguration, the tone covering the presidential inauguration was quite modest. The tone conveying the presidential joy during this period was "considerably limited" in this newspaper.

It may not be coincidental that both newspapers in America and Korea evaluated transition of new presidents. Why do news media assess presidency? Do they have the right? Newspapers may be institutions with unelected power. But this function may be part of the media's basic role as the surveillance provider of the (political) environment.

(2) The Image of a National Leader or Conciliator

A nation's president needs to show off to the people that he strives to talk to the opposition leaders, especially after the presidential election. President Roh's mandate was never overwhelming in the election (he received only 48.9% of ballots), just as Bush's was clearly not.

The first such story appeared on March 4th. The story titled "President Roh Extends His Arms to Mediate Opposition Parties; Roh Pursues a Caucus to Enact Special Prosecutor Bill" (03-04-03, #6, p. 5, +1). The story said that "President Roh extended his hands to hold a meeting with high-ranking officials in both parties to discuss news issues concerning the Special Prosecutor Bill. But the Hannara Pary killed the suggestion saying that there is no room for negotiation. It is not clear whether Roh's suggestion will provide a breakthrough in the convoluted political situation characterized by extreme confrontations (Paragraph 1)." Mr. Roh offered a conciliatory overture but was rejected, thus coded +1.

The following day another story on the same issue appeared with the title "Mr. Roh Pursues Direct Bi-Partisan Talks with High-Ranking Party Members; Roh Considers 'Live and Let Live' Politics by Discarding Authoritarianism; A New Paradigm in Korean Politics" (03-5-03, #5, p. 4, +2). The story went:

> The relationship between President Roh and the National Assembly shows signs of changes. The changes feature the attitudes for dialogues based on respects for the National Assembly, especially the opposition parties. What Mr. Roh declared a starting point for 'new politics' seems to be grounded in his perception that the relations with the opposition needs to be improved (Paragraph 1).
>
> Mr. Roh is presently pursuing a bi-partisan meeting with high-ranking party officials pertaining to the Special Prosecutor Bill purporting to probe the dispatch of money to North Korea (Paragraph 2).

A follow-up story appeared on March 10th. The story was anticipatory in nature with the title "Will the First bipartisan senior level meeting start smoothly?; Mr. Roh is Firm in Letting it Take Place; Formalities and Agenda Being Negotiated Behind the Scenes" (03-10-03, #11, p. 8, +1).

President Roh and a leading opposition politician met at the Blue House to discuss the bill. The two stories on March 13th reported that the meeting materialized and conveyed the warm climate the meeting. The titles of the stories say for themselves:

"President Roh and Opposition Party Leader Park Meet; Both Parties Say 'Not Conflicting Except on the Special Prosecutor Bill'; Behind-the-Curtain Contacts Busier" (03-13-03, #3, p. 4, +1) and

"Harmonious and Warm-Hearted Meeting Studded with Scathing Jokes; Roh Stresses, 'Only digestible words will be uttered'; Park Says, 'Let's compete in political merchandise' " (03-13-03, #4, p. 4, +1).

At last the bone of contention was solved. Five stories on March 15th reported that the contentious bill was enacted and promulgated. The first story on page one says "Special Prosecutor Act Concerning Investigation of Money Sent to North Korea Promulgated; President Roh Accepts the Original Without Exercising Veto; 'Appropriate Limitations in the Scope of Investigation Expected'; Special Prosecutor to Launch Investigation in the Middle of Next Month after One-Month Preparations" (03-15-03, #1, p. 1, +2).

An editorial offered lavish praises to this event. The editorial entitled "Special Prosecutor, Find Out the Truth Based on Trust" (03-15-03, #2, p. 2, +2) stated that "It was a natural and wise decision that President Roh promulgated the Special Prosecutor Act as was in the original."

A third story gave an explanation why Roh made that decision. This story titled "The Background of Acceptance of Special Prosecutor Act and Forecast of the Forthcoming Politics; A Bitter Decision to Avoid Political Impasse" (03-15-03, #3, p. 3, +2). The story said that "President Roh's acceptance of the bill could be interpreted that he chose a politics of 'live and let live' among the tense situation where pros and cons are clearly separated (Paragraph 1)."

A follow-up story carried a question and answer session conducted by Mr. Roh about this issue (03-15-03, #4, p. 3, +2).

And the last story on this day's edition carried the welcoming remarks by the opposition (03-15-03, #5, p. 3, +1).

The front page story on March 18th reported that President Roh intends to implement a special pardon to prisoners of conscience. The story with the title "Mr. Roh pursues special pardon for prisoners of conscience before the Buddha's Birthday celebration; 'A New Approach to Pro-Enemy Groups and Labor Issues Needed'; People Long on the Wanted List and Laborers Will Benefit from the Pardon" (03-18-03, #1, p. 1, +2). This straight story said that "Mr. Roh considers a special pardon marking his inauguration in the spirit of national reconciliation and integration (Para 1)." This seems to be a real conciliatory gesture as a political leader for a country still inflicted by ideological conflicts.

President Roh started to soothe leaders of Minju Party who felt alienated in the political games under the new president. The story on March 19th conveyed the atmosphere: "Roh Had Lunch With Leaders of Minju Party; He Accepted Requests for Party-Government Meeting; Roh Also Demanded Changes of the Party for a Future Perspective" (03-19-03, #1, p. 1, +1).

These stories describe Roh as a conciliator in political wrangling. George W. Bush also took conciliatory measures just after his inauguration as was shown in the previous chapter. In politics both of America and Korea, it seems that victors feel the need to lick the wounds of the defeated in the election.

(3) The Image of a Policymaker

The inaugural address provided broad policy objectives of the new administration. In addition to the straight story (02-26-03, #1, p. 1, +2) conveying President Roh's broad national policy objectives, this newspaper carried an analysis elaborating the blueprint of the policy objectives at the national level. Roh said that "the era of rule violation and privileges is over and national integration is a task of this era (02-26-03, #3, p. 3, +2).

A third story of Mr. Roh as policymaker could be found in his inaugural address. The story titled "President Roh Takes Office; Directions of Economic Policy As Extracted From The Inaugural Address; Roh Intends Draw Growth Locomotive Through Continued Reform; Roh Intends to Transform the Country Into One that Lures Foreign Investors" (02-26-03, #8, p. 5, +2). The story read that "President Roh allocated one third of his address in expressing his aspirations that Korea be the center of regional economy and contribute to the global prosperity and underlined that the starting line is the economy (Paragraph 1)."

Mr. Roh stressed the need to moderate the speed of bringing people to justice. This story showed that Mr. Roh exerted his power in moderating the speed of investigation. The story had the title "President Roh Emphasizes that People's Worries Should Not be Aroused by Prosecution at the Initial Days of Presidency at the First Aides' Meeting" (02-27-03, #2, p. 1, +2). According to the story:

President Roh underlined that the wrongs should be righted but that the process must be rational and cool-hearted. He said that if we can moderate the speed in investigation then we should do so in order not to arouse worries among people (Paragraph 1).

The story on March 5th issue implies how Mr. Roh directed his administration to make policies. The title itself says what he means: "Mr. Roh Instructs to Take Actions on Regulations in Foreigner Investment; He Directs Not to Take Short-Term Measures for Economic Recovery" (03-05-03, #2, p. 1, +1).

On the same day, Mr. Roh directed his administration to conceive of policy tasks for the 'Participatory Government' (Roh's Government). The title of the story said "Mr. Roh Directs His Administration to Conceive of Policy Objectives; Abstracts of Cabinet Meeting (03-05-03, #4, p. 3, +1)."

Why is policy making so late? This made a good contrast with Mr. Bush as a policymaker. Bush took concrete actions such as halting overseas spending on abortion, issuing education plan, proposing tax cut plan, etc.. In contrast Roh instructed his administration to set up policies. Why this difference happens needs to be overhauled.

When there arose controversies about the railroad track for high speed train, Mr. Roh directed to reexamine the planned track in controversy. The title went: "Mr. Roh Directs to Reexamine the Controversial High Speed Train Line (03-03-03, #7, p. 5, +1)."

When President Bush ordered invasion of Iraq, Mr. Roh stated his policy position. On page one of March 21, 2003 issue of this newspaper, the headline went "President Roh Supports America Considering National Interests: Today Cabinet Meeting Is Slated to Approve of the Motion to Send Korean soldiers to Iraq (03-21-03, #1, p. 1, +2)."

A follow-up story said that "Mr. Roh Will Persuade the Nation Personally to Put Down the Anti-War Public Opinion (03-21-03, #2, p. 8, +1)."

(4) The Image of a Decisive Leader, Person in Charge, and a Person Making Appointments

President Roh professed to implement reforms and in the process he met with resistance. Sometimes high-ranking officials resisted but was deposed in the reformist currents led by Mr. Roh. Stories depicting Roh's resoluteness in personnel management and making appointments belonged to this grouping.

On February 28th issue of the newspaper, there appeared a story of the first cabinet formed by Mr. Roh. The headline of the story went: "First Cabinet of the Participatory Government Is Launched; Kim Jin Pyo Named Minister of Finance and Economy, Minister of Justice Named Kang Kum Sil ; Minister of Unification Retained; Yun Young Kwan Named Minister of Foreign Affairs" (02-28-03, #1, p. 1, +2). The story read:

President Roh launched the first cabinet of his administration by naming 19 cabinet-level posts including naming Kim Jin Pyo, National Affairs Coordinator, as Deputy

Prime Minister cum Minister of Finance and Economy (Paragraph 1)."

On March 8th issue, the front-page story described a resolute Mr. Roh in confronting resisting prosecutors. See the headlines: "Mr. Roh Considering Reprimand of Rebelling Prosecutors 'Demands of Some Prosecutors Exceed Appropriate Limits'; Minister of Justice Says, Keeping the Original Principles but Will Reexamine Personnel Selection" (03-08-03, #1, p. 1, +2). See how decisive Mr. Roh was portrayed:

> In connection with the collective rebellion of prosecutors, President Roh Moo Hyun said that if this amounts to proper reasons for reprimand, then he would reprimand them (Paragraph 1).
> Mr. Roh confirmed this position after having reports about prosecutors from aides' meeting, presidential spokeswoman Song Kyung Hee said (Paragraph 2).

A related analysis appeared on page three. The title of this story went: " Angered Roh Says No to Collective Rebellion of Prosecutors; Grounds for Being Resolute to Prosecutors; Roh Says that He Will Not Ask Favors of Them His Highest Level Remarks Since Taking Office; Encourages Justice Minister by Saying the She is Iron Woman" (03-03-03, #5, p. 5, +2). The story went:

> The Blue House made a policy to confront directly the group rebellions by high-ranking prosecutors, regarding them as protests against president's personnel management rights and additionally as protests against reform demands of the new administration (Paragraph 1).

A follow-up story appeared on March 10th. The titles showed how resolute Mr. Roh was: "President Roh Does Not Trust High-Level Prosecutors He Vetoes Chief Prosecutor's Suggestion of Personnel Management. Personnel Placement

Plans Will Go Unaltered" (03-10-03, #2, p. 1, +2).

When there were worries afloat that North Korea might be the next target after the United States had attacked Iraq, President Roh made it clear that the worries were groundless. The front page story on March 25th issue had the titles: "Mr. Roh Laughs Away 'Next Target North Korea Theory' by Saying that The Worries are Groundless." The story said:

Mr. Roh laughed away the theory of American targeting of North Korea after Iraq war was completed by saying that he had repeatedly agreed with the United States leadership on the peaceful resolution of the Korean Peninsula issue. Roh also cited his agreement with American officials that North Korea is different from Iraq (Paragraph 1).

(5) The Image of an International Player

President Roh's role as an international player is not very conspicuous. During his first month in office he had only one coverage as an international player. March 14th issue of the newspaper carried a straight story titled "Roh and Bush Had First Telephone Conversation 'Peaceful Resolution of the North Korean Nuclear Issue'; Roh Supports American Efforts in Iraq; The Two Agree on the Earliest Visit of Roh to Washington" (03-14-03, #1, p. 1, +2). The story said:

President Roh had his first telephone conversation with the United States President George W. Bush since he took office and reaffirmed the principle of peaceful resolution of the North Korean nuclear issue through diplomatic efforts (Paragraph 1).

Mr. Roh said that although there were reports of differences between the two countries over the North Korean issue, he confirmed that there were no policy differences between both countries (Paragraph 2).

In a related analysis on page five, the reporter gave a favorable touch on the event. This analysis had a title "What Does Roh-Bush Dialogue Mean? Dialogue Was Meant to Suppress the 'Crisis Theory' Over Rifts in North Korean Policies; They Discussed Pending Issues Rated Timely; Assistance to Iraq War on the Horizon" (03-14-03, #4, p. 5, +2). The analysis read:

President Roh and President Bush had telephone conversations over pending problems such as Iraq war, North Korean nuclear issue, and the forthcoming American-Korean summit talks. The conversation between the two leaders was evaluated very useful in terms of timeliness (Paragraph 1).

(6) Personal Qualities: Roh's Candor and Anti-Authoritarianism

President Roh proposed an open debate with prosecutors to discuss matters of reform. A story about Roh's feelings described his personal aspects. The story had the title "Roh Talks About His Feelings Concerning Open Debate With The Prosecutors; Roh Said He Was Afraid When Prosecutors Accepted His Offer of Debate; He Did Not Realize that Prosecutors Were So Indignant" (03-13-03, #5, p. 4, +1). The story said:

President Roh expressed his feelings to Acting Representative Park Hee Tai of the Hannara Party about his heated debate with rank-and-file prosecutors (Paragraph 1).

Mr. Roh gave the background explanation that because lower level prosecutors complained about 'behind-the-curtain' personnel management and 'motivation to controlling the Prosecution Office,' he proposed an open debate with them (Paragraph 2).

Mr. Roh said that prosecutors would reject the proposal, but that he was worried that they accepted the proposal. He confessed that he once considered closed session with them (Paragraph 3).

With regard to the caustic remarks by the prosecutors, he said he did not anticipate that they would be so on the offensive. Although he has emphasized horizontal leadership, he did not realize that it was so hard to carry it out. He said that it hurt, in fact (Paragraph 4).

The piece on March 19th ran a perfectly personal qualities of Mr. Roh. The story with the title "Roh's Untraditional Behavior Is Talk of Every Day" (03-19-03, #2, p. 5, +2). The story read:

President Roh's anti-authoritarian behavior is creating subjects for talk everyday (Paragraph 1).

On the 18th, President Roh entered the cabinet conference hall 13 minutes ahead of the schedule. Half of the cabinet members did not yet arrive at the hall, and those in the hall were surprised at the sudden appearance of the President. Mr. Roh shook hands with cabinet members individually, while saying 'where can I have tea?' 'Does this government not serve tea to ministers?' (Paragraph 2).

When Minister of Environment Han Myung Sook said, 'What should we do, if you enter without any notice?,' Roh replied 'You all are dressed up.' At that, ministers burst into a roar of laughter (Paragraph 3).

(7) The Image of a New Style Leader: Open-Minded, Reformist

This newspaper ran lots of stories during Period I that described the new leader as nontraditional, anti-authoritarian, open-minded, or reformist.

The story titled "Nontraditional Personnel Recruitment; Women and People in the Forties Are Likely to Assume Cabinet Posts; Hierarchy and Male-Dominated Bureaucracies Eyed to be Uprooted" (02-26-03, #6, p. 4, +2) forewarned that Mr. Roh would show his untraditional style. In this newspaper "untraditional" was mainly to be interpreted as a favorable term. The story read:

The looming outlines of President Roh's cabinet shape-up is a series of the untraditional. The forthcoming emergence of women ministers and ministers in their forties predict an overall ebb of hierarchy- and male-dominated bureaucracies. Prime Minister designate Ko Keun, who assumed an Accountable Prime Ministership raised his opinion strongly and cabinet posts occasionally did not go to the intended persons (Paragraph 1).

This newspaper conveyed the climate of arguments over minister posts. The title of the story showed how much trouble the Roh's team took in selecting appropriate persons for cabinet posts: "Five to Seven Posts Still Being Weighed; Agonizing Overnight Over Cabinet Formation Education and Defense Posts Still Being Contended" (02-27-03, #4, p. 4, +1).

The following stories portrayed favorably the announcement of a new cabinet. The tone of description of unprecedented recruiting was mainly favorable:

"First Cabinet of Participatory Government Formed; Many Unprecedented Recruitments Whirlwind for Officialdom Forecast; Women Ministers Named to Powerful Ministries Four Women Ministers Means Experiments in Equality in Sexes" (02-28-03, #3, p. 3, +2);

"First Cabinet of the Participatory Government Roh Assures Two-Year Term for Cabinet Members; Roh Says No to Cabinet Shake-up for Climate Change Better Education Minister Being Sought" (02-28-03, #4, P. 4, +2); and

"Prime Minister Koh Offered His Opinion More Than Two Times; Prime Minister's Suggestion Features" (02-28-03, #6, P. 4, +2).

(However, the opposition Hannara Pary criticized that the new cabinet was experimental in nature disregarding the realities. The story (2-28-03, #5, p.4) just followed the positive story above. This comment proved valid when Mr. Roh made repeated cabinet reshuffles during his first and second year in office.)

The description of the new ministers appeared as the top story on the front page of the March 1st issue. The headlines showed how they were: "Solemn Ministers? Let's Break the Old-Fashioned Framework!; Untraditionally Recruited Ministers Show Unprecedented Path Bureaucracies Will Meet With Changes" (03-01-03, #1, p. 1, +2). The story said that the three young ministers expectedly showed informalities. These ministers offered instant corridor meeting with officials, vowed not to wear the minister badges, (Paragraph 1)."

An additional favorable story about recruiting personnel was about an aide whose mission was monitoring presidential relatives. The story titled "Post of Monitoring Presidential Relatives Went to an Unrelated Person; Talk of the Day about Mr. Yang, Presidential Aide" (03-01-03, #4, p. 4, +2). This person supported Mr. Lee Hoi Chang, opposition presidential contender, but was scouted for the post. Mr. Roh said, according to the story, he would rather pick the person who supported his rival and who does not know his relatives.

The March 3rd issue of the newspaper carried a front-page story about Mr. Roh's speech on reforms. The headline of this story went "President Roh Stresses Massive Reforms on Powerful Institutions; Flatters of the Power Will Have No Ground To Stand On" (03-03-03, #1, p. 1, +2). The story read:

> President Roh said that until very recently several powerful institutions served the political powers, thereby destroying internal order and lost people's trust. He said that these institutions should be reborn as institutions serving the people (Paragraph 1).
>
> Mr. Roh said that reforms are the task that must not stop above all things politics and administration must change (Paragraph 2).

Roh's remarks appear to be very reformist or revolutionary in that he disavowed the power structure of the predecessors. Whether or not he will lead his administration without the support of the powerful institutions remains to be seen.

On the March 4th issue, stories about internal promotions in the ministries appeared. One story was about presidential naming of vice ministers in ministries. This story said that 34 vice ministers were mainly in their fifties and people who have served in their respective ministries, representing their specialities in the areas. This story said that these bureaucrats will complement reform-oriented ministers with their specialties (03-04-03, #3, p. 3, +1). A related story talked about a new personnel system in recruiting vice ministers taking root (03-04-03, #4, p. 4, +1).

A story describing the processes about the first cabinet meeting appeared on the March 5th issue. The title says how the meeting proceeded: "Motion--Rebuttal--Re-rebuttal ; Three-Hour Debate Break during the Meeting; Youngest Minister of Local Autonomy Mr. Kim Shows Respect Towards Seniors" (03-05-03, #3, P. 3, +2).

A representative example of openness of this Roh's government appeared on the March 7th issue. Roh returned presidential retreat called Chong Nam Dai to the people. The story had this title: "Chong Nam Dai Returned To People's Arms in 20 Years; Roh Orders to Return it (03-07-03, #6, p. 5, +2)."

Roh government had a first workshop at minister level with 38 people attending. The title of the story read "Participatory Government Holds First National Affairs Debate; Roh Says that He Would Leave Affairs to Ministers and He Would Watch; It Was a Workshop to Share Ideas About National Policies" (03-08-03, #6, p. 4, +2).

President Roh had an open debate with low-ranking prosecutors. The newspaper had this title: "Mr. Roh-Prosecutors Open Debate; The Chief Prosecutor Resigns .. Aftershocks of Prosecutor Rebellion; Prosecution Office Anticipates Massive Personnel Purification" (03-10-03, #3, p. 3, +1).

(Just next to this story was printed a story about the heated debate between Roh and prosecutors. The story was titled "Hagglings For Two Hours Talks Exceed Danger Level; Mr. Roh Gets Angry and Says 'Do You Want to be Rude?' (03-10-03, #4, p. 3, -1)" This story was coded -1, for it lacked due respects to the president and revealed conflicts.)

President Roh's reform plans for the Prosecution Office surfaced on March 11th issue with the title "Chief Prosecutor Will Be Promoted Within the Prosecution Office Prosecution Will See New Faces Moving Upward; Roh's Reform Plans To Be Materialized; Large-Scale Personnel Turnover To Come To The Fore; After Personnel Management Will Come Systemic Reforms" (03-11-03, #2, p. 3, +2).

President Roh wanted to be an uncorrupted leader. So he ordered investigation of his mentor and predecessor's (Kim Dae Jung's) aides in connection to funds sent to North Korea. The story on March 13th issue said that Mr. Roh directed his administration to investigate in suspicion (03-13-03, #1, p. 1, +2).

A second story concerning the openness of the new government was about opening the main hall of the Blue House. The story had the title "Main Hall of the Blue House To Be Opened" (03-18-03, #7, p. 5, +2). The story read that "the Roh government plans to build his office near the secretarial office and open the previous main office after having remade it into a presidential memorial.

The newspaper said that President Roh's untraditional behavior was the talk of the day as described earlier (03-19-03, #2, p.5, +2).

When Mr. Roh invited assemblymen to the Blue House, the newspaper said that Roh's 'invitation politics' was in full track. The story titled "President Roh Invites 14 committeemen of Defense Committee of the National Assembly; American-Style Invitation Politics In Full Bloom" (03-20-03, #2, p. 4, +2). The story said that "Mr. Roh's invitation of rank-and-file assemblymen was another exception. His predecessors invited a group of committee chairmen but never invited ordinary committeemen without regard to party affiliation."

(8) The Image of a Hard Worker and Busy Person

A series of stories described Mr. Roh as a hard-working person. The first story in this category had the title "Breathless 'Four-Power' Diplomacy From the First Day; Roh Requests an

Aggressive Role of Koizumi, Japanese PM; Mr. Roh Coordinates U.S.-Korean Differences While Meeting Mr. Powell" (02-26-03, #7, p. 4, +2). Should he be breathless meeting a train of foreign VIPs? At any rate the story went: "President Roh began his presidency with a four-power diplomacy (Paragraph 1). Mr. Roh devoted most of his office hours to meeting Mr. Koizumi, Mr. Powell who participated in the inaugural ceremony (Paragraph 2)."

The second story on the inauguration day was titled "Roh Handled More Than 10 Events Until Late Into the Night; Description of the First Day" (02-26-03, #9, p. 5, +2). The story went that "President Roh handled more than ten events on his first workday (Para 1). The first event was paying tributes to (Paragraph 2)"

Mr. Roh and his aides worked overnight on selecting new cabinet members, according to the story on February 27th, as discussed above (02-27-03, #4, p. 4, +2). On the same day, a story said that Mr. Roh handled 16 events in one day. The story was titled "President Roh Handled 16 Official Events on the Second Day of His Presidency 'Busy and busy'; 'The Blue House Was Real Large' Was His First Words at Aides' Meeting; Help Required with North Korean Nuclear Issue, He Says to Foreign VIP's" (02-27-03, #6, p. 5, +2). The story began with "President Roh attended 16 events, counting in only official ones. (Paragraph 1)."

The image of a hard worker was also found in the portrayal of Bush during the Iraq War in the *New York Times* stories.

(9) Story About the First Lady

Only one story about the First Lady appeared during Period I. The story was titled "First Lady Kwon Yang Sook Emphasizes Monitoring Presidential Relatives; She Will Restrain Outdoor Activities For the Time Being; She Is Interested In Children's Welfare such as Childcare" (02-26-03, #12, +2). The story read:

Mrs. Kwon Yang Sook took her 'official office' as the First Lady on 25th (Pararaph 1).

Mrs. Kwon in traditional Korean costume watched his husband's swearing ceremony in expressionless outlooks (Paragraph 2).

It is said that she will take charge of affairs of presidential relatives (Paragraph 3).

Throughout the six research periods, this newspaper ran only one First Lady story. This made a good contrast with the *New York Times* coverage of Laura Bush. Laura Bush emerged on the newspaper when her role was required. This may represent the political culture that Koreans do not like the First Ladies perform outstanding roles as compared with American political culture.

(10) Roh's Attitudes to Media: Openness

President Roh made remarks on the press affairs on several occasions during Period I. The first was printed on the front page of the March 5th issue, but took little space and was coded +2. The story was titled "Mr. Roh Says 'He Will Not Meddle in Press Affairs'; Roh Emphasizes 'Do Not Look Towards the Political Power' "(03-05-03, #1, p. 1, +2). The story went:

President Roh said that these days freedom from the capital and advertisers is important to the press. He said that his government would not interfere in media affairs and he would not give calls to the media. Roh told the media not look to the political ower (Paragraph 1).

Mr. Roh said that he thinks that freedom from the political power is almost achieved and that Korean Broadcasting System does not need to look towards the political power in producing programs now that this institution is not constrained by the capital and advertisers (Paragraph 2).

On the March 18th issue, Mr. Roh said that the press guidelines prescribed by the Ministry of Culture and Tourism were inappropriate. Mr. Roh said that the guidelines make room for misunderstanding that the government tries to interfere in media affairs (03-18-03, #2, p. 1, +2).

A related analysis titled "President Roh Says 'Government Must Not Leave Room for Interference; He Restrains Minister Lee's press reforms" (03-18-03, #5, p. 4, +2).

A criticism followed this story. The story was about opposition Hannara Party's rebuke. Hannara opposed by saying that the press must not write as the press release dictates. The opposition criticized the closing of press rooms (03-18-03, #6, p. 4, -1).

Negative Coverage

(1) Opposition and Criticism from Political Opponents

The first criticism appeared on the inaugural day. The story was titled "Deformed Inaugural Festivities; Wrangling Over National Assembly's Special Prosecutor's Bill; Disorder Caused by Groups of Assemblymen's Stampeding; Diplomatic Corps Ridiculing the Disorderliness" (02-26-03, #11, p. 6, -2). This piece depicted the disorderliness of the inaugural ceremony. Assemblymen came and went to argue for and against the bill. Read how this piece reported:

> The war of nerves between Hannara and Minju Party over the confirmation of prime minister designate and the special prosecutor bill probing dispatch of money to North Korea reduced the climate of celebration to a half (Paragraph 1).
>
> Additionally, the locale of the ceremony was the entrance to the central hall of the second floor, increasing the disorderliness of the climate (Paragraph 2).
>
> Diplomatic corps in Seoul watched the scene and blurted out 'an interesting situation' (Paragraph 4).

This piece makes a good contrast with a story of protesters

cursing Bush's inaugural ceremony (01-21-01, #9, A17-1, -2). Just as the English counterpart was buried in p. 17, the Korean story was buried in p. 6. However, Korean version of cursing was less hurtful. *The New York Times* story depicted a scene where protesters threw eggs. American protesters waved signs proclaiming "Hail to the Thief." The thought that Mr. Bush thieved the presidency. See Period I of Chapter IV. On the February 28th issue, Hannara Party made caustic comments on the announcement of the newly-formed cabinet. The story with the title "Hannara Comments 'Experimental Cabinet Formation, Which Disregards Realities' " (02-28-03, #5, p. 4, -1). The story went:

Hannara Party made fiercely critical comments about the first cabinet of President Roh that it was an experimental cabinet formation, which disregards the realities (Paragraph 1).

The spokesman of Hannara Party said that naming women to important posts is commendable, but that the cabinet is so experimental and untraditional that it causes worries (Paragraph 2).

In a presidential system, the president can nominate cabinet members of his choice. The Congress or National Assembly then confirms the designates. In Korea, opposition parties make comment on the cabinet formation, which is not to be found in America.

The following stories showed critical comments from the political parties and forces:

"Minju Party Plans to Recommend Resignation of Mr. Jin, Minister of Information and Communication; Party Leaders' Meeting Will Convey the Negative Public Opinion" (03-08-03, #2, p. 1, -2);

"Minju Party's Old Mainstream 'Shall We Go Rough?'; Minju Fighting Over Special Prosecutor Bill" (03-17-03, #4, p. 4, -1);

"Minju's Internal Fight Serious; Conflicts Between Party and the Blue House Reach Dangerous Level" (03-18-03, #3, p. 3, -2); and

"Hannara Party Declares Total War on Press Policy, 'Should They Report As the Government's Press Release Dictates?'; Hannara Criticizes Closure of Press Rooms, Citing 'Meant to Control Under the Pretext of Reforms' " (03-18-03, #6, p. 4, -1).

(2) Resistance to Roh's Reforms from inside the Administration

Resistance to Mr. Roh's reforms was raised by prosecutors. On the day of Roh's inauguration, the newspaper reported about it with the title "Ms. Kang Kum Sil, A Woman Lawyer In Her Forties Speculated To Be Minister of Justice; Prosecutors Strongly Resisting, High-Ranking Prosecutors Worried About The Destruction of Hierarchy; Portions of Rank-And-File Prosecutors Say That It's An Opportunity For Prosecution To Secure Neutrality" (03-26-03, #15, p. 19, -1). The lead sentence of the story said that "With Ms. Kang Kum Sil being discussed as a prospective candidate to be minister of justice in the new government, the resistant currents from the prosecution grow high (Paragraph 1)."

Another case of resistance to the presidential nomination of a cabinet minister was about Mr. Kim Hwa Joong, candidate for Minister of Health and Welfare. On the same page the story appeared with the title "Rebellion Launched Against Naming Kim Hwa Joong, Candidate for Minister of Health and Welfare; Civic Organizations Disappointed with Consideration of Person Near to Him" (03-26-03, #16, p. 19, -1). The lead sentence of the story read that "With rumors being circulated that Mr. Kim Hwa Joong would be nominated to be minister of health and welfare, civic groups rebelled against the nomination (Paragraph 1)." A spate of resistance stories of this nature followed:

"Prosecutors Rebel En Masse Against Untraditional Personnel Policy by Minister; High-Ranking Prosecutors Plan to Submit Opposition Letter Citing Violation of Hierarchy" (03-07-03, #1,

p. 1, -2);

"Rank-and-File Prosecutors Also Rise Against Minister of Justice, Causing Whirlwinds; Statements Announced Asking For Referring Personnel Rights to Chief Prosecutor" (03-08-03, #3, p. 1, -2); and

"Abrupt Resignation of Chief Prosecutor Saying That He Realized The Roh Government's Will To Control Prosecutors Through Personnel Rights; Cross-Currents Generated Because of Disregarding Fair Personnel System" (03-10-03, #1, p. 1, -2).

(3) Conflicts Within the Blue House, Investigation of the Blue House Personnel and Presidential Relatives

The stories grouped under this subcategory can also be coded negative. These stories can cause credibility of the president to be reduced. The story about presidential aides and relatives who might be involved in irregularities are negative towards the president. The piece titled "Heads of Government-Owned Institutions Being Secretly Probed; Senior Secretary Moon Says 'Considerable Information Gathered and Being Confirmed; Presidential Aides Included in the Probe" (03-20-03, #1, p. 1, -1). The story went:

The anti-corruption team of the Blue House is carrying out a large-scale secret investigation of presidential aides and executives under its direct jurisdiction after it has gathered intelligence of their irregularities, it was learned (Paragraph 1).

A story conveying cacophony between the elderly and younger groups in the Blue House is a representative example of conflicts within. The story titled "Secretarial Office of the Blue House in Disharmony Between Elderly and Young; Disorder in the System Causes War of Nerves" (03-24-03, #3, p. 7, -2). Read the story:

The Secretarial Office of the Blue House of the new government is noisy. It is because of the still-unstable system although it took office almost one month ago. The noise originates mainly from senior group's worries that part of Mr. Roh's aides, including younger assistants called '386' generation, exerts excessive influence (Paragraph 1).

On the same page of the day's issue was carried story about an internal conflict about replacement of presidential spokeswoman. The story was titled "Internal Conflicts Over Replacement of Presidential Spokeswoman; Aftermath of Briefing Mistakes on Military Alerts; Voices of Sympathy and Replacement Mixed Over Worries of Reoccurrence" (03-24-03, #4, p. 7, -2). See how the story read:

Opinions suggesting replacement of presidential spokeswoman Song Kyung Hee are being raised. Ms. Song made an erroneous briefing just after the beginning of the American war on Iraq that the alert level of South Korean army was raised one notch higher. Because of this blunder, North Korea issued a denunciatory statement and foreign news media reported that the Korean Peninsula was reduced to a state of tension (Paragraph 1).

Stories about presidential apologies may represent candor of the president, thus may portray the president favorably (+1), but it may be undeniable that they are a bit damaging too (-1). The first story about presidential apology was published on the March 7th issue with the title "President Roh Apologizes For The Minister Jin's Trouble; Mr. Roh Seeks People's Understanding of the Trouble ... He Indicates Positive Approach to Double Nationality Issue" (03-07-03, #2, p. 1, -1). The story said:

In connection with Minister Jin's trouble, President Roh said that the government did its best to examine his trouble before nominating him Minister of Information and apologized sincerely that the government's decision of appointment may differ from the people's values (Paragraph 1).

Stories raising deep doubts about covert activities by the Blue House can be damaging to the president. A story about secret contacts with North Korea was printed with the title "Doubts Thicken About Secret Contacts with North Korea; Blue House Keeps Silent Saying That 'Nothing Particular' or 'No More to Say'; Mr. Rah Jong Il Maintains 'Personal Meeting' Whereas the Blue House Reasons 'Diplomat's Status'; Blue House Says that It Cannot Confirm Whether Contacts Were Ordered by Mr. Roh" (03-07-03, #4, p. 4, -1). The story read:

Deep doubts scarcely evaporates about covert contacts with North Korea of Mr. Rah Jong Il, national security adviser to the president. Without convincing explanations (Pararaph 1).

A related story appeared on the same day's issue with the title "Mr. Roh's Temperament Uneasy; Interrogates Mr. Jin, Minister of Information and Communications; Mr. Roh Stops Mr. Rah's Explanation Attempts" (03-07-03, #5, p. 4, -1). The story said:

President Roh expressed unsatisfactory state of mind about the controversies concerning Minister Jin's sons (meaning double nationality) and Mr. Rah's secret contacts with North Korea (Paragraph 1).

(4) Editorials and Columns Criticizing Roh

As was discussed earlier, an analysis (03-03-03, #3, p. 3, +2) marking one week of Mr. Roh's presidency was printed. The analysis praised anti-traditional style of Mr. Roh. On the contrary, a column marking one month of presidency was very critical (-2). The editorial marking one month was neutral (0).

The column titled "Failure of Amateurism" (03-25-03, #6, p. 10, -2) faulted fiercely how Mr. Roh conducted administration. Read how the columnist wrote:

The problem is that the people who took "a revolutionary change in life" after having been selected as those sharing "codes" with (Mr. Roh) do not perform smoothly as was expected. These people all created troubles just as if they all made a promise to. Those '386 generation' aides who nicely fitted in with Mr. Roh's codes and the troika ministers in their forties, Minister of Justice Kang Kum Sil, Minister of Administration and Autonomy Kim Du Kwan, and Minister of Culture Lee Chang Dong, who were recruited exceptionally showed their frailty immediately (Paragraph 4).

Minister Kang Kum Sil ... (Paragraph 6).

Minister Lee wreaked ... havoc by announcing reporting guidelines called 'methods of operation in public relations affairs' out of the blue (Last Paragraph).

In comparison, the editorial of this day was relatively neutral (0). The title was bland "One Month of Mr. Roh's Government; Changes and Tribulations" (03-25-03, #2, p. 2, 0). The editorial read in part:

One month has passed since Mr. Roh's government started with difficulties in national security and economic crisis. President Roh left lots of messages in personnel recruitment and suggestions of policy directions. The supersession of mainstream forces and powerful reform drives positive signs a kind of arrogance ... (Paragraph 1).

One editorial criticized the poor performance of a presidential spokeswoman. This piece titled "The Mouth of the Blue House Who Does Not Know" (03-07-03, #4, p. 4, -1). Read the editorial:

The amateurish briefings in which the spokeswoman says that 'she was at a loss' and the publicity system which merely resembles open style should not be allowed any longer. It is not tolerable that press office is a source of

confusion rather than a supplier of correct information...
(Paragraph 4).

In contrast, an editorial praised Mr. Roh's negotiations with
opposition (+1). The editorial titled "Negotiations for Special
Prosecutor Act and Conflicts within Minju Party" (03-17-03,
#1, p. 2, +1). The editorial read:

> With the promulgation of the special prosecutor act by
> President Roh, wranglings over this act came to an end.
> This was possible because promises were made by political
> forces about later revisions and because Mr. Roh trusted it.
> This kind of spirit of mutual trust provided a new frame-
> work of 'live and let live' in relations among the parties in
> and out of power (Paragraph 1).

Neutral Coverage

Predictions, anticipations, and explanations were coded neutral (0). One editorial titled "Epochal Tasks of Young
Government" (02-28-03, #2, p. 2, 0) was coded zero, because it
was about demands and.or advice to the new government. The
piece read:

> The first cabinet of President Roh's government was
> launched. The new cabinet can be characterized as respond-
> ing to national policy lines such as reform and stability and
> simultaneously as exposing untraditional aspects in person-
> nel management differing from predecessors. (Paragraph 1).
> We expect that the new government would be evaluated a
> dream team by serving the public and killing the private
> (Paragraph 5).

As was discussed above, the editorial of March 25th issue was
coded neutral (0). The title was a bland "One Month of Mr.

Roh's Government; Changes and Tribulations" (03-25-03, #2, p. 2, 0). This piece looked at both positive and negative aspects of the new government which began one month ago. Other neutral stories are not enumerated here.

Period II. President Roh's Proposal of Confidence Vote

This section is analysis of the *Kyunghyang Daily News* coverage of President Roh Moo Hyun from the issue of October 11, 2003 to that of November 10, 2003. This period was largely composed of coverage of President Roh's proposal of confidence vote, wranglings over confidence vote, decision to dispatch of Korean troops to Iraq, and revelations of illegal election funds during the presidential campaign.

During this period President Roh said suddenly that he would propose confidence vote of him to ask the will of the people again, considering that his approval rate fell to the bottom, which was caused by irregularities of his aides and relatives. This proposal was unprecedented, considering that he had served as president for only eight months out of the five-year term of office prescribed by the Korean constitution. Roh's low approval rate was a reflection of irregularities of his aides, and opacity of collecting presidential election funds. Mr. Roh received 48.9% of the votes at the presidential election and his approval rate once reached the 70% range, but it fell to 30% range just before his proposal of confidence vote. The term used for this occasion by the newspaper and Roh's government was "reconfidence" rather than "confidence vote" or "nonconfidence." This might imply that the Roh government used the term intentionally.

The newspaper coverage during this period was mainly about the proposition of confidence vote and opposition or criticism to confidence vote. Controversy went on for a while in the political circle. The newspaper conveyed what Mr. Roh said concerning his proposal of confidence vote and simultaneously opposition or criticism to his proposal. The former were coded favorable (+1, +2) and the latter unfavorable (-1, -2). This newspaper ran several columns attacking the proposal.

Whether or not to send additional Korean troops to Iraq was another issue that led to fierce argument among politicians. Roh's government did not sound firm in this policy, making conflicting remarks on this issue, thus inviting criticism from this newspaper.

Reports of conflicts among presidential aides grown out of the Blue House served negatively for the Roh government. This reminds one of the split of opinion among Bush aides over the scope of retaliation after September 11 attacks. Revelations of illegal election funds among politicians also caused damage to Roh government. Prosecutors at last declared that they would investigate the funds issue.

Roh's proposal of confidence vote originated from his intention to ask whether or not the people still had trust in him despite irregularities of his aides and relatives. However, Korean constitution does not have provisions pertaining to confidence vote of the president: Koreans are under presidential system, not parliamentary system. In this context, criticisms flooded against Roh's proposal. Although President Roh tried to define the political situation by proposing confidence vote, his power to define the situation was weak and nonetheless invited criticism. His intention to ask the people's will was deferred until the impeachment resolution was passed by the National Assembly in March 2004 and the general election was held in April 2004.

Positive Coverage

(1) Proposal of Confidence Vote and Follow-Up Stories

The October 11 issue of the newspaper ran a banner headline

about President Roh's remarks on his intention to ask the people's trust in him as the president. The headline was printed "President Roh Says He Will Ask People About His Reconfidence; Adviser Moon Voices 'Referendum Is Being Weighed': The Time Will Be Around General Election Next Year Apologies About Mr. Choi Do Sool's Irregularities" (10-11-03, #1, p. 1, +2). This straight story was coded +2, because it conveyed what the president said verbatim, although the reporter may contend that the article was written objectively. The message was strong. Read the paragraphs:

In connection with the suspicion on the former presidential aide Choi Do Sool about his receiving slush funds from SK corporation, President Roh announced that he could not claim ignorance of it and that he would like to ask the people whether they trust him as president, considering that people's distrust may have accumulated (Paragraph 1).

Touching on his former aide's problem, Mr. Roh said that he has to take the responsibility himself if his aide committed blunders and that he apologized to the people about the disgraceful incident (Paragraph 2).

It is the first time in Korean history of presidency that an incumbent president announced his intention to ask the people's trust in him concerning accountability for pending issues (Paragraph 3).

Mr. Roh had an emergency press conference at the Blue House and voiced his intention to ask people's will (Paragraph 4).

Related stories filled the following pages of the newspaper. A second story was a description of the scene of his announcement titled "The Shock of Roh's Remarks; Accumulated Distrust He Wants Judgment by the People; " (10-11-03, #2, p. 3, +1).

A third story was an analysis and prediction of the future political situations. The story was titled "The Shocks of Roh's Announcement; Declaration Like a Bomb Dropped Political

Situation Into the Whirlwind" (10-11-03, #3, p. 4, +1).

A follow-up story appeared on October 13th issue. The front page story was headlined "Special Act for Reconfidence Will Be Pursued; The Blue House Would Like a Referendum in January Asking Simply Confidence" (10-13-03, #1, p. 1, +1).

A story on polling about people's confidence in Mr. Roh appeared on the same day's issue. This story reported that the rate of popular confidence reaches 45%, higher than that of non-confidence 24%, that of abstinence reached 30% (10-13-03, #2, p. 1, +1).

A related analysis was printed on p. 5 of the same issue. The analysis was titled "Political Situation for Reconfidence; Poll Results Show That Dissatisfied But Have Reconfidence" (10-13-03, #6, p. 5, +1). The first paragraph read that "The first reaction of the people was leaning towards reconfidence to the card of reconfidence thrown by Mr. Roh."

Another related analysis connected with the above story was also a poll result that said that Mr. Roh's intention to seek reconfidence was not desirable (44.3%). This story was titled "Most People Think That Roh's Reconfidence Proposal Was Mistaken" (10-13-03, #7, p. 5, -1) and was coded -1, because the proportion of disapproving reconfidence was not polled to be overwhelming. This will be discussed later. The first paragraph read:

President Roh's declaration of reconfidence (sic) met with 44.3% of response that it is not desirable, whereas the proportion of the response 'desirable' reached 40.7% with the gap of 3.6% point (Paragraph 1).

The second part of a serial story about Roh's declaration was printed. This piece was titled "Future Procedures for Mr. Roh ; Large-Scale Counterattack on the Politicians" (10-13-03, #5, p. 3, +1). This story was a favorable interpretation of Roh's intentions:

Roh's suggestion of reconfidence can be seen as a large-scale counterattack against the political circle. Mr. Roh criticized the political circle by saying that the processes of reconfidence will never be as disorderly as the previous several months. (Paragraph 1).

An additional story saying that the proportion of people's confidence in Mr. Roh has increased is also a favorable story to Roh. the title of the story was "Public Opinion of Reconfidence Skyrockets; The Gap Widens Increasingly" (10-13-03, #8, p. 5, +2). See how this story developed in chronological order:

"President Roh Speaks to the Nation Vote of Reconfidence on around December 15th; Not to be Related to Policy" (10-14-03, #1, p. 1, +2);
"The Blue House Says Nothing to Opposition Criticism That Proposal of Reconfidence Vote is out of Political Ploy" (10-15-03, #9, p. 4, +1);
"Mr. Roh Keeps Silent We Will Win In Time; He Applies Gags to Aides" (10-16-03, #3, p. 3, +1);
"President Roh Indicates Political Compromise on Reconfidence Vote; Roh Seeks to Meet Opposition Leaders After Asia Pacific Economic Council Summit" (10-18-03, #1, p. 1, +1); and
"Roh Indicates Coordination in Scheduling of Reconfidence Vote; " (10-24-03, #1, p. 1, +1).

(2) Roh as a Policymaker and an International Player

There were a few policy stories. On October 18th issue, the newspaper printed a story titled "Decision Made to Send Security Forces (To Iraq); Official Announcement to be Made Today After National Security Council Meeting; Civic Groups etc Will Oppose" (10-18-03, #3, p. 1, +1). The President made a decision to send Korean troops to Iraq, which are security forces in nature.
A related story followed with the title "Mr. Roh Gave

'Soldiers' and Earned Bush's Heart; Stopgap Solution to Redeployment of U.S. Forces in Korea; Securing North Korea's Safety is Fruit" (10-21-03, #2, p. 3, +1).

Mr. Roh and Mr. Bush agreed in APEC summit to safeguard security of North Korea by signing multilateral documents. This drew attention because it may mean an American policy change (10-21-03, #1, p. 1, +2).

President Bush's comments on Mr. Roh made for stories. A story titled "Bush Says That Mr. Roh Is America's Friend and My Friend; Bush Praises Roh That His Speech Was Good" (10-21-03, #3, p. 3, +2). Read how Bush said to Roh:

> President Bush expressed his friendliness either by saying that he likes Roh as a human or by saying that Roh is America's friend or his personal friend perhaps because of Roh's decision to send Korean troops (Paragraph 2).

But an editorial on the same day criticized that South Korea did not get national interests in recompense to sending soldiers to Iraq (10-21-03, #6, p. 5, -1).

A breakthrough was reached concerning multilateral security. An analysis gave meanings and predictions to statement of chairman of APEC summit. The title read: "A Breakthrough Was Reached in Six- Party Talks That Did Not Proceed; Visible Results on Multilateral Security; North Korea Still Cold, Clinging to Nonaggression Pact" (10-22-03, #2, p. 5, +1).

Mr. Roh also predicted that six-party talks will be held soon. The story appeared with the title "Mr. Roh Says That Six Party Talks Will Be Held Soon; Foreign Ministry Suggests Step-by-Step Security Safeguard to North Korea" (11-01-03, #2, p. 2, +1).

Mr. Roh reestablished Korean history by apologizing for the 'April 3rd Incident of Cheju Island'. The story was titled "Mr. Roh Apologizes for the April 3rd Incident; Plain People of Jeju Island Were Victimized by Errors of National Power (11-01-03, #1, p. 1, +1).

A related analysis was printed on another page with the title

"Meaning of Roh's Apologies; He Puts Period to A Half Century of Unhappy Past" (11-01-03, #3, p. 5, +1).

As part of regional development, Mr. Roh proposed allocation of regional human resources in recruiting in public sectors. The story had the title "Public Sectors Will Employ Allocated Human Resources from Regions" (11-08-03, #1, p. 1, +1).

(3) Other Stories Favoring Mr. Roh

A story of Mr. Roh visiting Kwangju City described him very favorably and the story linked him to his predecessor Kim Dae Jung. The story had the title "President Roh Says That He Feels At Home Whenever He Comes To Kwangju" (11-08-03, #2, p. 5, +2). The story showed how warmly liked the region and how he was loked by the residents. See how the story read:

President Roh visited Kwangju and expressed a particular affection for the province Honam. Roh said at conversations with residents of Kwangju and Honam, which was held at the municipal museum, that whenever he comes to Kwangju he himself feels at home (Paragraph 1).

In front of the museum 40 odd members of Nosamo, his suppoter group, gathered and welcomed with placards, which said 'Citizens of Kwanju love Roh extremely' or 'Kim Dae Jung, Forerunner of Peaceful Reunification --- Roh Moo Hyun, Successor of Sunshine Policy (Para 9, Last Para).

A story about the opening of presidential library for his predecessor Kim Dae Jung also appeared to be supportive of Mr. Roh. The story was titled "Background for Opening of Library for Kim Dae Jung; Kim Pledges Roh Government's Policy of Peace and Prosperity" (11-04-03, #3, p. 5, +1). According to this story Mr. Kim said in his address that "we would encourage and assist so that President Roh's policy for peace on the Korean Peninsula and advancement of cooperation between North and South Korea (Para 3)." A follow-up analysis was printed about the meaning of the opening of the first presidential library (11-04-03, #3, p. 5, +1).

A dry (or favorable?) story about Mr. Roh's golfing was printed on the November 4th issue. The story had the title "President Roh's couple and Mr. Kang Kum Won's Play Golf" (11-04-03, #4, p. 5, +1). This story simply said that Roh played golf with his old friend:

> Mr. and Mrs. Roh played golf on the first of this month at Signus Golf Rink with Mr. and Mrs. Kang Kum Won, the owner of the rink and his long-time friend who runs Changsin Textile Company in Busan. President Roh's couple played golf on a newly trimmed cotton course with his friend's couple and returned to Seoul after eating supper (Paragraph 1).

But a follow-up column severely criticized his golfing four days later. A column titled "President's Inappropriate Golfing" (11-08-03, #3, p. 6, -2) said:

> The day when the facts were known that President Roh played golf with his old friend employees at the Blue House decried. One just said that he got angry without knowing why. presidential spokesperson Mr. Yun Tai Young confirmed that Roh played and shut up his mouth citing 'his privacy (Paragraph 1).

This story will be discussed later in the negative coverage section. Playing golf may be a commonplace sport for average persons in America. This would have made no story in America. But this piece takes issue with Roh's golf partner.

(4) Roh's Attitude to Media: Inviting Editors to Dinner

President Roh's efforts to have better relations with the press were found in this period. The November 3rd issue of the newspaper reported that the president would host a dinner for senior editors and news producers. The story was titled "President Roh

Invites Chief Editors/News Producers in Groups; He Wants to Hear Their Opinions and Public Opinion" (11-03-03, #2, p. 2, +1). According to the story, Presidential Public Relations Secretary Lee Byung Wan said that Mr. Roh wanted to hold a dinner to have a broad-ranging exchange of opinions on overall national affairs without formality. Mr. Lee said the to reduce the psychological hurdles the occasion will be held in the form of dinner at the Blue House (Paragraph 1).

A follow-up story appeared about the dinner on the issue of the fifth. The story titled "Mr. Roh Held Dinner With Chief Editors Roh Says Government and the Press Should Cooperate and End Conflicts" (11-05-03, #1, p. 5, +2) portrayed the change of climate and conveyed Roh's message. The story went:

> Delicate changes are being felt in Roh's relations with the press. President Roh had dinner with six chief editors of news organizations such as KBS, MBC, SBS, YTN, CBS, and Yonhap News. During the dinner served with wine and dongdongju, Roh said that his abrasive relations with the press caused unease to the people and that henceforth the press and the government should cooperate to offer hope and vision to the people (Paragraph 1).

A story on the next day described Mr. Roh saying to the elderly opinion leaders to the same effect with the title "President Roh Will Strive to Mend Relations with the Press During Lunch with Elderly Opinion Leaders" (11-06-03, #4, p. 5, +1).

Negative Coverage

(1) Criticism of Roh's Proposal of Confidence Vote

An analysis on the day of Roh's proposal discussed the shockwaves derived from it. The title was "Roh's Shocking Proposal of Confidence Vote; A Declaration of Megaton Bomb, Political Situation Turned Into Wild Currents" (10-11-03, #3, p. 4, -1). See how the story went:

> Chaos, unpredictability, whirlpool. President Roh's remarks on reconfidence are a bomb-like declaration, which is likely to bring tremendous shockwaves onto the whole nation. Naturally, it will drive the political situation into a state of visibility zero. It is hard to even guess where the shockwaves will reach with what strength. Vacuum of political power, political chaos resulting from it, (Paragraph 1).

A column criticizing his behavior was printed on the same day's issue. The column titled "Confusion of National Politics Must Be Avoided" (10-11-03, #5, p. 6, -1) raised a question why he did not seek other alternatives. The column additionally criticized that Mr. Roh did not bear the huge accountability and his political digestibility and endurance was not large enough.

A related story gave an explanation what might have led Roh to the remarks. The story was titled " Roh's Shocks of Reconfidence; Approval Rate Down To 30% Range In Eight Months; Repeated Scandals Surrounding Aides and Relatives Reflection of Accumulated Distrust from the People" (10-11-03, #6, p. 6, -1). This story explained that accumulated distrust of the people led to decrease of approval rate for Roh, and that led him to his decision t o ask people's trust again. According to this story, Mr. Roh was elected with 48.9% of the votes, enjoyed expectation of 92% from the people that he would conduct national politics smoothly, and he had 70% range of approval rate just after his taking office.

Another story appeared explaining why Roh came to the decision. The story said that the money scandal caused Choi Do Sool, Roh's former aide became a fatal blow to him. The title showed how "The Noose of Choi Became a Fatal Blow Was Choi a Nuclear Bomb; If Proven Unofficial Election Funds, It Will Deliver a Magaton Wave; If Proven Individual Bribery, Roh Cannot Escape From Political and Moral Responsibility"

(10-11-03, #7, p. 6, -1). In this story Roh was quoted as confessing that he could not run national politics in this situation. Choi's scandal was that serious, the story said.

An additional background story appeared. This story said that Roh's aides were all implicated in money scandals, resulting from his policy line of maintaining neutrality of the prosecution office. The story was titled "Roh's Five Close Aides Were Slashed by the Sharp Blade of Prosecutors; Aides Kwang Jai and Hee Jung Involved Intensive Investigation of Aides Unprecedented during President's Incumbency; Irony Created That Emphasis of Independence of Prosecutors Led to Cross-Currents to the Blue House" (10-11-03, #7, p. 6, -1).

The editorial of this day fiercely faulted Roh's behavior. The editorial took twice the space of ordinary ones with the title "Roh's Proposal of Reconfidence Was Not Serious" (10-11-03, #9, p. 7, -2). The editorial read:

> We are extremely dumfounded at Mr. Roh's bomb announcement that he would pursue reconfidence of the people on grounds of his aides' involvement in irregularities. We feel seriously disgraced that a president who has served merely eight months out of five-year term of office should seek reconfidence because he can no longer run politics. Roh's proposal is in a word an irresponsible proposal with neither cause nor practicality (Paragraph 1).

A follow-up analysis showed poll results that said that Mr. Roh's intention to seek reconfidence was not desirable (44.3%). This story was titled "Most People Think That Roh's Reconfidence Declaration Was Mistaken" (10-13-03, #7, p. 5, -1) and was coded -1, because the proportion of disapproving reconfidence was not polled to be overwhelming. This was discussed earlier. The first paragraph read:

> President Roh's declaration of reconfidence (sic) met with 44.3% of response that it is not desirable, whereas the proportion of the response 'desirable' reached 40.7% with

the gap of 3.6% point (Paragraph 1).

A column was printed to the effect that Mr. Roh must regain his declining trust for himself and not making recourse to the people. The column was titled "Reconfidence Card Not Tasty; Roh Must Regain His Trust For Himself Not Resorting to People" (10-13-03, #11, p. 5, -1).

Three opposition parties opposed Roh's confidence proposal and it became unclear whether his proposal will proceed as was planned. The story about it was titled "Mr. Roh Is Fast-Pedaling, But Met With Opposition; Whether Referendum Will Be Held Is Unclear" (10-14-03, #2, p. 3, -1).

In response to Roh's proposal, former president Kim Young Sam said that "Proposal of confidence vote is what befits dictator." Mr. Kim made caustic remarks on Roh's confidence proposal saying that there is no related article in the national constitution (10-14-03, #9, p. 5, -1).

Leading assemblyman of Hannara Party Mr. Choi Byung Ryol broached the idea of impeachment in connection with Roh's confidence proposal and irregularities of Roh's aides. Three opposition parties sought to form a joint committee to cope with the confidence issue. This story was coded -1, because opposition party leaders talked about impeachment of Roh (10-15-03, #1, p. 1, -1).

A related analysis explained that Mr. Choi intended to link Roh's confidence issue with his impeachment. In the story (10-15-03, #6, p. 3, -1), Mr. Choi said that "if Mr. Roh is implicated in the irregularities of his aides in whatever manner, then Roh can be the object of impeachment, and not just a matter of confidence. Impeachment was first mentioned (Paragraph 1)."

Foreign news media were cited to criticized Roh's proposal. A story based on foreign media was printed with the title "Foreign Media's Reaction to Confidence Vote; Financial Times Reports That People Are Baffled That President Resorted to Recall For Himself" (10-15-03, #3, p. 2, -1).

A follow-up story about opposition parties forming common front against confidence vote was printed with the title "Three Opposition Parties Get Together With Separate Calculations"

(10-16-03, #2, p. 3, -1).

An editorial followed with the title "It Is Feared That National Politics May Drift In The Midst of Confidence Vote Situation" (10-16-03, #4, p. 9, -1).

Opposition leader Kim Jong Pil criticized Mr. Roh in a lecture at Hosoh University that "a leader must step down when he lost trust of the people" (10-17-03, #2, p. 5, -1).

Assemblyman Kim Bu Kyum criticized Mr. Roh saying that "he must not find fault with opposition parties and the unfriend-ly press (10-18-03, #5, p. 4, -1). According to the story, Kim argued that "the people do not demand higher morality of the president, but they demand of Roh higher ability in handling national affairs."

A column titled "Politics As A Thriller Movie" (10-18-03, #8, p. 6, -1) argued that the people do not want to see the thriller-movie-like politics any longer."

Mr. Lee Hoi Chang, Mr. Roh's former contender in presiden-tial election, said that proposal of confidence vote was far-fetched. According to the story titled " Mr. Lee Returns Criticizes Roh's Proposal As Far-Fetched" (10-21-03, #5, p. 5, -1), Mr. Lee said that Roh's political gambling is unjustifiable considering that the country is in disorder and the people are ill at ease ... (Paragraph 1).

(2) Conflicts within the Blue House and Investigation of Aides

As discussed earlier, prosecutors' investigation of presidential aides can serve as negative coverage of the president. One of the examples was a story titled "Five Presidential Aides Were Hurt By Prosecutors; All Close Aides Are Implicated" (10-11-03, #8, p. 7, -1).

The offensive by opposition parties continued. The opposition forces agreed to seek investigation of national affairs by the National Assembly if Roh's explanation of the irregularities of his aides is unsatisfactory. See the story titled "Investigation of National Affairs Will Be Pursued If Roh's Explanation Is

Unsatisfactory; Three Opposition Parties Agree On Adoption of Special Prosecutors" (10-16-03, #1, p. 1, -2).

A story conveying the claims asking for replacement of presidential aides citing reforms shows that the aides did not carry out their roles as was hoped by the people. See the story titled "Voices for Replacement of Aides Grew Vocal; Personnel Reforms Sought" (10-17-03, #1, p. 4, -1). According to the story, politicians in power call for replacement of presidential aides publicly citing reforms in national affairs.

In response to the claims, Mr. Lee Kwang Jai, director of national affairs situation room of the Blue House, tendered his resignation to the chief of staff. The story was headlined "Director Lee Kwang Jai Resigned, Who Was Criticized As Having Monopolized Political Power Information; Roh Will Weigh Accepting His Resignation; Will It Lead to Resignation of the Young 386 Aides?" (10-20-03, #1, p. 1, -2).

A follow-up analysis appeared about the future of Roh's powerful young aides. The story was titled "Roh's 386 Aides Face Peril; A Series of Scandals and Rumors Drive Them To The Corner" (10-20-03, #5, p. 5, -1). The story said in part that " The 386 young aides of Mr. Roh at first symbolized youth and reform of the participatory government but they face a peril among a series of scandals and rumors."

A related story was printed that conveyed the gloomy climate of the young aides. The story titled "Gloomy Blue House" (10-20-03, #6, p. 5, +1) said in part that "young aides could not accept the accusation that they monopolized information and ower." The following stories fall under this group:

"Conflicts Within The Blue House Has Deepened Concerning Sending Korean Soldiers to Iraq; Despite Gag Order, Conflicts on Policy Lines About Troop Dispatch Sharpen" (10-22-03, #1, p. 4, -2). This story revealed a typical internal conflicts surrounding policy lines.

A related editorial titled "Are Presidential Aides Permitted to Behave Like This?" (10-22-03, #3, p. 7, -2) shed light on serious differences of opinion on sending Korean troops to Iraq about the nature of troops. One of the aides threatened to resign opposing the policy line.

A series of stories about illegal election funds appeared. The stories came out of opposing political forces and prosecutors, purported to inflict damage to Mr. Roh.

Assemblyman Kim Kyung Jai of the Minju Party charged that during the election campaign five corporations offered huge amounts of funds to Roh's camp (10-28-03, #1, p. 2, -1).

A related story was printed, conveying that Roh had double books for keeping tabs on election funds (10-28-03, #2, p. 4, -1).

"Business groups such as Samsung and Lotte Offered One Billion Won Respectively, Hyundai Motor and LG offered 500 Million to 1,5 Billion Won; Roh's Camp Received 6.5 Billion Won" (10-29-03, #1, p. 1, -2).

A related story was titled "Former Comrades at Arms Fight Desperately; Minju and Woori Party Engaged in Attack and Counterattack" (10-29-03, #2, p. 3, -1).

A related editorial demanded that doubts about election funds must be cleared (10-29-03, #4, p. 7, -1).

"Minju Party Maintained That Roh's Camp Money-Laundered 10 Billion Won; Woori Party Rebutted That High-Ranking Officials of Minju Party Embezzled 10 Billion Won" (10-30-03, #1, p. 1, -2).

"Roh Camp Handled Sponsoring Money Wrongly; Central Party Assembled Money and Distributed 14.9 Billion Won to Four Regions" (10-30-03, #5, -1).

"How Much Money Did Roh Camp Collect The Amount Could Reach 10 Billion Won Beyond The Declared 7.4 Billion" (10-31-03, #1, p. 1, -2). This story said that despite explanations from the party the doubts are deepening about the election funds of the Roh camp.

(In this wild-running current, President Roh said that investigation of election funds had better be started. Mr. Roh expressed his hopes that investigation should be launched with a view to reforming election funds gathering (11-03-03, #1, p. 1,

+1). This story was coded +1, because Roh expressed his views and his remark made a new turning point.)

The next day, a leading prosecutor declared that they will investigate the issue of presidential election funds on a broad scale. Mr. Ahn Dai Hee, a leading prosecutor said that the investigation will focus on political circles rather than business concerns. He also said that the prosecutors will investigate irregularities of presidential aides (11-04-03, #1, p. 1, -1).

A story about prosecutors' investigation of bank accounts of Roh's camp and Hannara Party appeared on November 6th issue of the newspaper. Central Investigation Department of the Highest Prosecution Office said that they launched a probe into a dozen bank accounts of the parties. But the story was place inside (11-06-03, #1, p. 2, -1).

A follow-up story was printed. It was about the investigation by the prosecutors titled "Prosecutors Penetrating The Center of Roh's Camp; Solid Clues May Be In The Prosecutors' Hands" (11-07-03, #1, p. 3, -1).

The following are stories about Prosecution Office but they are negative to Roh:

"Prosecutors Grasp Clues of Two to Three Companies Offering Billions of Won to Roh's Camp" (11-10-03, #1, p. 1, -1);

"Billions of Won to Regional Party Office of Roh Camp, Minju Party Discloses Additional Election Funds Suspicions" (11-10-03, #2, p. 4, -1); and

"Prosecutors Zeroing In On Roh's Election Funds" (11-10-03, #3, p. 5, -1).

The column titled "President Roh's Inappropriate Golfing Accused" (11-08-03, #3, p. 6, -2) was discussed earlier.

(3) Criticisms of Policymaking

During this period most of opposition or criticism was centered around sending Korean troops to Iraq, if not against Roh's proposal of confidence vote.

A story on the October 20th issue of the newspaper criticized Roh government's unclear decision on sending Korean troops to Iraq. The title said that "Roh's Government Said 'No Decision Made' During Daytime, But "Decided' During Nighttime; Roh Said No To Civic Organizations, But Notified Four Political Paties of His Decision; Credibility of Roh's Government Was Hurt" (10-20-03, #2, p. 3, -2). Read the story:

It is pointed out that credibility of Roh' government was seriously damaged concerning the processes of making a decision on sending troops to Iraq. Especially, criticisms are voiced that he has deceived the people seeing that he instantly made up his mind as if he were waiting for the United Nations resolution, although Mr. Roh has promised that he would make an informed decision after gathering broad public opinions (Paragraph 1).

A related story criticized that President Roh sent a letter to Mr. Bush to the effect that he would consider sending troops regardless of the six party talks on North Korean nuclear issue without fully gathering people's opinions (10-20-03, #3, p. 3, -1).

A third story about this problem was printed with the title "Assemblyman Lim Jong Suk Went On A Limitless Hunger Strike Against Troop Dispatch; Lim Declares That He Would Resign His Assemblyman's Post If Combat Forces Are Sent" (10-20-03, #4, p. 3, -1).

The editorial titled "U.S.--Korea Summit, What Is National Interest?" (10-21-03, #6, p. 7, -1) pointed out that even though Roh conceded to sending Korean troops to Korea, he did not get something in return from Mr. Bush.

Another editorial titled "President Roh Worried About Sending Troops" (10-31-03, #3, p. 7, -1) faulted Roh's uneasy stance after making a decision, saying that his indecisiveness will only spread fruitless arguments.

Neutral Coverage

A story on October 13th issue of the newspaper dealt with heated arguments over when and how to conduct referendum on President Roh's confidence. The story conveyed voices from the both of the opposing forces and is explanatory and predictive in nature with the title "Arguments Over Date and Methods About Referendum for Confidence Vote; Special Act With Time Limits Pursued ... Agreement Among Political Circle Is The Key" (10-13-03, #4, p. 3, 0). The following three articles may belong here:

"Political Parties Must Hurry to Agree on Referendum" (10-14-03, #10, Ed, 0);
"Political Skills of Mr. Roh and Other Four Party Leaders To Be Tested; Prediction of Political Situation Concerning the Serial Meetings" (10-25-03, #1, Straight, p. 5, 0); and
"The President Must Come Forward To Tackle Korea--Chile Free Trade Agreement" (11-10-03, #4, Editorial, p. 7, 0).

Period III. Pre-Impeachment of President Roh

This section is analysis of the *Kyunghyang Daily News* coverage of President Roh Moo Hyun from the issue of February 28, 2004 to that of March 12, 2004. This period was largely composed of coverage of political developments leading to the National Assembly's impeachment resolution of President Roh Moo Hyun.

President Roh's remarks on domestic politics incurred criticisms from opposition parties to the effect that he should not intervene in the forthcoming general election on April 15, 2004. The Central Election Monitoring Commission ruled that Mr. Roh violated neutrality obligation prescribed in the election law. Opposition parties voiced ideas of impeachment of Mr. Roh in this regard. However, Roh remained firm on his position that he did not "proactively" violate the election law, citing that he only gave answers to questions posed by reporters. For the 15 days leading to Roh's impeachment, Roh stayed firm and on occasion hinted that the constitutional court will be on his side.

This is a period during which the Central Election Monitoring Commission ruled that Mr. Roh failed to observe the obligation of neutrality. Opposition parties fiercely criticized Roh's behavior, discussed impeachment, and at last proceeded with impeachment procedures. Mr. Roh insisted that he did not violate neutrality obligation and he linked impeachment to people's confidence of him. Opposition parties succeeded in passing the impeachment motion at the National Assembly.

In the meantime, President Roh established himself as a patriotic leader by criticizing Japan's Prime Minister Koizumi Junichiro and also as a clean leader by ordering bad treatment for a bribing businessman. Prosecutors' investigation of presidential election funds and irregularities of Roh's aides continued even during this period.

This was a short period abruptly leading to presidential impeachment. Mr. Roh frequently showed his opinionated or obstinate temperament. Selecting this half-month period for analysis may be a bit arbitrary. However, impeachment offensives were launched and Roh was finally impeached. The proportion of negative coverage seemed as high as in Period II, but this abruptly changed when impeachment resolution was passed at the National Assembly as will be shown in Period IV. Roh was a strong-willed politician confronting impeachment motion head-on and was finally impeached.

Positive Coverage

(1) Image of a Strong-Willed Politician Confronting Impeachment Drive From Opposition Parties

When the Central Election Monitoring Commission ruled (March 3rd issue of the newspaper) that Mr. Roh violated obligation of neutrality, opposition parties floated the idea of impeachment of President Roh (March 4th issue). But Mr. Roh and his Blue House remained firm and steadfast against delivering any apologies demanded by opposition parties.

The first such story appeared on March 6th issue of the newspaper. The story was entitled "Blue House Says, We Did Not Consider Apologies; Roh Intends Head-On Confrontation, You Must Have Reasons Even When You Fire A Low-Ranking Official" (03-06-04, p. 2, #3, +1). According to the story, presidential spokesman Yun Tai Young said that "the Blue House has never examined and never discussed Roh's apologies demanded by the opposition parties (Paragraph 1)."

On March 8th issue of the newspaper, the Blue House said that "The President will not yield to opposition parties even though he will be removed from his post." The title said "Mr. Roh Will Not Yield Even Though He Will Be Removed From Post; Blue House Position, It Is Against National Interests, Publicity Warfare Will Be Launched Against Impeachment" (03-08-04, #2, p. 1, +2). The story read:

> The party in power expressed a steadfast policy of confrontation. The Blue House already had the advisers' meeting on legal affairs mindful of the situations after the impeachment motion was passed (Paragrpah 1).
>
> Public affairs adviser Lee Byung Wan said that in the past we heard talks of impeachment over a hundred times... (Paragraph 2).

On the March 9th issue, Mr. Roh said that opposition's demand for the president to stop presidential duties is excessive; he only gave answers to questions posed by reporters, not intending to interfere with the election procedures. Mr. Roh said that he cannot yield to impeachment pressures (03-09-04, #2, p. 1, +1).

Voices of opposing impeachment came out of the Blue House

and people in general. The following are the titles that show the developments:

"Party In Power Shocked And Angered; The National Assembly Is Crazy" (03-10-04, #3, p. 2, +1);
"National Assembly Must Rather Be Impeached Civic Groups Insist; The President Must Be Sobered, Some People Agree With Impeachment Movement" (03-10-04, #6, p. 4, +1);
"Mr. Roh Says That He Does Not Intend To Shrink From His Responsibility" (03-10-04, #8, p. 5, +1);
"Public Opinion Says That Impeachment Move Should Be Canceled; Old Wise Men and Civic Groups Say That He Should Apologize" (03-11-04, #1, p. 1, +2); and
"Advisory Board Of The Newspaper Says People Will Not Forgive Impeachment" (03-11-04, #3, p. 2, +1).

Faced with impeachment moves and pressures for his apologies, Mr. Roh intended to ask the people's judgement by means of general election on April 15th and he would not yield. A story on March 11th issue forewarned that Mr. Roh will deliver a speech on his position about impeachment and apologies (03-11-04, #2, p. 1, +2).

At last, Mr. Roh refused apologizing and delivered a speech, purporting to link results of the general election of April 15th to people's confidence of him (03-12-04, #1, p. 1, 0). In the meantime, assemblymen of Woori Party, affiliated to Mr. Roh, attempted to block the impeachment procedures through physical resistance in the National Assembly. His refusal to apologize infuriated opposition politicians and this very probably led to the eventual impeachment of Roh. Just before Roh's speech, this newspaper predicted that impeachment motion will not pass because of lack of the quorum but the prediction turned out to be wrong just in a few days. Such an abrupt turn of events!

(2) Image of a Patriotic Leader

On March 2nd issue of the newspaper, a story warning the

Prime Minister of Japan appeared. Top news on the front page, this story was about President Roh who warned Japanese Prime Minister not to pay tribute to Yasukuni Shrine, where Japan's chauvinistic war-mongers are buried. The story was titled "President Roh Warns Japan's PM Not To Visit Yasukuni Shrine; Roh Warns Him Not To Utter Words That Hurt Koreans on March 1st Speech; Roh Promises Better Treatment For Korean Independence Fighters and Their Posterity" (03-02-04, #1, p. 1, +2). The story said in part:

> President Roh expressed deep regrets that at least a national leader must not utter words that would hurt people in the neighboring country, pointing his address to Japanese leading politicians (Paragraph 1).
> Roh's address can be interpreted as carrying a strong warning to Japan's movements to revise the 'constitution for peace' and Japanese Prime Minister Koizumi Junichiro, who annually repeated his intention to visit the Yaskuni Shrine (Paragraph 3).

A follow-up story, which is interpretative in nature, provided a very positive touch to Roh's address. This story printed on page two had the title "Roh's Speech Was A Warning To Japan Pointing to Prime Minister Directly; Reestablishing History In His Own Style; Roh Personally Revised Manuscript Without Aides' Knowledge" (03-02-04, #3, p. 2, +2). This story said that Mr. Roh revised overnight for himself the manuscript that his aides wrote. Diplomats at the ceremony were surprised at his speech, the story said. This interpretative piece could have been written to throw a positive light on Mr. Roh's behavior, although why Mr. Roh revised the script himself overnight without his aides' knowledge or without consulting them remains unclear.

(3) Image of a Clean Leader

In his last speech before the impeachment (March 12th issue),

Mr. Roh divulged a high-ranking businessman's behavior asking favors from his older brother with briber money. Mr. Roh said that he ordered that the businessman receive bad treatment for that. The story had the title "Mr. Roh Instructed Ill Treatment After Getting Reports of Favor-Asking" (03-12-04, #3, p. 2, +1).

Negative Coverage

(1) Impeachment Offensives by Opposition Politicians

Mr. Roh's remarks about the general election of April 15th ignited un uproar in national politics. On March 3rd issue, a story appeared with a title "Presidential Remarks On General Election Create An Uproar; Opposition Cites Government's Intervention, But Roh Says Why Pick A Fight Against Me?" (03-03-04, #4, p. 4, -2). The story went:

> Just before the April 15 general election, President Roh's intervention in election emerges as a big controversy. Hannara Party and Minju Party took issue with Roh's recent election-related remarks, defined them as illegal election campaign, and floated ideas of impeachment of the President and Chairman of the Central Election Monitoring Commission (Paragraph 1).
> President Roh, on the contrary, confronted these suggestions with comments "Why pick a fight against me?" and the situation worsened. (Paragraph 2).

On the next day's issue, the newspaper carried a story about Roh's violation of neutrality obligation with the title "President Roh Violated Neutrality Obligation Central Election Monitoring Commission Demands Roh's Observance Of Neutrality; Opposition Party Pursues Impeachment" (03-04-04, #1, p. 1, -2). According to the story:

The Central Election Monitoring Commission ruled that President Roh's comments at the interview with the broadcast reporters' club violated article nine of election law which prescribes neutrality obligation for officials (Paragraph 1).

The Hannara Party and Minju Party professed their intention to pursue impeachment of the president and his apology citing that the president's violation became clear (Paragraph 3).

The above two stories signaled the start of an abrupt and convoluted process of impeachment. The president's position was that his violation was minor but that opposition parties demanded his apology. Mr. Roh insisted on refusing to apologize.

A related story appeared on the same day's issue. The story was about the ruling of the Commission. The story was titled "The Ruling Was In Fact A Warning, Brake Applied to Roh's Path To General Election; Aftershocks Of The First Ruling That The Incumbent President Violated The Neutrality Obligation" (03-04-04, #3, p. 2, -2). This story conveyed the fact that the Commission made a ruling concerning Roh's violation of neutrality obligation, and predicted that the effect thereof may spread widely.

A follow-up story said that while Roh refused to accept the ruling of the Commission, opposition parties entered virtually into impeachment process, thus causing starker situation (03-05-04, #1, p. 1, -2).

The editorial on this day demanded that Roh accept the ruling of the Commission. The editorial pointed out that Roh's argumentative comments alone cause political haggling and that Roh's political remarks are not productive.

On the next day's issue, opposition party warned seriously that if Mr. Roh does not apologize and make promises not to interfere in election, the party would move impeachment instantly by March 7th. The situation grew serious with this warning.

A final blow was made on March 10th issue. Impeachment

motion was made at the National Assembly. The story on this day was titled "Impeachment Motion Was Made Against President Roh; 159 Assemblymen Signed On The Motion First In History; Tomorrow Is Day For Voting Woori Party Professed To Block The Process; Blue House Says That They Will Watch The Process" (03-10-04, #1, p. 1, -2). The story reported that Hannara Party and Minju Party submitted impeachment motion to the Assembly with signatures of 159 lawmakers. (Paragraph 1).

A related story on the same day's issue said that the two parties made a common front in impeachment motion (03-10-04, #2, p. 2, -1).

(2) Investigation of Roh's Election Funds and his Aides

Even while the impeachment procedures were proceeding, investigation of election funds of Mr. Roh, irregularities of his aides and relatives was conducted by the prosecutors. Investigation of his aides or relatives has continued to this period. First of this series appeared on the March 1st issue. The story's titled "Two Or Three Politicians Will Be Summoned; Prosecutors Seriously Consider Handling Of Mr. Roh and Mr. Lee" (03-01-04, #1, p. 1, -1).

A related story (03-02-04, #2, p. 1, -1) said that one of the five business groups handed one billion won of illegal funds to Roh's presidential election camp.

A follow-up story (03-03-04, #1, p. 1, -1) said that prosecutors found out that Mr. Yo Tack Soo, presidential administrator, received 200 million won from Lotte business group and is going to detain him.

An editorial titled "Irregularities of Presidential Aides See No Ends" (03-04-04, #5, p. 4, -1) criticized that irregularities of Roh's aides continued without limits. The editorial said that Yo Tack Soo received ranging several hundred million won from Lotte business group and then Mr. Ahn Hee Jung, Roh's another aide, received six hundred million one from Lotte (Paragraph 1).

A related analysis on the same day's issue said that illegal funds flowing to Roh's election camp might have included other major business groups as part of their insurance money. The title explained itself: "Only Lotte Gave Illegal Funds to Roh's Camp?; It Was First Confirmed That One of the Five Major Groups Has Offered Funds; Other Four Major Groups May Have Offered Money; Roh's Aides' Reception of Money Divulged One By One" (03-04-04, #6, p. 4, -1).

A very controversial story (03-09-04, #1, p. 1, -2) appeared on March 9th issue. Prosecutors announced that the interim estimates of illegal election funds received by Hannara Party and Roh's camp reached 82.3 billion won and 11.3 billion won respectively, thus re-creating the controversy of 'one tenth of election funds.' President Roh has said that if his election funds exceed one tenth of that of Hannara Pary he would resign. This story predicted that on account of this finding political haggling will mount (Paragraph 4).

Prosecution's interim announcement of investigation seemed to be a stern warning to Roh's camp. The title showed how stern it was: "Interim Announcement of Election Funds Investigation Ahn Hee Jung's Role?; Ahn Handled 8.5 Billion Won Black Hole for Roh Camp; Ahn's Moral Relaxation Came to the Fore Scholarship Money from Home Towns" (03-09-04, #4, p. 3, -2).

On the same day's issue, another story said that Roh's older brother Roh Gun Pyong was summarily summoned to prosecutors to be probed about suspicions of 'Min Kyung Chan's Funds' of 65 billion won (03-09-04, #3, p. 1, -1).

Two opposition parties pressured Mr. Roh to step citing 'one tenth election funds.' The two parties maintained that now the election fund of Roh camp exceeded on tenth of that of Hannara Party Roh must step down as he has promised (03-10-04, #9, p. 5, -1). This was additional political offensive from opposition parties.

Mr. Roh's defending of his aides and relatives was criticized. In his speech to the nation, he said that ha cannot rescind his trust of his aides and relatives even though they were involved in irregularities. His speech was faulted for defending his close allies (03-12-04, #8, p. 4, -1).

Neutral Coverage

A story about supporters of Mr. Roh and Mr Lee, opposition presidential contender appeared. This story was about the two groups scheduled demonstrations. When idea of impeachment floated the two groups staged demonstrations separately and the coverage dealt with both groups fairly. The story was titled "Roh Sa Mo and Chang Sa Rang Stage Protests For and Against Impeachment" (03-11-04, #8, p. 7, 0).

A story criticizing both impeachment by the opposition and protest by Mr. Roh was coded 0. This story titled "Impeachment Situation, Only People Driven To Deathland" (03-12-04, #5, p. 3, 0) said that the people are driven to a land of death by political wrangling.

Period IV. President Roh Moo Hyun Impeached

This section is analysis of the *Kyunghyang Daily News* coverage of President Roh Moo Hyun from the issue of March 13th, 2004 to that of April 15, 2004. This period was largely composed of coverage of impeachment resolution at the National Assembly, people's protests against the impeachment and President Roh's personal qualities. Positive coverage of President Roh resulted from people's criticism of impeachment and columns and editorials attacking opposition parties, which impeached Roh.

President Roh Moo Hyun was impeached at the National Assembly by a majority of 193 to 2 on March 12, 2004. His office was suspended. Lawmakers of the Woori Party tried to stop the impeachment procedures with force but to no avail. This newspaper carried many stories about people's resistance to impeachment, symbolized by a series of their massive candlelight protests. This newspaper ran many columns and editorials that criticized impeachment resolution by the National

Assembly, thereby supporting President Roh indirectly.

In the meantime, Mr. Roh insisted that results of general election will be linked to his previous proposal of confidence vote. Several stories appeared that described Mr. Roh favorably, focusing on his personal qualities, conveying his personal feelings and hopes about future politics. The beat reporter wrote intimate stories of Roh's personal agonies about impeachment and general election. Roh went on a mountain-hike with beat reporters and expressed his feelings.

The stories mainly described the impeachment as a shock to the nation which occurred for the first time in constitutional history and then emphasized that the decision betrayed the true will of the people. Some stories were about polling results that disapproved of the impeachment.

In this period, stories not centered around the president, but those of reactions of the people and groups against Roh's impeachment provided positive coverage of Mr. Roh. There was not much of presidential politics during this period because his functions were suspended. Therefore a different categorization was adopted for analysis: (3) Columns and Editorials.

A few stories appeared that described Mr. Roh negatively. For example, he refused to negotiate with the opposition parties before impeachment. A story conveyed investigation of his older brother about money scandal. It should not be ignored that this newspaper carried stories of people who staged pro-impeachment demonstrations vis-a-vis with anti-impeachment protests, as will be discussed in the Neutral Coverage section.

President Roh was impeached by the National Assembly for charges of interference in the forthcoming election processes. The opposition forces took the majority of the Assembly and politicians supporting Roh was minority. What is important here is that the assemblymen's term of office is four years, whereas that of the president is five years. Roh's term began in February of 2003 and assemblymen's term ended in May 2004. The discrepancy in terms of office between that of the president and that of the assemblymen was part of the grounds that enabled impeachment. The power configuration of the National

Assembly and that of the administration did not correspond. After the general election of April 15th, the party in power, or the party supporting Mr. Roh, took the majority of the Assembly, as will be shown in Period V. The discrepancy disappeared after the general election. It is remarkable that the proportion of positive coverage soared suddenly after the impeachment.

Analysis of news coverage of this period (one-week period after the impeachment) was so polarized as was evidenced by a report of content analysis performed by Korea Journalism Society entitled "Content Analysis of Television Broadcasting Pertaining to Presidential Impeachment." The report said that "no matter how loosely the criteria may be applied, broadcast programs of impeachment were lopsidedly favorable to Mr. Roh." Analysis of three main airwave broadcasters' news and nonnews programs invited heated and fierce controversy. *The Chosun Ilbo* and other several conservative newspapers ran the report on the front page and broadcasters rebutted the analysis, raising questions about the ultimate motivation of the report. It was such a divisive report, and broadcasters and newspapers interpreted the report in their respective interests (*The Chosun Ilbo*, June 11, 2004, p. 1, p. 3).

Positive Coverage

(1) Criticisms of Impeachment and Anti-Impeachment Protests

On the day (March 13th, 2004) when the story about impeached Roh appeared, many stories criticizing the impeachment were published. The first reaction by President Roh to impeachment resolution was that "Although the impeachment is not justifiable, I accept the decision." Roh said that the decision of the constitutional court would be different, citing that the institution makes legal decisions." This implies that the ruling of the latter will reverse that of the National Assembly. The story was titled "Roh Says That The Constitutional Court Will Be Different" (03-13-04, #2, p. 1, +1).

On page two, the story and photos said that this situation cannot be. The story had the title "193 Opposition Votes Everything At An End in 43 Minutes" (03-13-04, #4, p. 2, +1). The story and the photo together described a scene where unjustifiable act was carried out. The caption of the photo said "lawmakers of Woori Party are forcefully being dragged away."

On page three, the title of a story said in part that " Confusion In Diplomacy and National Security May Occur" (03-13-04, #5, p. 3, +1).

The most critical story had this title: "Candlelight Protests Of Disobedience To Impeachment In The Whole Country; A Conflagration Of Resistance Movement Even Housewives Took Part; Civic Groups Profess That They Will Stage A Second June Protests" (03-13-04, #9, p. 5, +2). The story said:

> Groups with neckties, students, and housewives holding their children's hands bolted out into the streets. On the night of 12th, when impeachment of Mr. Roh was passed, streets in front of the National Assembly were turned into a ground for candlelight demonstration. Citizens with candlelights at hands stayed awake overnight shouting 'Impeachment Invalid' 'Dismiss The Assembly' (Paragraph 1).

Protests of citizens shouting that "the impeachment is invalid" may be very favorable coverage to Roh. This may be an indirect way to support imperiled Roh.

The whole of page 12 of the day's issue was devoted to photos describing shocks to the people. Five photos were carrying the message that the Assembly ignored the will of the people. The captions said in part that "There were no people (Meaning, they ignored the people's will). Cries of despair and shouts that the Assembly is dead! This offered a very positive coverage to Roh, showing "that the people opposed the impeachment." (03-13-04, #17, p. 12, +2).

On the next day's issue, a story about a nationwide protest occupied the top of the front page with the title "Nationwide Resistance Is Spreading, Shouting That Impeachment Is Invalid; 70,000 Demonstrators Participated In Yesterday's Protest; 56 Professor at Busan Kyungsung University Took Part" (03-14-04, #1, p. 1, +2). The story said in part that "Citizens' voices decrying the first impeachment of the president is spreading (Paragraph 1)."

On this day's issue another story about citizens opposing the impeachment was printed with the title "The Generation of June Rebellion Took To Streets; The Movement Of Civil Disobedience On Full Track; Ordinary Citizens With Neckties On and Housewives and Students Took Part; Conservative Groups Confronted These Groups With Their Own Protests" (03-14-04, #8, p.7, +1). This story had a photo which said "Return our president." This is undeniably positive to Mr. Roh and was coded +1.

On the March 15th issue, there appeared a story about poll results that described an emergency at the opposition parties that faced a sudden decline in approval ratings. This story conveyed a new climate in which the impeachment brought about a new formation of forces for and against Mr. Roh and the politicians who pushed ahead with impeachment faced internal criticism. This story had the title "Opposition Circles Faced With Sudden Decline In Approval Ratings; Cross-Currents Of Impeachment Rapidly Alters The Configuration Of General Election To Pro- vs Anti-Roh Division; Minju Party Members Demand Resignation Of Leadership" (03-15-04, #1, p. 1, +2).

On this day's issue again, the story about candlelight protests appeared. This story predicted that the protests will continue with a photo. This story (03-15-04, #4, p. 6, +1) said that "550 civic groups will stage a protest against the impeachment."

On the March 16th issue, a front-page story reported that many heads of local governments shifted to the Woori Party protesting against the impeachment. This story (03-16-04, #2, p. 1, +2) said that "because of the popular criticism against the impeachment, Minju Party faced a decline in popularity and that in Honam regions heads of local governments shifted to the Woori Party, which opposed the impeachment (Paragraph 2)."

Even a story appeared, which reported that university students gathered together to protest against the impeachment (03-16-04, #7, p. 7, +1).

According to a story (03-18-04, #1, p. 1, +2), a survey of recommendees for lawmaker at the three opposition parties said that "only 39% was positive to impeachment, while 61% was negative or reserving." This story said that 39.3% said yes to impeachment, whereas 19.8% said no and 40.9% was reserving any answer. The title said that "Only 39% Out Of Non-incumbent Recommendees For Lawmaker At The Three Opposition Parties Said Yes To Impeachment." This should not have been worded "only 39%." The tone should have been just "39%" instead of "only 39%," considering that double the proportion of potential opposition party lawmakers were also for impeachment and 40% did not make any judgment.

A series of stories about candlelight protests against impeachment were printed in favor of Mr. Roh. See the following titles of stories:

"Movement For Impeachment Invalidation Will Stage One Million Man Protest Today; Protests Will Be Held At 40 Odd Places Including 300,000 People; Conservative Groups Will Stage Confrontational Protests" (03-20-04, #3, p. 6, +2);
"A New Chapter Opens For Hilarious Protests; Protestors Exceeding Generations, Ideologies, and Occupations; Protestors Express Their Opinions In Festivity Mood Without Violence" (03-22-04, #1, p. 1, +2); and
"Protestors Put Out The Candlelights; 1.5 Million People Took Part For 16 Days Nationwide; A New Chapter for Peaceful Demonstration Demanding Impeachment Invalidation (03-29-04, #1, p. 1, +2)."

(2) Personal Qualities of Impeached Roh

On the day he was impeached, the newspaper reported that

Mr. Roh stayed calm. A very long title of this day's issue mentioned his calm mood in detail: "Roh Hoped To See The People In Several Months It Was A Long Day For Roh; He Maintained Affected Calmness; Roh Hopes To See The Ruling By The Constitutional Court Rather Than That Of The National Assembly" (03-13-04, #11, p. 7, +2). This offered a very personal aspect of Mr. Roh, which can be a very positive portrayal. Let's see how this story depicted Roh:

At eleven fifty-six a.m. of the 12th of March, the instant when President Roh was impeached, he was looking around Lottem Inc., a company in Changwon City, Kyungnam Province, which manufactures electrified trains. Five minutes later when he arrived at a place for lunch, he address the workers that he was impeached but that he would be all right until the evening. (Paragraph 1).

President Roh appeared firm in his will that he would fight the big opposition parties even when he became a vegetable president because of suspension of office. His close aides said that he seemed to *have made up his mind to become a martyr for political reform* (Seol's emphasis) (Last Paragraph).

A seemingly follow-up story appeared the next day's issue with the title "Roh Says That Nevertheless History Proceeds; His First Day Of Suspension Of Office; Roh Seriously Read Biography Of Former Brishc Prime Minister Margaret Thatcher After Having Got Up As Usual" (03-14-04, #5, p. 3, +2). This story was really personal in nature:

President Roh got up at around 5 am as usual at his residence at the Blue House. He began his day with a light exercise such as stretching. He had breakfast with his wife Kwon Yang Sook. He reportedly read stories closely about his impeachment in the morning newspapers. Mr. Roh went to sleep the night before after having watched television, which broadcast impeachment stories (Paragraph 1).

Another story about his agonies over his political future was printed on the March 22nd issue with the title "President Roh Troubled Over Confidence And Entry To Woori Party" (03-22-04, #5, p. 4, +2). See how the story portrays his state of mind in a very personal manner:

President Roh is agonizing over whether to link results of general election to confidence and whether to enter the Woori Party. It was learned that Mr. Roh recently said repeatedly to his close aides, 'I am really troubled. What should I do?' (Paragraph 1).

Although Mr. Roh expressed his position on confidence vote and entry to the party at the press conference and then said that he would soon present criteria for that on March 11th, he was driven into a dilemma as to which measure to take now that impeachment was passed (Paragraph 2).

As the date (April 15th) of general election drew near, Mr. Roh floated his idea of "new politics of integration." This tory had the title "President Roh Says That He Would Conduct Politics Of Integration Instead After General Election; He Would Turn Confrontation To Conversation He Would Discard Corruption and Provincial Politics" (04-12-04, #1, p. 2, +2). In this story, Mr. Roh said that he would pursue politics of conversation and compromise instead of life-or-death confrontation. His remarks were made on the way to mountain hiking with beat reporters.

Another related story about his state of the mind was printed nearby with the title "Roh Said Of Impeachment And General Election, Spring Has Come But Not Yet Spring; Roh Hints At Change Of His Mind That The Politics Will Be Transformed" (04-12-04, #2, p. 2, +2). This story portrayed Mr. Roh:

President Roh went on a mountain hiking with 50 odd beat reporters marking one month of his impeachment. This was his first event open to the press after the impeachment. Roh had three rounds of conversation on the mount while on two hours of the mountain hiking (Paragraph 1).

(3) Columns and Editorials Criticizing Impeachment

The editorial on the day when impeachment was passed was titled "Why Has This Country Been Reduced To This Situation?; Oppression Of The Majority Party, Violence Of The Assembly; Do Not Let National Affairs Drift" (03-13-04, #3, p. 2, +2). This editorial fiercely criticized the bigger opposition parties for passing the impeachment motion. Read how the editorial said:

> The shocking incident occurred, which is the first in the constitutional history. The National Assembly passed the impeachment motion of President Roh and his office was suspended. De facto suspension of constitutional politics occurred. Now political situation has sunken into a state where it is impossible to see one inch ahead. Great disorder is sure to come. We regret the behavior of the political circles who have lost reason (Paragraph 1).
> Why has this country come to this situation? (Paragraph 2).

One can compare this editorial with that of the *Chosun Ilbo*, also published in Korean. This newspaper seemed less fierce or mild in criticizing the impeachers. Read how it said in part:

> President Roh Moo Hyun was impeached by voting at the National Assembly yesterday. The Constitutional Court should determine whether or not to accept the impeachment of Roh within 180 days; All of Roh's presidential functions are suspended until then; The administration will be operated by Prime Minister Ko Keun in the capacity of the acting president. This is the first unhappy incident in the constitutional history and a tragedy that the unripe Korean society created (Paragraph 1).
> It forces a deep sigh of regret that our nation finally came to suffer from this state (Paragraph 2).

On this day's issue, one column decrying the impeachment appeared with the title "Coup d'etat under the name of congressionalism" (03-13-04, #19, p. 15, +1). This was a special contribution by a professor named Lee Jang Hee. Read how this column criticized the presidential impeachment:

Now the people are so tired of anger and disappointment that they are inclined to deny the existence of the National Assembly itself. The National Assembly, which ought to have been impeached itself, has approved impeachment of the president under the pretext of congressionalism and democracy, ignoring the opinion of the absolute majority of the people and scholars of constitution. (Paragraph 1).

The editorial on the next day's issue justified anger of the people raised by impeachment. The title itself was "Anger of the People is Just" (03-14-04, #11, p. 9, Editorial, +1).

A column contributed by Moon Soon Dae charged that the power of the national assembly must be stripped at the general election. See the title "The Sword of the National Assembly Must be Stripped" (03-15-04, #9, p. 12, Column, +1). This was a column that had the forthcoming general election in mind, meaning that people should not vote for the lawmakers who voted for the impeachment.

In a similar vein, an editorial appeared with the title "People's Will Should Be Translated To General Election" (03-15-04, #10, p. 13, Editorial, +1).

A related editorial contended that adding additional reasons for impeachment of Roh was not justifiable with the title "Addition of other counts to impeachment is not just" (03-18-04, #5, p. 13, Editorial, +1)

When candlelight protests became prevalent, editorials praised the candlelight events. See the title "Candlelights Aspire To Ripe Democracy" (03-22-04, #7, p. 13, Editorial, +1)

Another column criticizing the impeachment appeared with the title "Let us impeach lawmakers with votes who impeached Mr. Roh" (04-02-04, #1, p. 12, Column, +1). This column by

Professor Cho Ki Sook demanded that voters should ask candidates whether they were for or against the impeachment.

(4) Other Stories That Favor Roh

The news stories that follow are ones that collectively deliver a message that the impeachment was not just. See what these stories are about.

On the day when this newspaper reported on President Roh's impeachment, a story was printed that predicted Mr. Rohs political future in relation to the ruling of the Constitutional Court. This story said that "most of constitution scholars are opposed to the impeachment and that they predicted that the Court will reject the impeachment resolution (Paragraph 1)." This could signal a positive tone for Mr. Roh.

In a related story, a survey result by Korean Broadcasting System and Yonhap News was printed with the title "An Emergency Poll Says That Seven Out Of Ten Citizens Say That Impeachment Was Wrong" (03-13-04, #10, p. 7, +1). This story said that "seven persons out of ten responded that approval of impeachment was wrong. In particular, the approval ratings of the Woori Party soared to 30% range, which was above the sum of those of the three opposition parties (Paragraph 1)."

This story may merely say about a change, but it is undeniably positive to Mr. Roh.

A related story reported that Mr. Kim Dae Jung, Roh's predecessor, Said that it was "a very serious situation" (03-13-04, #12, p. 7, +1).

Another poll conducted by the newspaper and ANR had the title "68% Of Respondents Demand The Constitutional Court To Refuse The Impeachment" (03-14-04, #2, p. 1, +1). This might be an appeal to the Court that they reject the impeachment.

A story appeared about whether or not it was legal to impeach the president without questioning and debating at the Assembly. This story (03-14-04, #7, p. 5, +2) pointed out that "casting votes on a motion without questioning and debating was illegal." This story also said that the altering of session-opening time by the chairman was wrong. The story additionally contended that lawyers find fault with flaws on the impeachment document. This was favorable to Roh.

News reports in the foreign media were conveyed by this newspaper. This story (03-14-04, #9, p. 8, +1) quoted foreign news media that the latter reported that political infighting in Korea was life-or-death fight, thus attacking the opposition parties. A related story (03-14-04, #10, p. 10, +1) was about reaction by foreigners in Korea that despised the Korean situation.

On the March 16th issue, Ms. Kang Kum Sil, Justice Minister, said that the Assembly must cancel the impeachment. According to the story, Ms. Kang said that "The reason why the people are not worried is that they do not acknowledge the justness of the impeachment despite the suspension of constitutional politics." She said that the desirable thing is that the Assembly cancel the impeachment (03-16-04, #1, p. 1, +1).

A story about a conservative lawyer Lee Jong Wang joining Roh's lawyers' groups added more flavor to Roh's defense lawyer team for the case at the Constitutional Court. The title said that former conservative prosecutor joined the progressive lawyers' group, which was exceptional (03-23-04, #1, p. 6, +1).

Negative Coverage

During this period there was few negative coverage as compared with other periods. As was shown in the Positive Coverage section, a variety of stories seem to have provided favorable coverage to Mr. Roh. See the following limited number of stories that portrayed Mr. Roh negatively.

The first story was perhaps one that conveyed the fact that he was impeached. The story was headlined with big letters "President Roh's Office Is Suspended; The Resolution Was Passed With 193 Yeas and 2 Nays The First Incident in Constitutional History; Prime Minister Ko Kun Plays Acting President; Woori

Party Lawmakers Decided To Resign En Masse" (03-13-04, #1, p. 1, -2). This can never be a positive story to Roh and leaning towards negative tone, and at the least neutral. It was hard to code, but it was evaluated to be a negative one, because the National Assembly impeached President Roh. The impeachment was conducted by the National Assembly, meaning accusation of the president, and thus was coded -2. The story read:

> The impeachment motion of President Roh was passed at the National Assembly and Roh's functions were suspended (Paragraph 1).
>
> The lawmakers cast ballots on the impeachment motion while the Chairman Park Kwan Yong issued an authority of order maintenance; the motion was passed with 193 yeas and 2 nays, a total of 195 lawmakers took part in the vote. It is the first time that an impeachment motion was passed against the incumbent president and his function was suspended in the 56-year-long history of constitutional politics (Paragraph 2).

A related story explaining why this incident came about was carried on the same day's issue with the title "The Impeachment Resolution Was Forcefully Enforced On Account Of Roh's Refusal To Compromise; Chairman Park Took Sides With Opposition Parties" (03-13-04, #14, p. 8, -1). This is a critical story to Mr. Roh. See how the story described the background leading to the impeachment:

> Chairman Park tried draw a political solution by making overtures to the Blue House to have four party meeting after the first impeachment motion came to nought. But it was learned that the refusal by the Blue House led decisively to Park's strong attack on Roh (Pararaph 2).

On the March 25th issue, Park Kun Hye, representative of Hannara Party, said that Mr. Roh must be held accountable for his remarks about 'one tenth of funds.' According to this story (03-25-04, #1, p. 1, -1), Park said that Roh must either rescind his remarks of one tenth funds or take the full responsibility of this remarks. This story was an attack on Roh and was coded -1.

One more negative story about Roh's relatives or family members. This story (04-05-04, #1, p. 4, -1) was about Roh's eldest son and his father-in-law, who share a spacious and expensive apartment house in Yoido, Seoul. This story talked about privilege controversy about getting this apartment.

Neutral Coverage

Coverage during this period was so polarized that there was not much room for neutral stories to occupy. It is assessed that this newspaper largely favored Mr. Roh during this period, while there were neural stories that show the confrontation between pro-Roh and anti-Roh groups.

On the day impeachment stories were carried, there also appeared explanatory and predictive stories. A story (03-13-04, #6, p. 3, 0), which said that Mr. Roh will maintain his status and live in the Blue House as currently until the ruling by the Constitutional Court will be made, was coded 0.

A story about the first plenary session of the Constitutional Court was coded neutral. This story (03-14-04, #3, p. 1, 0) said that the first meeting will be held on 18th of March and Roh's lawyer groups will be formed including Mr. Moon Jae In.

Stories about confrontation between pro-Roh and anti-Roh groups were printed. One story (03-15-04, #3, p. 6, 0) was about face-offs on the websites between the two groups. Another story (03-25-04, #3, p. 7, 0) was about candlelight demonstrations of the two camps, which were to be held at Kwanghwamoon, Seoul.

Period V.
Victory in General Election on April 15, 2004

This section is analysis of the *Kyunghyang Daily News* coverage of President Roh Moo Hyun from the issue of April 16th, 2004 to that of May 14th, 2004. This period was largely composed of coverage of general election to Roh's resumption of his presidential functions.

When election results showed that the Woori Party took a majority of the seats at the National Assembly, President Roh judged that he won the confidence of the people and that the people had trust in him. Stories about election results discussed adverse effects of impeachment resolution and Roh's victory. Although Roh was not expected to talk politics while impeachment was in effect, he met high-ranking Woori party members and talked about future politics and administration, including his second cabinet formation.

Roh's reaction to general election was conveyed in an indirect manner through his aides. His ideas of future politics were floated via his aides too. During this period he considered new cabinet formation. He continued to talk about reforms.

A column criticized Roh's indulgence in election victory. He and his party were full of joy at the election results. The Constitutional Court ruled that the disputed impeachment procedures were lawful, thus rejecting arguments of opposition that the procedures were unlawful. Negative stories about Roh's aides and relatives continued.

Overall, during this period there were fewer stories concerning coverage of the president. The higher proportion of positive coverage of Roh continued into this period.

Positive Coverage

(1) Roh Regaining Confidence and Adverse Effects of Impeachment

On the day election results were known, this newspaper reported that most of opposition party leaders who led impeachment processes were defeated in the election. This story indicated that the impeachment resolution was refused by the people's will, and thus this was committed against the will of the people and was unjustifiable. The story occupied the front page with the title "Kim Jong Pil, Cho Soon Hyung Defeated; Proponents of Impeachment, Lawmakers Hong Sah Dug, Park Sang Chun, and Choo Mi Aie Lost Their Seats" (04-16-04, #1, p. 1, +2). This story said:

In this election, in particular, high-ranking politicians of Hannara Party and Minju Party who led impeachment resolution, mostly failed to keep their seats at the Assembly, thus a judgment whether or not the impeachment was just is assumed to have been made (Paragraph 3)."

A related story on this day's issue reported that the adverse effects created by the impeachment formed a new political configuration in which the party in power became bigger than opposition parties. The story (04-16-04, #2, p. 2, +2) said that "The impeachment of the president became the dividing line between victory or loss of the election. The theory of no need to have a bigger opposition party overwhelmed that of need to restrain the bigger party in power (Paragraph 1)."

A third story on this day's issue was interpretative in nature in saying that this was a 'revolutionary election.' The story said that incumbent lawmakers who got reelected reached only 37% and that a total shift in generation was evident. The title said that "A Revolutionary Election Biggest Changes In Seats; Only 37% Of Incumbents Reelected A Typhoon Created By Impeachment; A Period For Young Politics Is Wide Open; Older Generation Of Three Kims Completely Receded" (04-16-04, #5, p. 9, +2).

On this day's issue, a story about reactions from the citizens appeared with the title "Now Conduct Politics Of Harmony, Transcend Victory Or Loss; Strong Adverse Effects Of

Impeachment Creates Advancement of Minno Party; Nosamo Group Acclaims Victory" (04-17-04, #6, p. 10, +1). This story was about reactions from the citizens or citizen groups, but it played positively for Mr. Roh.

Two stories were printed on the next day's issue. One was a column evaluating the election results. This column with the title "Hannara, Throw Your Towel" (04-17-04, #1, p. 12, +1) said that the election had two issues at stake; impeachment and confidence of the president. The column argued that on these two issues, Hannara Party failed. The column said that "As a result, the people reconfirmed confidence in President Roh and they passed a death sentence on the impeachment resolution (Paragraph 1)."

A related editorial (04-17-04, #2, p. 13, +1) said that now the election victory has gone to the Woori Party, the Constitutional Court must respect the decision of the people which was reflected by the general election. The editorial also said that the politicians can solve this problem among themselves while respecting the ruling of the Court. The editorial can be an appeal to the Court that because the people gave victory to the party in power, the ruling must in favor of Mr. Roh, meaning that their ruling must refuse the impeachment resolution.

(2) Image of Roh as a Conciliator

On the day the newspaper reported election results, a story about Roh's political ideas for 'live and let live' was published. This may belong to coverage of the president with an image of a *national conciliator*, as discussed earlier. According to the story (04-16-04, #3, p. 6, +2), President Roh's politics will be provided with support of a larger party in power and his political ideas for reconciliation will thrive. This story said that after monitoring the exit polls, Mr. Roh reportedly emphasized politics of integration and 'live and let live' (Paragraph 5)."

(3) Roh as a Political Leader Contemplating Future Courses

A story of President Roh as party leader was presented on the April 19th issue of the newspaper. Mr. Roh encouraged Mr. Chung Dong Young, Chairman of the Woori Party, for his devotion in a one on one conversation. This story (04-19-04, #1, p. 3, +1) described Mr. Roh as making daily contacts with figures in political circles and as collecting opinions in preparation of resumption of his office.

A related story appeared the next day. Mr. Roh met Mr. Kim Kun Tai, Representative of the Woori Party, in a one-on-one conversation and discussed reforms. The story (04-20-04, #1, p. 4, +1) said that Mr. Roh might have suggested that Mr. Kim join Roh's cabinet.

A quasi-formal reaction from Mr. Roh was published on the April 21st issue. According to the story (04-21-04, #1, p. 1, +2), Roh regarded the results of the general election as people's confidence in him. This was not a report of Roh's official declaration of his resumption of political activities, but the reporter attached a serious meaning to Roh's remarks. See how the story was written:

> It was confirmed that President Roh said to his close allies that election results reassured people's confidence in him (Paragraph 1).
> Roh expressed his ideas for the first time that if the opposition parties had grasped more than half of the seats at the Assembly he might have resigned from the presidency after giving up the political power (Paragraph 2).

A related interpretative story appeared with the title "Roh Stretching Himself to Start on a Political Path" (04-21-04, #2, p. 4, +2). According th this story, "Mr. Roh *declared* dismantlement of confidence constraint. And Roh thought that he was released from one of two constraints, that is, political (confidence) and legal (pending impeachment in the Constitutional Court) (Paragraph 1)."

Mr. Roh did not issue any declaration. But the beat reporter made an interpretation of the event based on his gathering of remarks who are Roh's close allies.

A follow-up story was printed about Roh's ideas of 'a big frame politics' the next day with the title "Has Roh Completed Contemplation Of Political Path?; Roh Says He Would Play An Influential Party Member, Although He Would Separate Party And Administration; His Ideas About Party Personnel Makeup Soon To Emerge" (04-22-04, #1, p. 4, +1). This story described Roh:

President Roh invited 20 leading lawmakers of the Woori Party for a dinner with them. This can be interpreted that Mr. Roh has embarked on a full-scale political path after his previous assessment that he was released from political constraint. Summarizing his remarks at the dinner, Roh might have completed his deliberations on his future political initiatives (Paragraph 1).

Preparations for Mr. Roh to resume his office may also belong here. The story described Roh's aides preparing for his return. This story (05-11-04, #2, p. 5, +2) said that "although employees of the Blue House are very cautious, they are busy preparing things in case the president resumes work with a view to the ruling of the constitutional court to that effect.

(4) Roh in Charge of Affairs Contemplating Cabinet Reshuffle

A story of Mr. Roh deliberating on a new cabinet formation appeared on the May 3rd issue of the newspaper with the title "Cabinet Shakeup Expected at the End of This Month Affecting 6~8 Ministries; Mr. Chung Dong Young and Kim Kun Tai To Take Posts in the New Cabinet; Mr. Kim Hyuk Kyoo de facto Designated Next Prime Minister; Posts Such As Unification, National Defense, and Local Autonomy Will Change Hands" (05-03-04, #1, p. 1, +2). See how the story reported:

President Roh is scheduled to reformulate his Blue House secretarial office and his cabinet at the end of this month after the Constitutional Court has passed a ruling on his impeachment. Under his new plan, 6~8 cabinet posts will be changed, including Prime Minister's post. It was learned that the successor to Prime Minister Ko Kun will in effect be presidential economic advisor Kim Hyuk Kyoo as a managerial PM (Paragraph 1).

A related analysis appeared on the same day's issue. This analysis provided an explanation about the new cabinet shake-up. This story (05-03-04, #2, p. 3, +2) said that leading politicians will take the cabinet posts, that two future presidential contenders will enter the cabinet, and that secretarial office will be strengthened, etc.
A third story (05-03-04, #3, p. 3, +1) on this day said that the representative of the Woori Party will be determined by Roh's decision.
When Hannara Party opposed Roh's intention to designate Mr. Kim Hyuk Kyoo as prime minister, Mr. Roh reconfirmed his decision to go ahead with Mr. Kim as PM. The title of the story said "Designation of Kim Hyuk Kyoo Unaltered" (05-07-04, #1, p. 1, +2). Mr. Roh showed his strong and unflinching will to designate his favorite person as prime minister.

(5) Roh as a Reformer Again

A few days before President Roh resumed his office, this news paper reported that he will pursue reforms. This story had the title "President Roh Will Pursue High-Intensity Reforms; When He Resume Office, He Will Address The Nation" (05-11-04, #1, p. 1, +2). Reform was a main them when he took office in February of 2003. With the refusal of the impeachment by the constitutional court impending and with his party occupying the majority at the National Assembly, Roh and his aides broached the topic of reform again:

In case where President Roh resumes office through the ruling of the Constitutional Court, he will embark on a second national affairs initiative purported to bring about high-intensity reforms such as recovery of grassroots economy, governmental innovation, eradication of irregularities (Paragraph 1).

President Roh would reportedly deliver an address suggesting high principles concerning national affairs administration with these objective in mind, if the Court rejects the impeachment resolution (Paragraph 2).

Mr. Roh also would make an apology concerning the incident of impeachment and conclude his confidence problem by mentioning results of the general election (Paragraph 3).

This story may be a forewarning of the forthcoming events. President Roh began to discuss reforms again when he resumed office.

Negative Coverage

There appeared few negative stories in this newspaper during this period. But stories cautioning self-conceit of the Woori Party were printed. Check the following stories.

(1) Criticisms against Self-Conceit of Roh and his Party

A column appeared which criticized retrogression of the reform motives professed by the party in power. This column had the title "Party In Power Indulged In Election Victory And Loses Reform Motives" (04-26-04, #1, p. 13, -2). The story read:

> Some media report that President Roh, who professed to remain an ordinary party member even after his entry into the Woori Party, has already designated a certain lawmaker as de facto chairman of the National Assembly. If the President designates the head of the National Assembly,

how is it related to reforms that they so frequently mentioned? If we look into reports originating from the party in power, the flamboyant terms of reform uttered by the Woori Party manifest how flimsy a foundation they are based on (Paragraph 2).

A very interesting story was printed about Roh's genius in his childhood. A story (05-08-04, #2, p. 7, -1) datelined Kim Hae City said that this city had distributed about 5,000 books on Roh's childhood genius and his growth. According to the story, Kim Hae City is causing a controversy by publishing tourism guidebooks, which described President Roh's birthplace as a mystery and extolled his growth processes. This story said that 2,000 books were already distributed among elementary, middle, and high school students.

A third story was about whether the impeachment processes were legal. One judge at the Constitutional Court said that the legal procedures were not flawed, meaning that arguments by the Woori Party and the Blue House about the flawed impeachment procedures were not accepted. This story (05-14-04, #1, p. 1, -1) was a minus for them.

A related interpretative story said that the next day's ruling will be either firing the president or rejection of the impeachment. This story (05-14-04, #2, p. 3, -1) presupposed that the impeachment procedures were legal. Now what remained to be seen was whether the Constitutional Court will accept the impeachment resolution or reject it. This story appeared on the May 15th issue of the newspaper.

(2) Persistent Irregularities of Roh's Aides and Relatives

Negative stories about Roh's aides and relatives persisted even during this period. One story (04-29-04, #2, p. 6, -1) was about Mr. Song In Bae, Roh's former Blue House secretary, who received illegal political funds and was defeated in the general election.

The other story was about Mr. Roh Kun Pyong, President

Roh's older brother. This story (05-08-04, #1, p. 6, -1) said that the court will formally deliberate on Roh's brother's case next mont. This story had a negative tone.

Neutral Coverage

A story just one day before the ruling of the Constitutional Court described pro- and anti-Roh groups on an equal basis, thus coded 0. See how the title was displayed "Constitutional Court On Full Alert Marking The Day of Judgment; Nosamo Groups Preparing A Welcoming Ceremony For President Roh; Conservative Groups Convinced Of Acceptance Of The Impeachment" (05-14-04, #4, p. 7, 0).

Period VI. Roh's Resumption of Presidential Office

This section is analysis of the *Kyunghyang Daily News* coverage of President Roh Moo Hyun from the issue of May 15th, 2004 to that of May 29th, 2004. This period was largely composed of coverage of resumption of presidential office after the ruling of the Constitutional Court.

President Roh Moo Hyun resumed his functions when the Constitutional Court ruled that "the case failed to get approval from enough number of judges to substantiate the impeachment." But the ruling warned that Roh should be more cautious in uttering his words. With this ruling Mr. Roh resumed his presidential office and began his functions as President. In this period President Roh discussed reforms, national conciliation, policies, and suggested ideas of cabinet shakeup for the second time in his term. With majority of lawmakers at the Assembly backing him and his functions fully reinstated, a story said the real term of his office started.

A story said that although the ruling of the Constitutional

Court reinstated Roh's functions, it gave a sting on his careless mouth. His words were not cautious enough. Roh's handling of outgoing Prime Minister Ko Kun was also criticized. Roh's new media policy of restraining pool reporters from covering president's meeting with aides and assistants was faulted.

Positive Coverage

(1) Constitutional Court Upholds Roh's Presidency and Celebration

The first story about President Roh's resumption of office was printed on the May 15th issue as the top news. The story had the title "Impeachment Rejected President Roh Will Return To His Office; The Constitutional Court Pronounces That Roh Violated Part Of The Election Law But It Does Not Constitute Serious Reasons For Relieving Him Of His Office; Three Judges Reportedly Raised Minority Opinions But Not Made Public" (05-15-04, #1, p. 1, +2). This quite lengthy headline shows what the story is all about. See the story:

> The impeachment of the president, which is the first in Korean constitutional history, finally ended in the rejection of impeachment in 63 days (Paragraph 1).
> The Constitutional Court pronounced that this request of judgment failed to get the required number of judges to substantiate the impeachment and that the Court rejects it (Paragraph 2).
> President resumed his office with this ruling, which was suspended with the impeachment resolution at the National Assembly. This ruling made the politicians of Hannara and Minju Party susceptible to criticisms that they forced the impeachment in an irrational manner (Paragraph 3).

A related story (05-15-04, #2, p. 1, +1) was about apologetic comments from Ms. Park Kun Hye, representative of the Hannara Party. She apologized that the politicians caused trouble to the people at a press conference.

A related analysis said that the Court issued a yellow card to Roh, but a red card to opposition parties. This analysis (05-15-04, #4, p. 3, +1) said that the ruling was a very sophisticated eclectic solution to the impeachment resolution. The story said in part:

> The final conclusion by the Constitutional Court's ruling is summarized that although the President violated parts of the election law, this does not constitute serious reasons to impeach the president. The Court's ruling is evaluated to be meaningful in that it permitted the president to return to office but that it sent a powerful message (Paragraph 1).

A related story (05-15-04, #7, p. 4, +1) said that the ruling reflected the will of the people at the general election and that the impeachment procedures were just. This means that because the people elected the majority of politicians at the general election, the people wanted Mr. Roh to be reinstated, and that the Court made the ruling to that effect.

A story (05-15-04, #11, p. 6, +1) said that foreign heads of state had sent congratulatory messages to Mr. Roh and that foreign media filed dispatches from Seoul about the Roh's news.

Two stories conveyed reactions from the citizens. One story (05-15-04, #13, p. 8, +1) said that citizens received this ruling as an anticipated result and appealed to the politicians that they should now address people's lives discarding their political infighting.

The other story (05-15-04, #14, p. 8, +2) was from Kim Hae, Roh's home town, This story conveyed the celebratory mood of the town, where townspeople shouted out of joy.

The editorial (05-15-04, #15, p. 15, +1) of this day's issue said that the rejection of the impeachment was never surprising news. It said that the ruling of the Constitutional Court is merely legal reconfirmation of a fact that relieving the President was mistaken, which everybody with rational thinking would expect so. But this editorial ignored that perhaps three judges might have favored the impeachment resolution. Those three may be lacking in rational thinking?

(2) Roh's Personal and Intimate Qualities

Two personal descriptions appeared on the day of resumption of office. One story titled "Mr. Roh Said, Thank You For Your Lots Of Trouble; Mr. Ko Replied That You Should Let Me Leave Now; Mr. Roh Had Dinner With Mr. Ko" (05-15-04, #9, p. 5, +1) was about the conversation between Mr. Roh and Mr. Ko Kun, interim acting President. Read the story:

Mr. Roh had dinner with Mr. Ko Kun, on the first day of his reinstatement. The dinner lasted for one hour and thirty minutes over wine in a warm spirit (Paragraph 1).

Mr. Ko consoled Mr. Roh 'What a heartache you had! You must have felt suffocated.' Mr. Roh replied 'You experienced lots of trouble. You must have born too heavy a burden. I feel grateful for your excellent performance of administration (Paragraph 2).'

A related story followed. The story said that employees of the Secretarial Office at the Blue House gave a welcoming ceremony to Mr. Roh. The title of the story was "Employees Of The Secretarial Office Had Returning Ceremony For Roh With Claps Of Hands" (05-15-04, #10, p. 5, +2). Check the story:

Employees gave a welcoming ceremony with applause when Mr. Roh arrived at the Main Building of the Blue House (Paragraph 1).

President Roh said during the lunch, 'You had endured a lot of trouble and thanked them. With this self-abstinence, we could achieve more.' The employees presented Roh with a fountain pen to the effect that he would have to work a lot (Paragraph 2).

(3) Roh as a Reformer and Policymaker

A story said that Mr. Roh now begins his real term of office. This story had the title "Roh's New Term In Real Sense Of The Word Begins Silent Reform Pursued" (05-15-04, #8, p. 5, +1) predicted that Roh will pursue 'silent reform', 'powerful hands-on administration' and 'systematic government.' The story said:

> President Roh has entered into his second phase of the term with the ruling of the Constitutional Court. Some officials at the Blue House even say that his real term has begun (Paragraph 2).
> Mr. Yun Tai Young, presidential spokesman, declared that the spirit at the inauguration must be realized. Roh's second phase of the term can be summarized in the concepts such as 'silent reform,' 'powerful hands-on administration' and 'systematic government (Paragraph 2).'

A follow-up story appeared that described Roh as driving economic reform in his second phase of the term. This story (05-17-04, #1, p. 1, +1) said that Roh will pursue the second phase of reform in the areas of grassroots economy and innovation of national government with high intensity.

A related interpretative story (05-17-04, #2, p. 3, +1) said that Roh will not give up economic reforms. Roh also said that he will not use short-term stimulation policy.

A story (05-17-04, #4, p. 5, +1) about reformation of the aides system could belong here. Roh got rid of political affairs assistant and participatory innovation assistant and set up new assistant posts.

The following titles show that they fall under stories of president as the reformer and policymaker:

"Roh Presided Over Economic Examination Meeting; He Talks About Stock Prices Meeting Will Be Held Monthly" (05-18-04, #1, p. 2, +1);

"Roh's Economic Keywords Are Principle and Reforms; Roh

Is Confident That He Will Overcome Crisis Progressive Policies Toward Conglomerates Looming" (05-18-04, #2, p. 5, +1);

"President Roh Instructs Meeting Of Security Ministers To Construct Cooperative Autonomous National Defense" (05-21-04, #1, p. 1, +2);

"Rohs Says That Reforms Will Continue Limits On Investment Total: He Will Relax Restraints Of Enterprise Radically: He Converses With Heads Of Businesses" (05-26-04, #1, p. 1, +1); and

"Roh Says That He Would Pursue Economic Growth And Reform Simultaneously; He Also Argues That Theory Of Economic Crisis Distorts The Substance Of The Matter" (05-26-04, #3, p. 3, +1).

A story (05-26-04, #4, p. 3, +1) about Roh appealing to business leaders may also belong here. Roh said to business leaders that the economy has come out of a long tunnel and that we have to start again.

(4) Image of National Conciliator: "Live and Let Live"

President Roh attended the ceremony commemorating the uprising of the May 18th and appealed that we open a new age of harmony and "live-and-let-live." This story (05-19-04, #1, p. 1, +1) described Mr. Roh as a national conciliator.

A related story (05-19-04, #2, p. 5, +1) also said that Mr. Roh and other politicians gathered together to mark the May 18th. Roh said at the ceremony that "To overcome divisions is the most important task left to us."

(5) Roh in Charge of Affairs Contemplating Cabinet Reshuffle

Stories about Roh's consideration of cabinet reshuffle may belong here. A story said that Mr. Roh was considering a two-phase cabinet reshuffle. The title of the story shows itself: "President Roh Considering Two-Phase Cabinet Reshuffle; Posts of Three Ministries Will Be Changed This Week Additional Reshuffle After Confirmation Of A New Prime

Minister" (05-24-04, #1, p. 1, +1).

A related story (05-24-04, #2, p. 5, +1) was interpretative in nature. This story said that because Prime Minister Ko Kun refused to recommend ministers, the cabinet reshuffle will take place in two steps.

Mr. Roh insisted that Mr. Kim Hyuk Kyoo become new Prime Minister. A story (05-26-04, #2, p. 2, +1) said that despite objections from the opposing parties, Roh clang to Mr. Kim as Prime Minister. This story was written quoting political sources.

The next day, presidential spokesman Lee Byung Wan said that Mr. Kim Hyuk Kyoo is the strongest candidate for Prime Minister's post. The story was titled "Mr. Kim Hyuk Kyoo Will Be Officially Designated As Prime Minister" (05-27-04, #1, p. 1, +1).

[A related story (05-27-04, #2, p. 4, -1) was about controversies concerning Mr. Kim as candidate for Prime Minister. Hannara Pary said that Mr. Kim will not pass the confirmation process, while arguments over Kim expanded.]

(6) Other Stories That Favor President Roh

Mr. Roh entered the Woori Party. The story said that his entrance into the party rebuilt the party-administration channel. This story (05-21-04, #3, p. 3, +1) predicted that Roh's second phase administration will seriously start.

A related editorial (05-21-04, #5, p. 13, +2) argued that Roh's entrance into the party should have happened earlier. The editorial said that Mr. Roh left the Minju Party eight months ago while a new party was being formed, but it was unavoidable. This editorial argued that if the President does not belong to a political party, it is against the principle of responsible politics. Since the political situation came back to normal, the return of the President to the political party is absolutely natural.

Negative Coverage

(1) Roh's Careless Words and his Narrow-Mindedness

The newspaper ran a story about Mr. Roh's careless words on the day the Constitutional Court delivered the ruling. The story sounded like a warning and was titled "A Sting On Roh's Careless Mouth" (05-15-04, #6, p. 3, -2). The story said:

> If the President does not respect and observe laws, he cannot demand the people and other officials to observe laws (Paragraph 1).
> The Constitutional Court criticized Roh's careless words before the final ruling. The Court took issue with Roh's remarks on four occasions count by count and criticized that he violated the articles prescribing obligations of neutrality in elections and observance of the constitution (Paragraph 2).

An interesting coincidence was discovered here. Out of a slew of stories covering Roh's reinstatement, only one story was negative. The same holds true for coverage of Bush's inauguration and that of Roh's. This kind of consideration in laying out stories may arise from journalistic sense of balance. 100% positive stories may not attract readers' attention.

Ms. Park Keun Hye, Representative of the Hannara Party, attacked President Roh citing that he intentionally turns away from economic crisis under the pretext of reform. According to the story (05-18-04, #3, p. 5, -1), she urged that Roh perceive the economy correctly.

A column criticized Roh for inviting only his political allies. The column titled "American Forces in Korea and the Blue House" (05-24-04, #3, p. 11, -1) said that lawmakers of the Woori Pary cannot easily oppose Roh's policy lines, and so he needs to discuss affairs with conservative and progressive politicians (Paragraph 9).

(2) Roh's Ill Treatment of Ko Kun and Insistence on Kim Hyuk Kyoo

Roh's insistence on Mr. Kim Hyuk Kyoo as candidate for Prime Minister's job caused a series of controversies. Roh also created trouble by forcefully urging outgoing Prime Minister Ko Kun to recommend cabinet members.

A story about Ko's resignation showed what a trouble Roh's administration had. The story was titled "Prime Minister Ko Kun Tendered Resignation; Roh's Hope Of Early Cabinet Reshuffle Shattered" (05-25-04, #1, p. 1, -2). Examine the story:

> Prime Minister Ko Kun officially refused President Roh's request to recommend three cabinet members for Roh's reshuffle. PM Ko tendered his resignation via presidential chief of staff, presidential spokesman Yun Tai Young said (Paragraph 1).
>
> Accordingly, Roh's intention to implement an early cabinet reshuffle was shattered and Roh's cabinet reformulation will be postponed to the end of this month (Paragraph 2).

A related background story about Ko's resignation appeared with the title "Ko Does Not Like To Be A Rubberstamp; He Refused And Left The Administration" (05-25-04, #3, p. 3, -2). This story said that although Mr. Ko usually respects common sense, it was an unexpected behavior.

A related story (05-25-04, #4, p. 3, -1) originating from the Blue House was about the bafflement. Presidential aides became troubled by Ko's refusal and talk of violation of the spirit of the constitution: Outgoing prime minister cannot recommend cabinet members.

A Story sharing similar vein was "Cabinet Reshuffle Not Going Smoothly (05-25-04, #5, p. 3, -1).

A column criticized Roh's behavior. This column (05-26-04, #5, p. 5, -2) written by the beat reporter said that Roh's intention to pursue stable policies with both the administration and the party in concert with each other floundered at the inception. The column criticized that "Roh's reform drive met with a red light and affairs of several ministries became paralyzed."

A final touch on Roh's blunder on cabinet reshuffle was the story about Ko's bitter parting ceremony. The editorial titled "Prime Minister Ko's Bitter Departure And Cabinet Reshuffle" (05-26-04, #6, p. 13, -2) said that "Ko's bitter departure leaves bad aftertastes. It is really regrettable that Roh's second phase of the term started with squeaky sounds."

A follow-up story (05-27-04, #2, p. 4, -1) was about controversies concerning Mr. Kim as candidate for Prime Minister. Hannara Pary said that Mr. Kim will not pass the confirmation process, while arguments over Kim expanded.

(3) Roh's Restriction on Media Access Faulted

A story said that using pool reporters at the Blue House was stopped, causing difficulties in filing stories with the title "Blue House Prevents Pool Reporters From Covering Events And Causes Trouble" (05-18-04, #4, p. 5, -1). See how the story criticized the Blue House:

> The Blue House in its second phase of Roh's term restrains beat reporters' coverage, causing conflicts with the press corps. The Blue House did not permit coverage of the meeting of aides and assistants presided by the President, which was in fact the first event after Roh resumed office. Until now this meeting has been customarily covered by two or three pool reporters for about ten minutes just before the meeting was held and reporters talked to aides and assistants (Paragraph 1)

Neutral Coverage

A story (05-15-04, #3, p. 2, 0) of description on the scene at the Constitutional Court was coded 0, because the story said that it took just 25 minutes in reading the ruling, etc.

The speculative story about the ratio of judges who approved or disapproved of the impeachment resolution, that is, 6:3 or 5:3:1 was also coded 0.

An editorial (05-15-04, #16, p. 15, 0) was coded 0, because it made an appeal that Roh devote himself to economy.

Quantitative Analysis: How Much Favorable Was the Newspaper Coverage to Roh?

The number of total stories for each period and their break-down of coding based on the qualitative analysis is shown in the following table. The table below also shows the trend of coverage of the newspaper.

Table 4:

Tone of Kyunghyang's Coverage of Roh Moo Hyun

Period Tone	Inaugural n= 125	Confidence n=130	PreImpeach n=58	Impeached n=97	Election n=28	Resumption n=56
Very Positive	37.6%	6.2%	6.9%	17.5%	28.6%	10.7%
Positive	30.4	30.0	24.1	53.9	39.3	55.4
Neutral	11.2	12.3	20.7	20.6	10.7	5.4
Negative	13.6	42.3	32.8	7.3	17.9	16.1
Very Positive	7.2	9.2	15.5	1.0	3.5	12.4

$$X^2 = (20, N=494) =$$

Note:

1. Period I (Inauguration and One Month): Data were collected from February 26 to March 25 in 2003.
2. Period II (Proposal of Confidence Vote and One Month): Data were collected from October 11 to November 10 in 2003.
3. Period III (Pre-Impeachment and A Half Month): Data were collected from February 28 to March 12 in 2004.
4. Period IV (Impeachment Resolution and One Month): Data were collected from March 13 to April 15 in 2004. Roh was impeached on March 12.
5. Period V (General Election and One Month): Data were collected from April 16 to May 14 in 2004. General election was held on April 15.
6. Period VI (Resumption of Office and A Half Month): Data were collected from May 15 to May 29 in 2004. Impeachment resolution of President Roh was rejected by the Constitutional Court on May 14, and Roh resumed his office on that day.

As the above table shows, positive (very positive+positive) coverage of President Roh during Period I reached 68.0%. It can be said that Roh enjoyed "honeymoon" with this newspaper. That plummeted to a whopping 36.2% in eight months. The low number reflects that Roh's proposal of confidence vote met with strong objection. The low rate of positive coverage continued until just before the impeachment resolution by the National Assembly. During the pre-impeachment period, the figure remained low at 31.0% of positive coverage. However, the impeachment resolution passed by the coalition of opposition parties turned everything upside down. The rate of positive coverage suddenly soared up to 71.4%. This level of positive coverage lasted until the general election period at 67.9%, reflecting that the aftershocks of impeachment resolution persisted. When Mr. Roh recovered his functions, the level of positive coverage returned to the inaugural period, that is, upper 60s in percentage.

In terms of negative coverage, Mr. Roh started with reletively low level of negative (very negative+negative) coverage at 20.8%. That, however, skyrocketed to 51.5% during period II, when he proposed confidence vote. There were many stories that attacked his proposal of confidence vote. This high level of negative coverage almost lasted until pre-impeachment period, at 48.3%. But when he was impeached, negative stories almost disappeared, down at 8.3%. Bur after general election, negative coverage mounted again to 20.4%. When Mr. Roh resumed his office, the rate of negative coverage again rose to 28.5%. The vicissitudes of positive and negative tone also shows Roh's fortune at politics.

Triangulation: Comprehensive Interpretation of Roh Coverage

Period I. Roh's Inauguration

During the period of President Roh Moo Hyun's inauguration and one month, it is evaluated that he enjoyed one-month honeymoon with this newspaper. The rate of positive coverage (very positive+positive) reached 68.0% (37.6%+30.4%). The rate of negative coverage (very negative+negative) amounted to 20.8% (7.2%+13.6%). As compared with coverage of inauguration period of President Bush by the *New York Times* (positive 62.5%, negative 20.0% respectively), Mr. Roh enjoyed honeymoon with this Korean newspaper for one month.

The areas of positive coverage comprised 10 story groupings as discussed in the qualitative analysis; those of negative coverage consisted of four story groupings, as discussed earlier.

During this period, this newspaper described Mr. Roh holding a low-key inauguration, considering that the country had a tragedy just before the inauguration (?). In one week and in one month his performance as president received mixed evaluations: good and bad. Mr. Roh was largely welcomed as reformer, a new-style leader, and a national conciliator after a bitter and close election result. The country was so divided and unpredictable during the election campaign. He was also described as a policymaker, but this story said that Mr. Roh directed his cabinet to conceive of policy objectives.

This made a contrast with Bush story about his directions to implement his policy plans! Examine stories about Bush's image as policymaker in Period I of Bush's inauguration.

Mr. Roh was also depicted as a decisive leader in making cabinet appointments. He proceeded with his own candidates for ministers despite some opposition from ministries and civic groups. He showed his image as an international leader by having a phone conversation with Mr. Bush. As was the case with

Mr. Bush, this newspaper too ran personal stories about Roh. Mr. Roh was portrayed as confiding his feelings frankly about his debate with prosecutors to an opposition leader. This newspaper focused on Mr. Roh as a new-style leader, open-minded and anti-authoritarian. These terms in the stories seemed to have been used objectively, but the connotation was positive tone, and that very positive.

Roh's image as a hard-worker seemed a bit odd. Stories said that Mr. Roh handled 10 events or 16 events and described him as a very busy person. These stories never sounded as criticizing Roh. The tone was positive. Just one story was allocated to the First Lady Mrs. Kwon Yang Sook, which was about her role as person to care about relatives. Even his attitude to news media was positively depicted. He said that he would not meddle in press affairs. But this did not last long. He gradually turned into a president grumbling about media reports.

In negative stories, this newspaper ran reports about criticisms from opposition parties and resistance to his reforms. One negative story was printed on his inauguration, which was about the disorderliness of the celebration. When Roh's first cabinet formation was announced, opposition parties criticized that it was an "experimental" cabinet. Stories of opposition and resistance from within the government ministries also were negative to Roh. Stories about conflicts or irregularities among his aides and those of Roh's relatives and family members damaged Roh's image as president. These stories continued to pester Roh during his six periods for this research. One stinging column that marked one month of Roh's presidency said that Roh's cabinet formation was a "failure of amateurism."

Period II. Confidence Vote?

The decline of positive stories and the increase of negative stories were both remarkable during this period. The rate of positive coverage (very positive+positive) sank to 36.2%

(6.2%+30.0%). And the rate of negative coverage (very nega-tive+negative) soared to a whopping 51.5% (9.2%+42.3%), the highest point out of the six research periods. The rate of nega-tive coverage was a lot higher than that of positive coverage: a difference of 15.3% point. This was a period of hardship for Mr. Roh. He floated the idea of confidence vote to ask the will of the people whether they still trusted him as president despite repeated news reports of his aides' irregularities. This newspa-per criticized Roh citing that the Korean constitution does not have the relevant provision. This period was selected for analy-sis because Roh's proposal of confidence vote marked an important event.

In this period, Roh's abrupt proposal of confidence vote start-ed a series of stories. Stories of his proposal and his following intentions were coded +2 or +1. Roh insisted on his confidence vote but at last came to a compromise: that is, the confidence vote did not materialize.

Mr. Roh was also described as a policymaker and an interna-tional player. He made a decision to send Korean troops to Iraq and he was praised by President Bush "as Bush's best friend" during the APEC summit. Roh's visit to Kwangju was warmly described.

Mr. Roh, who had maintained creaky relations with the media, offered a peace initiative to media people to mend fences. Although he professed his open media policy after his inaugura-tion (03-05-03, p. 1), his relations with the media were largely rough.

During this period, this newspaper's attack on Roh's proposal of confidence vote was relentless. A series of straight stories, analyses, columns, and editorials were printed to attack the idea of confidence vote. Poll results were cited to report that most people did not regard confidence vote as a good idea. An editor-ial said that in the midst of the confidence vote, national politics may drift.

As in the Period I, conflicts within the Blue House continued to be reported. In addition, stories of investigation of presiden-tial aides and relatives continued to appear. Investigation of presidential election funds also continued. These stories were all considered negative to Mr. Roh. President Roh also met with criticism about his prevarication in decisionmaking on sending Korean troops to Iraq. He did not declare in a manifest manner that he would send Korean troops to Iraq.

On the whole, Period II was a situation created by Mr. Roh. This differed from September 11 attacks in that he initiated the situation. However, Roh's power to define the situation was not strong enough to quel the criticisms. He was considered a person who does not respect the constitution.

Period III. Pre-Impeachment

This was a period of heated wrangling about whether to impeach the president. The duration of a half month may sound arbitrary, but this was to see how the tone of coverage changed over the development of the presidential impeachment. This was a period leading to the sudden impeachment of Mr. Roh.

During this period, the rate of positive coverage (very positive + positive) reached 31.0% (6.9% + 24.1%), the lowest point out of the six research periods. This figure reflects that Mr. Roh was attacked by opposition parties about his violation of neutrality obligation in election. The rate of negative coverage (very negative + negative) stayed 48.3% (15.5% + 32.8%), still very high and higher than that of positive coverage: a difference of 17.3% point. The reason for this seems that Mr. Roh invited criticisms by his violation of neutrality obligation.

The image of Mr. Roh during this period was a strong-willed person who confronted the impeachment proposals, although the portrayal of him sometimes leaned towards a somewhat opinionated and uncompromising person. When the Central Election Monitoring Commission ruled that Mr. Roh violated the "neutrality obligation," Roh and his aides stood steadfast against the ruling. This incited opposition politicians to broach the idea of presidential impeachment. Mr. Roh and his aides refused to consider apologetic remarks demanded by opposition parties. Civic groups sided with the Blue House and Mr. Roh did not intend to concede. When Roh finally refused to apologize for the "neutrality violation," the National Assembly dominated by opposition parties went ahead with the impeachment procedures.

Even during this period, Mr. Roh warned Japanese Prime Minister Koizumi Junichiro not to visit the Yasukuni Shrine, citing that this could hurt Korean people (03-02-04, p. 1). In his address to the nation just before the impeachment, in which he never uttered apologetic remarks, he said he took punitive measures to a bribing businessman.

Negative stories occupied almost a half of the whole coverage. Large-scale impeachment offensives were launched by opposition parties. Opposition parties criticized that President Roh's election-related remarks amounted to interference in the election processes. Additionally, the ruling of the Central Election Monitoring Commission poured oil into the fire: the ruling said that Roh violated neutrality obligation. An editorial demanded that Roh accept the ruling of the Commission and stop political haggling. Opposition lawmakers seriously warned that Roh should not interfere in general election and demanded that Roh apologize, but to no avail. Stories of Roh's final refusal to apologize instantly started the impeachment procedures. Opposition made the motion and was about to pass the motion. The stories involving this development were all assessed to be negative to Roh.

In the meantime, stories about irregularities of Roh's aides continued to appear. Stories of investigation of Roh's election funds also persisted. An editorial said that "irregularities of Roh's aides see no ends." A very controversial story about Roh's remarks on "one tenth of election funds" was published. The Prosecution Office announced that Roh's election funds exceeded one tenth of the funds used by opposition presidential contender. Roh's defense of his family member and aides in his last address before the impeachment invited criticism.

Period IV. Roh Impeached!

The figures in quantitative analysis of Period IV show that the ratios were very striking. The rate of positive coverage (very positive + positive) abruptly skyrocketed up to 71.4% (17.5% + 53.9%), the highest out of the six research periods. That of the Period III was only 31.0%. The rate of negative coverage (very negative + negative) suddenly declined to 8.3% (1.0% + 7.3%), the lowest out of the whole six research periods. That of Period III was 48.3%. What a sudden change in tone! In terms of statistical figures and significance of the presidential impeachment, this period was very special.

A variety of stories appeared which could support President Roh in direct and indirect manner. On the one hand, a spate of stories describing citizens' massive candlelight protests against the impeachment could surely be interpreted to be positive to Roh. Stories that worried about "forthcoming" confusion in policy and "shocks" originating from the impeachment may belong here. Read a series of stories that justified and supported anti-impeachment protests staged by the people. Even a story about "putting out candlelights" (meaning stopping the candlelight protests) was featured as a new chapter in peaceful demonstration.

On the other hand, portrayals of intimate and personal qualities of Mr. Roh appeared. There appeared a series of stories that described Mr. Roh, who was politically out of function: Roh reading biography of former British Prime Minister Margaret Thatcher, Roh discussing a martyr for his political reforms, Roh agonizing over results of general election and his confidence problem, and Roh expressing hopes of getting rid of corruption and provincial politics while on a mountain hiking, etc.. These stories were direct descriptions of Roh in a positive light.

During this period, a slew of columns and editorials appeared in support of Roh. One editorial said that the impeachment was a shocking incident and it was oppression by the political majority. One contributing columnist said that "it was coup d'etat under the name of congressionalism." Another editorial said that anger of the people is just. An ensuing editorial said that people's will must be translated to the general election. An editorial glorified that candlelights aspire to ripe democracy. One contributing columnist finally urged, "Let's impeach the lawmakers who impeached the president."

There were other stories that affected Roh in a favorable light. An emergency poll result was reported, which was conducted by pro-Roh news media: "Seven out of ten citizens responded that the impeachment was wrong." A poll conducted by this newspaper said that citizens demand that the Constitutional Court reject the impeachment resolution. A story said that most of the constitution scholars are opposed to the impeachment.

In contrast to mountains of positive stories, there were few negative stories. There was a story that reported that Roh was impeached by the National Assembly. This may belong to the category of negative tone. An explanatory story said that this incident came about by Roh's intransigence. A negative story about Roh's relatives was also printed.

Content analysis of this period produced by Korea Journalism Society said that reports by the three airwave broadcasting companies were very prejudicial in favor of Roh. The analysis was reported by the *Chosun Ilbo* (June 11, 2004, p.1+p.3) and other newspapers. This was later refuted by broadcasters, e.g., by the Korean Broadcasting System. The nature of broadcast reports during this period created such a controversy. The present author thinks that impeachment was implemented pursuant to the prescribed provisions of the constitution and law, that the impeachment was never a shock, and that the function of the Korean constitution never was suspended. The writers of the constitution made astute preparations for the presidential impeachment, either in Korea or in the United States. The present author thinks that deliberation of the impeachment motion should have happened had it not been for physical blocking by the Woori Party members. They should not have tried to block the procedures. They should not have thrown shoes to the chairman of the Assembly. Woori Party members should have participated in the voting for or against the impeachment. Korean National Assembly could not have the deliberation procedures because of the physical blocking by the Woori Party members. The present writer also thinks that the reason why impeachment resolution was passed was that the configuration of the National Assembly reflected power structure of the previous period. The term of office for lawmakers and that for the president do not coincide. Additionally, President Roh made frequent lapses of words and his intransigence made for his impeachment.

Period V. Victory in General Election

This period may be an extension of Period IV, seeing that the impeachment was still valid. But since Woori Party members occupied the majority of the Assembly, this clearly marked a turning point in Korean domestic politics. The Woori Party backed by President Roh won the general election, and Roh judged this to mean that he won the confidence vote. The rate of positive coverage (very positive + positive) stayed high at 67.9% (28.6% + 39.3%). The rate of negative coverage (very negative + negative) reached 20.4% (3.5% + 17.9%). But the number of stories pertaining to presidential coverage decreased to just 28, even though the duration of Period V lasted almost one month. The number of stories was 125 (Period I, one month), 130 (Period II, one month), 58 (Period III, a half month), 97 (Period IV, one month), and 56 (Period VI, a half month).

The spillover effect of the impeachment resolution and the victory in general election for the Woori Party may have combined to influence the tone of coverage during this period. Impeachment resolution was still in effect. While conveying the election results, this newspaper said that major proponents of impeachment lost their seats. A related story said that the impeachment resolution became the dividing line between victory or loss in the election. The tone of this newspaper, in general, was that the impeachment resolution was unjust and proponents of impeachment lost in the election. One column contended that the loss of Hannara Party means that impeachment was wrong. An editorial went further, urging that the Constitutional Court should respect the will of the people as represented by the election results.

Relieved by favorable election results, one story said that Mr. Roh will pursue politics of mutual prosperity based on his new power base at the National Assembly. Roh deliberated on future political courses while meeting with party cadres of Woori Party. Roh thought that he was freed from political constraint by election results. He contemplated new cabinet formation in case he is freed from the impeachment. Roh broached topics of reform again in view of his resumption of office with the ruling of the Constitutional Court.

As negative coverage, one column said that the new party in power lost momentum in reforms and the party members already are indulged in self-conceit. Negative stories of Roh's relatives and aides appeared in this period too.

Period VI. Resumption of Presidential Office

The duration of a half month may appear a bit arbitrary, but the selection of this period was to see if the ruling of the Constitutional Court caused any change in coverage of Roh's presidency. The figures seem to represent that things came back to normal. The rate of positive coverage (very positive + positive) stood at 66.1% (10.7% + 55.4%). The rate of negative coverage (very negative + negative) was 28.5% (12.4% + 16.1%).

Just as the story of impeachment resolution conducted by the National Assembly was assessed a negative story, the story of the ruling passed by the Constitutional Court was assessed a positive story to Mr. Roh. This story said that "the case failed to get the sufficient number of judges to validate the impeachment resolution." An interpretative story said that the ruling reflected the will of the people as shown by the general election. Another story said that citizens anticipated this result. An editorial said that this was never surprising.

Intimate stories appeared. Acting President Ko Keun during the impeachment period had dinner with reinstated President Roh Moo Hyun. Blue House employees gave a welcoming ceremony to Roh.

Roh entered into a real presidential term with new power configuration at the National Assembly. He began to talk about reforms, this time a "silent reform" in the economic area. He met with heads of businesses. Relieved from the impeachment, he expressed his hopes of mutual prosperity in politics. Roh began to consider a cabinet reshuffle as a reinstated president. When Roh entered the Woori Party, which he backed in a declared manner but not yet entered, an editorial said that Roh should have done so earlier. What a fawning story!

The ruling of the Constitutional Court criticized Roh in part that he did not observe the laws. This story was titled "A Sting on Roh's Careless Mouth." How symbolic! Roh met with opposition in trying persistently to designate Mr. Kim Hyuk Kyoo as Prime Minister. Roh was also attacked for his handling of Ko Kun and cabinet reshuffle. Roh demanded the outgoing Prime Minister Ko Kun to recommend candidates for ministry posts and Ko tendered his resignation in defiance. A column criticized Roh's manner of handling of affairs. An editorial said that Ko had a bitter departure. Roh's new media policy of restricting access to aides' meeting to beat reporters generated criticisms.

Research Questions Revisited

One needs to return to the four research questions raised at the end of Chapter II at this point. First, did Roh enjoy honeymoon for one month with this newspaper? As the figures in Table 3 shows, the ratio of positive tone (+2 and +1) reached 68.0%; This is a bit higher than that enjoyed by Bush with the *New York*

Times (62.5%). The ratio of negative tone (-2 and -1) for Roh amounted to 20.8% and that of Bush was 20.0%. The levels of negative coverage were almost the same. Consider that Roh's hard-driving reform incurred resistance within the government and opposition parties.

Second, about the ratio of positive and negative coverage? The total number of stories which can affect Roh's image amounted to 494 out of 126 days' issues of the newspaper. The calculation of the author found that very positive stories reached 90 (18.2%), positive 185(37.4%), neutral 68 (13.8%), negative 112(22.7%), and very negative 39(7.9%). The overall ratio of positive stories per one negative story (275 to 151) reached 1.82 stories. In summary, this newspaper ran 1.82 positive stories per one negative story for President Roh. In comparison, Bush enjoyed 2.64 positive stories per one negative story (359 out of 575 stories). The reason Roh had low rate of positive coverage may result from critical stories of him when he proposed confidence vote and attacks from opposition parties just before the impeachment, as shown in Period II and III.

Third, what is the presidential image of Roh in each period? As was shown in the Qualitative Analysis section, Roh was portrayed as a reformer with a strong willpower and new style leadership in Period I. After that, Roh was described as a fathomer of public opinion of him but he incurred criticism by his proposal of confidence vote; Korean constitution does not have any provision for that. During Period III, Roh quarreled with opposition party members over his alleged intervention in general election by his remarks. In Period IV, Roh received indirect support from this newspaper that attacked opposition parties for impeaching Roh and conveyed popular protests against the impeachment. President Roh was portrayed as a victim of minority party member. In Period V, Roh-backed Woori Party won the election. This newspaper conveyed the message that most of the impeachment proponents lost their seats, thereby justifying Roh's stance. After Roh resumed his office, he was again described as a reformer who will take measures in earnest.

Fourth, was there superficial coverage of Roh? The expression "superficial" may mean that intrinsically superficial aspects of presidency such as president's haircut, habits, and expressions. But in this newspaper's coverage of Roh, sometimes analytical stories themselves were not thought to be in-depth, as was discussed earlier. For example, this newspaper did not elaborate why Roh's new style was better, whether his new seating arrangement brought about more efficient discussion of affairs, or his transition and administration was more efficient than before. One can compare this subject with that of Bush stories discussed earlier.

CHAPTER **VI**

The more powerful or successful people or groups are, the more negative news coverage of them will be. Coverage of political candidates is more negative toward front-runners and incumbents than toward the underdog. Looking for flaws in potential winners and in the powerful has become a routine part of investigative journalism. Journalists may feel that they can be magnanimous toward losers (Routines of Media Work 6: Shoemaker & Reese, 1996, p. 266).

POSITIVE OR NEGATIVE PORTRAYAL OF PRESIDENCY

Presidential Coverage in Review

Chapters IV and V analyzed how *the New York Times* and *the Kyunghyang Daily News* portrayed the president either positively or negatively. Can one draw a generalization of how news media portray the president in either way? To have an attempt at this, one needs to look back at the categorizations in the previous two chapters. One needs to review how presidential images were conveyed by the two newspapers. The previous two chapters served as case studies of media's presidential coverage. Let's review the categories and make an attempt at generalization. The categories of presidential coverage in each section may serve as bases for theorizing presidential coverage.

Portrayal of George W. Bush

Period I (Inauguration)

Positive Coverage
1. Inauguration, Jubilation, Successful Transition: "Bush Taking Office" "Smooth Start"
2. National Leader, Conciliator, and Unifier: "Bush the Conciliator"
3. Policymaker: "Bush Halts Overseas Spending on

Abortion"

4. Decisive Military Leader: "Bush Approves Air Raids on Iarq"
5. Person in Charge, Making Appointments: "Bush Appoints Powell's Son to Lead F.C.C."
6. International Leader: "Bush Due to Visit Mexico"
7. Personal Qualities: "Proud Father and Son Bask in History's Glow"

Negative Coverage

"Protest against Bush's Inauguration"
"Editorial Criticizing Bush's Faith-based Services"
"Bush Team under Attack on Emissions"

Period II (September 11 Attacks)

Positive Coverage

1. Crisis Leader, Military Leader: "Bush Vows to Exact Punishment for Evil" "Bush Tells the Military to Get Ready" "National Crisis Changes Bush's Presidency"
2. National Soother: "Bush Leads Prayer, Visits Aid Crews" "Bush Visits New York City"
3. Personal Qualities and First Family: "Bush's Father Depicting Burden of Presidency" "Laura Bush Playing the Soother"
4. Others: "Congress Supports Bush" "Al Gore Backs Bush"

Negative Coverage
"Column Criticizing Bush for Not Coming back to Washington sooner"
"Bush Advisers Split on Scope of Retaliation"
"Analysis Attacking Bush for not having Military Plan"
"Column Criticizing Bush for Adopting New Foreign Policy without Systematic Analysis"

Period III (Afghan War)

Positive Coverage

1. Decisive Military Leader: "Bush Warns Taliban" "Bush Offers Taliban Second Chance to Yield"
2. International Leader: "Bush Meets Jian Zemin and Vladimir Putin"
3. First Lady: "Laura Bush Reading a Storybook to Kindergarteners"
4. Others: "Bush Winning High Praises of Gore Backers"

Negative Coverage

1. Stories and Columns Criticising Bush's War Plan: "A Military Quagmire Remembered" "Guns Won't Win the Afghan War" "Pakistanis Shout, Bush is a Dog" "Europeans Apprehensive about the War"
2. Others: "Bush not Attending Domestic Affairs" "Bush's Foreign Policy Turned Upside Down"

Period IV (Iraq War)

Positive Coverage

1. Military Leader: "Bush Issues Ultimatum and Vows to Attack" "Doctrine of Pre-Emptive Strike Justified" "Bush Declares One Victory in a War on Terror"
2. International Leader: "Japanese Prime Minister Supports Bush" "Bush Meets Blair in Belfast to Discuss War"
3. Personal Qualities: "TV Watch; Bush's Soft Words That Convey a Hard Line" "President Keeps Battlefield Close" "Another Bush Watches on the Sidelines" "War Looked from the Oval Office" "White House Memo; Bush Shows Looser Side in an Interview"
4. War Reports Favoring Bush: "Military Successes Give Bush a Boost" "U.S. Forces Take Control in Baghdad, Bush Elated"
5. Others: "Congress; Both Parties Close Ranks Behind Bush" " Even Critics of War Say the White House Spun it with Skill"

Negative Coverage

1. Bush's War Decision Criticized: "War in the Ruins of Diplomacy" "Antiwar Resolution Jolts a Rural Township" "Critics Say U.S. Lacks Legal Basis for Attack" "Senator Deplores Attack on Iraq" "As a Quick Victory Grows Less Likely, Doubts Are Quietly Voiced in Washington" "Thousands Join in Boston to Demand End of War"
2. Others: "Bush's New Asylum Policy Under Fire" "Secrecy; the Bush Byword"

Portrayal of Roh Moo Hyun

Period I (Inauguration)

Positive Coverage

1. Low-Key Inauguration, Not Much Celebration, Transition with Mixed Evaluations: "Roh Takes Office, Let's Build Peace and Prosperity" "Modest Celebration" "One Week of Roh Presidency Brings Mood of Changes" "One Month of Roh Presidency Brings Changes and Tribulations"
2. National Leader and Conciliator: "Roh Pursues Bi-Partisan Talks, Seeks Live-and-Let-Live Politics" "Roh Pursues Special Pardon for Prisoners of Conscience"
3. Policymaker: "Roh Directs Administration to Establish Policy Objectives" Roh Decides to Send Korean Soldiers to Iraq"
4. Decisive Leader, Person in Charge and Making Appointments: "First Roh Cabinet Launched" "Roh Considering Strong Measures for Revolting Prosecutors" "Angered Roh Says No to Collective Revolt of Prosecutors" "Roh Vetoes Chief Prosecutor's Personnel Placement"
5. International Player: "Roh and Bush Had Their First Telephone Conversation"
6. Personal Qualities (Roh's Candor and Anti-

Authoritarianism): "Roh Says He Was Concerned When Prosecutors Accepted his Offer of Open Debate" "Roh's Untraditional Path is Talk of Every Day"

7. New-Style Leader (Open-Minded, Nontraditional, and Reformist): "Nontraditional Personnel Recruitment; Women and People in the Forties to Assume Cabinet Posts" "Roh Stresses Massive Reforms" "First Cabinet Meeting Heated With Debates" "Main Hall of the Blue House to be Open to the Public"

8. A Hard Worker or a Busy Person: "Breathless Four-Power Diplomacy from the First Day" "Roh Handled More Than Ten Events Until Late into the Night" "Roh Handled 16 Official Events on the Second Day"

9. First Lady: "First Lady Will Monitor Presidential Relatives"

10. Roh's Media Policy: "Roh Will Not Meddle in Press Affairs"

Negative Coverage

1. Disorder in Inauguration, Opposition from Political Opponents in Cabinet Formation and Measures: "Hannara Party Criticizes Experimental Cabinet Formation" "Hannara Faults Media Guidelines by the Roh Government"

2. Resistance to Roh's Reforms inside the Administration: "Prosecutors Strongly Resisting Ms. Kang Kum Sil as Justice Minister"

3. Conflicts Within the Blue House Aides and Investigation of Presidential Relatives: "Secretarial Office of the Blue House in Disharmony between Elderly and Young"

4. Editorial and Columns: "Failure of Amateurism" criticizing one month of Roh presidency.

Period II (Proposal of Confidence Vote)

Positive Coverage

1. Proposal of Confidence Vote and Follow-Up Stories: "Roh

Proposes Confidence Vote" " Polls Show People Still Trust Roh"
2. Policymaker and International Player: "Decision Made to Send Korean Troops to Iraq" "Bush Praises Roh as America's Friend"
3. Others: "Roh's Visit to Kwangju"
4. Roh's Media Policy: "Roh Invites Journalists to Blue House for Dinner"

Negative Coverage
1. Opposition to Roh's Proposal of Confidence Vote: "Column, Confusion Must be Avoided" "Editorial, Roh's Proposal was not Serious" "Poll Results not Favoring Confidence Vote" "Opposition Parties Opposed to Confidence Vote"
2. Conflicts Within the Blue House and Investigation of Irregularities of Aides and Relatives: "Five Presidential Aides Hurt by Prosecutors" "Voices for Replacement of Aides" "Differences Among Aides About Sending Korean Troops to Iraq" "Scandals and Rumors Originating from Aides" "Disclosures of Roh's Election Funds"
3. Opposition to Policymaking: Stories of opposition to sending Korean soldiers to Iraq.

Period III (Pre-Impeachment)

Positive Coverage
1. Strong-Willed Politician Confronting Impeachment: "Roh Did Not Consider Apologies" "Roh Did Not Violate Election Law"
2. Patriotic Leader: "Roh Warns Koizumi about Visiting Yaskuni Shrine"
3. Clean Leader: "Roh Instructs Ill Treatment of Businessman for Bribing his Brother"

Negative Coverage
1. Impeachment Offensives Launched by Opposition

Politicians: "Roh's Violation of Neutrality Obligation Cited" "Impeachment Motion Submitted"
2. Investigation of Roh's Election Funds and His Aides: "Roh's Election Funds Exceed One-Tenth of Mr. Lee Hoi Chang" "Irregularities of Roh's Aides See No End"

Period IV (Roh Impeached)

Positive Coverage

1. Various Stories Criticizing Impeachment and Conveying Anti-Impeachment Protests: "Candlelight Protests"
2. Personal Qualities: "Roh's Agonies" "Roh Discussing Politics of Integration"
3. Columns and Editorials Faulting Impeachment
4. Others: Constitution scholars opposed to impeachment, Poll results showing that people want Roh's reinstatement, etc.

Negative Coverage

Few negative stories: "Impeachment Proceeded because of Roh's Refusal to Apologize"

Period V (General Election)

Positive Coverage

1. Roh Regaining People's Confidence by Winning General Election, Adverse Effects of Impeachment Proven
2. Roh as Conciliator: "Live and Let Live"
3. Political Leader Contemplating Future Political Courses, Big-Frame Politics.
4. Person in Charge, Contemplating a New Cabinet Formation
5. Rohs as a Reformer

Negative Coverage

1. Criticisms Against Self-Conceit of Roh and His Party
2. Irregularities of Roh's Aides and Relatives: "Aide

Received Illegal Funds"

Period VI (Resumption of Presidential Office)

Positive Coverage

1. The Constitutional Court Upholds Roh's Presidency, Celebration of Reinstatement and People's Reaction, Editorials Welcoming Roh: "Impeachment Resolution Rejected" "Roh's Comeback Welcomed"
2. Personal Qualities: "Roh Talking to Ko Kun"
3. Reformer and Policymaker: "Roh's Real New Term Begins"
4. National Conciliator: "Live and Let Live"
5. Person in Charge, Contemplating Cabinet Reshuffle
6. Others: "Entrance into the Woori Party"

Negative Coverage

1. Roh's Careless Words and His Narrow-Mindedness Criticized: "A Sting on a Careless Mouth" "Roh Inviting Only His Allies"
2. Roh's Mishandling of Ko Kun and Insistence on Mr. Kim Hyuk Kyoo as Prime Minster Criticized.
3. Roh's Media Policy Faulted.

Comparison of Two Newspapers

As was shown above, *the New York Times* and the *Kyunghyang Daily News* used various ways of portraying the presidency either positively or negatively. Categories of presidential images overlap in part and sometimes the two newspapers have their own distinctive ways of portraying the presidency. Let's compare and contrast presidential coverage over the research periods briefly to have a feel about it.

During the inaugural period, how did the two newspapers describe the festive mood of inaugural period? Bush called for civility, compassion, unity, and a nation of character in his address. Roh appealed to the nation to build peace and prosperity on the Korean Peninsula. The two newspapers conveyed perfectly positive coverage of both presidents. Roh's inauguration was made a bit low-key, considering the tragic accident in Daegu City. In contrast, the *New York Times* ran a story describing Americans staging a protest against Bush and throwing an egg to the president's car. The Korean newspaper ran a story describing a disorderly spot at the inaugural ceremony. But both stories were buried deep inside. The festive mood was conspicuous in the *Times*, which ran several stories of the First Family, including "Father and Son Bask in History's Glow" and inaugural ball in Crawford. But it was not the case in *the Kyunghyang Daily*.

The two newspapers carried stories of the president as a national conciliator, leader, and unifier. The *Times* had a story titled "Bush the Conciliator" and the Korean newspaper had a story titled "Roh Considers Live and Let Live Politics." The newspapers also carried stories describing the president as a decisive leader and an international player. Bush was described as being decisive in ordering an air raid against Iraq and Roh was described as being decisive in insisting on his personnel reforms at the Prosecution Office. In terms of policy making, the *Times* described Bush taking concrete measures and issuing orders such as halting overseas spending on abortion, whereas Roh was instructing his newly-formed cabinet to conceive of new policy plans. This may reflect the structural differences in both countries in designing and implementing policies. But one wonders why Roh instructed his cabinet to design policies instead of already having policy ideas or lines ready to implement.

Both of the newspapers ran personal-quality stories of the president, but differently. The *Times* conveyed more joyous mood by employing various ways of describing the First Family: "Bush's inaugural ball", "father and son", "refitted Oval Office", and "Oval Office with a hue", and so forth. And the style of the story sounded more personal and intimate. In contrast, the Korean newspaper ran stories of Roh with merely personal traits. President Roh was portrayed as a person of candor and anti-authoritarianism. Roh's candor or naivete could be found when he said that he was worried that the prosecutors unexpectedly accepted his offer of an open debate with them. The newspaper focused on Roh's new style: open-minded, untraditional, reformist, and so on. These personal styles of Roh may surely connote positive tone.

Roh was additionally described as a hard worker. The stories were dry in nature as compared with those in the *Times*, but it is undeniable that these stories conveyed positive image of Roh. No Korean story discussed Roh's "tears of joy" in winning the presidential election. It was remarkable that there was only one story about the First Lady Mrs. Kwon Yang Sook, which only said that "she will take care of relatives issues". The story did not describe any personal quality of Mrs. Kwon. The story about Mrs. Kwon was printed only once all through the six research periods.

Both newspapers carried stories that evaluated one-week transition. The Korean daily ran stories of one-month presidency of Roh, but *the Times* did not. The *Times* ran seven stories evaluating Bush's "smooth start" at the end of the first week. The first such story was printed on the first page citing all sides. It had the headline "BUSH'S TRANSITION LARGELY A SUCCESS, ALL SIDES SUGGEST; Careful Planning Seen; Analysts Find a Few Missteps but Note a Deft Touch in Dealing With Congress" (01-28-01, #1, A1-1+A14, +2). The story said that "prominent Republicans and even many Democrats agree that Bush has presided over one of the most orderly and politically nimble White House transitions in at least 20 years." Various transition stories followed.

In contrast, the Korean newspaper ran just one story at the end of the first week, and a very critical column and a neutral editorial marking one month. The story of one-week presidency was placed on page three of the March 3, 2003, issue with the title "The Anti-Authoritarian Blue House Comes Nearer to the People; One Week of Roh Presidency Brings Mood of Changes;

Conference Hall's Seating is Rearranged Parallel as that of the White House..." (03-03-03, #3, p. 3, +2). This story marked the first week of Roh presidency, but did not seem to have evaluated Roh's transition in a substantial and profound manner. The story focused on newly-fetched changes, but did not discuss Roh's performance in transition. It sounded a bit superficial by mererly touching on the new seating arrangement modeled on that of the Oval Office of the White House and a new atmosphere for discussion among the president and his aides. It was not a transition evaluation. A column marking one month of Roh presidency scathingly criticized the amateurish performance of Roh government. The editorial marking one month sounded neutral in mixing both positive and negative comments. Roh's initial weeks at the Blue House appeared to resemble those of Bill Clinton in that he had designated problematic cabinet members and faced opposition from the military about the gay soldiers, and so forth. However, Roh differed from Clinton in insisting on his reform policies (personnel change included) in his administration despite opposition from the establishment.

Should the news media run stories of presidency evaluation and why? What is the ground allowing the media to do that? One media scholar said that this kind of role for the media originates from media's innate role as monitor of power: the so-called surveillance of the environment. Although news media are not elected power, they voluntarily assume this responsibility.

It is noticeable that the Korean newspaper frequently ran stories of Roh's attitude (or policy) to news media. The newspaper said that Roh will not meddle in media affairs, and it's a positive tone. It may be paradoxical, however, that Roh afterwards frequently vented dissatisfaction with news reports, creating frictions with conservative newspapers (but not with broadcasters).

How did the two newspapers attack their president respectively? The *New York Times* largely ran policy stories such as opposition to Bush's tax plan, Bush's overseas abortion policy. In contrast, the *Kyunghyang Daily* ran relatively many negative stories about Roh's performance, policy, and doubts of election funds. Roh's first cabinet formation was criticized by opposition parties as being "experimental." Roh's reforms met with deep-rooted objection from the establishment. Conflicts were featured between Roh's senior and junior aides, his relatives and aides were incessantly involved in irregularities.

Positive and negative stories may be mere reflections of social events affecting the president. But it is undeniable that newspapers convey news stories of certain categories that fit their editorial policy, thus trying to play a role in shaping the public opinion and policymaking.

When September 11 attacks occurred, the *Times* described Bush as a crisis or military leader. This was a national crisis originating from outside the American soil. Bush was described as "vowing" to retaliate, ordering the military to get ready, pledging to attack Afghanistan if bin Laden is not delivered, and so on. The newspaper portrayed Bush as a "transformed leader", who became steadier and more confident. In this national crisis, Bush was portrayed as a national soother, and his wife played the same role. In critical stories, Bush was criticized for not returning to Washington sooner, and his advisers were split over the scope of retaliation. He was also attacked for not having a military plan. Later he took the military measure, that is, attack of Afghanistan.

In comparison, Roh's proposal of the confidence vote was a self-inflicted (or, self-induced) crisis inside this country. The Korean newspaper conveyed Roh's words pertaining to the confidence vote and reported poll results showing that people still have trust in Roh. Conflicts within the Blue House aides persisted and investigation of irregularities of Roh's aides and relatives did not cease. Coverage of continued troubles among presidential aides and relatives may never be positive to the president.

In Roh's pre-impeachment period, Roh was described as a person of strong will. His violation of neutrality obligation continuously provided grounds for opposition's criticism. Doubts about Roh's election funds also provided fodder for attack against him.

The war situations were the occasion where American news media could show their patriotism. During the periods of Afghan War and Iraq War, Bush was certainly portrayed as a decisive military leader. He was described as meeting foreign leaders to seek military cooperation from foreign countries. First Lady Laura Bush was described as attending to children by reading a storybook to kindergarteners. In going to war against Afghanistan, a column recalled the Vietnam-style quagmire and another advised that "guns won't win the war."

During the Iraq War, the *Times* seemed to justify the war by printing Bush's pre-emptive war doctrine. In this period, this newspaper ran several stories that described Bush very positively: Bush always keeping the battlefield close, Bush making hard war decisions, Bush showing looser human side, etc. These stories almost approached flattery in nature. There were reports that the war went smoothly. Simultaneously, the newspaper ran stories that criticized Bush's war decision: going to war because of diplomatic failure, thousands of people protesting against the war, etc. This was a reflection that Iraq War was such a controversial one.

When Roh was impeached, it was a crisis for a president and a political party. It was never a crisis to the proportions of September 11 attacks. But the Korean newspaper carried many stories of people's protests against the impeachment. Poll results were printed which were supportive of Roh. Columns and editorials faulted the impeachment resolution of the National Assembly. Even during this period, the newspaper described Roh's agonies and his ideas of future domestic politics. There were few negative stories.

When results of the general election were known, this newspaper linked the results to adverse effects of the impeachment of Roh, implying that the impeachment was unjustifiable. During this period, Roh was still described as one trying to be a conciliator, talking about 'live and let live.'

When Roh resumed presidential functions with the ruling of the Constitutional Court rejecting the impeachment resolution, there appeared stories of celebration and personal dialogues, which were positive to Roh. However, a story of Roh's careless words (intervention in general election politics) was printed, but it did not deliver a heavy impact, because Roh was reinstated. Roh was described as a conciliator again. This time Roh's media policy was faulted for restraining activities of beat reporters.

How do News Media Portray the President?

To generalize the ways in which news media portray the president positively or negatively is never an easy task. So this temporary generalization is based on results of this research and the previous analysis and research by other theorists and media scholars. As was discussed previously, media contents pertaining to presidential coverage are results that come from negotiations between journalists on the one hand and the president, presidential assistants, and others on the other. As this study included all stories that may affect the presidential images, other stories written by reporters outside of the White House or Blue House beat can also be candidates for stories of presidential coverage.

Here, a temporary scheme for positive and negative coverage is offered based on the research results. An overall scheme is that the nearer the reporter is to the president, the more positive stories he or she writes, and vice versa. The portion of positive stories may depend on the proximity of the reporter to the president. The following are temporary generalizations of positive and negative coverage of the president.

1) Stories about the president's personality and presidential spouse: As was shown previously, stories about the president's personal aspects were usually (very) positive. These stories are written by presidential beat reporters and they are in a better position to do so. Because the White House or the Blue House has enormous resources to control the journalists, it will not be easy for beat reporters to write negative stories about the presi-

dent consistently. Stories of personal aspects were normally positive. But president's behavior or speech is still open to criticism or praise by the beat reporters.

2) Stories about presidential relatives, aides, and cabinet members: As was shown, conflicts among presidential aides were reason for media criticism either in the *Times* or the *Kyunghyang*. Conflicts among Bush's aides about the scope of retaliation made for a negative story. There were much more stories about internal conflicts in the Korean newspaper than in the *Times*. These were negative stories to the president. In the Korean newspaper, many negative stories about presidential aides and relatives were also printed. But the stories were largely written by reporters covering the Prosecution Office that investigated irregularities of presidential aides and relatives. Stories of cabinet members were written with positive or negative tone. In the *Times*, stories of presidential relatives (e.g. Bush's father) and presidential spouse were normally positive, whereas in the Korean newspaper stories of presidential relatives (e.g. brother) and presidential aides were largely negative. But it should be noted that these negative stories were written by other reporters than the Blue House beat reporters.

3) Others (third parties, events, policies, and political actors): News media are freer to praise or criticize the president's policy and behavior rather than personal qualities. News media can affect the president's image positively or negatively in an indirect manner by conveying people's reactions towards president's policies (e.g., demonstrations for or against the president). Columnists and editorial writers are freer to criticize, praise, or support the president's policies or behavior. Newspapers can affect presidential images by conveying positive or negative messages of the political allies or opponents. Usually newspapers convey presidential policies and then reactions from the people who are affected by the policies. The reactions can be either positive or negative to the president. Poll results are useful means of conveying newspapers' support or criticism of the president.

Kumar (1981) was insightful in elucidating publicity strategies (i.e., squeezing more juice) of the White House. Her scheme was useful in conducting analysis of presidential images in both the *New York Times* and the *Kyunghyang*. However, as this research defined positive or negative stories as those affecting the presidential image broadly, stories of anti-war demonstration (negative to Bush) and those of candlelight protests (positive to Roh) were also regarded as presidential coverage.

From a theoretical point of view, Daniel Hallin's idea can be drawn on (Reese, 1996, p. 227-28). Media scholar Hallin introduced a useful model to help understand the ways in which the news maintain ideological boundaries: sphere of consensus, sphere of legitimate controversy, and sphere of deviance. Most of the negative stories may belong to the sphere of controversy. When there are small or large portions of population that are opposed to the president, then news stories conveying their message can deliver the negative tone to the president.

Another way of looking at the positive or negative coverage of the president may be a technical approach by the journalist. The newspapers may claim that they do an objective reporting, but they have their leeway in placing which story on which page. They may also claim that their conveying of what the president says and does is objective, but this also increases or decreases the positive or negative impact of the story. Stories describing anti-war or anti-impeachment protests may indirectly affect presidential image.

Stories describing the inaugural ceremony of President Bush occupied the front page, but a story of fierce protest against his office-taking was placed on an inside page. A negative story was also printed in President Roh's inauguration, but it was not conspicuous. The newspapers might have tried to strike a sophisticated balance in describing the jubilant event. A news analysis of the pre-emptive strike doctrine was printed on the front page of the *New York Times*, whereas a straight story criticizing America's lack of legal basis in attacking Iraq was buried inside. The latter said that the United States did not have the legal basis to attack Iraq and disarm Saddam Hussein. Suppose that this story was printed on the front page! In the same vein, a column marking one month of Roh presidency, which attacked the amateurish performance of President Roh, had less impact although it was a direct attack to Roh. Suppose this column was printed on the front page.

Stories about presidents carrying out their presidential functions may sound objective reporting and journalists may claim as such. But as was discussed earlier, based on Kumar's (1981) analysis, presidential images such as man of the people, national leader, international player, and policymaker are those that publicity officials strive represented in the news media. In this respect, collaboration of publicity officials and White House or Blue House beat journalists could be found in the news reports. In the research, presidential images as national conciliator, national soother, and crisis leader were discovered. These stories were largely positive to the president. These stories may be produced by reporters as an observer or insider.

Negative stories originating from presidential functions were filed by reporters who cover other beats as reactions from the people affected by presidential policies. Stories of anti-war (Iraq War) protests in and out of America are good examples. In Korea, reports of revolt against Roh's reform may fall under this group. These can convey negative images to the president by describing others' reactions to the presidential policies or politics. In this case newspapers can portray the president negatively by describing others actions (i.e., indirectly). But newspapers may claim objective reporting and balanced stance here, too.

In terms of president's personal stories, full collaboration between the beat reporter and the president (or publicity officials) may be needed, as Kumar (1981) indicated. See how intimate the stories are in describing Bush conducting Iraq War, seen from the Oval Office: "Bush unwaveringly confident" "Bush with a little shake of his fist" "Bush absorbed in every detail of the news from Iraq," and so forth. The Korean newspaper, in this vein, did the same thing: "Roh an anti-authoritarian, reformer, new-style leader" "Roh open to the press (early in his presidency)" "Roh a hard worker," and so on.

Stories about irregularities of Roh's aides and relatives were frequently printed, providing negative image to Roh. In contrast, stories of Laura Bush and Bush senior occasionally were published to buttress President Bush's images.

In addition, poll results, columns, or editorial are useful means of conveying a message. Polls either criticize or assist the president indirectly. Columns and editorials have a distinctive status in portraying the president.

Reiteration of the thesis of this research on presidential image is in order here. Although the White House and the Blue House exert considerable control over media coverage of them, news organizations have their own framework to generate presidential images (i.e., media's framing power). President Bush's images conveyed by the *New York Times* is definitely the end product of complex and active interactions between the *Times* journalists on the one hand and the White House, the Bush administration, the American public, and the world community on the other. The same may hold true for the Korean newspaper. President Roh's images conveyed by this Korean newspaper is the end product of complex and active interactions between the reporters of this newspaper on the one hand and the Blue House, the Roh administration, the Korean public, and the world community on the other.

When and How Can News Media Criticize the President?

(1) Presidential Loss of Credibility with the Media and Public

In what circumstances and in what manner can media criticize the president? This question may never be easy to answer. Grossman and Kumar (1981, pp. 7-13) wrote that the adversary aspects of the White House-media relationship broke into open conflict during the years 1965 to 1974 (roughly the period between President Johnson's implementation of his decision to send large numbers of American troops to Vietnam and

President Nixon's resignation). This period can be characterized as that during which presidents lost their credibility with the media and the public for that matter. The reputation of the president as the public's servant was tainted by Johnson's furtive escalation of the unsuccessful intervention in Vietnam and by urban racial disorders that some critics attributed to the dislocations of Great Society social programs. The political and constitutional crises of Watergate convinced many journalists, scholars, and other members of the attentive public to revise their opinions of the presidency. The loss of confidence in the believability of White House officials experienced by many reporters during the Johnson and Nixon administrations was reflected in titles of their books about the era: *Anything But the Truth; The Politics of Lying; The Great Coverup*; and *No Thank You, Mr. President*. The credibility gap that these presidents created made sufficient room for media criticisms. When the public thinks that the president does not attend to their interests, the media have grounds to criticize the president.

In the case of President Roh Moo Hyun, he lost credibility with the public for corruption charges of his aides and relatives, and his repeated slips of the tongue. This was addressed in the research section.

(2) Personal Crises, Scandals, or Power Struggles

While discussing media's feeding frenzy on former President Bill Clinton, Bennett (1996, pp. 131-35) indicated that when politicians, presidents included, become caught up in personal crises, scandals, or power struggles, the news media may descend like a pack of hungry dogs to devour the political prey. If any hint of a sex scandal is added or the smoking gun of political corruption is produced, then the frenzy can bring down the high and mighty. During the 1992 presidential election campaign, the news was spiced by charges of Clinton's extramarital affairs, pot smoking, draft dodging, and other personal issues. Clinton's character became a major preoccupation of the press. The resulting challenge for the Clinton communication team was to reassure voters about the character defects raised in the news and reinforced by opponents during the primaries and the general election.

After the election, embittered Clinton closed the corridor between the press room and the White House communication office, which was was regarded as a declaration of war by the White House press corps. The icy relations left the press pack surly and ready to pounce at the slightest hint of a scandal or personal failing. The press pounced on such items such as Clinton's expensive haircut aboard an Air Force One on a Los Angeles International Airport taxiway and a scandal in the management of the White House travel office that was quickly dubbed "Travelgate" in the media.

In the case of President Roh Moo Hyun, scandals pertaining to his aides and relatives became the target of media attack. Conflicts within Roh's aides were also targeted by the media. Opposition forces such as Hannara Party and Minju Party continued to attack President Roh on charges of intervention in general election and on suspicions of his election funds, etc.. This was discussed earlier.

(3) Organized Political Opposition and Lack of News Management

According to Bennett (1996), there are at least three reasons for the series of feeding frenzies that plagued the Clinton presidency. Stated in general terms: i) Cooperative relations between the politician's communication staff broke down; ii) The politician's communication staff seemed to think it unnecessary (or beneath the dignity of the office) to follow the basic rules of news management; and iii) The politician was implicated in questionable activities that, whether due to incompetent communication strategy or the magnitude of the offenses, resulted in uncontrolled news situations. Additionally, Clinton's supporters accused political opponents of feeding the frenzy with well-orchestrated accusations.

(4) Divided Elite

On issues where the elite is seriously divided, there will be dissenting voices allowed in the news media, according to Herman and Chomsky (2002, p. 346, n. 125). Herman and Chomsky noted that if stories that do not fit the elite consensus (government-business-military interests), they are less likely to appear in the media. But when elite consensus is nonexistent or their opinions are divided, media can take sides with the opposing forces and they can criticized the president. In America, divided elite opinions during the Vietnam War and Iraq War can be examples for negative presidential coverage. In Korea divided elite opinions on moving administrative capital, sending Korean troops to Iraq, and impeachment procedures of President Roh can be good examples of negative coverage. Conservative newspapers persistently and consistently criticized Roh's plan to move the administrative capital. But one of progressive newspapers, which shared Roh's values, criticized Roh's plan to send Korean troops to Iraq.

As was discussed earlier, it is hard for White House beat reporters to attack the president directly, if not in exceptional situations where hard evidence is at hand. They can be instantly exposed to the pressure of the White House publicity officials. In attacking the president, reporters who cover other beats that are affected by presidential policies or measures are freer to criticize the president than presidential beat reporters. Columnists and editorial writers are also freer to attack the president.

In explaining reasons for criticizing the president, Hallin's theory of "sphere of legitimate controversy" may be useful (Shoemaker & Reese, 1996, p. 227-28). Hallin divided journalistic world into three spheres: legitimate controversy, consensus, and deviance. The sphere of legitimate controversy is where objectivity and balance are sought. Following Hallin's argument, this is the region of electoral contests and legislative debates, of issues recognized as such by the major established actors of the political process. When an issue is regarded as within the sphere of controversy, news media can run stories written by their columnists and editorial writers more freely (positively or negatively). They can also take an indirect means of running stories about those who oppose presidential policies and measures. In attacking the president, larger news organizations with ample human resources are in a more favorable position to do so. Small news organizations with limited resources cannot afford to, because they are more dependent on publicity operations of the White House, as was discussed earlier.

According to Hallin, at the core is the sphere of consensus, "the motherhood and apple pie" domain. Within this region journalists do not feel compelled either to present opposing views or to remain disinterested observers. The journalist's role is to serve as an advocate or celebrant of consensus values. Beyond the sphere of legitimate controversy is the sphere of deviance, the realm of people and ideas outside the mainstream of society. Hallin noted that in this region journalism casts off neutrality. It plays the role of exposing, condemning, or excluding from the public agenda those who violate or challenge the political consensus. It marks out and defends the limits of acceptable conflict.

On the whole, if presidential stories do not fit the story frames of media, they are apt to become negative stories. As was discussed previously, the ideal story frames are the president as a problems solver, an international leader, and a representative of the people. As Dick Cheney's foregoing observation implies, the present author thinks that if the president fails to define the situation, in other words, fails to set the public agenda, then the media will begin to set their own agenda and begin to criticize the president.

When and How Can News Media Flatter the President?

In what circumstances and in what manner can media criticize the president? This question may not be easy to answer, either. The above-mentioned "Four Frames of Presidential Images" theorized by Cook and Ragsdale (1995) was a view from a journalist's standpoint, whereas "White House Strategies for Projecting Presidential Images" by Grossman and Kumar (1981) was a view from a White House publicity official. As was examined in the research sections (Chapter IV and V), stories of positive presidential coverage can also be analyzed with other theoretical frameworks. And the categorization of positive coverage attempted here may not be final and definitive. But a temporary suggestion of framework is attempted here, which combines theories by Cook and Ragsdale, Grossman and Kumar, and Bennett.

The image of the president as "a problem solver" may be the basic starting line. This may include the leadership qualities of the president. The president diagnoses problems and presents solutions (i.e., policies and measures), and shows his various leadership roles. Stories of a variety of presidential leadership roles can become positive stories. In the process of this research, various kinds of leadership roles were found. Sometimes stories of the people or opposition parties backing the president or the president's policies can carry positive tone to the president. The presidential image as an international leader (or, player) can also be part of the leadership role for a president.

The story of the president as a representative of the people partly overlaps with the technique of projecting "personal qualities". Stories of the president acting like an ordinary person, agonizing over problems, and making hard decisions, showing loose sides can all be positive stories. Intimate descriptions of president's human aspects can be achieved through close cooperation between journalists and the White House, thereby producing very positive coverage of the president. Stories of human aspects of the president normally tends to be positive. However, presidential errors, slips of the tongue, or corruption can be targets for fierce media attack. As was shown earlier, corruption of President Roh's aides were fodder for fierce media criticisms in Korea.

Reversed conditions of the negative coverage discussed earlier can also be conducive to positive coverage. If the president is fully trusted by the people, enjoys support from opposition forces, and efficiently manages press relations, then this could lead to positive media coverage of the president. These are the conditions conducive to positive stories, but conditions met may not necessarily create positive stories that publicity officials hope for.

In discussing media's positive or negative coverage of the president, Reese and Shoemaker (1996) needs to be included. The two media scholars argued that media contents are shaped through various filters: news judgement of individual reporter, media routines, editorial policy of corporate organizations, outside influences, and so forth. Therefore, news stories that are positive or negative to the president are all the end products of these filters. The presidential news stories are produced by the editorial policy of news organizations and a myriad other filters.

CHAPTER **VII**

The longer people work for a media organization, the more socialized they are to the policies---stated and unstated---of the organization. Media workers learn what their organizations want by observing others, by receiving feedback from their superiors, and by observing what makes it into the finished communication product (Links between Influences from Individuals and Those from Routines 1: Shoemaker & Reese, 1996, p. 265).

CONCLUDING REMARKS

Summary of Book

Today presidential news is available anywhere and anytime. People cannot read newspapers, watch television, or access the Internet without encountering news about presidential remarks or presidential photographs. Presidential communication emanating from the White House or the Blue House may be the utmost form of political communication. More and more people are involved in disseminating presidential messages and getting positive coverage from media can make or break the presidency. That is why presidents are so eager to get favorable media coverage. Very often media image of the president can mean political reality for the people who have scarce opportunity to experience the reality.

For over two hundred years of U.S. history, presidents have been discontented with media portrayal of them. Korean presidents may be no exception in this respect. But as Grossman and Kumar (1981) showed, American news media have run "unexpectedly" favorable coverage of their presidents. Photographs of the presidents were more favorable than stories. As Grossman and Kumar showed, there exists a certain temporal pattern in presidential coverage, although this pattern is growing harder to observe these days. The two scholars conceptualized "the honeymoon period" of the presidents with the media. But the honeymoon is becoming shorter recently. President Bill Clinton and Roh Moo Hyun may be people with shortened honeymoon with the media.

In order to get positive media coverage, presidents are keenly interested in "controlling and manipulating" the media. According to political scientist John A. Maltese (1992), Vice President Dick Cheney (vice presidency, 2001-09) previously emphasized the importance of controlling media agenda. Cheney said that "to have an effective presidency the White House must control the media agenda. Any appearance of disunity among the president's ranks will be seized upon by the media for a story." In this vein, the administration of George W. Bush has tightly-knit communications operations (Kumar, 2003). The presidential publicity machine uses a variety of tactics: win favor, shape news flow, orchestrate coverage, full control, partial control, or no control. At the same time, presidential office use tactics of negotiation and cooperation. Sometimes publicity officials use intimidation and they need to manage news. Political scientist W. Lance Bennett (1996) said that "the sheer growth of the news media that cover the White House requires considerable daily news management."

President George W. Bush has a demonstrated interest in communications (Kumar, 2003). Bush operates a well-organized publicity machine: Press Office, Office of Communications, Office of Media Affairs, Speechwriting Unit, Coalition Information Centers, Office of Global Communications, and Office of Strategic Initiatives. Bush's publicity team employed Bush loyalists and this team operates as a communications team for the Executive Branch of government (in the words of Bush's Chief of Staff Andrew Card).

Grossman and Kumar (1981) presented techniques of projecting positive presidential images. According to them, presidential assistants use techniques of projecting personal qualities, leadership qualities, policymaker's images, etc.

From media's perspective, presidential stories need to fit their story frames. News media personalize or dramatize stories and journalists need to write interesting stories for editors and audiences. Cook and Ragsdale (1995), in this regard, presented four frames of presidential images: the problem solver, the international leader, the representative of the people, and a person who makes mistakes. Sometimes stories tend to become superficial rather then serious.

Bennett was insightful and penetrating in pointing out limitations of adversarial role of the media. He went so far as to say that the adversarialism is ritualistic. He said that "a ritualistic posture of antagonism between press and government creates the appearance of mutual independence without throwing open the content of the news to the serious coverage of a broad range of political perspectives. Such ritualistic posturing dramatizes the myths of a free press and an open government." Long-time White House correspondent Helen Thomas of the United Press International may be an example. She was known for posing harsh questions to presidents but her stories carried by the wire service were usually bland.

The White House as a newsbeat for reporters may be the most prestigious place. But it may not be attractive to enterprising reporters. Correspondents allow officials to herd them to briefings, ceremonies, and conferences where they are fed a diet of statements. They may not roam freely as they do in the beats such as the city council. However, it is true that editors allow prominent position for stories that come out of the White House. Beat reporters find it hard and tiring to cover the White House. Many of the White House correspondents get promoted after their stint at the White House. Most reporters did not regard the White House beat as requiring expertise.

When can news media criticize or flatter the president? Media can criticize the president when they lose credibility with the media and the public. Personal crises, scandals, or power struggles of the president can be targets for media attack. Presidents can also be criticized by media when political opponents stage organized attacks on them and when they fail to manage news. On the contrary, media may flatter the presidents when they fit the journalistic story frames.

As part of research, this book conducted a case study of two newspapers. This author examined presidential coverage of *the New York Times and the Kyunghyang Daily News* to discover how they portrayed the president either positively or negatively.

First, this book examined 575 stories out of 134 days' issues of the *New York Times* which might have affected the image of President George W. Bush. As the research findings showed, the positive (+2 and +1) coverage during the four periods amounted to 359 stories (62.4%). The ratio of positive coverage on the whole was "much higher" than that of Grossman and Kumar's study, or 48.7%. It was calculated that the *New York Times* carried 2.64 positive stories per one negative story during the four research periods.

Given that the first "one hundred days" (or six months) are popularly believed to be a period of presidential "honeymoon" with the news media, it is understandable that a fairly high percentage (62.5%) of the stories during Period I were positive (+2 and +1). However, even during this honeymoon period, new policy lines proposed by the incoming president incurred opposition from the public or interested parties. Period I can be characterized by Bush's image as a victor in the presidential election, a new national leader, a conciliator, a proponent of new policy lines, a military leader, a person with power to appoint federal officials, an international leader, and a new occupant in the White House. During this period, his image as a policymaker was a bit marred by opposition to his new policy on tax, abortion, emission, and religion.

During Period II, everything changed following September 11 terrorist attacks. Mr. Bush was transformed into a national crisis leader and national soother. President Bush was granted by the Congress broad powers to declare war on terrorism. He was portrayed as a military commander conducting an anti-terrorism war. Positive coverage of him soared to 70.9% in this period. However, disputes were revealed among his aides pertaining to the scope of retaliation, and the order of the whole world was being reorganized forcefully and without deep foreign policy analysis under the imperative of the anti-terrorism war led by Bush. Complaints were reported about the harsh security measures pursued by the Bush administration.

During Period III, President Bush was mainly portrayed as a military leader. The *New York Times* said that he was transformed into a confident leader. Mr. Bush was described to be focusing on anti-terrorism operations. He flatly refused negotiations with the Taliban regime in Afghanistan. He gave an order to send special forces to this region. *New York Times* reporter Elisabeth Bumiller described how "carefully and deliberately" Mr. Bush prepared for the war. The newspaper also portrayed him as an international leader who met with Jiang Zemin of China and Vladimir Putin of Russia to seek support to his war on terrorism. The newspaper conveyed the opposition to Bush's ground war plan and reminded the public about the nightmare of the Vietnam quagmire.

During Period IV, President Bush was mostly portrayed as a resolute wartime leader and simultaneously a much-hated leader by large portions of Arab people. He issued an ultimatum to Saddam Hussein asking him to go into exile and warned Americans about the prospects of a longer war. The *New York Times* carried an analysis justifying Bush's pre-emptive strike logic and traced this logic in another story. Mr. Bush was described as an international leader. *Times'* reporter Bumiller gave several intimate descriptions of Mr. Bush. Finally, Mr. Bush declared that "military phase in Iraq ended and America gained one victory in a war on terror" (*New York Times*, 05-02-03, A1-1).

Through all these three critical periods (Phase II, III, IV), it is quite clear that President Bush "defined the situations." The *New York Times* mostly conveyed verbatim what he said or described what he did. In this manner, this newspaper portrayed President Bush as a national leader, a national unifier, a crisis leader, and a decisive wartime leader. Sometimes the newspaper provided very intimate descriptions of how he reached a war decision, how he conducted the war, and how seriously he was involved in the war. Although the *New York Times* provided intimate and personal aspects of Mr. Bush, this newspaper did not reveal the trivial aspects of him. Mr. Bush was assessed to be a "serious" office-holder, differentiated from his predecessor Bill Clinton, whose image was marred with a variety of scandals. That is what Mr. Bush might have wanted the news media to do. The agenda of the *New York Times* were set by Mr. Bush who handled the dramatic crises and wartime situations. But during Period I, the *New York Times* arguably portrayed Bush in a positive light on a voluntary basis.

Next, this book examined images of President Roh Moo Hyun of South Korea as portrayed by *the Kyunghyang Daily News*. The research of the Korean newspaper examined 494 stories out of 126 days' issues of the *Kyunghyang*, which might have affected the images of President Roh Moo Hyun. *The Kyunghyang* is published in Seoul, Korea and distributed nationwide. As the research findings showed, the positive stories (+2 and +1) amounted to 275 (55.6%) and negative stories (-2 and -1) to 151. The number of positive stories per one negative story was 1.82. This was lower than that of the figures of Bush portrayal (2.64 positive stories to one negative story).

During the first month of Roh's presidency (i.e., Period I), this newspaper portrayed Roh in a favorable light. The ratio of positive to negative coverage was 68.0% to 20.8%. It may be safe to say that Roh enjoyed honeymoon with this newspaper. The positive coverage consisted of stories describing Roh as a national leader or conciliator, a policymaker, a decisive leader and person in charge, an international player, a person of candor, a new style leader who is open-minded and anti-authoritarian, and a hard worker, etc. He was depicted as being considerate in keeping the celebration low-keyed, given the tragedy prior to the inauguration. Evaluation of Roh's one week and one month presidency was mixed in this newspaper. The beat reporter focused on changes that Roh brought about (positive tone implied), but a columnist scathingly criticized Roh as an amateurish politician in running the administration. Roh's appointment of cabinet members created trouble and his reform drive met with strong resistance from the establishment, from senior prosecutors, in particular. His first cabinet formation was decried as being "experimental" by opposition parties. Stories of presidential aides involved in irregularities and internal conflicts among aides provided a negative tone to the presidential image.

Political haggling continued into Period II, when Roh proposed a confidence vote out of the blue. But Roh's proposal was based on accumulated criticisms against him regarding irregularities or corruption of his aides. Instantly, Roh incurred criticisms. The ratio of negative stories soared to 51.5%, the highest figure out of the six research periods, while that of the positive stories declined to 36.2%. This newspaper ran developing stories of confidence vote and conveyed changes in Roh's ideas and words. This newspaper ran columns and editorials criticizing proposal of confidence vote. The newspaper also cited opposition parties and even polls, which were opposed to the confidence vote. The proposal of confidence vote finally did not materialize.

Periods III, IV, V, and VI can be discussed in a lump. The two weeks of pre-impeachment period (Period III) was indicative of the future impeachment resolution. The impeachment offensives launched by opposition lawmakers was grounded in the violation of neutrality obligation committed by Roh. The ruling by the Central Election Monitoring Commission provided momentum to the impeachment motion. While the ratio of positive coverage sank to the lowest point (31.0%), the ratio of negative coverage stayed still very high (48.3%). During this period, this newspaper carried many stories discussing Roh's violation of neutrality obligation and impeachment offensive by the opposition parties.

During Period IV, when impeachment motion was passed, it is remarkable that this newspaper ran lots of stories criticizing the impeachment resolution as soon as the resolution was passed by the National Assembly. A series of candlelight protests were staged, and this was carried into the pages of the newspaper. In addition, this newspaper ran columns and editorials criticizing the impeachment resolution, showing that this newspaper was fiercely against the impeachment. Poll results were drawn on to support Roh. As a result, the ratio of positive coverage suddenly soared to 71.4%, making a conspicuous contrast with Period III. There were several stories that portrayed Roh's personal aspects very intimately after the impeachment went into effect. This newspaper also tried to strike a balance by carrying stories that described Roh as being unyielding in making apologies, which ultimately led to the impeachment resolution.

Period V may be an extension of Period IV in that the impeachment was still in effect. As the Roh-backed Woori Party took the majority of the Assembly, the newspaper gave an interpretation that Roh won his confidence vote. The newspaper said that losers of Assembly seats were those who advocated impeachment of Roh. This newspaper again conveyed images of Roh as a conciliator, a reformer, and a person contemplating cabinet reshuffle. In this period the number of stories reached the lowest point (28 stories) for the duration of one month, reflecting that Roh was still under impeachment and that people were waiting for the ruling of the Constitutional Court about the impeachment.

In Period VI, Roh resumed his presidential functions with the ruling of the Constitutional Court. The editorial welcomed the ruling and a story said that the ruling reflected the will of the people. The newspaper again portrayed Roh as a policymaker, a reformer, and a conciliator. Roh was described as having a heartfelt dialogue with the outgoing Prime Minister Ko Kun. But Roh was criticized for treating Mr. Ko badly by forcing him to recommend ministers.

How can Media Portray Presidents Positively or Negatively?

How can the news media portray the president positively or negatively? As was shown in the actual analysis of the presidential coverage of the two newspapers and as was discussed in Chapter VI, news media have a variety of means to describe the president either positively or negatively, and even neutrally.

Means of positive portrayal of the president may comprise stories of the president as a problem solver. This means that the president who shows "leadership qualities" can be portrayed in a positive light. As was enumerated in the analysis of the two newspapers, news media can convey a variety of presidential images as a national leader, conciliator, and unifier; a policy-maker; a decisive military leader; an international leader (or, international player); a person in command or in charge; a national soother; a reformer; a new style (anti-authoritarian, nontraditional) leader; a hard worker; a patriotic leader; a clean and honest leader, etc. These are presidential images extracted from this research and there may be other positive presidential images not included here.

Stories of personal aspects of the president may deliver a positive image of the president. As was discussed, drawing a personal and intimate picture of the president or the first lady (or, president's relatives) requires close cooperation of the two sides. As was shown, there are various ways of doing this: father and son rejoicing in the glow of honor on the inaugural day; a Texas inaugural ball; Bush senior talking about the loneliness of the Oval Office; Bush engrossed in war details; Bush making a hard decision on Iraq war with Colin Powell. And coverage of Roh as follows: Roh as a person of candor revealing his worries over debates with prosecutors; Roh's agonies over interpretation of general election results; Roh's long day when he was impeached; Roh having dinner with Ko Kun after impeachment was annulled, and so forth.

Stories describing other subjects but have the effect of favoring the president may also be included in this group. Various forms are found: congressional support for Bush's war policy; reports saying that the war progresses smoothly; massive anti-impeachment candlelight protests of the Korean people; constitution scholars opposed to the impeachment; poll results showing that people still trust Roh, etc.

Columns and editorials have their own independent ability to praise or criticize the president's policies. One column contended that Iraq War might be illegal but still be legitimate, presenting good reasons for going around the U.N., while the editorial said that war resulted from failure of diplomacy. Stories of evaluation of the presidency may lie within the media's self-entrusted role emanating from the media's proper function of surveillance of the environment. It may not be merely coincidental that the *New York Times* and the *Kyunhyang Daily News* offered assessment of the transition for Bush and Roh.

Means of negative portrayal of the president may comprise stories of the presidential policies or measures opposed by people who have different views or are adversely affected by them. As president's policies cover all imaginable sectors of a country's administration, opposition may occur in any of the sectors. Stories of negative tone to the president may comprise: Bush's abortion policy will cost lives overseas; opposition to Bush's war plans (Afghan War and Iraq War); politicians and people opposed to the war; prosecutors revolting against Roh's reform; opposition parties criticizing Roh's first cabinet; criticisms of Roh's proposal of confidence vote; opposition to sending Korean troops to Iraq; impeachment offensive by opposition parties; Roh's violation of neutrality obligation; Roh's media policy of restriction criticized, and so forth.

Conflicts or corruption within the White House or Blue House could have negative effects to the president. The *New York Times* ran few such stories during the research periods but *the Kyunghyang* ran a slew of them. Stories of this group are following: Bush advisers split over scope of retaliation; cacophony between senior and younger aides in Roh's Blue House and suspicion of corruption involvement by Roh's aides; Roh's five aides hurt by prosecutors; Roh's young aides involved in scandals and rumors and investigation of them, etc.

Sometimes presidential words or behavior can become the object of media criticism. Stories of this nature include: investigation of Roh's election funds; announcement that Roh's election funds exceeded one tenth of his election contender's; Roh's careless words criticized; Self-conceit of Roh's party faulted; Roh's disrespectful treatment of Ko Kun criticized, etc..

One needs to be assured that columns and editorials are freer to criticize the president. One column said that all three of Roh's handpicked cabinet members caused trouble. An editorial decried that Roh was not serious in proposing confidence vote.

As was shown in the analysis of the *New York Times* stories during the Period II, III, and IV, Bush had the power and skills to "define the situation". It forced the *Times* to follow his lead. It has to be admitted that Bush had exerted presidential leadership during these periods. It also has to be acknowledged that the situation was critical. The *Times* could not set its own agenda during these three periods. However, when Bush failed to find the evidence of weapons of mass destruction (WMD) and American casualties in Iraq continued to increase in the second half of 2003, the *Times* began to set its own agenda. It began to focus on American casualties. Here, the power to "define the situation" may be interchangeable with the power to "set the agenda".

In stories portraying Roh, the *Kyunghyang* might have voluntarily described him positively in Period I. While the popularity of Roh was declining with the passage of months in his first year in office, it seems that he wanted to test his chances by proposing a vote of confidence. But he failed to define the situation and incurred torrents of criticisms instead. The impeachment resolution by the National Assembly posed a crisis to Roh. The nature of this crisis differs from that of September 11 attacks in that the former was generated by the inside forces. This time again Roh could not define the situation but he was portrayed as a victim of conservative aggression. This in turn assisted him (or, his party) in the general election. Results of the general election and then the ruling of the Constitutional Court revived Roh's presidential functions.

One needs to be reminded of Cheney's remarks about setting the agenda discussed earlier. He said that if the White House fails to set the public agenda, then the media set their own agenda. In the same vein, Knight Ridder journalist Warren Strobel (1997) argued that "if policymakers, including the president, create policy or communication vacuum, news media begin to create their own policy (or policy agenda) and fill the gap." This means that if media begin to set their own agenda, they tend to be critical to the president. Five months after the end of military phase of the war in Iraq (as of October, 2003), there developed a "credibility gap" between Mr. Bush and the public, pertaining to the existence of weapons of mass destruction and the unstable Iraqi war situation. The U.S. media began to raise questions about the existence of WMD and be critical of the war.

Generally speaking, if the president has the power to "define the situation", then the news media may very probably follow his lead. If the president has the power and skills to lead the country, then news media as well as the public will follow his lead. But if the president lacks the power and skills to set the public agenda, then news media will set their own agenda and begin to criticize the president. And the public will begin to voice opposition. Whether news media portray the president positively or negatively depends on the power of the president to define the situation, that is to say, presidential leadership. One of the key components of presidential leadership is his communication skill.

Limitations and Future Questions

This research has been conducted by the author alone. Professor Kumar advised the present author to conduct the qualitative analysis by recruiting at least two more coders apart from the present researcher in her email on June 28, 2003. According to her, "there are a lot of people who do content analysis. Robert Richter does regular counts of coverage for favorability. There are those who look at the individual words, which are coded as being favorable and unfavorable, and others who seek to measure a story's favorability by the impression left by the piece." For that, she wrote that the author needs at least three coders."

However, considering that this is research conducted by the author to write a book and that this is not a project sponsored by an academic institution, the author could not help but do it alone. This implies that the coding of stories might be subjective to a limited extent, no matter how the author strove to be objective in evaluation of stories. And the author has to admit that the coding in this research can never be definitive, except for conspicuously negative or positive stories.

All the more, the use of additional coders might not have been functional. If the evaluations of additional coders turned out to be highly correlated with this research, then their results will be taken to corroborate this research as a matter-of-fact finding. On the contrary, if their findings are significantly less correlated with this research, they may only detract from the value of this research. Or they might mean that this research is less "valuable" than this researcher thinks. The author thinks that readers can also play coders of stories while reading this book, just as advisors of the author's master os science thesis did. The readers may agree or disagree with my coding while they go on reading this book.

Social research expert Earl Babbie (2001) did not spell out whether content analysis can be valid only if conducted by more than one coder. Babbie simply wrote that newspaper articles are appropriate topics for content analysis and that the coding can be done by analyzing the manifest and latent content (Babbie, 2001, pp. 303-30).

Grossman and Kumar (1981) admitted that their "content analysis does *not provide a definitive portrait* (Seol's emphasis) of media coverage of the presidency" (p. 254). The two authors wrote that their content analysis, however, "does produce a clear picture of how the president and the White House were treated" by the news media. In this vein, *this author will be satisfied if a rough picture of the New York Times' portrayal of President Bush was drawn by this research, and if a rough picture of the Kyunghyang Daily's portrayal of Roh was drawn.* In this book, content analysis of the two newspapers served as groundwork for theorizing positive or negative presidential coverage.

The present author discovered that negative stories were comparatively easier to code. But there was some wiggle room for positive (+2 and +1) stories to be coded neutral (0). The *New York Times* or the *Kyunghyang Daily* journalists may insist that they make it a principle to adhere to objective reporting. In this case, the viewpoint of public relations practitioners (or, publicity officials) was adopted to code the stories: How would a public relations officer assess this particular story? Will this story please the White House or Blue House publicity officials?

Additionally, this study has adopted a five-step scale in coding the stories instead of three. This enabled the author to extract conspicuously positive or negative pieces. And a more detailed and refined definitions of the positive and negative images were provided for this research. In this respect, *this research was an attempt to be an objective analysis of the intrinsically subjective material in that every newspaper has their own color.*

This research has adopted a different approach from that taken by the Grossman and Kumar's study (1981). The definition of the scope of presidential coverage differs from their study. The "presidential image" in this research means the news coverage of the president and those stories that can affect the president's image. The two scholars conducted a content analysis of stories of the president and the White House, that is, "who he is, what he does, and what his programs, actions, and goals are." But as discussed in Chapter II, it is fairly difficult for White House correspondents to portray the incumbent president in a negative light, except in some exceptional cases. As shown earlier, reporters who wrote the largest number of intimate (and thus favorable) stories of the president were the White House reporters. It is understandable because they are physically nearest to the president and they are in a better position to do it. The same may be true of the Korean case.

Another difference from Grossman and Kumar's study is that this research has adopted a mix of evaluation methods: (1) To grasp the overall impression of the story by perusing the titles, subtitles, and the locus (page and place within the page) of the story in the newspaper and see whether there is a relevant photo, (2) To read the story lines and extract impressive ones, and extract the impressive words or phrases. But this research did not count the number of individual words. To borrow Babbie's words, this book tried to analyze the manifest and latent content in a comprehensive manner.

This research could be more profound if the scope of research ranged from the inauguration of Bush and Roh to their retirement, including the above developments. Future researchers may study the whole term(s) of the Bush and Roh presidency. Considering that television is increasingly more important in political communication, content analysis of the television news of President Bush and Roh may also be very meaningful.

Last but not the least important, the writing styles of the *New York Times* articles and those of the *Kyunghyang* may need to be studied. The author realized that sentences and descriptions of the *New York Times* were sophisticated and highly refined. These sentences need to be compared with those of Korean newspapers. Some stories were thought to be emotion-rousing, especially when they described intimate aspects of the First Family. The question of how reporters wrote straight stories, analyses, and columns may be additional topics of comparison for future research.

What topics reporters write about can also be a matter of concern in that the topics covered may represent differences in political culture in both countries. This book briefly touched on this but this topic may need further study.

CHAPTER

국문 요약 : 대통령과 언론, 친구인가 적인가

들어가면서_

노무현 대통령은 2003년 2월 취임 직후부터 지금(2004년 12월)까지 줄곧 일부 보수적 국내 신문과는 원만한 관계를 갖지 못한 것 같다. 이 기간에 노 대통령이 사석에서 "대통령 노릇 하는 데 위기감이 든다"고 한 발언이 어느 신문에 대서특필됐다. 그는 취임 1주년을 맞은 2004년 2월 "언론과 원만한 관계를 갖도록 노력하겠다"면서 청와대 출입기자들을 다독거렸다. 이것은 그동안 그의 언론관계가 좋지 않았음을 반증한 것이다. 노 대통령은 지속적으로 발생한 친인척 및 측근비리로 자신의 인기가 하락하자 2003년 10월 자신에 대한 신임을 묻겠다는 폭탄 발언으로 정국을 흔들었다. 우리 헌법은 '대통령이 신임'을 묻는 규정을 두고 있지 않다. 이로 인해 국내 언론과 정치인과 국민은 모두 한바탕 소동에 휩싸였다. 2004년 3월엔 노 대통령의 '총선개입 발언' 논란이 정쟁으로 비화해 갑자기 국회에서 탄핵 논의가 본격화됐다. 국회의 탄핵 소추가 성립되자 국내 언론(신문과 방송)은 탄핵을 강력히 비난하는 방송사들과 일부 진보적 신문, 그리고 탄핵을 묵인 또는 방조하는 듯한 보수적 신문 등 두 그룹으로 크게 나눠졌다. 말하자면 일부 언론매체는 대통령에게 친구였고 다른 일부 매체는 그에게 적이었다. 탄핵 직후 방송의 내용이 노 대통령에게 너무 우호적(편파적)이라고 분석한 한국언론학회의 보고서는 조선일보를 비롯한 일부 신문에 크게 보도되면서 보도의 공정성을 둘러싼 논란을 다시 일으켰다.

　대통령에 대한 언론 보도가 왜 이렇게 큰 문제가 되는가. 나아가 대통령들은 왜 언론 보도에 이처럼 큰 관심을 기울이고 있을까. 대부분의 국민은 대통령의 메시지를 직접 접할 기회가 거의 없다. 따라서 국민들은 신문이나 방송과 같은 대중매체가 비춰주는 대통령의 모습(미디어 이미지)을 실제로 받아들이게 된다. 이들에게는 '미디어의 실제'(media reality)는 '정치의 실제'(political reality)처럼 인식되는 것이다. 이 때문에 보도기관들이 대통령의 어떤 모습을 국민에 전달하는가에 의해 대통령의 정치나 정책이 매우 중요한 영향을 받는다. 미국의 학자들은 보도에 의해 대통령의 정책이 성공하거나 실패할 수도 있다고 지적했다. 한국의 행정수도 이전과 한국군의 이라크 파병에 관한 논쟁도 그 사례일지 모른다. 미국 정치학자 도리스 그레이버(Doris Graber, 2002) 교수는 "미디어는 정치환경을 전달하는 이상의 역할을 한다. 미디어란 바로 정치환경이다"라고 말했다. 그레이버에 의하면 대통령들은 후보 시절부터 자신을 좋게 알리기 위해 언론의 우호적 보도를 필요로 한다. 대통령에 취임한 후에는 정책의 성공과 실패, 정치나 정책의 활력이나 효율성, 국민의 정부 여부 등은 언론의 보도에 크게 좌우된다. 따라서 대통령이 우호적 언론 보도를 확보하는 것은 자신의 정책 시행을 위한 최우선 과제로 대두한다. 여러 전직 백악관 참모들의 말을 들으면, 백악관의 회의과정이나 행정부의 정책결정 과정에서 미디어에 대한 고려는 매우 중요한 위치를 차지한다. 모든 정책이 언론의 반응을 염두에 두고 개발되거나 발표된다(Graber, 2002, p. 277-78).

　언론과 대통령, 그리고 대통령과 언론. 이 양자의 관계는 친구일까 적일까. 언론은 언제 대통령에게 친구가 되고 언제 적이 되는가. 그리고 언론은 어떤 방법으로 우호적 또는 적대적인 보도를 하는가. 본서는 대통령과 언론의 상호관계에 관한 이같은 의문에 접근하기 위해 미국과 한국의 사례를 들어 그 해답을 구하려 시도했다. 본서는 뉴욕타임스가 조지 W 부시 대통령을 어떻게 묘사했는지, 그리고 경향신문이 노무현 대통령을 어떻게 묘사했는지를 중요한 의미가 있는 일정기간을 선정해 보도내용을 분석했다. 그 뒤 언론은 어떤 상황에서 어떤 방법으로 대통령에게 우호적–적대적 보도를 하는지에 관해 이론화를 시도해 보았다. 본서는 저자가 2003년 12월 미국 캘리포니아주 새너제이 주립대 저널리즘 스쿨에 제출한 석사학위 논문 '뉴욕 타임스가 묘사한 조지 W. 부시의 대통령 이미지(Presidential Image of George W. Bush as Depicted by the New York Times)'를 기초로 했다. 저자는 2004년 5월부터 11월 사이 이 석사 논문에 국내 언론(경향신문)의 사례 연구를 추가하고 이론적 논의를 더욱 보완해 이 책을 구성했다. 특히 언제 어떤 방법으로 대통령을 우호적 또는 적대적으로 묘사하는지 범주화한 것은 다소 이론적으로 취약할 수 있겠으나 저자 나름 대로 이론화를 시도해 본 것이다.

본론: 논의에 들어가며_

1. 대통령의 시각

가. 대통령의 전통적 언론 적대감과 그 허실

두 세기가 넘는 미국 대통령사에서 모든 대통령들은 신문(그리고 최근에는 방송)들이 자기들에게 우호적인 보도를 해줄 것을 기대했다. 국정을 이끌어 나가는데 "언론이 도와줬으면"하고 바라는 이런 기대는 이해할 만하다. 한국 대통령들도 이 점에서는 마찬가지일 것이다. 그렇지만 건국 초창기의 미국 대통령들은 지극히 당파적인 신문 보도로 상당한 고통을 받았다. 당시 발행 부수가 낮은 신문들은 대부분 정파적 이해관계를 가진 사람들이 발행했기 때문에 노골적으로 편파적 기사를 실었다. 독자들도 신문이 어느 대통령에 우호적인지 적대적인지 이해한 상태에서 신문을 사서 읽었다.

신문의 대량 인쇄가 가능해진 20세기와 21세기엔 이런 사정이 달라졌을까. 신문들은 지난 세기 '객관적 보도'의 기치를 들고 대통령과 관련한 보도를 한다고 자랑해 왔다. 하지만 대통령들은 여전히 대통령과 관련한 언론 보도에 대해 불만을 가졌다. 실제로 미국 정치학자 랜스 베넷(W. Lance Bennett)은 '객관적 보도' 준칙들이 전문적 언론이나 언론 윤리의 확립과 함께 자리잡지 않고 신문의 대량판매를 위한 수단으로 내세워졌다고 밝혔다(Bennett, 1996, pp. 146-149). '객관적 보도'나 '공정 보도'는 애당초 전문적 보도를 위한 언론윤리나 정치적 고려에서 나온 것이 아니었다. 어쨌든 미국 역사를 돌이켜 보면 미국 대통령들은 언론이 객관적 보도를 한다고 선전하는 동안에도 언론 보도 내용에 여전히 불만을 가졌다. 전반적으로 말해 미국 대통령들의 눈에는 미국 언론이 자신들에게 친구가 아니었다는 얘기다.

초창기의 사례를 보자. 토머스 제퍼슨 대통령(재임 1801-09)은 "만약 신문 없는 정부를 가져야 할 것인지 아니면 정부 없는 신문을 가져야 할 것인지 결정하는 선택권이 나에게 맡겨진다면 나는 주저 없이 후자를 택할 것이다"라는 발언을 한 인물이다. 이처럼 극도의 친언론적 발언도 드물 것이다. 제퍼슨 대통령은 우리에게 언론자유 수호의 대표적 옹호자로 알려져 있다. 하지만 제퍼슨 대통령은 자신에 관한 언론 보도에 대해 엄청난 불만을 가졌다. 그는 당시 신문의 편파적 보도에 너무도 심하게 시달린 나머지 언론 보도에 대해 격렬한 독설을 퍼부었다. 제퍼슨 대통령은 신문 보도의 가치에 대해 "아무리 무식한 사람이라도 신문 보도를 믿지 않을 것"이라고 악평했다. 그는 나아가 "신문 보도는 세상사에 실망한 사람들의 한 단면을 보여주는 것에 불과하며 언론자유의 남용은 사상 유례 없이 적정 수준을 넘어섰다"며 언론을 강하게 질타했다(Edwards and Wayne, 1994, p. 138).

언론보도에 대한 대통령의 불만은 최근에도 찾아볼 수 있다. 로널드 레이건 대통령(재임 1981-89, 사망 2004년)은 언론을 능숙하게 조작한 정치인으로 평가받고 있다. 그는 언론이 자신을 탁월한 지도자로 묘사하도록 유도한 것 때문에 '위대한 전달자'(Great Communicator)라는 별칭까지 얻었다. 그럼에도 불구하고 레이건 대통령은 언론에 대해 뿌리 깊은 불만을 갖고 있었다. 그는 어느 날 방송 출연을 마친 뒤 마이크 전원이 켜져 있는 줄 모르고 근처의 기자들에게 안 들리는 작은 목소리로 "개자식들"(Sons of bitches)이라고 욕설을 했다. 자신이 모르는 사이에 녹음된 레이건 대통령의 이 발언이 널리 알려지자 기자들이 "이게 무슨 말이냐"라며 따져 물었다. 당시 래리 스피크스 백악관 대변인은 "대통령은 그런 발언을 했는지 기억하지 못한다. 아마 날씨가 좋다는 얘기이며, 귀하들이 부유하다는 것을 말했을 것이다(It's sunny, and you are rich)"라고 해명하면서 얼버무렸다(Sons of bitches와 sunny... rich는 두운과 각운이 맞아 이런 해명을 했을 것이다. 저자 주. Smith, 1990, p. 1).

빌 클린턴 대통령(재임 1993-2001)도 자신에 대한 미국 언론의 보도에 깊은 불신감을 가졌다. 대통령 당선자 시절 클린턴은 "언론의 감시견 기능을 인정한다. 그러나 기사의 제목 거리를 찾느라 도를 넘는 일이 흔하다. 이런 언론을 매개자로 삼아 자신의 뜻을 국민에게 전달하려는 사람은 아마 미친 사람일 것이다"라고 말했다(Nelson, 1995, p. 297).

노무현 대통령도 한국 언론에 큰 불만을 가진 인물로 널리 알려져 있다(그는 방송은 아니고 주로 보수적 신문에 불만을 표시했다). 노 대통령은 취임 직후엔 언론보도에 대해 개방적 자세를 보였다. 그러나 그는 취임 후 몇 달 안돼 "대통령 역할을 못해 먹을 정도의 위기감이 든다"면서 한국의 보수 신문들에 대해 노골적 불만을 드러냈다. 그는 2004년 6월 주한 외교 사절들을 청와대로 초청한 자리에서 "한국 신문의 제목을 그대로 믿지 말라" "본국으로 한국 사정을 보고할 때 나에게 또는 공무원에게 먼저 문의한 뒤 보고해 달라"고 주문했다(경향신문 2004년 6월 5일 2면). 노무현 대통령은 몇차례 언론과 화해를 시도한 것으로 평가되지만 언론에 대해 여전히 깊은 불신을 가진 것으로 보도되고 있다. 특히 2004년 행정도시 이전 추진 계획과 관련해 "정권의 명운을 걸고 하겠다" "서울 중심부에 있는 일부 신문들이 수도 이전을 반대한다"며 노골적인 반감을 드러냈다. 하지만 저자는 노 대통령이 국내 방송사들의 보도 내용에 대해서는 별로 불만을 토로하지 않는 것을 중시한다. 방송사들의 대통령 보도는 보수 신문들에 비해 상대적으로 우호적 논조를 가졌음을 반증한다고 풀이할 수 있다.

그렇다면 학자들은 대통령과 언론의 관계를 어떻게 평가하고 있을까. 미국 언론은 이렇게 욕먹을 정도로 대통령들을 적대적으로 묘사했는가. 미국의 정치학자 마이클 그로스먼과 마싸 쿠마르(Michael Grossman & Martha Kumar, 1981)는 그들의 공저 '대통령 묘사(Portraying The President)'를 통해 미국 주요 언론 매체의 대통령 보도 논조에 관한 흥미 있는 연구 결과를 발표했다. 두 정치학자는 1953년부터 1978년까지 25년 간 게재된 뉴욕타임스(New York Times) 및 시사주간지 타임(Time)의 대통령 기사, 그리고 1968년부터 1978년까지 방송된 CBS저녁뉴스(CBS Evening News)의 대통령 보도의 내용을 분석했다. 이들은 연구 결과 "3개 매체가 예상과는 달리 미국의 대통령을 상당히 우호적으로 보도했다"고 결론지었다. 그들이 분석결과가 절대적인 것은 아니라고 말했지만 일단 이들의 주장을 읽어 보자.

25년 동안 뉴욕타임스와 타임이 보도한 백악관 기사를 분석한 결과 보도내용이 예상보다 매우 우호적임이 드러났다. 두 매체는 부정적 기사 한 건에 대해 긍정적 보도 두 건을 보도했다. CBS 저녁뉴스의 경우 베트남전 보도가 포함돼 부정적 보도가 많은 편이었다. 하지만 연도별 분석을 하면 긍정 보도 대 부정 보도의 비율은 다른 두 매체와 같은 유형을 보였다 (Graber, 1982, p. 89).

그로스먼과 쿠마르는 '2 대 1'의 비율에 대해 "예상 외로 우호적 보도가 많았다"고 말했다. 하지만 저자는 우선 미국(또는 한국의) 대통령들이 이런 정도의 비율에는 절대 만족하지 않을 것으로 믿는다. 저자가 그렇게 믿는 이유는 백악관과 정부가 우호적 보도를 최대한 많이 얻기 위해 방대한 공보조직을 갖추고 조직적으로 공보(홍보)활동을 전개하기 때문이다. 백악관에는 대통령에 대한 우호적 보도를 이끌어내기 위해 언론담당관실(Press Office, 매일 출입기자를 상대로 공보활동을 하는 곳으로 백악관 대변인은 이 조직의 책임자다)과 커뮤니케이션 딤딩관실(Office of Communications, 백악관의 중장기 공보활동 및 공보전략을 세우는 곳, 공보담당관 Director of Communication이 책임자다) 등 여러 기구를 운영하고 있다. 쿠마르와 설리번(Kumar & Sullivan, 2003)은 공저 '백악관의 세계(The White House World: Transitions, Organization, and Office Operations)'를 통해 백악관 공보조직, 활동내용, 그리고 소속원들의 업무 등을 매우 상세하게 기술하고 있어 내용을 참고할 만하다.

그로스먼과 쿠마르(1981)에 따르면, 백악관 공보 직원들은 우호적 보도를 하는 기자에게는 적절히 취재 편의를 봐준다. 그러나 적대적 보도를 하는 기자에게는 직접-간접으로 취재에 불편을 주거나 눈에 보이지 않는 규제를 가하기도 한다. 초지일관 대통령에 적대적 기사를 쓰는 기자들은 백악관 공보담당 직원들의 취재 편의를 받지 못할 각오를 해야 한다. 아울러 백악관 직원들이 흘려주는 정보를 받지 못할 준비가 돼 있어야 한다. 따라서 독자적으로 백악관을 비판할 역량(즉 재력이나 취재력, 예컨대 뉴욕타임스나 워싱턴포스트 등 큰 언론매체들은 역량을 갖췄다고 평가됨)을 가진 언론사에 소속한 기자가 아니면 백악관 출입기자나 그 기자가 소속된 언론사는 지속적으로 백악관을 비판하는 일이 어렵다고 그들은 지적했다. 취재 역량이 부족한 지방 언론들이 백악관에 대해 비판 일변도의 보도를 하기가 어려운 것은 백악관에 대한 의존도가 높기 때문이라는 설명이다. 이런 맥락에서 저자는 백악관 공보 직원들은 '2 대 1' 보다 훨씬 높은 비율로 대통령에 관련한 우호적 보도를 기대한다고 믿는다.

두 학자가 분석대상으로 삼은 '대통령과 관련한 보도' 는 백악관 기자들이 쓴 기사를 그 내용으로 하고 있다. 하지만 저자는 '대통령을 우호적으로 또는 적대적으로 보도' 하는 기사의 범위가 백악관 출입기자들이 행하는 보도활동에만 한정되지 않는다고 생각한다. 예컨대 2003년 3월 부시 대통령의 대 이라크 전쟁 개시를 전후해 미국언론이 미국 내외의 대규모 반전시위를 보도한 것은 부시 대통령의 전쟁 정책에 반대하는 적대적 보도로 볼 수 있기 때문이다. 당시 뉴욕타임스는 "미국의 대 이라크 전쟁은 국제법적 근거가 약하다"는 유엔 출입기자의 기사를 게재한 바 있다. 이 기사도 부시 대통령에게 부정적 영향을 준다고 평가할 수 있다.

그로스먼과 쿠마르(1981)에 따르면, 대통령의 리더십을 부각하는 보도, 가정에 충실한 가장으로서 대통령을 묘사하는 보도, 희로애락 감정을 가진 인간적 측면을 부각한 보도, 갈등과 분쟁을 해결하는 보도 등이 우호적 보도로 평가된다. 이건 이해할 수 있다. 예컨대 지미 카터 대통령이 1978년 8

월 뉴욕시를 방문해 정치인들이 지켜보는 가운데 파탄에 빠진 시의 재정을 구제하기 위해 서명한 것은 대통령에 우호적인 보도로 평가된다. 반면 대통령이 뭔가 잘못을 저지르거나, 행정부가 어떤 공표된 목적을 성취하지 못하거나, 대통령에 대한 비난이나 반대를 담은 보도 등은 대통령에 대한 적대적 보도로 평가된다.

그로스먼과 쿠마르는 사진 보도도 언급했다. 두 사람에 따르면, 대통령과 관련한 사진 보도는 백악관 측 실무진이 사진 촬영의 여건을 유효하게 통제할 수 있다. 따라서 사진 보도의 대부분은 구조적으로 대통령에 우호적인 측면을 전달할 수밖에 없다는 것이다. 두 사람은 우호적 사진 보도의 비율이 우호적 기사 보도의 비율보다 훨씬 높았다고 분석했다. 두 학자는 아울러 대통령과 관련한 기사가 적대적인 경우에도 사진의 내용은 우호적인 내용이 많아 기사와 사진의 내용이 불일치하는 경우도 흔했다고 썼다. 이것은 텔레비전 방송 보도에 있어서도 화면 보도에 관한 한 어느 정도 유사한 평가를 할 수 있다고 생각된다. 스틸 사진 보도와 ENG 카메라 보도는 대체로 백악관 실무진의 협조를 필요로 하기 때문이다. 이런 상황은 청와대의 경우에도 해당한다고 말할 수 있다.

그로스먼과 쿠마르(1981)는 아울러 "언론의 대통령 보도에 일종의 패턴(추세)이 존재한다"고 주장했다. 두 학자는 대통령의 취임 초기(밀월 기간)에 가장 많은 수의 우호적 기사가 등장하며, 차츰 그 수가 줄었다가, 임기 종료시 다시 우호적 기사가 많아진다고 썼다. 그러나 이런 추세는 닉슨 정부에 들어서면서 적용되지 않기 시작했다. 워터게이드로 통칭되는 불미스런 정치공작으로 닉슨 대통령에 대한 부정적 보도는 급증했다. 이 사건을 계기로 미국의 언론과 대통령간의 관계는 전임 대통령들이 정착시켜 놓은 조심스런 상호존중 또는 상호협조 관계에서 대통령 불신 관계로 급변했고 이것이 현재까지 지속한다고 말할 수 있다.

정치학자 마크 로젤(2003)에 의하면, 프랭클린 루스벨트(FDR) 대통령은 언론을 자신의 의도대로 좌지우지한 인물이었다. 당시 미국 언론은 루스벨트 대통령에게 상당한 존경심을 갖고 있었다. 다음은 로젤이 루스벨트 대통령의 '언론 다루기'를 묘사한 것이다.

루스벨트 대통령은 자신의 인품과 전문가적 언론 지식을 이용해 기자들을 매료시켰으며 자신의 정책에 백악관의 시각을 투영하기 위해 기자들을 효율적으로 이용했다. 기자회견에 참석하는 기자들은 오늘날이라면 받아들이기 어려운 규칙들을 수용했다. 루스벨트 대통령은 어떤 내용을 말하기 전 보도 전제 또는 비보도 전제를 지시했고 어떤 내용은 출처를 밝히지 말라고 요청했다. 말하자면 그는 상세한 '보도지침'을 내렸다. 대통령의 취재규칙을 준수하지 않는 기자들에게는 백악관에 대한 접근이 금지됐다. 루스벨트 대통령이 판단하기에 어리석은 질문을 하는 기자들에게는 종이로 만든 원추형의 '바보 모자'(dunce cap)를 씌웠다. 루스벨트는 우호적인 기자들을 자신의 백악관 가족 만찬에 초대했다. 특정 사안에 관해서는 그들의 의견을 구하기도 했다. 사진기자들은 소아마비로 다리를 못 쓰는 루스벨트 대통령이 휠체어로 옮겨지는 모습을 절대 촬영하지 못하도록 했다. 그는 1936년 필라델피아의 프랭클린 필드에서 연설하기 위해 연단에 올라가기 직전 넘어져 진흙구덩이에 얼굴을 들이박았다. 이때 어느 누구도 이 사건을 보도(사진 보도 포함)하지 못했다. 루즈벨트 대통령이 언론의 우호적 보도를 향유할 수 있었던 것은 당시 시대상황이 국가적 경제위기를 맞은 데다 외국의 무력 위협(2차 세계대전)이 있었고 그 시절 기자들은 요즘처럼 워싱턴 정계를 의심의 눈길로 보지 않았기 때문이다(Pfiffner & Davidson, 2003, pp. 137-38).

조지 W. 부시 대통령의 전임자인 빌 클린턴 대통령은 밀월기간은 커녕 취임 초기부터 언론의 심한 공격을 받았다. 클린턴은 취임 초기 수개월간 동성애자 군 복무 제한 완화 문제, 순조롭지 못한 장관 임명, 백악관 여행 담당직원의 독직 문제, 클린턴 대통령 자신의 200달러 고가 이발 문제 등으로 언론의 지속적이고도 집중적인 공격을 받았다. 특히 그는 '르윈스키 스캔들'로 모든 미국 언론으로부터 공격을 받게 됐다. 급기야 그는 1999년 2월 의회의 탄핵 소추까지 당할 뻔했으나 위기를 겨우 모면했다. 그는 탄핵 표결이 정족수를 넘기지 못해 겨우 대통령직을 유지했다. 저자는 당시 CNN의 존 킹 기자가 "어떻게 하면 대통령이 자신의 딸 정도의 나이인 어린 처녀와 희롱할 수 있느냐"면서 클린턴 대통령의 행위를 맹렬히 공격했다. 존 킹 기자는 2004년에도 '백악관 출입 선임 전문기자'(Senior White House Correspondent)라는 직책으로 백악관 보도를 계속하고 있다.

정치학자 도리스 그레이버는 조지 W. 부시 현 대통령도 그다지 초기 밀월을 즐기지 못했다고 평가했다. 그레이버 교수는 "부시 대통령이 클린턴이나 아버지 부시보다 훨씬 언론의 관심을 끌지 못했으며 적대적 보도로 인해 그의 취임 초기는 밀월과 거리가 멀었다"고 말했다(Graber, 2002, p. 283).

나. 우호적 보도를 이끌어내기 위한 대통령의 언론 다루기

대통령들은 언론을 제어-조종해 항상 우호적 보도가 나오도록 유도하려 한다. 정치학자 존 몰티즈(John Maltese, 1992)는 딕 체니 부통령이 언론 조종을 어떻게 생각하는지 예전의 일화를 통해 보여주었다. 체니 부통령은 아버지 부시 정권 시절 국방장관 취임 직전에 몰티즈를 만나 언론에 관한 대화를 나누었다. 체니는 몰티즈에게 "언론에 의한 의세 설정을 통제할 필요가 있다"고 강조했다. 포드 대통령 시절 백악관 비서실장을 지낸 체니 부통령의 조지 W. 부시 행정부의 언론 정책이 어떨 것일지 충분히 짐작하게 한다.

백악관을 효율적으로 운영하려면 언론의 의제를 통제해야 한다. 통제를 위해 필수적인 것은 행정부내 기강을 유지해야 한다는 점이다. 대통령의 보좌진이 외견상 불일치를 드러내면 이것은 반드시 대통령이 설정하려는 의제를 훼손할 기회를 언론에 제공하고야 만다(Maltese, 1992, p. 1).

미국 메릴랜드주 타우슨(Towson) 대학의 정치학자(대통령학) 마싸 쿠마르(2003) 교수는 저자에게 이메일로 보낸 미발표 논문을 통해 "조지 W. 부시 대통령은 미디어의 의제 통제에 깊은 관심을 가지고 있다"고 평가했다. 이같은 언론관을 가진 부시 대통령과 체니 부통령이 입성한 백악관이 전례 없이 꽉 짜인 미디어 제어정책을 쓰는 것은 당연한 일이 아닐까 싶다. 정치학자 에드워즈와 웨인(Edwards & Wayne, 1994)에 따르면, 백악관은 우호적인 보도를 이끌어 내기 위해 직원의 약 3분의 1을 언론 관계의 일에 투입하고 있다. 정치학자 도리스 그레이버(1997)는 대통령이 언론의 우호적 보도를 이끌어 내기 위해 다음과 같은 3가지의 전술을 구사한다고 썼다.

1)언론의 호감을 얻기: 백악관은 기자들에게 좋은 기삿거리를 주거나 특종감을 제공해 우호적 관계를 형성하려 한다.
2)뉴스의 흐름을 장악하기: 대통령은 촌철살인의 논평을 가하거나 언론과 접촉을 제어함으로써 뉴스의 흐름을 이끌어 가려 한다.
3)보도 과정을 잘 조정하기: 대통령들은 보도가치가 있는 행사를 갖거나 중요 발표를 앞두고 뉴스를 통제하거나 공식적 의전행사를 갖는 등 여러 방법으로 보도 과정을 효율적으로 제어하려 한다(Graber, 2002, pp. 281-83).

대통령이 우호적인 언론 보도를 얻기 위해 의제 통제와 언론조작 등 방법을 구사하는 도중에도 백악관과 출입기자들 사이에는 기사 가치에 관한 끊임없는 교섭과 협조가 진행된다고 말할 수 있다. 정치학자(대통령학) 티머씨 쿡과 린 랙스데일(Timothy Cook & Lyn Ragsdale, 1995)은 대통령과 언론의 상호 관계에 관해 "동시에 서로 의존적이면서도 서로 독립적

(simultaneously interdependent and independent)"이라고 규정했다. 두 학자에 따르면 "대통령은 그들의 메시지를 보내고, 정치적 의제를 설정하고, 우호적인 여론을 조성하며, 정치적 반대자에게 압력을 가하는 등 여러 목적을 위해 언론의 우호적 보도를 필요로 한다. 대통령의 공보 공작에 대응하는 언론측은 매일의 뉴스제작을 위한 중요 인물로 대통령을 인식한다. 이런 면에서 언론에는 대통령 관련 기사가 매우 중요하다(Nelson, 1995, pp. 297-330)."

전술한 바와 같이 양자는 상호 의존 관계가 성립하는 가운데에서도 상호 독립적이다. 대통령은 다른 정치인들과 마찬가지로 우호적인 보도가 많기를 원한다. 하지만 언론인들은 독자(시청자)에 대한 봉사정신, 보도의 균형과 중립성에 대한 신념, 성취 의욕 등을 갖고 있다. 언론인들은 이런 이유로 백악관이 제공하는 보도자료에만 의존하는 '백악관 홍보기자'(flack)에 머무르려 하지 않는다. 그 결과 백악관과 언론은 여러 사안에 대해 뉴스가치가 있는지 없는지를 둘러싸고 끊임없이 상호 절충과 교섭을 진행한다고 말할 수 있다.

어떤 사안이 보도가치를 가졌느냐에 대해 백악관과 언론의 판단이 상이한 것은 당연할지 모른다. 흔히 뉴스는 중요성과 재미를 가져야 한다고 말한다. 레이건 대통령 시절의 래리 스피크스 대변인은 이 문제에 관해 한마디로 적확하게 표현했다. "우리에게 뉴스를 어떻게 연출해야 하는지 말하지 말라. 우리는 당신들에게 어떻게 보도해야 하는지 요청하지 않겠다." 스피크스 대변인은 백악관 출입기자들에게 보란 듯이 이 문구를 자신의 사무실벽에 붙였다.

다. 우호적 보도를 이끌어내기 위한 대통령의 책략

그로스먼과 쿠마르(1981)는 백악관이 언론의 우호적 보도를 이끌어내기 위해 어떤 전술(기술)을 구사하는지 유형별로 상술했다. 이런 전술은 구체적으로도 언론의 보도 내용에서도 확인되고 있어 매우 흥미롭다.

첫째, 인간적 특성을 묘사하도록 하는 방법이 있다. 언론이 대통령을 '평범한 사람'처럼 묘사하도록 유도하는 방법이다(이것은 한국에서 한때 노태우 대통령이 '보통 사람' 이미지를 내세운 것과 같은 맥락이다, 저자 주). 대통령은 수많은 보좌진을 거느린 행정부 수반으로 당연히 힘 있는 유명인사인데도 언론이 이렇게 묘사하도록 유도하는 이유는 국민에게 친근감을 주기 위한 데 있다. 예컨대 지미 카터 대통령은 한때 매사추세츠주의 작은 도시 클린턴(Clinton)과 캘리포니아주의 소도시 살리나스(Salinas)를 방문했다. 그는 이곳의 농가에서 평범한 농부들과 함께 식사하면서 자연스럽게 대화하는 장면을 연출했다. 전국에 생중계되는 이 행사를 위해 백악관 직원들은 여러 주 전부터 현장 답사와 경호 활동 등 준비에 만전을 기하느라 너무도 분주했을 것임은 말할 필요가 없다.

대통령을 가족의 일원으로 묘사하도록 하는 방법도 있다. 아버지로서 남편으로서 아들로서 묘사하는 기사는 대체로 우호적일 수밖에 없다. 가끔 영부인을 내세워 대통령이 좋은 이미지를 갖도록 할 수도 있다. 예컨대, 백악관 직원들은 포드 대통령의 무뚝뚝한 이미지를 보완하기 위해 인생의 유유자적한 멋과 맛을 추구하는 베티 포드 여사를 언론에 노출시켰다. 존 F 케네디 대통령이 1961년 파리의 국제회의에서 별로 내세울 만한 성과를 거두지 못하자 백악관 공보직원들은 재클린 케네디 여사를 언론에 노출시켰다. 케네디 대통령은 "재클린을 파리로 모셔온 신사"라는 언론의 묘사에 별 불만을 표시하지 않았다. 2003년 가을 조지 부시 대통령이 로라 여사를 파리로 보내 미국의 유네스코 재가입 행사에 참여하도록 한 것도 같은 맥락으로 보면 된다. 당시 뉴욕 타임스는 늙은 얼굴의 프랑스 신사 자크 시라크 프랑스 대통령이 상대적으로 젊은 로라 부시 여사의 손등에 입맞추는 사진을 1면에 크게 썼다. 타임스는 당시 "미국 주도의 이라크 전쟁으로 인한 미국과 프랑스 사이의 갈등이 해소될 것인가"라는 내용의 기사를 게재했다. 대통령은 간혹 천진난만한 어린이들을 안아주거나 이들을 귀여워하는 모습을 보여준다. 이런 종류의 기사와 사진이 보도된다면 그것은 분명 대통령에게 우호적인 묘사라고 말할 수 있다.

둘째, 대통령의 지도력(리더십) 발휘 장면을 묘사하도록 하는 방법이 있다. 여기에는 단호한 모습의 군사적 리더십을 드러내는 것과 어떤 사태를 완전히 장악하는 모습을 드러내는 것이 있다. 군대를 파견하거나 공격을 명령하는 등 군 통수권자로서 보여주는 단호한 모습은 언론의 찬사를 유도하고 국민의 지지를 이끌어 낼 수 있다. 예컨대 뉴욕 타임스는 조지 W. 부시 대통령의 9-11 테러 공격 이후의 리더십을 '위기를 처리하는 지도자'(crisis leader)또는 '군사적 지도자'(military leader)로 묘사했다. 이것은 부시에게 매우 우호적인 보도였다(Edwards & Wayne, 2003, xvii). 프랭클린 루스벨트 대통령과 해리 트루먼 대통령은 2차대전 중 군사 지도자로서의 이미지를 확립했다. 트루먼 대통령과 드와이트 아이젠하워 대통령은 한국전에서의 군사 지도자로서의 강력한 이미지를 세웠고, 존 케네디 대통령은 '쿠바 위기'를 통해 단호한 군사지도자의 모습을 미국민(나아가 세계인)에게 각인했다.

대통령이 자신에게 도전하는 각료급 보좌진을 결연히 해직하는 것도 같은 맥락이다. 제럴드 포드 대통령은 기자회견을 통해 헨리 키신저 안보 보좌관과 제임스 슐레싱거 국방장관을 단호하게 해임했다. 당시 한 백악관 관리는 "대통령의 권위를 확립하기 위해 대통령의 권위를 넘으려는 보좌진을 해임했다"고 말했다. 대통령이 지식인의 모임이나 과학자들의 모임에 모습을 나타내 행사를 주재하거나 발언을 하는 것도 우호적 보도를 이끌어 내기에 좋은 기회다. 아울러 국제회의에 참석해 다른 국가의 정상들과 회담성과를 내는 것도 국제적 리더십에 관한 보도를 이끌어 내는 좋은 기회가 된다.

셋째, 정책 결정자의 이미지를 그리도록 유도할 수도 있다. 대통령은 상하 양원 합동회의에 참석해 정책 연설을 행할 수 있고 매년초 연두교서를 발표할 수 있다. 대통령은 이를 통해 행정부가 관할하는 국정 전반에 관한 정책적 입장을 밝힐 수 있으며 나아가 국가의 모든 사안에 대해 입장을 밝혀 정책을 세워나갈 수 있다. 백악관은 언론이 이런 사안에 대해 대통령을 정책 결정자로서 묘사하도록 유도한다.

넷째, 기자회견을 이용해 우호적 보도를 이끌어 낼 수 있다. 대통령이 출연하는 거의 모든 행사는 뉴스 기관에 대해 어떤 형태로든 기삿거리를 제공한다. 대통령은 기자회견에서 여러 가지로 자신에게 유리한 규칙을 세워 언론 보도가 자신을 우호적으로 보도하도록 유도할 수 있다. 전술한 바와 같이 프랭클린 루스벨트 대통령은 언론인들과 격의 없는 대화와 농담을 주고받는 가운에 언론의 우호적 보도를 유도했다. 최근 텔레비전과 통신수단의 발달로 인해 대통령의 연두 기자회견 방송 직후 반대파 정치인의 반박이 거의 동시에 보도된다. 이 때문에 대통령 발언이 가지는 정치적 위력이 다소 떨어졌다. 하지만 대통령은 여전히 언제 어떤 방법으로 어떤 내용의 기자회견을 할지를 결정할 수 있는 등 여전히 유리한 여건에서 기자회견을 가질 수 있다.

2. 언론의 시각

가. 대통령 보도를 보도형식에 꿰어맞추기-- '제왕적' 언론

정치학자 로버트 엔트먼(Robert Entmann, 1990)은 "미국언론이 대통령 기사를 억지로 기사 보도의 틀에 짜맞추려 한다"(story framing을 지칭함. 저자 주)고 지적한 바 있다. 그는 이같은 언론의 행태를 '제왕적 언론'(imperial media)이라고 규정했다. 엔트먼은 논문 '제왕적 언론'에서 다음과 같이 기술했다.

보도 매체들은 대통령 보도에서 뉴스의 틀에 짜맞추려 하는 관행을 갖고 있다. 대통령이 언론 보도를 관리하는 행위는 간혹 언론인들의 보도목적상의 필요에 부합하기도 한다. 그러나 언론이 기사를 선택하는 과정에서 기자들은 독자를 끌 수 있는 기사의 틀에 맞추기 위해 강력한 인물, 정치인들 사이의 갈등이나 논란, 독자에 대한 충격 등을 찾아내려 한다(DiClerico, 1990, p. 155).

엔트먼의 이같은 말은 아래에서 상술하는 언론 보도의 틀에 대통령 관련 기사를 짜맞추려는 경향을 잘 짚어낸 것이라 할 만하다. 이같은 보도의 틀 짜기를 인정한다면, 백악관이 언론의 우호적 보도를 이끌어 내려면 언론 보도의 틀(기사의 틀)에 맞도록 공보활동을 전개해야 한다는 얘기가 된다. 언론은 나름 대로 독자(시청자)의 관심을 유발하고 이를 유지하기 위해 대통령 보도를 어떤 틀에 짜맞추는 경향이 있음은 사실이라 하겠다.

이 문제에 관해 쿡과 랙스데일(1995)은 대통령에 대해 국민이 가지는 이상적 이미지(보도의 틀)는 '한 사람의 외로운 지도자 이미지'라고 정의했다. 그들은 언론에 나타나는 보도유형을 아래의 4가지로 정리했다.

첫째, 문제 해결자로서 나타난 대통령 기사. 언론은 대통령이 복잡하고 어려운 국내 문제를 시원히 해결하는 모습을 보여주고 싶어한다. 이것은 언론이 대통령에 대해 가지는 이상적인 지도자형이라 할 수 있다. 예컨대 씨어도어 루스벨트의 '스퀘어 딜' 정책이 나온 이래 우드로 윌슨의 '뉴 프리덤' 정책, 프랭클린 루스벨트의 '뉴 딜' 정책 등은 대통령이 문제해결에 나선 모습을 한마디로 묘사한 것이다.

둘째, 국제적 지도자로서 나타난 대통령 기사. 비록 국가 위기시에 국방장관, 국무장관, 중앙정보국장이 중요한 실무적 역할을 수행하지만 미국 언론은 결국 자유세계를 지키는 최고 책임자는 미국 대통령이라고 묘사하고 싶어한다. 냉전 기간 대통령은 자유세계를 공산주의로부터 보호하는 궁극적인 지도자로 묘사됐다. 냉전체제 붕괴 이후에는 조지 H. W. 부시 대통령(아버지 부시)은 '바그다드의 도살자'인 이라크의 사담 후세인 대통령이 미국에 가하는 위협으로부터 국민을 보호하려고 노력하는 지도자로 묘사됐다.

셋째, 미국 대통령은 '미국의 꿈'(American dream)을 상징하는 사람으로 묘사된다. 대통령은 평범한 미국인을 대표하기도 하고 수많은 국민들을 대신해 크리스마스 트리를 점등하기도 한다. 대통령은 가슴 뭉클한 성공담의 주인공이기도 하며 미국을 대표해 우주 여행에서 귀환하는 우주인을 환영하기도 한다.

넷째, 대통령의 모습이 이상의 3가지 보도의 틀(frame)에 잘 맞지 않을 경우 언론은 대통령의 잘못, 실수, 스캔들을 흥미 위주로 보도한다는 것이다. 미국 언론은 지미 카터 대통령이 이란에 억류된 미국인 인질 구출작전에서 실패한 것을 부각해 지속적으로 보도했고, 아버지 부시 대통령이 "새로운 세금은 없다"는 선거공약을 어기자 이를 집중적-지속적으로 비판했다. 미국 언론은 베트남전 도중 린든 존슨 대통령에 대해 "몰래 대규모 공습을 하도록 명령하는 등 확전을 지시해 놓고도 이를 모르는 척한다"고 맹공격했다. 언론은 이른바 존슨 대통령의 '신뢰도 격차'(credibility gap)를 문제 삼았던 것이다.

나. 언론의 대통령 비판은 '의례적'인가?

정치학자 랜스 베넷(W. Lance Bennett, 1996)은 (대통령에 대한)언론의 적대적 역할이 제한적이며 '의례적'일 수밖에 없다고 지적했다. 베넷 교수의 주장에 따르면 만약 언론이 진정으로 지속적으로 정치인 보도를 적대적으로 한다면 심각한 딜레마에 빠질 것이라는 얘기다. 그는 적대적 보도가 계속된다면 언론이 신뢰성의 근거로 삼는 기존의 사회조직에 대한 심각한 불신이 생긴다고 말했다. 정치인이나 관리의 발언이 언론에 의해 일관되게 공격을 당하고 불신을 당한다면 언론은 스스로의 보도내용에 관한 공식적인 확인을 받을 수 없게 된다는 지적이다. 따라서 '뉴스의 객관성(객관적 보도)'은 어느 사회에서 기사에 허용되는 '한정된' 시각과 이 시각이 신뢰할 만하다고 확인하는 정부의 공식적 견해에 의해 유지된다는 것이다. 이 범위 내에서 뉴스의 객관성이라는 언론적 환상이 만들어진다고 그는 설명했다.

기자들이 공직자나 정부기관의 뻔한 선전을 해주는 것도 객관적 보도에서 일탈하는 모습이다. 만약 진정한 언론의 적대성과 이의 완전한 상실이 뉴스의 객관성을 해친다고 한다면 이것은 중요한 의미를 갖는다. 환언하면, 언론이 보여주는 어떠한 적대적 행위도 무제한의 공격이 아니라 '적대적 태도표명' 정도로 평가절하해 수용할 필요가 있다는 것이다. 언론과 정부 사이의 '의례화'된 적대적 태도는 정치적 문제를 진지하게 다루지 않고도 상호독립적이라는 외양을 창출해 낸다. 이런 의례적 태도는 '자유로운 언론과 공개된 정부'라는 가공적인 허상을 만들어 낸다는 게 베넷의 주장이다. 저자는 베넷의 의례적 적대성 논리에 공감한다.

베넷 교수는 의례적 적대성의 증거로 케네디-존슨-닉슨의 기자회견 분석결과를 제시했다. 그가 잭 오르(Jack Orr)의 조사를 인용-소개한 바에 따르면, 케네디-존슨-닉슨 등 3개 행정부에서 공격적이거나 비판적 질문의 비율은 거의 일정했고, 공격적 질문은 개인적인 성질의 것에 한정됐다. 이런 개인적 질문들도 많은 경우 대통령 직책에 대한 예의를 갖춰 제기됐다. 게다가 강력한 정치적 공격이 될 만한 질문은 대통령이 문제를 새로 정의하거나 의문을 완전히 해소할 수 있도록 기자늘이 '개방형 질문'을 제기했다는 것이다. 언론은 대통령 직책에 대한 존경심을 나타내면서 공격적 질문을 제기해 결국은 언론의 공격성이 서로 존재가치를 확인하기 위한 '의례적' 행위라는 설명이다. 베넷 교수의 이같은 주장은 언론이 대통령을 공격할 수 있는 범위의 제한성을 지적하는 예리한 통찰이라고 볼 수 있다. 백악관을 가장 오래 출입한 UPI통신의 헬렌 토머스(여)는 공격적인 질문을 하는 기자로 널리 알려졌다. 그러나 그가 쓴 통신기사는 그의 질문과는 달리 그다지 공격적이지 않다고 평가받았다. 토머스 기자의 사례는 베넷 교수의 이런 예리한 통찰력을 증명하는 한 사례라 할 만하다. 토머스 기자는 자신의 백악관 출입 시절을 정리한 '백악관의 맨 앞줄에서(Front Row at the White House; My Life and Times; 한글 번역판 1999, 도서출판 답게)'를 출간했다.

다. 언론의 대통령 보도는 양자간 길항작용의 결과물

이상에서 보았듯이 대통령은 자신의 대선 승리, 임기 중 정책수행, 또는 대통령 재선을 위해 우호적 언론보도를 절실히 필요로 한다. 대통령은 이를 위해 엄청난 공보조직을 운영하고 여러 공보책략을 구사한다. 그러나 언론은 독자(시청자)들의 관심을 끌기 위해 대통령 관련 기삿거리가 보도의 틀에 부합하면 더욱 빈번히 기사화하고 그렇지 않으면 기사화하지 않거나 비판적 보도를 하게 된다. 앞서 살펴본 바와 같이 대통령과 언론은 서로 의존적이면서도 서로 독립적이다. 따라서 신문이나 방송에 나타나는 대통령 기사는 대통령과 언론이 서로 지속적으로 특정 사안의 기사 가치를 놓고 교섭과 협조와 논쟁을 한 끝에 만들어지는 결과물이라고 말할 수 있다. 이 결과물은 대통령에 우호적일 수도 있고 적대적일 수도 있다.

저자는 어느 국가에서 대통령의 이미지에 영향을 주는 언론 보도(대통령 보도)는 대통령(행정부 포함)을 한 당사자로 하고 이에 대응하는 언론과 독자(시청자, 유권자, 국민)를 다른 당사자로 하는 상호작용을 통해 이뤄진다고 생각한다. 간혹 한국 대통령에 관한 우호적-적대적 보도는 외국 언론에서도 찾아볼 수 있다. 200여 년 전과 달리 요즘 자리잡은 언론의 '객관적 보도' 준칙에서 보면 언론은 정당한 근거 없이 주관적으로 대통령에게 적대적 기사를 쓸 수는 없다. 적대적 기사를 쓰려면 누군가(국민의 일부나 다수, 또는 야당정치인) 대통령을 비난하는 입장을 가져야 한다. 따라서 언론이 대통령에 대해 적대적 보도를 했다면, 그것은 대통령의 정책에 반대하는 세력이 국민 중 일부라도 존재했음을 전제한다. 언론의 사설이나 칼럼 등 대통령에 대한 우호적–적대적 논평성 기사도 결국 상술한 근거에 기초해 성립한다 하겠다. 국민이 압도적으로 지지하는 대통령을 특정 언론이 적대적으로 보도했을 경우 그 언론은 국민의 외면을 당할 것이다(예컨대, 대통령과 관련한 보도는 아니지만 2003년 캘리포니아 주지사 소환투표 당시 투표일 수일 전 아널드 슈워제네거 후보의 '여성 가슴 만지기' 스캔들을 보도한 로스 앤젤레스 타임스는 독자 수천 명을 잃은 것으로 보도된 바 있다, 저자 주). 특히 미국처럼 상업적 언론이 주류를 이루는 사회에서는 상업적 목적을 위한 대통령 비판 보도는 있을 수 있겠다. 그러나 국민 대부분이 대통령을 지지할 경우 그에게 적대적 보도를 한다면 언론이 스스로 상업적 또는 정치적 존립 근거를 상실할 수 있다.

3. 뉴욕 타임스의 조지 W. 부시 대통령 보도 분석

가. 분석 대상, 조사 방법, 분석 결과

저자는 미국의 유력 신문 중 하나인 뉴욕 타임스가 조지 W. 부시 대통령을 우호적으로 묘사했는지 적대적으로 묘사했는지 소사해 보았나. 마이크 필름에 수록된 '부시 대통령에게 영향을 미칠 수 있는' 기사와 사진을 분석 대상으로 삼았다. 저자는 이 연구를 2003년 수행했다. 뉴욕 타임스의 기사 중 분석 대상 기간은 아래와 같이 4개 기간이었고, 이 기간에 기사에 대한 내용 분석(Content Analysis)을 수행했다. 아래의 기간 중 보도물을 분석 대상으로 삼은 것은 이 기간의 보도가 부시 대통령에 관한 적대적 또는 우호적 보도의 양상을 잘 보여줄 것으로 판단했기 때문이다.

1) 부시 대통령의 취임과 한 달간 보도: 2001년 1월 20일자에서 2월 19
   일자까지
2) 9-11 대미 테러 공격과 한 달간 보도: 2001년 9월 12일자에서 10월
   7일자까지
3) 아프가니스탄 탈레반에 대한 전쟁과 한 달간 보도: 2001년 10월 8일
   자에서 11월 7일자까지
4) 부시 대통령의 대 이라크 최후통첩과 부시 대통령의 주요전투 종결
   선언 보도: 2003년 3월 18일자에서 5월 2일자까지

　저자는 이 4개 기간 중 보도물로서 부시 대통령에게 긍정적 또는 부정적
묘사를 하는 기사와 사진을 모두 추출했다. 그 수는 총 575건에 달했다. 저
자는 분석대상에 속하는 기사의 범위를 백악관 출입기자가 쓰는 기사(그로
스먼과 쿠마르는 이 범주의 기사를 분석대상으로 삼았다)를 포함해 부시에
관한 우호적 또는 적대적 보도라고 판단되는 많은 다른 기사들을 폭넓게
분석대상으로 삼았다. 예컨대 '부시 대통령' 표현뿐만 아니라 '부시 보좌
관들' '부시 행정부' 등을 포함시켰고 부시 행정부의 행정이나 정책의 영
향을 받는 측의 환영, 반발 등에 관한 기사도 이 범주에 포함했다. 저자는
대통령에 대한 우호적 또는 적대적 보도의 범위를 상당히 폭넓게 규정했
다. 예컨대, 부시 대통령의 특정 정책에 반대하는 기사가 게재됐다면 이것
이 우리가 아는 '사회부 기자'가 쓴 기사일지라도 이것을 부시 대통령에게
적대적인 기사로 평가했다(미국 언론에서는 국가문제부 National Desk에
소속된 기자들이 주로 이런 성격의 중요한 기사를 쓴다. 저자 주).

　저자는 또한 부시 대통령에 대한 기사 및 사진을 다섯 단계로 분류했다.
보도 내용을 매우 우호적(매우 긍정적), 다소 우호적(다소 긍정적), 중립적,
다소 적대적(다소 부정적), 매우 적대적(매우 비우호적)으로 평가—분류했
다. 아울러 이같은 특정 기사가 1면에 게재됐는지 신문 중간쯤에 게재됐는
지 신문의 마지막 쪽에 게재됐는지 등도 평가 내용에 포함했다. 흔히 기사

평가는 3단계로 실시하지만 필자는 적대적-우호적 기사의 대표적 사례를 추출하기 위해 5단계 평가법을 채택했다. 저자는 우선 보도에 대한 우호적-적대적 보도에 관한 질적 분석을 했고, 그 다음 몇건의 기사가 우호적-적대적인지 수량적 분석을 했고, 이어 종합적인 분석을 가했다. 그러나 여기서는 수량적 분석의 결과를 먼저 제시하고 질적-종합적 분석 결과를 정리한다.

나. 수량적 분석(Quantitative Analysis)

저자는 모두 575건에 이르는 기사와 사진에 대한 분석-평가결과를 아래의 표〈표1〉로 정리해 나타낼 수 있었다. 아래는 수량적 분석으로 부시 대통령에 대한 뉴욕 타임스의 긍정-부정 보도의 비율과 시기에 따른 긍정-부정 보도의 추세를 잘 보여준다.

〈표1〉

기간별 우호-적대 보도	취임 및 한달 n=160	9-11 테러공격 n=160	아프간 전쟁 n=160	이라크 전쟁 n=160
매우 긍정적	17. 5%	31. 4%	12. 3%	27. 4%
다소 긍정적	45. 0	39. 5	50. 5	28. 1
중립적	17. 5	8. 9	13. 7	14. 5
다소 부정적	11. 3	11. 3	22. 5	18. 9
매우 부정적	8. 7	8. 9	1. 5	11. 1

저자 주: 전체 기사 건수는 575건.

위의 표를 보면 다음의 사항들을 알 수 있다.

1)취임 초기의 우호적 보도(매우 우호적 보도+다소 우호적 보도)는 62. 5%로 적대적 보도(다소 적대적 보도+매우 적대적 보도)의 20. 0%보다 3배 가량 많았다.

2)9-11 테러 기간 중 우호적 보도는 70. 9%로 적대적 보도 20. 2%보다 3. 5배 가량이었다.

3)아프간 전쟁 중 우호적 보도는 62. 8%로서 적대적 보도 24. 0%보다 3배에 좀 덜 미쳤다.

4)이라크에 대한 전쟁 초기의 우호적 보도는 55. 5%로서 적대적 보도 30. 0%의 2배에도 미달했다.

다. 질적 분석(Qualitative Analysis)

ㄱ. 부시 대통령의 취임초기 보도 분석

뉴욕 타임스는 2001년 1월 21일자 1면에 '부시 취임, 부드러움과 온정과 품위 있는 나라 만들기를 호소하다' 라는 제목의 스트레이트 머리기사를 실었다. 타임스는 또 이날 1면 해설기사를 통해 부시의 대통령 취임에 합법성을 부여했다. 해설기사의 제목은 '전통과 합법성: 미국의 오랜 의식이 처절했던 선거전의 어두운 구름을 걷기 시작하다' 라고 돼 있다. 이 해설기사는 "조지 W. 부시가 오른 손을 들고 '미국의 헌법을 보전하고 보호하고 방어하겠다' 고 선서하는 중에도 그의 머리 위에는 의문부호가 드리워져 있었다. 그러나 선서의 순간, 그리고 선서의 바로 그 행위를 통해 대통령은 자신의 합법성에 대한 도전을 제거하기 시작했다. 합법적 대통령인지 여부에 관한 논란은 국민이 백악관 집무실에 걸린 부시의 사진에 차츰 익숙해지면서 약화될 것이고……"라고 표현했다. 이런 내용은 부시 대통령에 대해 참으로 우호적이고도 세밀한 묘사라 아니할 수 없다.

다른 '취임 축하' 기사는 부시 부자가 기쁨에 못 이겨 눈물을 흘리는 것을 어떻게 처리해야 할지를 전한 내용이다. 기사는 "자랑스러운 아버지와 아들, 역사의 작열하는 밝은 빛을 마음껏 누리다"(Proud Father and Son Bask in History's Glow)라는 제목을 갖고 있다. 저자는 이런 제목에 대해서도 타임스가 부시 대통령에게 '엄청난 아첨'을 했다고 평가한다. 이런 기사는 객관적 보도, 담담한 보도의 적절한 수준을 훨씬 넘는 제목이며 너무도 연성화된 기사라고 필자는 생각한다. 기사의 내용은 매우 부드러운 감성에 호소하고 있다. 내용을 보자. "취임을 수일 앞두고 부자는 눈물 흘리는 문제를 얘기했다. 아버지와 아들은 눈물이 눈을 촉촉히 적시는 정도를 넘어 얼굴을 완전히 적셔버릴까 걱정했다. 대통령이 될 아들은 눈물둑이 무너질까봐 시선을 너무 아빠쪽으로 고정시키지 않겠다고 말했다. 아버지 부시는 눈물을 마르게 할 수 있는 처방약이 없겠느냐고 의사에게 상의했다고 농을 던졌다……." 이 정도면 이만저만한 아부의 정도를 뛰어넘는다고 생각된다. 저자는 이런 아첨성 묘사는 아직 한국 언론의 보도에는 등장하지 않았다고 생각하고 싶다. 여러 해 전 김대중 대통령이 청와대에 입성할 때 국내 언론은 그가 차량 여러 대 분량의 장서를 옮겼다고 보도한 바 있다. 저자는 이것이 김씨의 독서량을 은근히 홍보해 준 약간의 아첨성 기사가 아니었나 하는 느낌을 갖고 있다. 시각에 따라서는 이런 기사에 대해 "사실을 전하는 객관적 보도였다"고 주장할 근거도 물론 있다고 필자는 인정한다. 그러나 타임스의 이런 아첨성 기사와는 차원이 전혀 다르다.

이날 보도 중 부시 대통령은 매우 적대적으로 묘사한 기사도 있었다. 하지만 이 기사는 신문의 안쪽으로 들어간 지면인 A17면 상단에 게재돼 있었다. 이같은 지면 배치는 타임스가 반대 의견을 실어주는 대신 추후 대통령 취임의 합법성에 관한 논란을 제기하지 말 것을 의도하는 게 아닌가 하는 느낌을 준다. 어쨌든 부시의 취임 반대기사는 매우 강도 높은 표현으로 돼 있다. 기사의 제목은 "시위: 수천명의 반대자들이 수도에서 항의하다"로 돼 있다. 기사는 "부시의 리무진이 지나가자 많은 사람들은 '도둑놈에게 만세를'(Hail to the Thief)이라는 플래카드를 흔들었다. 다른 사람들은 성조기의 별 50개를 같은 수의 회사 로고로 바꾼 국기를 들고 흔들었다. 누군가 리무진에 달걀을 던졌다"라고 돼 있다. '도둑놈에게 만세를' 은 한국의 대통령 찬가에 해당하는 미국의 '대장에게 만세를(Hail to the Chief)' 을 패러디처럼 바꿔놓은 것이다. 별 50개를 회사 로고로 바꾼 것은 대기업 경영자 출신이 많은 부시 정권의 인물들을 비꼰 것이다. 취임하는 대통령의 리무진 승용차에 달걀을 던졌다는 것도 상당히 새로운 느낌을 준다. 한국에서 이런 정경이 벌어질 가능성이 있는지 궁금하다.

이 기간 중 뉴욕 타임스는 부시 대통령을 선거전의 승자, 새로운 국가적 지도자, 선거후유증을 치료하는 화해무드 조성자, 연방 고위공직자들을 임명하는 국정의 최고 책임자, 국제무대에 나서는 국제적 지도자, 백악관의 새로운 입주자 등 상당히 우호적인 모습으로 그렸다. 타임스는 동시에 감세정책을 추진하지만 강력한 반대에 부딪치는 모습, 해외 낙태자에 대한 지원 중단 등으로 반발에 부딪치는 모습을 적대적으로 그렸다. 그러나 굳이 밀월기간을 해칠 만큼 많은 적대적 보도는 하지 않았다고 저자는 평가했다. 이것은 앞서 기술한 그레이버의 평가와는 조금 다르다. 하지만 다수의 미국 언론 관계자들은 부시가 초기 밀월을 어느 정도 향유했다고 평가하고 있다. 타임스는 부시의 취임 1주일을 맞아 여러 건의 기사를 게재, 앞선 몇몇 행정부의 정권 교체 중 가장 매끄러운 정권 인수 작업을 마쳤다고 매우 우호적 기사를 게재했다.

ㄴ. 9-11 테러공격기 보도 분석

2001년 9월 11일 미국은 건국 후 하와이를 제외하고는 처음으로 본토에 대한 테러공격을 당했고 미국민은 엄청난 충격을 받았다. 미국민 사이에는 한때 위기의식이 만연했다. 타임스는 부시 대통령을 위기에 처한 미국을 이끌어 나가는 지도자(위기 지도자 또는 군사적 지도자)의 모습으로 우호적으로 보도했다. 테러 발생을 보도한 2001년 9월 12일자 타임스는 1면에서 "부시가 임기 중 처음으로 중요한 위기에 직면했다"면서 "부시는 비열한 테러범들을 찾아내 처벌하겠다고 굳게 다짐했다"고 전하고 있다. 부시 대통령이 "테러범들에게 복수하겠다고 다짐했다"는 구절도 나온다. 9월 13일자 15면 기사는 부시가 9-11 테러에 대해 "전쟁행위"에 해당한다고 규정하는 것을 묘사했다. 이후 타임스는 부시가 뉴욕의 와해된 세계무역센터 현장을 방문하는 기사 등 국가적 슬픔을 치료하는 지도자의 모습을 그리는 기사도 다수 실었다. 이 기간 중 우호적 보도의 비율은 무려 70. 9%에 달했다. 당시 여론조사는 이같은 언론의 논조를 반영한 것인지 부시 대통령 지지도가 테러 직전 51%에서 테러 직후 수일 만에 86%까지 껑충 치솟았다(갤럽 조사, 9월 14-15일). 위기시에는 지도자에 대한 지지율이 상승한다는 것이 다시 입증됐다. 이런 현상은 아마 미국에만 국한되지는 않을 것이다.

이 기간 중 뉴욕 타임스는 부시 대통령이 위기를 관리하는 지도자의 모습으로 묘사했다. 타임스는 "국가적 위기는 나흘 만에 부시의 대통령 직무 수행 행태를 바꾸었다"(9월 16일 A1면 해설)는 기사를 포함해 부시의 강력한 리더십 구축에 관해 여러 차례 기사를 게재했다. 이 기간 중 타임스는 부시를 국민을 위로하는 국가적 위로자, 군사공격을 준비하는 군사적 지도자 등 매우 우호적 모습으로 그렸다. 이 신문은 "부시가 9-11을 계기로 완전히 달라졌으며 강력한 리더십을 가진 새로운 인물로 거듭났다"고 묘사했다.

한 번은 테러 수일 후 "부시 대통령의 참모들이 보복의 범위를 정하지 못해 분열돼 있다"(9월 20일 1면)는 기사가 있었다. 부시에 적대적 내용이라 할 만하다. 그러나 이 기사는 사흘 후 "부시 참모들, 여러 목소리에서 하나의 전략을 수립했다"(9월 23일 1면)는 기사로 완전히 희석됐다.

ㄷ. 아프간 전쟁 초기 보도 분석

아프간 전쟁 초기에 부시 대통령은 아프간을 공격하는 군사적 지도자, 반 테러 전선을 구축하기 위해 국제적 협력을 요청하는 국제적 지도자 등의 모습으로 묘사됐다. 타임스의 기사들은 기까이에서 본 부시 대통령의 테러전쟁 지휘 모습(10월 9일, "The Planning: A Look Behind the Scenes, From White House Aides")을 친근하고 밀도 있게 그렸다. 부시가 아프간의 탈레반 정부의 교섭제의를 단호히 물리치고 빈 라덴을 내놓으라고 일갈하는 강력한 모습(10월 15일 A1)도 그렸다. 엘리자베스 뷰밀러 백악관 출입기자는 부시 대통령이 얼마나 주도면밀하게 아프간전을 준비했는지(10월 8일자 B1) 섬세하게 묘사했다. 타임스는 부시 대통령이 국제적인 테러진압 전선을 구축하기 위해 장쩌민 중국 국가주석을 만나는 모습도 그렸다. 그러나 이런 기사와는 대조적으로 "베트남의 수렁을 회상하라"(10월 31일자 B1)며 부시 대통령의 개전을 반대하는 적대적 칼럼도 실렸다.

ㄹ. 이라크 전쟁 기간 보도 분석

2003년 3월 시작된 미국의 이라크 전쟁은 그 후유증이 2004년에 들어서도 계속됐다. 하지만 이 전쟁에서는 2003년 3월 17일(타임스 18일자)부터 5월 1일(타임스 2일자)까지 실질적 적대행위가 있었다고 말할 수 있겠다. 3월 17일 부시 대통령은 최후통첩을 발령해 이라크에 대해 개전을 선언했고, 5월 1일 사담 후세인 타도를 위한 '주요 군사적 작전'의 종료를 선언했다. 이 기간 중 부시에 대한 보도는 우호적 보도가 55. 5%였고, 적대적 보도는 30. 0%로 2배에 좀 미달했다.

타임스는 전쟁 기간 중 여러 차례 부시 대통령을 결단성 있는 전쟁지휘자로 묘사했다. 이라크의 사담 후세인 대통령에게 48시간의 시한을 준 최후통첩을 보도(3월 18일 A1, 스트레이트 기사)해 강력한 전쟁 지휘자의 이미지를 그렸다. 타임스는 나아가 부시 대통령의 선제공격을 정당화하는 장문의 해설기사(3월 18일 A1, "A New Doctrine of War: In an Age of Unseen Enemies, President Says, Waiting for Opponent to Attack is Suicide")를 실었다. 수일 후에는 이라크에 대한 '선제 공격' 논리가 어떻게 형성돼 이번 전쟁에 적용됐는지 자세히 보도했다. 엘리자베스 뷰밀러 기자는 몇 건의 기사를 통해 부시 대통령이 전쟁을 지휘하는 모습을 매우 친밀하고 우호적인 이미지로 묘사했다. 이런 기사들을 보면 뷰밀러 기사는 백악관 출입기자임이 분명했다(사실이 그렇다). 그녀의 기사 중에는 백악관 보좌관들의 말을 인용해 작성한 기사들이 많았기 때문이다.

그러나 타임스는 부시의 개전 결심을 비난하는 여러 적대적 칼럼들을 동시에 실었다. 3월 18일자는 A32면에 "외교적 노력의 실패로 인한 개전"이라는 칼럼을 통해 부시 대통령이 외교적 노력을 성사시키지 못해 이라크에 대한 무력행사에 들어가게 됐음을 비난했다. 수많은 반전 시위 기사들은 부시 대통령을 적대적으로 묘사했다. 타임스는 동시에 이라크 전쟁 찬성자들의 집회도 잘 보도했다. 그만큼 이 전쟁은 미국 내외에서 격심한 찬반논란을 일으켰고, 그런 사회적 여론 분열 현상이 대체로 지면에 잘 반영됐다. 앞에 든 통계 수치 55. 5% 대 30. 0%는 이를 반영했다고 보인다.

타임스는 이라크전 초기에 선제공격 논리를 정당화해 부시 대통령에 우호적 보도를 했었다. 그러나 타임스는 2003년 5월 이후에도 이라크 주둔 미군이 계속적으로 자살 테러로 희생을 당하고, 대량파괴무기의 증거가 발견되지 않자 적대적 보도를 하기 시작했다. 아래 기사들의 제목은 이같은 논조의 변화를 잘 보여준다. 아래의 기사들은 1면에 보도된 것으로 뉴욕 타임스의 보도가 어떻게 변화했는지 드러내고 있다.

2003년 9월 13일 A1: "신속한 전쟁, 그러나 유혈의 평화"

2003년 9월 23일 A1: "장병의 용기에는 훈장, 그러나 그 아내에게는 장병의 유해"

2003년 9월 25일 A1: "초기보고, 대량파괴무기 발견 실패"

라. 뉴욕 타임스는 부시 대통령에게 언제 우호적–석대적이있나?

미국 언론은 항상 미국 대통령에게 우호적이거나 적대적이었을까. 아니면 우호적 보도와 적대적 보도는 어떤 상황에 의해 만들어지는 것일까. 대통령이 국민의 압도적 지지를 받고 있으면 언론이 쉽사리 대통령에 적대적 보도를 할 수 있을까.

전술한 바와 같이 미국민은 9–11 직후 부시 대통령에 대해 급작스럽게 높은 지지율을 보였다. 그렇다면 대통령에 대한 높은 지지율과 언론(뉴욕 타임스)의 부시에 대한 우호적 보도는 어느 정도 상관 관계가 있음을 짐작할 수 있다. 지지율 상승과 우호적 보도 중 어느 쪽이 다른 쪽을 야기했는지 저자가 명시하기는 어렵다. 하지만 저자는 아무래도 언론의 우호적 보도가 지지율 상승을 이끌어냈다는 강한 느낌을 갖고 있다.

이상의 사례 연구에서 본 바와 같이 뉴욕타임스는 부시 대통령의 취임초기에 다수의 우호적 보도를 했으며, 9-11 이후와 아프간 전쟁 초기에도 다수의 우호적 보도를 했다. 타임스는 미국의 이라크 전쟁에 대해서는 상대적으로 우호적 보도를 많이 하지 않았다. 타임스는 2003년 9월 이라크에서 대량파괴무기의 증거가 발견되지 않자 이라크 전쟁의 정당성을 의심하는 일련의 기사와 사설을 게재하기 시작했다. 타임스는 이라크전 개전을 전후해 부시 대통령의 이라크 전쟁 정책에 대한 반대시위도 중요하게 보도했다. 유엔발 기사로 이라크전의 법적 근거가 없다는 보도도 했다. 유엔 출입기자가 쓴 "이라크 전쟁은 국제법적 근거가 없다"는 기사는 신문 안쪽(2003년 3월 20일 A19면)에 실렸다. 만약 이런 내용이 1면 머리기사로 게재됐다면 분명 상당한 정도의 파괴력을 가졌을 것이다.

부시 대통령의 선제공격에 대해 정당성을 인정하는 해설기사를 게재한 뉴욕 타임스가 왜 부시에 대한 적대적인 보도로 선회했을까. 부시의 대량파괴무기(WMD)의 존재에 관련된 발언이 신뢰성을 차츰 잃었기 때문이다. 이른바 신뢰도의 격차(Credibility gap)가 생겼다고 말할 수 있다. 베트남 전쟁 당시에도 린든 존슨 대통령의 신뢰도 격차가 거론됐다. 존슨 대통령이 미국민에게 전달하는 베트남 전쟁 상황과 베트남 현지의 사정이 상이했고 이런 사실을 언론이 보도했기 때문이다. 베트남전 당시 많은 젊은이들은 반전 시위를 벌이는 가운데 미국은 점차 베트남전의 수렁으로 빠져들었다. 반전 시위의 확산과 전황에 대한 신뢰도 격차는 미국 언론이 당시 대통령들을 적대적으로 보도할 수 있는 정당한 근거를 제공해 주었다고 저자는 생각한다.

미국 나이트-리더 언론사의 워런 스트로벌 기자는 이 문제에 관해 통찰력 있는 주장을 했다. 그는 저서를 통해 "대통령을 포함한 정책 결정자들이 정책이나 공보의 공백을 만들면 언론은 자체 힘으로 그 공백을 메운다"고 썼다(Strobel, 1997, Late-Breaking Foreign Policy). 저자도 스트로벌 기자의 이런 주장에 완전히 공감한다. 스트로벌 기자의 지적은 앞서 언급한 딕 체니 부통령의 발언과 어느 정도 맥이 통한다. 체니는 백악관이 의제를 설정하지 못하면 언론이 의제를 설정하기 시작해 부정적 보도를 한다고 지적한 바 있다. 그는 아울러 백악관 보좌진이 서로 다른 목소리를 내면 언론공격의 먹이감이 된다고 말하면서 "의제를 통제"할 필요성을 강조했다. 백악관내 보좌진들의 서로 다른 목소리란 결국 스트로벌의 정책상 공백을 말하는 것이다. 저자는 스트로벌 기자의 주장에 다음을 첨언하고 싶다. 대통령이나 그의 정책이 권위를 잃거나 정책에 반대하는 세력이 생겨날 경우 언론은 이들의 의견을 반영하게 된다. 이런 여건은 결국 언론에 대통령을 공격할 수 있는 정당한 근거를 제공하게 된다. 언론은 이에 근거를 두고 대통령에게 적대적인 보도를 할 수 있다.

저자의 뉴욕 타임스 보도 분석으로 다시 돌아가 보자. 부시 대통령의 취임초기, 9-11 테러 공격, 아프간 전쟁, 이라크 전쟁 등 4개 기간은 상당히 극적인 기간이다. 부시 대통령의 취임은 새로운 백악관의 주인을 맞는 일이다. 이 기간 중 부시의 취임을 반대하는 기사도 있었지만 타임스는 부시의 취임과 순조로운 정권이양을 우호적으로 보도했다. 이런 우호적 보도는 타임스가 자발적으로 한 것으로 보인다. 그러나 9-11 테러, 아프산 전쟁, 이라크 전쟁은 극적인 사건이 벌어진 상황이다. 국가적 위기나 국가가 다른 나라에 대해 전쟁을 벌이는 급박한 상황에서 대통령에 적대적 보도를 한다는 것은 그만큼 정당한 근거가 필요하다. 예컨대 베트남전처럼 전쟁이 오랜 기간을 끌어 반전 여론이 높아진다거나 이라크전처럼 반대여론이 많으면 언론이 적대적 보도를 할 근거가 생긴다. 이런 여건은 딕 체니 부통령이나 워런 스트로벌 기자가 말하는 바와 같이 "대통령이 의제를 통제할 힘"

이 약해진 상황이어서 언론이 스스로 의제를 설정하기 때문이다. 9–11 직후의 우호적 보도는 그만큼 미국내 여건이 대통령에게도 극적이었기 때문이다. 이런 극적인 여건에서는 대통령이 "상황을 규정"할 수 있다. 환언하면 극적인 여건에서 대통령은 상황을 규정해 언론의 우호적 보도를 이끌 수 있다. 하지만 대통령이 스스로 신뢰도 격차를 만들면 언론은 그 틈새를 비집고 들어가 스스로 의제를 설정해 대통령에 적대적인 보도를 할 수 있게 된다.

4. 경향신문의 노무현 대통령 보도 분석

가. 분석대상, 조사방법, 결과해석

경향신문의 노무현 대통령과 관련한 기사를 분석하는 데 있어 저자의 분석 방법과 결과 해석을 앞서 행한 뉴욕타임스의 것과 동일했다. 따라서 아래에서 분석대상 기사들의 기간만을 표시한다.

1) 노무현 대통령의 취임과 한 달간 보도: 2003년 2월 26일자에서 3월 25일자까지
2) 노무현 대통령의 신임투표 제안과 한 달간 보도: 2003년 10월 11일자에서 11월 10일자까지
3) 탄핵 전 2주 보도: 2004년 2월 28일자에서 3월 12일자까지(3월 12일 국회 탄핵가결)
4) 노무현 대통령 탄핵 후 한 달 보도: 2004년 3월 13일자에서 4월 15일자까지(4월 15일은 총선일, 열린우리당 1당 부상)

5) 총선 후 한 달 보도: 2004년 4월 16일자에서 5월 14일자까지(5월 14
일은 헌법재판소가 탄핵기각을 결정한 날)

6) 노무현 대통령 탄핵 기각 후 2주간 보도: 2004년 5월 15일자에서 5
월 29일자까지(대통령 업무 복귀와 반달)

나. 수량적 분석

긍정과 부정적 기사의 기준에 맞춰 해당 기간의 기사들을 평가해 표로
만들어 본 결과 아래의 〈표2〉와 같이 나타났다.

〈표2〉

기간별 보도내용	취임 n=160	신임투표 n=160	탄핵전 2주 n=160	탄핵한달 n=160	총선거 n=160	직무복귀 n=160
매우 긍정적	37.6%	6.2%	6.9%	17.5%	28.6%	10.7%
다소 긍정적	30.4	30.0	24.1	53.9	39.3	55.4
중립적	11.2	12.3	20.7	20.6	10.7	5.4
다소 부정적	13.6	42.3	32.8	7.3	17.9	6.1
매우 부정적	7.2	9.2	15. 5	1.0	3.5	12.4

저자 주: 전체 기사 건수는 494건에 달함.

위의 표는 다음과 같은 사실들을 보여준다. 우선 취임과 한 날 기간 중
노 대통령은 이 신문에서 68. 0%의 긍정적(매우 긍정적+다소 긍정적) 보
도를 향유했다. 이 정도면 밀월임을 충분히 보여준다 하겠다. 조지 W. 부
시 대통령 취임과 한 달 동안 뉴욕타임스의 부시 보도는 긍정 보도가 62.
5%였음을 상기하면 꽤 높은 비율의 긍정 보도이다. 취임 기간 중 부정적
(매우 부정적+다소 부정적)보도는 20. 8%로 부시에 대한 부정적 보도(20.
0%)와 거의 같은 수준이었다. 이 기간 매우 긍정적 보도가 37. 6%에 달했

음도 눈에 띈다.

다음으로 노 대통령이 신임투표를 돌연 제의했을 당시의 보도를 분석하면 긍정적 보도가 36. 2%에 불과했다. 이에 비해 부정적 보도는 무려 51. 5%에 달했다. 노 대통령의 신임 투표 제의에 대해 이 신문은 여러 형태의 기사를 통해 비난했음이 숫자로 드러났다. 이 기간 중 부정적 보도의 비율이 매우 높았다.

국회 탄핵 전 2주 동안의 보도를 보면, 긍정적 보도가 31. 0%로 여전히 매우 낮다. 반면 부정적 보도는 48. 3%로 여전히 매우 높았다. 이는 대통령의 총선 개입에 대한 보도가 많아서 그런 것으로 보인다.

노 대통령이 국회에서 탄핵되자 신문의 논조가 반전했다. 탄핵 직후 한 달간 긍정적 보도는 71. 4%로 급격히 상승했다. 이것은 탄핵반대 촛불시위 등 대통령에 대한 간접적 지원 성격의 보도가 많았기 때문으로 분석된다. 반면 이 기간 중 부정적 보도는 8. 3%로 급격히 줄었다.

총선 직후의 기사도 대통령에 대한 간접 지원 성격의 기사가 많았다. 경향신문은 열린우리당의 승리를 탄핵의 역풍으로 기술했다. 이 기간 부정적 기사도 비율이 낮았다.

헌법재판소의 결정으로 국회 탄핵이 무효로 처리되자 긍정적 보도는 취임초의 수준에 가까운 66. 1%에 달했다. 상생의 정치 등 새로운 개혁에 관한 대통령의 구상 등이 보도됐기 때문이다. 이 기간 부정적 보도는 28. 5%로 다소 높아졌다. 고건 총리에 대한 각료 추천 강요 및 김혁규 총리 카드를 고집한데 대한 비판성 기사가 있었기 때문으로 분석된다.

다. 질적 분석

ㄱ. 노 대통령 취임과 한 달간 보도
긍정적 보도: 이 기간 중 신문은 대구 지하철 참사를 고려해 경건한 취임식을 갖고 난 뒤 첫날부터 숨가쁜 4강 외교에 들어가는 모습을 그렸다.

대통령 취임 1주와 1개월에 맞춘 신문의 대통령 평가는 긍정과 중립과 부정으로 일관성을 갖지 못했다. 신문은 취임 1주년을 맞은 평가 기사(3월 3일 3면)에서 "탈권위 청와대 국민 곁으로; 노 대통령 입성 1주일 변화의 바람; 백악관식 맞보기식 자리 배치; 수석회의 토론식 진행"이라는 기사를 통해 달라진 청와대의 모습을 보여줬다. 당연히 긍정적 보도로 평가된다.

신문은 또 야당에 손을 내미는 '화해자'로서 또 상생의 정치를 말한 대통령을 묘사했다. (부시도 취임 직후 야당 지도자들을 상대로 대화를 제의했다.)신문은 노 대통령이 내각에 "참여정부의 정책과제를 구상하라"고 지시(3월 5일 3면)하는 정책입안자로의 모습도 그렸다. 뉴욕 타임스는 부시 대통령이 취임 후 바로 해외 낙태 지원을 중단하라는 정책조치를 취하는 모습을 그렸다. 이것은 미국과 한국간 차이를 보여준다. 신문은 대통령이 첫 내각을 발표하고 고위공직자를 임명하는 행정부 수반의 모습을 전달했으며 부시와 전화통화(전화외교)를 하는 모습(3월 14일 1면)도 전했다. 대통령이 검사들과 벌인 공개 토론에 관해 "검사들이 토론 제의를 덜컥 받자 걱정이었다"고 묘사한 부분(3월 13일 4면)은 인간적 측면을 우호적으로 그렸다고 평가된다. 이 기간 중 특히 대통령은 여성과 40대를 장관으로 파격 등용하는 등 새로운 스타일의 지도자이며 개혁적 정치인으로 줄곧 묘사됐다. 영부인 권양숙 여사는 조사 기간 중 단 한 번만 기사화됐다. 그는 "대통령 친인척 관리를 우선과제로 삼겠다"(2월 26일 6면)는 제목 아래 신문에 보도됐다. 부시 대통령의 부인이 중요한 시점에 타임스에 등장하는 것과는 너무 비교된다. (탄핵 무효화 직후 출근하는 대통령을 배웅하는 사진이 한 번 실렸다.)대통령은 언론 보도에 대해 간여하기 않겠다(3월 5일 1면)고 밝혔다. 대통령의 대언론 입장은 이후에도 수시로 나타났다.

부정적 보도: 국회에서 열린 취임식과 축하연에서 의원들이 몰려다녀 어수선했으며 특검법을 둘러싼 진통이 있었다. 기사(2월 26일 6면)에 따르면 외교사절들이 "웃긴다"고 조소를 보냈다고 돼 있다. 이것은 취임식날 부시 대통령의 승용차에 계란을 던지는 정도의 매우 부정적 기사는 아니지

만 어쨌든 상당히 부정적 함의를 가졌다. 한나라당은 첫 내각이 발표되자 "현실을 무시한 실험적 내각"(2월 28일 4면)이라고 비난했다. 신문은 행정부내에서 대통령의 개혁에 반발하는 모습을 전달했고 청와대 내부 청장년 간 갈등도 묘사했다. 한 칼럼(3월 25일 10면)은 "아마추어리즘의 실패"라는 제목으로 취임 한 달을 맞은 대통령을 맹렬히 공격했다. 이날 사설과 8면 칼럼은 중립적 성격을 띠었다.

ㄴ. 대통령의 신임투표 제의와 한 달간 보도

긍정적 보도: 최도술씨가 개입된 정치자금 수수의혹의 여파로 대통령은 "축적된 국민불신에 대해 국민에게 재신임을 묻겠다"(10월 11일 1면)고 선언했다. 이후 신문은 신임 여부에 관한 일련의 기사를 실었다. 이를 둘러싼 여야간의 공방이 신문지면에 전달됐다. 이 기간 중 한국군 이라크 정책이 결정됐으며 대통령은 아시아−태평양 경제협력체(APEC)회담 중 부시 대통령에게서 "미국의 친구이며 나의 친구"(10월 21일 3면)라는 찬사를 받았다. 대통령의 광주 방문은 "광주에 올 때마다 고향처럼 느껴진다"(11월 8일 5면)는 제목으로 우호적으로 보도됐다. 대통령은 통신−방송사의 국장들과 만찬을 하면서 "그동안 언론과의 불편한 관계로 국민께 다소 불안을 드린 점이 있다"면서 정부와 언론이 서로 협력해 나가겠다(11월 5일 5면)고 말했다.

부정적 보도: 신문은 재신임을 묻겠다는 발언이 "정국을 시계 제로의 상태로 몰아넣을"(10월 11일 4면)일이라고 해설했다. 같은 날 칼럼은 "국정혼란은 안 된다"고 비난했고, 이날 사설은 "대통령 재심임 제안은 경솔했다"고 공격했다. 한나라당은 탄핵을 거론했다. 신문은 이 와중에도 청와대의 측근 5명이 모두 부정에 연루해 상처를 입었다(10월 11일 7면)고 전했다. 대통령이 검찰 독립의 강조하다 역풍을 맞았다는 분석도 실었다. 대통령이 한국군의 이라크 파병 결정을 분명히 발표하지 않아 대통령의 신뢰성에 문제가 생겼다는 신문의 비판(10월 20일 3면)도 받았다. 대통령 외유중

한국군 파병을 놓고 청와대 내부 참모들간 갈등이 심화했다는 보도(10월 22일 4면)는 앞서 논의에서 제기한 대표적 내부 갈등으로 언론의 좋은 기사감이 된다. 이 기간 386세대 참모들의 스캔들과 소문이 그치지 않았다.

ㄷ. 탄핵 직전 2주간 보도

긍정적 보도: 이 기간은 탄핵 결정을 향해 줄달음치는 과정이었다. 중앙선관위가 대통령이 중립 의무를 위반했다고 결정을 내리자 대통령은 선거에 개입하지 않았다고 주장하면서 야당측의 사과 요구를 거부했다. 기사 "사과는 검토한 바도 없다: 청와대 불퇴전 결의"(3월 6일 2면)는 대통령의 강경한 입장을 잘 보여주었다. 사과를 거부한 대통령은 마침내 회견을 통해 "총선과 재신임을 연계하겠다"고 밝혔다. 대통령의 강경한 모습을 보여주는 기사들이다. 대통령은 동시에 고이즈미 준이치로 일본 총리에 대해 "야스쿠니신사를 참배해 한국인에게 상처를 주지 말라"고 경고했다.

부정적 보도: 신문은 야당 정치인들의 지속적인 대통령 공격을 전달했다. 선거 중립 의무 위반을 거론하는 야당의 움직임을 자세히 전했다. 이어 국회에서 탄핵 동의안이 제출됐다. 이런 와중에도 대통령의 대선자금 문제가 불거져 나왔으며 '10분의 1'이 넘는다는 검찰의 발표도 있었다. 대통령 측근들의 비리 문제도 계속 터져 나왔다.

ㄹ. 탄핵과 한 달간 보도

긍정적 보도: 이 기간의 긍정적 보도는 대부분 탄핵을 비난하는 형태로 나타났으며 이것이 대통령을 간접적으로 지원하는 의미에서 긍정 보도라 할 수 있다. 이 기간 대통령을 직무가 정지돼 공식활동을 전하는 기사는 없었다. 대통령에 대한 국회 탄핵이 있던 날 대통령은 "헌법재판소 결정은 다를 것"이라고 말했다. 대표적인 대통령 지지 시위에 관한 기사는 "전국 곳곳에 탄핵 불복종 촛불 행렬"(3월 13일 5면)이다. 이것은 제2의 6월항쟁을 일으키겠다는 시민단체들의 모습을 전했다. 이날 사설은 "나라꼴 왜 이 지

경이 됐나; 다수당의 횡포이자 의회의 폭거; 국정 표류 막아야"라는 제목으로 돼 있다. 사설은 "헌정사상 초유의 충격적 사태가 벌어졌다"며 심각한 논조를 띠었다. 이어 여러 형태의 대통령 지지 시위를 전달하는 기사들이 여러 건 보도됐다. 1백만 명이 탄핵반대 시위를 갖겠다는 기사(3월 20일 6면)가 보도됐는가 하면 1백 50만 명이 참여한 시위가 촛불을 끄면서 종료됐다는 기사(3월 29일 1면)도 실렸다.

이 기간 대통령의 인간적 측면을 우호적으로 묘사한 기사가 몇 건 있었다. 탄핵 직후의 모습을 그린 "몇 달 뒤 국민 앞에 다시 서게 되길;대통령의 길었던 하루"(3월 13일 7면)라는 기사를 보자. 기사는 탄핵 가결 당시 대통령이 경남 창원의 한 공장에 있었다고 전하면서 이렇게 전했다. "노 대통령은 직무정지로 식물 대통령이 됐음에도 거야와 정면승부하겠다는 의지가 확고해 보였다. 핵심측근들은 노 대통령이 정치개혁의 순교자가 될 것을 결심하고 있는 것 같다고 말하고 있다." 꽤나 우호적 묘사인 것같다. 대통령이 총선-재신임 연계와 열린우리당 입당을 놓고 측근들에게 "난감하다. 어떻게 하면 좋겠느냐"고 말한 것을 전달한 기사(3월 22일 4면)도 인간적 고뇌를 우호적으로 묘사한 기사로 평가됐다. 대통령이 출입기자들과 함께 산행하면서 총선 후에는 통합정치를 펼치겠다고 말하는 장면을 전달한 기사(4월 12일 2면)도 긍정적 묘사였다.

탄핵 결정에 대해 반대하는 칼럼과 사설도 잇따랐다. 칼럼(3월 13일 15면)은 "의회주의를 빙자한 쿠데타"라고 격렬히 비난했고, 사설(3월 15일 13면)은 "탄핵 민심을 4-15 총선에 담자"고 주장했다. 탄핵 당일 대부분의 헌법학자들이 탄핵이 무효라는 입장을 전한 기사(3월 13일 4면)와 응답자의 68%가 헌법재판소에 대해 탄핵 기각을 요구한다는 여론조사 보도(3월 14일 1면)도 있었다.

부정적 보도: 이 기간 대통령에게 부정적 내용의 기사는 별로 없었다. 탄핵을 가결하는 기사(3월 13일 1면)는 부정적인 내용이라 할 만하다. 그 외 대통령이 타협을 거부했기 때문에 탄핵이 가결됐다는 기사(3월 13일 8

면)가 있었다. 대통령의 장남이 거주하는 50평 아파트에 대한 특혜 논란(4월 5일 4면)을 전달한 기사도 있었다.

ㅁ. 총선과 한 달 보도

긍정적 보도: 총선 결과 김종필 조순형 씨 등 야당 거물들이 낙선하자 신문은 탄핵을 주도한 중진들이 패배했다고 보도(4월 16일 1면)했다. 신문은 4-15의 선택으로 '탄핵 역풍'이 여대야소라는 형국을 만들었다고 전했다. 거여(큰 여당)를 업은 대통령의 '상생의 정치'가 탄력을 받을 것이라고 전망했다. 사설(4월 17일 13면)은 "헌법재판소가 탄핵이 부당하다는 주장에 손을 들어준 총선민의를 존중해야 한다"고 썼다. 이날 칼럼은 "국민은 대통령을 재신임한 만큼 한나라당은 수건을 던져야 한다"고 지적했다. 이 기간 대통령은 총선 민의를 자신에 대한 재신임으로 간주한다고 발언(4월 21일 1면)했다. 이에 따라 직무복귀를 앞두고 김혁규씨를 총리로 하는 내각 개편을 구상하는 모습(5월 3일 1면)을 보였다. 신문은 아울러 대통령을 고강도의 개혁을 추진하겠다는 개혁자로서(5월 11일 1면) 다시 그렸다.

부정적 보도: 칼럼(4월 26일 13면)은 총선의 승리에 도취한 여권의 개혁의지가 후퇴하고 있다고 꼬집었다. 이 칼럼을 보자. "열린우리당에 입당하더라도 평당원으로 있겠다던 대통령이 아무개 의원을 국회의장으로 사실상 낙점한 것 같다는 보도도 있다. 대통령이 입법부 수장을 내정한다면 이것은 여당이 입만 열면 외쳐온 정치개혁과 어떤 관계가 있는가. 총선이 끝나고 불과 며칠 사이 여권발 보도를 들여다 보면, 열린우리딩의 현란한 개혁 언어들이 얼마나 빈약한 실체에 기반하고 있는지 드러낸다"고 비판했다. 대통령의 고향인 김해발 기사(5월 8일 7면)는 "6세 때 천자문을 뗀 대통령은 천재"라는 제목으로 보도하고 있으나 좀 부정적 여운을 남겼다.

대통령의 비서 출신인 송인배씨가 강금원 씨에게서 5천만 원을 받아 검찰에 소환됐다는 측근 의혹 기사(4월 29일 6면)는 이 시기에도 계속됐다.

ㅂ. 대통령 직무 복귀와 2주간 보도

긍정적 보도: 헌법재판소의 탄핵 기각 결정 보도(5월 15일 1면)를 계기로 여러 보도가 쏟아져 나왔다. 이 결정은 총선 민의를 반영한 것이라는 해설기사도 게재됐다. 탄핵 기각 직후 고건 총리와 노 대통령간 만찬분위기를 전하는 기사는 인간적 측면을 드러냈다. 두 사람은 "그동안 고생 많았다"(대통령) "이젠 졸업시켜 주셔야죠"(고건 총리)라는 대화를 나누었다. 청와대 비서실 직원들은 복귀 의식을 가졌다. 이 기간 대통령은 진정한 새 임기를 맞아 '조용한 개혁'을 하겠다며 향후 정국을 계획했다. 상생의 정치를 하겠다는 발언(5월 19일 1면)도 나왔고 개각 구상에 관한 여러 기사도 나왔다. 대통령이 열린우리당에 입당하는 기사도 있었다.

부정적 보도: 헌법재판소의 결정이 대통령의 가벼운 입에 일침을 주었다는 비판성 해설기사(5월 15일 3면)도 있었다. 이 기사는 "헌재는 기각 결정을 내리기에 앞서 노 대통령의 가벼운 입에 대해 쓴소리를 쏟아냈다. 지난해 말부터 올해 초까지 노 대통령이 한 4가지 발언을 조목조목 들춰가면서 선거중립 의무와 헌법수호 의무 위반을 문제 삼은 것이다"라고 지적했다. 신문은 대통령이 김혁규 총리후보에게 집착하는 것도 비판했고, 물러나는 고건 총리에게 각료를 제청하라고 무리하게 요구하는 것도 비판했다. 대통령의 무리한 개각 집착에 대해 비난하는 칼럼(5월 26일 5면)도 있었다. 대통령이 관례로 해 오던 풀기자단의 수석회의 취재를 막은 것을 비판하는 기사도 있었다.

5. 언론은 언제 어떻게 대통령을 비판하거나 칭찬할 수 있나?

이 부분은 저자가 나름대로 전문가들의 견해와 필자의 연구를 종합해 정리해 본 것이다. 전문가들의 견해는 이론적인 것으로 어떤 상황에서 대통령을 비판하거나 칭찬할 수 있는지에 관한 것이다. 그 다음 저자는 뉴욕타임스와 경향신문의 사례 연구에서 추출된 것을 정리해 언론이 어떤 주제를 묘사함으로써 대통령을 비판하거나 칭찬할 수 있는지 정리해 본다.

가. 비판적 보도를 할 때

ㄱ. 언론과 국민이 대통령을 신뢰하지 않을 때: 그로스먼과 쿠마르는 1965년에서 1974년(대체로 말해, 존슨 대통령이 대규모 병력을 베트남에 파견하겠다는 결정을 이행했을 때부터 닉슨 대통령이 사임했을 때) 사이 백악관과 언론의 적대적 양상이 공개적 갈등으로 드러났다고 말했다. 이 기간은 미국 대통령들이 언론과 국민으로부터 신뢰를 상실한 때였다. 그때까지 대통령은 국민의 공복이라는 평판을 누려왔다. 그러나 존슨 대통령의 은밀한 병력 증파와 '위대한 사회' 건설 정책의 여파로 생겨난 인종갈등으로 이미지 손상을 입었다. 또한 닉슨 대통령은 워터게이트 사건으로 정치적-헌법적 위기를 초래했다. 이 때문에 언론인 학자 국민들은 종전에 갖고 있던 대통령의 이상적 이미지를 수정했다. 백악관 관리들에 대한 신뢰 붕괴는 존슨-닉슨 시대의 많은 언론인들이 쓴 책의 제목에서도 드러난다. 예컨대, "결코 진실은 아니다" "거짓말의 정치" "위대한 은폐" 등이 있다. 이런 대통령들이 만든 신뢰도 격차는 언론이 이들을 비판할 수 있는 공간을 마련했다. 동시에 많은 국민이 대통령은 국민의 문제에 관심을 기울이지 않는다고 생각하면 언론은 대통령을 비판할 근거를 갖게 된다.

노무현 대통령의 경우 여러 측근 참모들의 부정부패, 친인척들의 비리 개입, 잦은 발언 실수 등으로 인해 국민의 신뢰를 잃었다고 평가된다.

ㄴ. 개인적 위기, 스캔들, 권력투쟁: 정치학자 랜스 베넷(1996)은 빌 클린턴 대통령에 대한 언론의 집중 공격을 논하면서 정치인들이 개인적 위기나 스캔들이나 권력투쟁에 연루되면 언론이 배고픈 개들처럼 정치적 희생

양에게 달려든다고 썼다. 조금이라도 섹스 스캔들의 조짐이 있거나 정치적 부정의 증거가 조금이라도 드러날 경우 언론의 집중 공격이 높고도 힘 있는 자들을 파멸로 몰아 간다고 그는 말했다. 1992년의 미국 대통령 선거전 동안 미국의 뉴스는 클린턴 대통령의 혼외정사, 마약흡입, 징집도피 등 개인적 문제로 뒤덮였다. 이 때문에 클린턴 진영 공보팀의 최대 과제는 개인적 흠결을 덮고 이에 관해 유권자들의 신뢰감을 심어주는 것이었다.

대선전에서 승리한 클린턴 후보는 백악관에 입성한 뒤 백악관 기자실과 공보조정실(communication office)사이의 통로를 막아 버렸다. 기자들은 이것을 언론에 대한 선전포고로 받아들였고 양자간에 긴장감이 고조했다. 그 결과 언론은 클린턴의 값비싼 이발료(200달러)를 비난하거나, 백악관 여행담당실 관리상의 문제를 '트래블게이트' 라는 이름으로 집중 공격했다.

노무현 대통령의 경우 대선자금에 관한 의혹, 측근—친인척 비리, 그리고 참모들간 갈등이 주로 언론의 비판을 받았다. 총선을 앞두고 열린우리당을 지원하는 발언을 한 데 대해 한나라당이 공격했다. 이 보도는 권력투쟁에 관련된 대통령에 대한 비판이었다.

ㄷ. 야당의 공격과 뉴스관리의 실패: 랜스 베넷에 의하면, 클린턴 대통령을 괴롭힌 언론의 집중 공격은 3가지다. 첫째, 공보 직원들이 언론과 협력적 관계를 유지하는 데 실패했다. 둘째, 대통령이 언론 관리를 하는 것은 품위에 어울리지 않는다는 이유로 기본적인 뉴스 관리에도 소홀히 했다. 셋째, 대통령이 의심을 살 만한 행동에 연루해 있어서 공보 전략 부족이나 사안의 중대성에 무관하게 뉴스를 통제할 수 없는 상황에 빠졌다. 클린턴 공보팀은 정적들이 정치 공세를 조직적으로 전개했다고 비난했다.

ㄹ. 대니얼 핼린(Daniel Hallin)의 '합법적 논쟁의 영역' 이론: 핼린은 저널리즘의 세계를 '합법적 논쟁의 영역' '의견일치의 영역' '일탈의 영역' 의 3개 영역으로 나눈 뒤 선거 과정이나 입법 논의 등 여러 정치과정은

기존의 정치세력들이 벌이는 합법적 논쟁의 영역에 있다고 말했다 (Shoemaker & Reese, 1996, p. 227). 이 영역에서는 대통령에 대한 비판과 칭찬이 이뤄질 수 있다고 하겠다. 예컨대, 노 대통령의 행정수도 이전에 관한 찬반 논쟁도 이 영역에 속한다. 한국에서 행정수도 이전문제를 놓고 여야간-시민간 논쟁이 벌어지는 이유는 이것이 이 영역에 속하는 문제이기 때문이다. 언론도 이 문제를 놓고 대통령의 수도 이전에 우호적인 언론과 적대적 언론으로 크게 양분됐다. 국내에서 이 문제가 정책 논의를 넘어 정쟁으로 비화하는 양상을 보였다. 노 대통령 탄핵 문제나 국군의 이라크 파견도 언론사간 논조를 갈라놓은 사건이었다. 언론은 대통령이 관련된 이들 사안에 대해 대통령에 대해 우호적 또는 적대적으로 보도했다.

ㅁ. 엘리트들이 특정 사안을 놓고 분열할 때: 허먼과 촘스키(Herman & Chomsky, 2002, p. 346, n. 125)는 어떤 이슈를 놓고 국가 엘리트간 분열이 있을 때 언론은 비판적 목소리를 낼 수 있다고 말했다. 따라서 이슈를 놓고 우호적 논조도 나올 수 있다는 얘기다. 예컨대, 한국의 행정수도 이전을 놓고 지배 엘리트들은 찬반 양 진영으로 나뉘어 서로 다른 목소리를 냈다. 이를 반영한 듯 한국의 언론도 행정수도 이전을 놓고 엇갈린 논조를 보였다. 이전 반대의 일부 민의를 업고 보수 신문들은 집요하게 수도 이전 반대 논리를 폈다. 수도 이전 반대는 결국 노 대통령의 수도 이전 정책을 반대한 것이고, 나아가 대통령에 대한 비판으로 해석됐다.

나. 우호적 보도를 할 때

대통령에 대한 우호적 보도는 사례 연구에서 본 바와 같이 참으로 다양하다. 한마디로 말하자면, 인간이 생각할 수 있는 모든 방법으로 우호적 보도를 할 수 있다고 하겠다. 하지만 이론적 연구와 사례 연구를 종합해 이곳에서 일단 이론화를 시도해 보자.

우선 대통령은 모든 문제의 해결자로서 묘사될 수 있다. 이것은 대통령의 리더십 자질들을 포함한다 하겠다. 대통령은 나라의 문제를 진단하고 해결책 즉 정책방안을 제시하며 리더십을 보여준다. 사례 연구에서 본 바와 같이 대통령은 여러 리더십 역할을 수행했다. 가끔 국민 또는 여야당의 대통령 지지, 대통령의 정책에 관한 보도도 우호적 보도가 된다. 국제 무대의 지도자(또는 참여자)로 묘사하는 것도 우호적 보도이다.

대통령을 국민 중 한 사람으로 묘사하는 것은 대통령의 '인간적 자질'을 묘사하는 것과 유사한 점이 있다. 어쨌든 대통령을 보통사람처럼 묘사하거나, 어떤 문제에 대해 고뇌하는 모습을 묘사하거나, 어려운 결정을 내리거나, 느슨한 인간적인 면을 드러내는 것으로 그리는 것은 우호적 보도에 속한다고 하겠다. 전술한 바와 같이 대통령에 관한 세밀한 인간적 묘사는 대통령과 언론간 긴밀한 협조를 통해 실현될 수 있다. (그러나 대통령의 실수, 부정, 의심스런 행동 등은 언론의 공격 목표가 된다.)

비판적 보도의 반대 여건이 우호적 보도를 위한 여건으로 뒤집어 볼 수도 있겠다. 대통령이 국민의 신뢰를 받고 있거나, 반대 세력의 지지를 받는다거나, 언론 관계를 잘 관리한다면 대통령에 대한 우호적 보도를 기대할 수 있겠다. 예컨대 9-11 이후 공화당원인 부시 대통령은 테러전을 위한 정책을 제시해 민주당원들의 지지를 받았다고 보도한 것은 우호적이다.

대통령에 대한 비판적-우호적 보도를 논하는 데에는 슈메이커와 리즈(Shoemaker & Reese, 1996) 교수의 논의를 함께 고려할 필요가 있다. 두 저자는 언론을 통해 나타나는 보도 내용은 여러 여과 과정을 거쳐 나왔다고 주장했다. 말하자면 보도 내용은 개별 기자의 뉴스가치 판단, 언론 보도의 관행, 외부의 영향, 언론사의 편집 방향 등을 거쳐 생산된 것이다. 따라서 대통령에 대한 긍정-부정적 보도는 모두 이런 요소들이 함께 작용해서 나온 종합적 생산물이라 할 수 있다.

다. 우호적 보도에서 나타나는 대통령의 모습(이미지)

다음은 뉴욕타임스와 경향신문이 묘사한 대통령의 긍정적 모습을 열거한 것이다. 이것은 두 신문의 사례 연구에서 추출한 것이다.

〈부시〉

(1) 대통령 취임과 축하, 성공적인 정권이양, 순조로운 출발

(2) 국민적 지도자, 위기의 지도자, 국민적 화해자, 국론통합자

(3) 정책입안 및 집행자

(4) 과단성 있는 군사적 지도자

(5) 전권을 가진 지도자, 공직 임명자

(6) 국제무대의 지도자(참여자)

(7) 인간적 모습을 보이는 가족의 한 사람(아버지와 아들), 영부인을 통한 희생자 위로

(8) 국가적 위로자(슬픔에 잠긴 국민을 위로한)

(9) 의회 지지를 받는 대통령, 야당 지지를 받는 대통령

(10) 전장의 보도를 통한 승리자 모습

(11) 여야당의 지지를 받는 대통령

〈노무현〉

(1) 조촐한 취임, 그리고 취임 후 변화의 바람을 몰고 온 지도자

(2) 국가적 지도자 겸 화해자: 상생의 정치

(3) 정책 입안과 집행자

(4) 단호하고 강력한 지도자와 책임을 가진 지도자: 검찰 반발 돌파, 각료 임명, 탄핵 위협에 맞서는 모습 등

(5) 국제적 참여자

(6) 새로운 스타일의 지도자: 개혁주의자, 마음이 열린 사람, 솔직하고 탈권위적인 지도자

(7) 열심히 일하는 지도자

(8) 영부인의 역할을 통한 우호적 이미지: 친인척 관리에 전념

(9) 신임투표 제의로 심판을 원한 지도자

(10) 애국자, 민족주의적 지도자: 고이즈미 일본 총리에 경고

(11) 국민 지지를 받는 지도자: 탄핵 항의 시위를 통한 모습, 총선에 승리
    하는 모습

(12) 인간적 모습: 탄핵에 관한 고뇌

(13) 언론 지지를 받는 대통령: 칼럼과 사설이 탄핵을 비판

라. 비판적 보도에서 나타나는 대통령의 모습(이미지)

두 신문에서 추출한 대통령에 대한 비판적 보도에서 나타나는 대통령의
모습을 정리해 보면 다음과 같다.

〈부시〉

(1) 취임에 반대하는 시위대

(2) 사설과 일반 기사: 정책에 대한 비판, 부시의 행위를 비판, 군사계획
    을 갖지 못했음을 비판, 부시의 전쟁 계획을 비판, 국내문제에 신경
    쓰지 않음을 비판, 외교 실패로 인한 이라크전 개전을 비판

(3) 보복전(아프간전)의 범위를 둘러싼 부시 측근들의 갈등

〈노무현〉

(1) 취임식의 어수선함

(2) 개혁 정책에 대한 조직적 반발, 국군 해외 파병에 반대

(3) 청와대 내부 참모들간 갈등과 측근들에 대한 비리수사

(4) 칼럼과 기사의 비판: 아마추어리즘의 실패, 신임투표 제의 비판

(5) 신임투표에 대한 반대

(6) 야당의 탄핵공세, 사과 거부로 탄핵 강행

(7) 대통령 선거자금 수사

(8) 총선 승리에 대한 여당 자만을 경고

(9) 대통령의 경솔한 언행에 대한 비판

(10) 고건 처리 및 김혁규 고집에 대한 비판

(11) 청와대 보도 제한에 대한 비판

글을 끝맺으며_

이상의 본론에서 살펴본 바와 같이 미국과 한국의 대통령들은 언론 보도에 대해 지속적으로 불만을 가져왔다. 대통령들의 불만은 편파적 보도에 대한 불만에서 피상적 보도에 대한 불만까지 여러 이유에 근거한다. 대통령들은 언론이 행정부의 정책을 국민에게 잘 설명하지 않고 지엽적인 보도에 매달린다고 불평해 왔다. 그러나 정치학자 쿡과 랙스데일(1995)이 갈파한 바와 같이 대통령과 언론은 "상호 의존적이면서도 서로 독립적"임을 부인할 수 없다. 프랭클린 루스벨트 대통령과 미국 언론의 관계에서 살펴보았듯이 미국 언론은 결국 미국 대통령의 정책을 국민에 전달하는 중요한 역할을 해 온 것도 사실이다. 이런 맥락에서 쿡과 랙스데일의 말은 궁극적으로 미국 언론이 미국 대통령에게 때로는 적대적이기도 하고 때로는 우호적이기도 했다는 뜻으로 되새겨 볼 수 있다. 문제는 언론이 언제 대통령에게 우호적이거나 적대적 보도를 하는가 하는 점이다. 이것은 앞서 논의됐다.

뉴욕 타임스는 대통령이 강력한 리더십을 발휘해 국민을 이끌어 나가는 동안('상황을 규정'해 나가는 동안)에는 대통령을 우호적으로 묘사했다. 그러나 대통령의 발언이 거짓인 것으로 의심을 사거나, 다수의 미국민이 미국 대통령의 정책에 반대하거나, 백악관내에서 정책상 공백이 생기는 경우(신뢰도 격차가 생기는 경우) 미국 언론은 그들의 대통령에게 적대적 보도를 했다. 이런 맥락에서 미국 언론은 대통령의 지도력(리더십)에 따라 대통령에게 친구가 되기도 했고 적이 되기도 했다고 정리할 수 있겠다.

이런 논의는 한국에서도 적용 가능하다고 생각한다. 미국에서나 한국에서나 대통령이 확고한 권위와 강력한 리더십을 발휘하면 언론이 우호적 보도를 하게 된다. 그러나 대통령의 권위가 흔들리거나, 리더십을 발휘하지 못하거나, 그의 정책이 상당수 국민의 지지를 받지 못하면 언론은 이를 근거로 삼아 대통령에 대해 적대적으로 보도할 수 있다. 대통령 측근이나 친인척 비리, 청와대 내부갈등, 정책을 둘러싼 여야당의 마찰 등은 언론이 대통령을 적대적으로 묘사할 근거를 제공한다. 친일 과거청산 문제나 행정수도 이전 문제 등은 정책을 둘러싸고 엘리트가 양분된 대표적 갈등 사례였다. 일부 언론은 이를 근거로 노 대통령을 공격했다.

국내 언론은 이런 와중에 정치적-정책적 논쟁의 중요 당사자처럼 행동했고, 사실상 중요 정책의 참여자가 됐다. 이것은 언론이 공공 의제(public agenda) 설정에 참여한 것으로 언론의 정당한 기능이기도 하다. 이런 관점에서 경향신문은 취임이나 탄핵 등 분석 대상 기간 중 우호적 보도를 통해 노무현 대통령의 리더십을 인정하는 논조를 보였다고 평가할 수 있다.

본서가 논의한 대통령에 대한 언론 보도의 우호적-적대적 묘사란 궁극적으로 언론이 대통령의 리더십을 인정하느냐 부정하느냐에 관련돼 있다. 이 책에 인용된 여러 전문가들은 언론 보도에 나타난 대통령의 모습이 정책의 성패, 나아가 대통령의 정치적 생명을 좌우한다고 지적했다. 강력한 공보기관을 포함해 강력한 정치력과 행정력을 가진 대통령들이 자신에 관한 언론의 보도를 어떻게 유도하느냐 하는 문제는 결국 대통령들의 정치적-정책적 리더십에 달려있다. 아무리 대통령의 정책이 훌륭해도 이것을 전달하는 의사 소통 기술이 서투르다면 대통령은 정치적-정책적으로 성공할 수 없다.

이 책은 대통령의 리더십 중 매우 중요한 부분을 차지하는 대통령의 의사 소통 기술(presidential communication skills)에 관한 논의를 모아 정리한 것이다. 저자는 이 논의를 기초로 대통령의 의사 소통 기술이 어떻게 미국과 한국의 사례에서 언론 보도로 나타나는지 연구-분석해 보았다. 대통령의 리더십은 종국적으로 정치적 의사 소통 기술에 의해 평가될 수밖에 없다. 현대 정치에서 대통령의 의사 소통 기술은 바로 대통령의 리더십을 의미한다. 대통령이 세련된 의사 소통 기술을 갖지 못했다면 그는 리더십을 갖지 못했다고 말해도 좋다.

주: 국문요약 부분은 '관훈 저널' 2004년 여름호(pp. 265-290)에 저자가 기고한 '미국 대통령과 언론, 친구인가 적인가'에 대한 후속편의 성격을 갖고 있다. 관훈 저널 기고문은 저자의 저널리즘 석사 논문을 요약해 정리한 것으로 언론이 언제 대통령을 긍정적 또는 부정적으로 묘사하는지 기초적 의문만 제기한 것이었다. 본서는 여기에 한국의 사례를 새로 추가했다. 영문으로 된 본서와 국문요약 부분은 경향신문의 노무현 대통령 보도를 분석한 내용을 비롯해 대통령에 대한 언론의 긍정-부정적 보도에 관한 이론화 또는 일반화를 새롭게 담고 있다. 저자는 앞으로도 대통령과 언론의 관계에 관한 연구를 계속해 본서를 더욱 보완할 생각이다.

EPILOGUE

This is a book born from months of physical backache and personal agonies. Sitting up late into the night writing the manuscript, the author developed a chronic backache, which is not so serious as to go see the doctor but which is a bit of occasional discomfort and slight pain in the vertebral area. While examining and coding stories of the *New York Times*, the author could do the job in a mental state of calmness.

However, while the author examined stories of the *Kyunghyang Daily News*, something weighed heavy on the head. Should the research result turn out to be critical of the newspaper's overall coverage of Roh, senior editors and co-workers may get angered or disappointed. Should the research result turn out to be flattering to the presidential coverage of this newspaper, this may incur criticism from others that the author has failed to maintain due objectivity and neutrality by cutting off the corporate relations.

It should be stressed that the same research methods were used for Korean data. It should also be underscored that the author did his best to maintain objectivity and neutrality in the analysis of data.

It needs to be emphasized that the purpose of selecting the *Kyunghyang Daily* for analysis was to make a modicum contribution in improving presidential coverage, regardless of the research results which may be critical or flattering to news coverage of this newspaper. In the eyes of the author, heated and partisan wrangling over research report by the Korea Journalism Society about Korean broadcasters' programs just after the presidential impeachment resolution was simply appalling. The author realized that content analysis of news media could be so divisive and controversial.

Why did the author write this book in English and publish it in Korea? The foundation of this book is the author's Master of Science thesis in journalism entitled "Presidential Image of George W. Bush as Depicted by the New York Times." The thesis was submitted to San Jose State University, San Jose, California, U. S. A. in December, 2003. This book has an additional chapter on President Roh Moo Hyun's images as portrayed by the *Kyunghyang Daily*. In addition, one more chapter was added about how news media portray the president positively or negatively.

This book is an attempt to categorize and generalize presidential coverage. The author judged that translation of my thesis into Korean and adding analysis of the Korean newspaper would take more time than continuing to write in English. Personally, translating my own thesis into Korean appeared to be a duplication of the original work. If this book should attract sufficient readers, then the author would consider writing in Korean with more supplementation.

REFERENCES

APPENDICES
Appendix A (The New York Times)
Appendix B (The Kyunghyang Daily News)

REFERENCES

Babbie, Earl (2001).*The Practice of Social Research*. Belmont: Wadsworth Thomson Learning.

Bagdikian, Ben H. (2004). *The New Media Monopoly*. Boston, Beacon Press.

Bennett, W. Lance (1996). *News: The Politics of Illusion, Third Ed.* Longman Publishers USA.

Cook, Timothy E. & Ragsdale, Lyn (1995). The President and the Press: Negotiating Newsworthiness at the White House. In Michael Nelson (Ed.), *The Presidency and the Political System* (4th ed. , pp. 297-330). Washington D.C. : Congressional Quarterly Inc.

Edwards III, George C. & Wayne, Steven J. (1994). *Presidential Leadership: Politics and Policy Making*, 3rd Ed. , New York: St. Martin Press

Edwards III, George C. & Wayne, Steven J. (2003). *Presidential Leadership: Politics and Policy Making*, 6th Ed. , Belmont: Wadsworth/Thomson Learning

Entmann, Robert M.(1990). The Imperial Media. In Robert E. DiClerico (Ed.), *Analyzing the Presidency*. Guilford: The Dushkin Publishing Group, Inc.

Fallows, James (1997). *Breaking the News*. New York: Vintage Books,A Division of Random House, Inc.

Gans, Herbert J. (1979). The messages behind the news. *Columbia Journalism Review*, January-February 1979, pp. 40-45, adapted from *Deciding What's News*.

Graber, Doris A. Ed. (1982). *The President and the Public*. Philadelphia: Institute for the Study of Human Issues

Graber, Doris A. (1997). *Mass Media and American Politics*. Washington D. C. : Congressional Quarterly, Inc.

Graber, Doris A. (2002). *Mass Media and American Politics*, 6th Ed. Washington D. C. : Congressional Quarterly, Inc.

Grossman, Michael Baruch & Kumar, Martha Joynt (1981). *Portraying the President: The White House and the News Media*. Baltimore and London: The Johns Hopkins University Press.

Grossman, Michael Baruch & Kumar, Martha Joynt (1982). Images of the White House in the Media. In Doris A. Graber (Ed.) *The President and the Public*. Philadelphia: Institute for the Study of Human Issues

Herman, Edward S. & Chomsky, Noam (2002). *Manufacturing Consent: The Political Economy of the Mass Media*. Pantheon Books, New York.

Kerbel, Matthew Robert (1991). *Organizational Efficiency and Presidential Power*. Sunny Series in the Presidency. State University of New York Press

Kernell, Samuel (1997). *Going Public: New Strategies of Presidential Leadership*. Washington D. C. : Congressional Quarterly Inc.

Kessel, John H. (2001). *Presidents, the Presidency, and the Political Environment*. Congressional Quarterly, Inc.

Kovach, Bill & Rosenstiel, Tom (1999). *Warp Speed: America in the Age of Mixed Media*. The Century Foundation Press, New York.

Kumar, Martha Joynt (2003). Communications Operations in the White House of President George W. Bush: Making News on His Terms, unpublished paper.

Kumar, Martha Joynt & Sullivan, Terry Ed. (2003). *The White House World: Transitions, Organization, and Office Operations*. Texas A&M University Press.

Maltese, John Anthony (1992). *Spin Control: The White House Office of Communications and the Management of Presidential News*. The University of Northern Carolina Press.

McQuail, Dennis (2000). *Mass Communication Theory*. Thousand Oaks, CA: SAGE Publications.

Milkis, Sidney M. & Nelson, Michael (1984). *The American Presidency: Origins and Development, 1776-1993*. Washington D. C. : Congressional Quarterly Inc.

Pfiffner, James & Davidson, Roger H. Eds. (2000). *Understanding the*

Presidency, 3rd Ed. , Addison-Wesley Educational Publishers, Inc.

Pfiffner, James (2003). The Transformation of the Bush Presidency. In Pfiffner, James and Davidson, Roger H. (Eds.), *Understanding the Presidency*, 3rd Ed. , 2003, Addison-Wesley Educational Publishers, Inc.

Rozell, Mark J. (2003). The Press and the Presidency. In Phiffner, James & Roger H. Davidson (Eds.), *Understanding the Presidency*.
   Addison-Wesley Educational Publishers, Inc.

Shoemaker, Pamela J. & Reese, Stephen D. (1996). *Mediating The Message: Theories of Influences on Mass Media Content, Second Ed.* Longman Publishers USA.

Smith, Carolyn (1990). *Presidential Press Conferences: A Critical Approach.* New York: Praeger Publishers.

APPENDICES

Appendix A (The New York Times)
1. List of Very Negative (-2) Stories

Period I (January 21, 2001 to February 20, 2001)

01-21-01, #9, A17-1, Straight: "THE DEMONSTRATIONS; Protesters in the Thousands Sound Off in the Capitol" by David E. Rosenbaum.

01-23-01, #9, A20-1, Editorial: "Opposing the Ashcroft Nomination."

01-26-01, #3, A17-2, Analysis: "Adding a Financial Threat to Familiar Promises on Education; Failure will be sanctioned, the new president says" by Jacque Steinberg.

01-27-01, #4, A15-1, OP-Ed, "A Deadly Global Gag Rule: Bush's abortion policy will cost lives overseas" by Daniel E. Pellegrom.

01-29-01, #2, A1-2+ A21, Straight, "Questions Raised On New Bush Plan To End Estate Tax" by David Cay Johnston.

01-30-01, #6, A22-1, Ed, "Faith-Based Services"

01-31-01, #3, A14-1, Analysis, "By Resisting Ashcroft, Democrats Send a Signal; This nomination appears clinched" by Alison Mitchell.

01-31-01, #4, A14-2, "Excerpts from Remarks (of Opposition) by Hatch and Schumer on Ashcroft Nomination"

01-31-01, #10, A20-1, Ed, "Wrong Way on Energy"

02-03-01, A12-2, #2, Ed, "Editorial Observer; How George W. Bush Can Reach Black Voters; John Ashcroft makes racial detente much more difficult" by Brent Staples.

02-10-01, A10-1, #4, Str, "A Bush Aide Faults Plan To Repeal Estate Tax" by Elizabeth Becker.

02-16-01, #3, A12-1, Str, "Bush Team Under Attack on Emissions Talks" by Andrew C. Revkin.

02-16-01, #4, A12-1, Str, "Critics Seek To Overturn Abortion Rule; Oppose Bush Limits On Aid Sent Abroad; And old policy, newly reinstated, rekindles an old debate" by Robin Toner.

02-19-01, #2, A13-1, Str, "Federal Panel Warns Bush Of Social Security Problems; Service Inconsistent and Slow, Reports Say" by Robert Pear.

Period II (September 12, 2001 to October 07, 2001)

09-12-01, #5, A27-1, Op-Ed, "New Day of Infamy; The questions we must answer" by William Safire.

09-13-01, #7, A27-1, Op-Ed, "Inside The Bunker; The view from the PEOC" by William Safire.

09-19-01, #2, A1-1+B6, Str, "World Leaders List Conditions On Cooperation" by Patrick E. Tyler and Jane Perlez.

09-20-01, #2, A1-1+B5, Str, "Bush Advisers Split on Scope of Retaliation" by Patrick E. Tyler and Elaine Sciolino.

09-20-01, #5, B6-2, Str, "Senate Democrat Opposes White House' s Antiterrorism Plan and Proposes Alternative; Concerns that citizens' rights might be curtailed unnecessarily" by Neil A. Lewis.

09-25-01, #5, B7-1, Str, "Lawmakers Tap Brakes on Bush' s Hurtling Antiterrorism Measure" by Neil A. Lewis.

09-26-01, #3, B2-2, Str, "CHARITY; Islamic Aid Organization Expresses Anger at Its Inclusion on Bush Terror List" by Barry Bearak.

09-27-01, #3, A1-1, Anal, "Issue Now; Does U. S. Have a Plan?" by R. W. Apple Jr. .

09-28-01, #2, A1-1+B5, Str, "Bush Law-Enforcement Plan Troubles Both Right and Left" by Robin Toner.

09-28-01, #3, B2-1, Photo, Captioned "Indonesia protesters chanted anti-American slogans outside the United States Embassy," Slogans such as "Bush dog" and "Big Satan."

10-02-01, #2, A25-1, Op-Ed, "New Fears, New Alliances" by Edward N. Luttwak.

Period III (October 08, 2001 to November 06, 2001)

10-13-01, #1, A23-1, Op-Ed, "Abroad at Home; Mr. Bush' s New World; His foreign policy has turned upside down" by Anthony Lewis.

10-25-01, #1, A1-1+B8, Str, "White House Memo; Home Front Is a Minefield For President" by Elisabeth Bumiller and David E. Sanger.

/Period IV (March 19, 2003 to May 02, 2003)/
03-18-03, #10, A32-1, Ed, "War in the Ruins of Diplomacy"

03-18-03, #12, A33-1, Op-Ed, "Things to Come; Is this war only the beginning?" by Paul Krugman.

03-19-03, #2, A1-2+A15, Str, "A Worried World Shows Discord; World Reaction" by Alan Cowell in London.

03-19-03, #5, A22-1, Str, "Immigration; New Asylum Policy Comes Under Fire" by Philip Shenon.

03-19-03, #6, A29-1, Op-Ed, "D-Day" Thomas Friedman.

03-20-03, #4, A19-1, Str, "Threats and Responses; United Nations; Critics Say U. S. Lacks Legal Basis for Attack" by Felicity Barringer

03-20-03, #7, A29-1, Str, "Drilling in Alaska, A Priority for Bush, Fails in the Senate" by David Firestone.

03-26-03, #1, A1-2+A12, Str, "Senate Votes to Reduce Bush' s Tax Plan" by David E. Rosenbaum.

03-26-03, #2, A12-2, Anal, "How the President' s $726 Billion Plan Was Cut in Half" by David Firestone.

03-28-03, #3, A16-2, Ed, "Secrecy; The Bush Byword"

03-30-03, #1, A1-1+B11, Anal, "Bush Peril; Shifting Sand and Fickle Opinion" R. W. Apple Jr. .

03-30-03, #3, B10-2, Str, "The Mood; As a Quick Victory Grows Less Likely, Doubts Are Quietly Voiced in Washington" by David Sanger.

04-12-03, #2, A1-2+A8, Str, "Senate Vote Could Sharply Reduce Bush Tax Cut" by David E. Rosenbaum.

04-14-03, #2, A19-1, Op-Ed, "A Senseless Salute; It' s a mistake for presidents to act like soldiers" by John Lukacs.

04-16-03, #1, A1-1+A14, Str, "IN A CONCESSION, BUSH LOWERS GOAL OF TAX PLAN; Proposing $550 billion; White House Talks Tough, but Final Deal May Well be Closer to $350 Billion" by Elisabeth Bumiller.

04-19-03, #2, A12-1, Ed, "And the Winner Is Bechtel."

04-21-03, #2, A23-1, OP-Ed, "What Is It Good For?; The war pushers turn out to be the profit takers" by Bob Herbert.

2. List of Very Positive (+2) Stories

Period I (January 21, 2001 to February 20, 2001)

01-21-01, #1, A1-1+A14+A16, Str, "BUSH, TAKING OFFICE, CALLS FOR CIVILITY, COMPASSION AND 'NATION OF CHARACTER'; Unity Is A Theme; In Inauguration Speech, He Asks Citizens to Seek 'a Common Good' " by Frank Bruni & David E. Sanger.

01-21-01, #2, Anal, "Tradition and Legitimacy; A Nation's Rituals Begin to Dissolve Lingering Clouds of a Bitter Election Battle" by R. W. Apple Jr.
.

01-21-01, #3, A1-1+A17, Str, "Proud Father and Son Bask in History's Glow" by Frank Bruni.

01-21-01, #5, A1-2+A13, Str, "Inaugural Diary; Great Political Theater With a Touch of Pomp" by Guy Trebay.

01-21-01, #7, A14-2+A15, Transcript of inaugural address.

01-21-01, #8, A16-2, Str, "THE SPEECH; In His Inaugural Address, Bush Lingers on a Promise to Care" by Melinda Henneberger.

01-22-01, #1, A1-1+A12, Str, "On First Day, Bush Settles Into a Refitted Oval Office; He Greets Public After Touring New Home" by David E. Sanger.

01-24-01, #1, A1-1+A14, Str, "Bush Pushes Ambitious Education Plan; Would Use U. S. Aid to Force Schools to Meet Standards" David E. Sanger.

01-24-01, #2, A1-1+A15, Anal, "School Book Balancing Act; The logic behind annual test" Diana Jean Schemo.

01-24-01, #4, A14-2, Excerpt from Bush's education initiative.

01-26-01, #1, A1-1+C1, Str, "IN POLICY CHANGE, GREENSPAN BACKS A BROAD TAX CUT; White House Is Pleased; Guarded Endorsement by Fed Chief" by Richard W. Stevenson.

01-28-01, #1, A1-1+A14, Str, "BUSH' S TRANSITION LARGELY A SUCCESS, ALL SIDES SUGGEST; Careful Planning Seen; Analysts Find a Few Missteps but Note a Deft Touch in Dealing With Congress" Richard L. Berke.

01-30-01, #1, A1-1+A20, Str, "President Offers Plan to Promote Oil Exploration; Uses California Crisis to Sell Energy Policy" by Joseph Kahn & David E. Sanger.

01-30-01, #4, A18-1, Str, "Nudging Church-State Line, Bush Invites Religious Groups to Seek Federal Aid" by Laurie Goodstein.

01-30-01, #5, A18-1, Excerpt, "Bush on the Creation of a White House Office Tied to Religion. "

02-02-01, #1, A1-1+A16, Str, "SENATE CONFIRMS ASHCROFT AS ATTORNEY GENERAL, 58-42, CLOSING A FIVE-WEEK BATTLE; Victory for Bush; But Tally of Democrats Hints at New Fights Over Court Picks" by Alison Mitchell.

02-02-01, #4, A16-2, Excerpt from "Remarks in the Senate Debate on the Ashcroft Nomination"

02-03-01, #1, A10-1, Str, "Bush, the Conciliator, Meets With Democrats" by David E. Sanger & Alison Mitchell.

02-07-01, #3, A18-1, Ed, "Smart Start on Defense Budgeting"

02-09-01, #1, A1-1+A10, Str, "BUSH IN FIRST STEP TO SHRINK ARSENAL OF U. S. WARHEADS; To Order Defense Review; But Commitment to a Missile Shield Seems Firm, Even in Face of Allies' Worries" by Steven Lee Meyers.

02-10-01, #1, A1-1+A12, Str, "White House Memo: Presidency Takes Shape With No Fuss, No Sweat" by Frank Bruni.

02-11-01, #1, WK16-1, Ed, "Between Two Eras"

02-14-01, #1, A1-1+A26, Str, "BUSH DETAILS PLAN TO FOCUS MILITARY ON NEW WEAPONRY; A Break With Orthodoxy; President Joins Defense Debate on New vs. Old Technology --- Billions Are at Stake" by David E. Sanger.

02-14-01, #2, A26-1, Excerpt from "Bush' s Remarks on the Military"

02-17-01, #2, A1-1+A4, Anal, "THE WORLD STAGE, ACT I, First Act For Bush; Declaring Leadership" Frank Bruni with David E. Sanger.

02-17-01, #4, A4-2, Excerpt "In the President' s Words on the Bombing; 'It' s a Routine Mission. ' "

02-17-01, #7, Op-Ed, "No Choice But To Strike; To contain Iraq, expect more air strikes" by Anthony H. Cordesman.

02-20-01, #2, A1-1+A12, Pho+Str, "A Day of Remembrance in Oklahoma City; Bush Dedicates Museum at the Site of Oklahoma Bombing" by Frank Bruni.

Period II (September 12, 2001 to October 07, 2001)

09-12-01, #1, A1-1+A14, Str, "U. S. ATTACKED; HIJACKED JETS DESTROY TWIN TOWERS AND HIT PENTAGON IN DAY OF TERROR; President Vows to Exact Punishment for 'Evil' " by Serge Schmemann.

09-12-01, #2, A1-2+A4, Str, "A Somber Bush Says Terrorism Cannot Prevail" by Elisabeth Bumiller with David E. Sanger.

09-12-01, #3, A4-2, Transcript of "Bush' s Remarks to the Nation on the Terrorist Attacks"

09-13-01, #2, A16-1, Str, "AFTER THE ATTACKS; Washington' s Response; THE PRESIDENT; Bush Labels Aerial Terrorist Attacks 'Acts of War' " by Katharine Q. Seelye & Elisabeth Bumiller.

09-13-01, #3, A15-1, Transcript of "Bush' s Remarks to Cabinet and Advisers (on Attacks)"

09-14-01, #1, A1-1+A18, Str, "BUSH AND TOP AIDES PROCLAIM POLICY OF 'ENDING' STATES THAT BACK TERROR; LOCAL AIRPORTS SHUT AFTER AN ARREST; President to Visit New York --- bin Laden Singled Out" by Elisabeth Bumiller & Jane Perlez.

09-14-01, #2, A1-1+A4, Anal, "No Middle Ground Exists In War Against Terrorism" R. W. Apple Jr. .

09-14-01, #3, A18-1, Excerpts from "President' s Remarks on Investigation Into Attacks; 'This nation is sad. But we' re also tough and resolute. ' "

09-15-01, #1, A1-1+A6, Str, "BUSH LEADS PRAYER, VISITS AID CREWS; CONGRESS BACKS USE OF ARMED FORCES; A Day of

Mourning; President, in New York, Offers Resolute Vows Atop the Rubble" by Robert McFadden.

09-15-01, #2, A1-1+A16, Str, "U. S. Demands Arab Countries 'Choose Sides' by Jane Perlez.

09-15-01, #3, A6-1, Transcript of President's Remarks "We Are in the Middle Hour of Our Grief"

09-15-01, #4, A6-2, Column, "WHITE HOUSE MEMO; Two Strangers, Bush and New York City, Meet and Embrace in Calamity's Wake" by Elisabeth Bumiller.

09-15-01, #6, A7-1, Str, "Heartened by a Visit By Bush" by Clyde Haberman.

09-16-01, #1, A1-1+A5+A6, Str, "BUSH TELLS THE MILITARY 'GET READY' ; BROADER SPY POWERS GAINING SUPPORT; Long Battle Seen; 'We' re at War,' He Says --- Support in Poll for Armed Response" by Elaine Sciolino.

09-16-01, #2, A1-2+A19, Str+Pho, "In Four Days, A National Crisis Changes Bush's Presidency" by David E. Sanger & Don Van Natta Jr. .

09-16-01, #4, A5-2, Text of Bush's radio address "A Different Battle Awaits"

09-17-01, #1, A1-1+A13+C6, Str, "NATION SHIFTS ITS FOCUS TO WALL STREET AS A MAJOR TEST OF ATTACK' S AFTERMATH; Bush Is Confident; Officials Seek to Avoid Sell-Off and Bolster Investors' Resolve" by Richard W. Stevenson with Jonathan Fuerbringer.

09-18-01, #1, A1-1+B4, Str, "Bin Laden Is Wanted in Attacks, 'Dead or Alive,' President Says" David E. Sanger.

09-19-01, #6, B11-2, Str, "THE PRESIDENT; In This Crisis, Bush Is Writing His Own Script" by Elisabeth Bumiller & Frank Bruni.

09-20-01, #1, A1-1+B6, Str, "BUSH ORDERS HEAVY BOMBERS NEAR AFGHANS; DEMANDS BIN LADEN NOW, NO NEGOTIATIONS; Deploys Warships; President Is Addressing Congress Tonight to Lay Out His Aims" by David E Sanger.

09-21-01, #1, A1-1+B4, Str, "BUSH PLEDGES ATTACK ON AFGHANISTAN UNLESS IT SURRENDERS BIN LADEN NOW; HE CREATES CABINET POST FOR SECURITY; Bars Talks, Saying Hosts Will Share the Terrorists' Fate" by Elisabeth Bumiller.

09-21-01, #3, A1-1+B5, Anal, "A Clear Message; 'I Will Not Relent' ; A Vow to Root Out All Global Threats" by R. W. Apple Jr. .

09-21-01, #4, A34-1, Ed, "Mr. Bush' s Most Important Speech"

09-21-01, #5, B4, Transcript of Mr. Bush' s Address on Terrorism Before a Joint Meeting of Congress; 'We will not tire. We will not falter and we will not fail. "

09-21-01, #6, Str, "THE SCENE; Joint Congress Transformed Into a United Showcase of Courage and Resolve; A defining moment for America, with few precedents" by Alison Mitchell.

09-21-01, #8, B6-1, Str, "WASHINGTON RESPONSE; Congress Joins In Support Of President" by David E. Rosenbaum.

09-22-01, #3, A1-1+B2, Col, "WHITE HOUSE MEMO; For President, a Mission and a Role in History; Role Finds Bush Onstage, Waiting; Shoulders that once shrugged now broaden with weighty resolve" by Frank Bruni.

09-22-01, #4, A3-2, Str, "Democrats in Senate Back Down on Missile Shield Issue; Opposition to Bush on any defense issue dissipates" by Adam Clymer.

09-23-01, #3, A1-1+B2, Str+Pho, "From Many Voices Advising Bush, One Battle Strategy" by Jane Perlez & David Sanger & Thom Shanker.

09-25-01, #1, A1-1+B4, Str, "BUSH FREEZES ASSETS LINKED TO TERROR NET; RUSSIANS OFFER AIRSPACE AND ARMS SUPPORT; Banks 'On Notice' ; President Says Foreign Financial Institutions May Be Punished" by David E. Sanger & Joseph Kahn.

09-28-01, #1, A1-1+B6, Str, "Bush to Increase Federal Role in Security at Airports; National Guard and Oversight of Screening" by Elisabeth Bumiller.

09-28-01, #7, B6-1, Str, "THE NATIONAL GUARD; Bush Proposal Is Welcomed by Governors and Travelers" by Kate Zernike.

09-29-01, #1, A1-1+B4, Str, "PRESIDENT SAYS U. S. IS 'IN HOT PURSUIT' OF TERROR GROUP; A Guerrilla War; Allied Units Reportedly Entered Afghanistan --- No U. S. Word" by David E. Sanger & Steven Lee Meyers.

09-29-01, #3, A19-1, Op-Ed, "Abroad at Home; Progress and Problems; Mr. Bush has set exactly the right tone" by Anthony Lewis.

09-30-01, #1, A29-1, Str, "Bush 'Is My Commander,' Gore Declares in Call for Unity; Urging support for the president in an effort to seek justice, not revenge" by Richard L. Berke.

10-01-01, #1, A1-1+B2, Str, "Bush Approves Covert Aid for Taliban Foes; $100 Million to Help Refugees Is Also Set" by Michael R. Gordon & David E. Sanger.

10-07-01, #1, A1-1+B5, Str, "BUSH SAYS 'TIME IS RUNNING OUT' ; U. S. PLANS TO ACT LARGELY ALONE; Rumsfeld Returns; Administration Says It Has Enough Backing for Long Campaign" by Elaine Sciolino & Steven Lee Meyers.

Period III (October 08, 2001 to November 06, 2001)

10-08-01, #1, A1-1+B3, Str, " U. S. AND BRITAIN STRIKE AFGHANISTAN, AIMING AT BASES AND TERRORIST CAMPS; BUSH WARNS 'TALIBAN WILL PAY A PRICE' ; Bomb and Missile Attacks --- Bin Laden Issues Threat" by Patrick E. Tyler.

10-08-01, #5, A17-1, Op-Ed, "Essay: Our 'Relentless' Liberation; Afghans now, Iraqis soon" by William Safire.

10-08-01, #6, B6-1, Str, "THE PLANNING; Quietly, Carefully,
President Worked Toward a Decision on Attack-Aid Combination" by David E. Sanger & Elisabeth Bumiller.

10-09-01, #1, B7-1, Str, "THE PLANNING; A Look Behind the Scenes, From White House Aides" by Elisabeth Bumiller & David E. Sanger.

10-12-01, #1, A1-1+B5, Str, "BUSH OFFERS TALIBAN '2ND CHANCE' TO YIELD; SAYS HE' D WELCOME U. N. IN NATION-BUILDING; FBI ISSUES ALERT ON SIGNS OF NEW TERROR; 'Just Bring Him In' ; President Hints He Will Halt War if bin Laden Is Handed Over" by Patrick E. Tyler & Elisabeth Bumiller.

10-12-01, #2, A1-1+B14, Pho+Str "Honoring Pentagon Victims, and Survivors; President Bush and his wife, Laura, at a ceremony"

10-12-01, #5, A24-1, Ed, "Mr. Bush' New Gravitas"

10-12-01, #6, B4, Excerpts from "the President' s Remarks on the War on Terrorism"

10-12-01, #7, B5-1, Str, "MEDIA WATCH; To Reassure World, Bush Flies Confidently and Forcefully Without a Net" by Alessandra Stanley.

10-15-01, #1, A1-1+B2, Str, "PRESIDENT REJECTS OFFER BY TALIBAN FOR NEGOTIATIONS; Demands Surrender of bin Laden --- U. S. Bombs Fall in Kabul" by Elisabeth Bumiller.

10-19-01, #1, A1-1+B4, Pho+Str, "THE PRESIDENT; Bush Meets China' s Leader" by David Sanger.

10-20-01, #1, A1-1+B4, Str, "BUSH MEETS JIANG; Citing Support for War, President Plays Down Contentious Issues" by David E. Sanger in Beijing.

10-20-01, #2, A4-1, Str, "Rome Journal: A Bush Admirer Longs to Join America' s A-List" by Melinda Henneberger.

10-20-01, #5, B1-1+B6, Str, "Bush Winning Gore Backers' High Praises; Foreign Policy Choices Seen as Ideal for Crises; Many Democrats are having a quiet change of heart on the president" Richard L. Berke.

10-20-01, #6, A1-1+B2, Str, "More Than 100 G. I. 's in Afghan Ground Raid; NIGHTTIME ASSAULT; 2 Die in Copter Accident at Pakistan Base --- Taliban Site Hit" Eric Schmitt with Steven Lee Meyers.

10-24-01, #3, B1-1+B2, Str, "Bush' s War Troika Seeking Blend of Military and Civilian Decision-Making; An old issue of how much oversight to impose on field commanders" by Eric Schmitt.

11-07-01, #2, B4-1, Excerpt from Bush' s speech "In President' s Words; 'Lift This Dark Threat' ; 'An international coalition of unprecedented scope' "

Period IV (March 19, 2003 to May 02, 2003)

03-18-03, #1, A1-1+A15, Str, "Bush Gives 48 Hours, and Vows to Act; READY TO ATTACK; Diplomatic Effort Ends --- Terror Alert Level Is Raised for U. S. " by Richard W. Stevenson.

03-18-03, #2, A1-1+A14, Anal, "A New Doctrine for War; In Age of Unseen Enemies, President Says, Waiting for Opponent to Attack 'Is Suicide' ; Allies say the gunslinging image is now an advantage" by David Sanger.

03-18-03, #5, A14-2, Transcript of Bush' s Speech on Iraq "Saddam Hussein and His Sons Must Leave"

03-18-03, #6, A14-1, Str, "Congress; Both Parties Close Ranks Behind the President" No reporter' s name.

03-18-03, #9, A18-2, Str, "TV Watch; Soft Words That Convey a Hard Line" by Alessandra Stanley.

03-20-03, #1, A1-1+A20, Str, "BUSH ORDERS START OF WAR ON IRAQ; MISSILES APPARENTLY MISS HUSSEIN; President Warns of Difficulty --- Airstrikes on Baghdad" by Dvid E. Sanger with John F. Burns.

03-20-03, #2, A1-2+A20, Str, "Days of Waiting and Wondering Ends With Word From President" by Richard W. Stevenson.

03-23-03, #2, B1-2+B10, Str, "Pre-emption; Idea With a Lineage Whose Time Has Come" by Steven Weisman.

03-23-03, #3, B10-1, Str, "Bush Warns That the War in Iarq May Last Longer Than Expected" by David Sanger.

03-24-03, #1, A1-2+B2, Str, "Lowering Expectation; As Iraqi Resistance Stiffens, Bush Moves To Prepare U. S. Public for a Harder War" R. W. Apple Jr. .

03-24-03, #2, B12-2, Str, "Commander in Chief; Bush, Pleased by Progress, Tries to Lower Expectations" by Richard Stevenson.

03-28-03, #1, A1-2+B13, Str, "War to Keep Going Until Regime Ends, Bush and Blair Say" by Tom Shanker & Elisabeth Bumiller.

03-28-03, #2, A11-1, Str, "White House Proposes New Rules for Overtime" by Steven Greenhouse.

03-28-03, #4, B12, Transcript from news conference by Bush and Blair "Speeches and Testimony; Bush and Blair at Camp David; 'Acting Together in a Noble Purpose' "

03-29-03, #1, A1-1+B11, Str, "WHITE HOUSE SAYS WAR IS 'ON TRACK'; SHOW OF SUPPORT; Bush Assails Hussein --- Syria and Iran Warned Not to Interfere" by Richard Stevenson.

03-29-03, #2, B11, Excerpts from Bush' s Speech to Veterans Groups at the White House.

03-30-03, #2, B1-1+B11, Str, "President, No Matter Where, Keeps Battlefield Close" by Elisabeth Bumiller.

03-30-03, #10, Week in Review p. 1, Feature, "The End of Texas as We Know Them; Bush' s fiscal revolution has just begun, and the economy may never be the same" by Daniel Altman.

04-04-03, #3, B9-2, Str, "Paying for the War; House and Senate Approve Bush's Wartime Spending Request" by David Firestone.

04-05-03, #1, A1-1, Anal, "Dash to Baghdad Leaves Debate in Dust; Military Successes Give Bush a Boost" by R. W. Apple Jr. .

04-07-03, #1, A2-2, Str, "Bush Visit Is Viewed as Hopeful Sign for Ulster Impasse" by Warren Hoge in London.

04-07-03, #3, B2-2, Col, "White House Letter; Another President Bush Watches on the Sidelines" by Elisabeth Bumiller.

04-09-01, #1, A1-2+B6, Anal, "Bush's War Message; Strong and Clear" by R. W. Apple Jr. .

04-09-03, #4, B7-2, Excerpts from Remarks by Bush and Blair "Iraq Will Soon Be Liberated"

04-10-03, #1, A1-2+B10, Str, "U. S. FORCES TAKE CONTROL IN BAGHDAD; BUSH ELATED; SOME RESISTANCE REMAINS; Bush Tunes In And Sees Iraqis in Celebrations" Elisabeth Bumiller & Douglas Jehl.

04-11-03, #2, B8-2, Transcript of taped statements by Bush and Blair "We Will Help You Build"

04-12-03, #1, A1-2, Pho+Str, "SOLDIERS' HONOR; Visiting troops wounded in Iraq, President Bush gave a Purple Heart yesterday to Army Sgt. First Class Thomas Douglas . . . " by *New York Times* Photographer

04-14-03, #1, A1-2+B1, "How 3 Weeks of War in Iraq Looked From the Oval Office" by Elisabeth Bumiller et al. .

04-15-03, #1, B1-2+B10, Str, "Americans See Clear Victory in Iraq, Poll Finds; Baghdad's fall has fortified Bush's political standing" by Adam Nagourney & Janet Elder.

04-15-03, #2, B10-1, Str, "POLITICAL STRATEGY; Bush to Use Ratings in War To Sell Proposed Tax Cut" Richard W. Stevenson.

04-16-03, #2, A1-1+B3, Str, "BUSH SAYS REGIME IN IRAQ IS NO MORE; SYRIA IS PENALIZED; Cutting an Oil Pipeline; U. S. Is Also Pressuring Iran" by David Sanger & Thom Shanker.

04-17-03, #1, A1-1+B6, Str, "BUSH URGING U. N. TO LIFT SANCTIONS IMPOSED ON IRAQ; 12 Years of Trade Curbs; Oil Money Seen as Paying for Rebuilding, but Plan Could Reignite Council Feud" by

Richard Stevenson with Felicity Barringer.

04-17-03, #1, A1-1+B6, Str, "BUSH URGING U. N. TO LIFT SANCTIONS IMPOSED ON IRAQ; 12 Years of Trade Curbs; Oil Money Seen as Paying for Rebuilding" by Richard Stevenson.

04-17-03, #2, A1-2+A8, Str, "White House Is Pressing Israelis To Take Initiatives in Peace Talks" by Steven R. Weisman.

04-19-03, #1, A1-1+B6, Str, "Bush Plans to Ask U. N. to Lift Penalties Against Iraq in Phases" by Steven Weisman.

04-20-03, #1, B14-1, Str, "THE ADMINISTRATION; Even Critics of War Say the White House Spun It With Skill; A battlefield narrative that worked at home, if not everywhere" by Elisabeth Bumiller.

04-22-03, #1, A1-1+A18, Str, "BUSH' S AIDES PLAN LATE SPRINT IN '04; Formal Campaign Would Start Near Sept. 11 Anniversary" Adam Nagourney & Richard W. Stevenson.

04-26-03, #1, A13-1, Str, "WHITE HOUSE MEMO; Bush Shows Loose Side in an Interview" by Elisabeth Bumiller.

04-28-03, #1, A18-1, Col, "White House Letter; Playing It Straight at an Odd Washington Ritual" by Elisabeth Bumiller.

04-29-03, #2, A19-2, Excerpt "In Bush' s Words; 'Superb' Progress in Iraq"

05-02-03, #1, A1-1+A16, Str, "Bush Declares 'One Victory in a War on Terror' ; He Says Military Phase in Iraq Has Ended" by David E. Sanger in San Diego.

05-02-03, #2, A16-2, Transcript from President Bush' s Remarks on the End of Major Combat in Iraq"

05-02-03, #3, A17-2, Str, "THE SCENE; In Full Flight Regalia, the President Enjoys a 'Top Gun' Moment" by David Sanger.

Appendix B (The Kyunghyang Daily News)

목록 1: 매우 부정적 기사(-2)의 제목

기간 1 (03년 2월 26일자에서 3월 25일자까지)

2. 26, # 11,6면, " 모양새 구긴 '축하연' ; 국회특검법 등 진통 영향; 의원들 몰려 다녀 어수선; 외교사절 '재미있네' 조소"

3. 07, # 1,1면, "검찰 '서열 파괴 집단 반발; 강 법무 '파격 인선' 방침에 간부들 반대 건의서"

3. 08, # 2,1면, "민주 진 정통 퇴진 건의 -- 당직자 회의, 청와대에 부정 여론 전달키로"

3. 08, # 3,1면, "평검사들 가세 '파문' 확산 -- '총장에 인사권 이관' 잇딴 성명 -- 대검 간부들도 건의서"

3. 10, # 1,1면, "김각영 총장 전격 사퇴 -- 새정부 인사권 통해 검찰 통제 뜻 확인"-- '인사 파동은 공정한 시스템 무시 탓' "

3. 18, # 3,3면, "민주 내홍 파열음 심상찮다 -- 당-청 갈등 중첩 위험 수위"

3. 24, # 3,7면, "청와대 비서실 '청-장 불협화음' -- 체계 혼선 잇단 신경전"

3. 24, # 4,7면, "청와대 '대변인 경질' 속앓이 -- 군 경계 브리핑 잘못 파문 -- 재발 우려 교체-동정 엇갈려"

3. 25, # 6,10면 내부 칼럼, "아마추어리즘의 실패" 강한 비판

〈비교〉

3. 25, # 2,2면 사설, "노무현 정부 한 달, 변화와 시련" 중립적(0).

3. 25, # 4,8면, "노무현 대통령 취임 한 달 -- 새 정치 '기대 반' ; 개혁 역풍 우려 '우려 반' -- 파격 인사변화 부응 큰 박수; 경제난 우려 재벌 개혁 주춤" 중립적(0).

〈추가: 다소 부정적(–1) 기사 목록〉

2. 26, # 15,19면, "새 법무장관 40대 여변호사 강금실 씨 내정설; 검찰 강력 반발, 고위간부들 '서열 파괴, 조직 와해 우려'; 평검사 일부 정치 중립성 확보 호기다"

2. 26, # 16,19면, " '김화중 복지 내정'도 반발. 시민단체들 '측근 배려 차원' -- 실망스럽다"

2. 28, # 5,4면, "한나라, 현실 무시한 실험 내각"

3. 07, # 2,1면, "노 대통령, '진 장관 파문 송구' -- 국민 양해 당부 -- 이중 국적 문제는 전향적 검토"

3. 07, # 3,2면 사설, "모르는 것 많은 '청와대 입' "

3. 07, # 4,4면, "대북 비밀 접촉 의혹 증폭 -- 청와대 '별일 아니다' '더할 얘기 없다' 침묵 일관 -- 라종일, '사적 만남'에 청와대 '외교관 신분' -- 노 지시 여부엔 '확인해 줄 수 없다' "

3. 07, # 5,4면중, "심기 불편한 노 -- 진 정통 불러 따져 묻고, 라 보좌관 해명 제지하고……"

3. 17, # 2,4면, "특검법 정국, 북 송금 절차 수사 암초 만났다"

3. 17, # 4,4면, "민주 구주류 특검법 싸고 갈등 -- 이젠 막 가자는 거죠"

3. 18, # 6,4면, "대 언론 정책 전면전 선언 -- '개혁 이름으로 다각 통제' -- 기자실 폐지 등 비난 -- 한나라 '써준 대로 보도하란 말이냐' "

3. 20, # 1,1면, "정부 산하 단체장 비리 내시   문 수석 상당한 첩보 확인 중 -- 대통령 측근도 포함"

기간 2 (03년 10월 11일자에서 11월 10일자까지)

10. 11, # 9,7면 사설, "대통령 재신임 제안 경솔했다"

10. 13, # 7,5면, "노 재신임 선언, '잘못한 일' 우세"

10. 16, # 1,1면, "노 비리 해명 미흡 땐 국정조사 -- 3야 대표 합의 -- 특검제 도입도 추진"

10. 20, # 1,1면, " '권력 정보 독점' 지목 이광재 실장 사표 -- 노 대통령 수리

여부 주목--386 참모 거취 가늠자"

10. 20, # 2,3면, "이라크 파병--낮엔 결정된 바 없음, 밤엔 확정 -- 노 시민단체엔 부인, 4당엔 파병 통고 -- 상처받은 노 정부 신뢰성"

10. 22, # 1,4면, "노 외유중 청와대 파병 갈등 심화; 일부 수석 외교-국방 라인 독주에 견제구; 함구령에도 파병성격 등 노선 충돌 첨예화; 박 수석 전투병 보내면 사퇴 가능성 거론"

10. 29, # 1,1면, "삼성-롯데 10억씩, 현대차-LG 5억~15억; 노 캠프 65억 이상 받았다; 민주 '이상수 의원 영수증 안 돌려줘' "

10. 29, # 3,5면, "또 불거진 파병 혼선; 청와대 정부 강온파 규모 성격 신경전"

10. 30, # 1,1면, "민주 '노 캠프 128억 돈 세탁 의혹' ; 우리 '민주 고위당직 100억 횡령' "

10. 31, # 1,4면, "노 캠프 얼마나 걷었기에……; 개한 74억 넘어 100억대 달할 수도;이 의원 '50억은 여러 계좌 합한 것' "

11. 04, # 1,1면, "대선 자금 무제한 수사; 5대 기업 + 알파; 검찰 '기업보다 정치권 초점' ; 노 대통령 측근 비리도 엄정 수사키로; 최도술씨 SK 외 7~8곳서 금품 수수"

11. 08, # 3,6면 칼럼, 대통령의 부적절한 골프

〈추가: 다소 부정적(-1) 기사 목록〉

10. 11, # 5,6면 칼럼, "국정 혼란은 안 된다" 비판적

10. 11, # 6,6면, "노 재신임 충격 -- 취임 8개월 만에 30%대 추락 -- 측근, 친인척 등 잇단 파문 -- 축적된 국민 불신 반영"

10. 11, # 7,6면, "노, 최도술 덫 치명타 인식 -- 최씨 '핵폭탄' 이었나 -- 비공식 대선 후원금 확인 팬 메카톤 파장 -- 개인 수뢰 결론 나도 노 정치-도덕적 책임"

10. 11, # 8,7면, "날선 검에 측근 5인 상처 -- '좌 광재, 우 희정' 등 모두 연루 -- 집권 중 강도 높은 수사 이례적 -- 독립 강조하다 역풍 아이러니"

10. 13, # 12,7면 사설, "재신임 투표 정략 연계 말라"

10. 14, # 2,3면, "노 고속 주행 3야에 막혀 '안개 속' -- 재신임 정국, 국민투표 불투명"

10. 14, # 3,3면, "38분 내내 박수 한 번 없어"

10. 14, # 7,5면, "재신임 국민투표 -- 독재자나 하는 것, YS '헌법에도 없는 일' 독설"

10. 15, # 1,1면, "3야 재신임 공대위 추진 -- 오늘 대표 회동 -- 최대표 '노 비리 연루 땐 탄핵' 국회 연설"

10. 15, # 3,3면, "재신임 국민투표 외신반응 -- FT지 '소환 자처 국민 당황' 신화통신 '정면 돌파 배수진' "

10. 15, # 6,3면, "반격-퇴로 다목적 카드 -- 최대표 탄핵 연설 안팎"

10. 15, # 8,4면, "개헌론 등에 중진들 잇단 제동 -- 민주 위상 찾기 속앓이"

10. 15, # 11,7면 사설, "대통령에 대한 예의라니 -- 최도술 공격"

10. 16, # 2,3면, "셈 다른 3야 -- 어색한 입맞춤 -- 3당 지도부 회동 안팎-전망; 노 대통령 공격 -- 2시간 만남 -- '노 때문이야' 한 목소리에 만족"

10. 16, # 4,3면 사설, "재신임 정국 국정 표류 우려된다"

10. 17, # 1,4면 "목소리 커지는 청와대 물갈이 -- 인적 쇄신 요구"

10. 17, # 2,5면, "민중 의사 앞에서 독재 확립 -- JP, 카이사르 빗대 노 비판"

10. 18, # 2,1면, "신당 청와대에 인적 쇄신 요구 -- 이광재 상황실장 겨냥 -- 반드시 경질해야"

10. 18, # 3,3면, "청 각본 있는 혼선? -- 이쪽선 이 말, 저쪽선 저 말 -- 오락가락 수차례 말 바꾸기"

10. 18, # 4,4면, "통합신당 김부겸 의원 쓴 소리 -- '노 대통령 야-언론 탓하지 말라' "

10. 18, # 6,5면, "노 소신에 신당 쇄신 반기 -- 여권내 신적 쇄신 파장"

10. 18, # 7, "스릴러 같은 정치와 통치"

10. 18, # 8, "국민투표가 합헌이 되려면"

10. 22, # 3,7면 사설, "청와대 참모들 이래도 되나"

10. 28, # 1,2면, "현대차도 노쪽에 기부금; 대선 낭시 5개 기업시 50억--75억 제공;민주 김경재 의원 주장"

10. 28, # 2,4면, "노 대선자금 이중 장부 있다?; 민주 의혹 제기, 반환 촉구; 이상수 '말도 안 돼' 반박"

10. 28, # 3,7면 칼럼, "노 이제는 희망을 주십시오; 정쟁에 망가지는 리더십 답답; 실사구시 정치로 경제 챙기길"

10. 29, # 2,3면, "옛 동지 사활 건 진실 게임; 민주-우리당 의혹 해명"

10. 29, # 4,7면 사설, "노 대선 자금 의혹도 밝혀야"

10. 30, # 2,1면, "노 대통령 전 운전기사 소환; 검찰, 최도술 11억 나눠 쓴 혐의 추궁"

10. 30, # 4,4면, "노 대선 자금 민주-우리당 사활 건 공방"

10. 30, # 5,4면, "노 캠프 후원금 편법처리; 중앙당 일괄 모금 149억 4개 지역 분산"

10. 30, # 6,5면, "노 측근 비리 눈덩이 되나; 이번엔 전 운전기사 선봉술씨 소환; 수수명목-사용처 등 집중 추궁"

10. 31, # 3,7면 사설, "노 대통령, 파병 걱정스럽다"

11. 04, # 5,7면 칼럼, "미국의 늪, 한국의 덫; 이라크 저항에 미 베트남 악몽; 추가 파병 덜컥수에서 손 빼야"

11. 06, # 1,2면, "노 캠프 계좌 10여개 추적; 검찰 한나라 전 재정국 간부 2명 체포영장"

11. 06, # 2,3면, "본 게임은 거여; 몸 푸는 강 검찰; 민주 계좌 추적 배경과 전망; 노 캠프 먼저 손대 야 탄압 주장에 쐐기; 한나라 추적 초읽기"

11. 06, # 3,4면, "명의 없는 2억 영수증 발견; 민주 노관규, 노 캠프 자금 또 폭로"

11. 07, # 1,3면, "노 캠프 핵심 찌르는 검; 정대철 소환 방침 등 연일 강수; 확실한 단서 쥔 듯 -- 특검 봉쇄 목적도"

11. 07, # 2,7면 사설, "노 캠프 차명 계좌 철저히 밝혀야"

11. 08, # 4,7면 사설, "노 측근 비리 특검 할 만하다"

11. 10, # 1,1면 2단, "노 캠프 비선 라인 불법 모금; 검찰 2~3개 기업 수십 억대 포착"

11. 10, # 2,4면, "노 캠프 지구당에 수십억 비자금; 민주, 대선자금 의혹 추가 폭로 공세"

11. 10, # 3,5면, "노 대선자금 옥죄는 검; 비선 라인-정대철 모금 두 갈래에 수사 초점 맞춰"

기간 3 (04년 2월 28일자에서 3월 12일자까지)

3. 03, # 4,4면, "대통령 총선 관련 발언 쟁점화; 야 '관권 개입' -- 노 '웬 시비냐'"

3. 04, # 1,1면, "노 선거 중립 의무 위반; 선관위 준수 강력 요청; 사전 선거 운동은 아니다; 야선 탄핵 추진; 정국 대치 심화 예고"

3. 04, # 3,2면상, "사실상 경고, 노 총선 행보 제동; 현직 대통령 선거법 위반 첫 인정 파장"

3. 05, # 1,1면, "민주 '조건부 탄핵' 결의; 청 '이성 잃은 정치 공세'; 선관위 선거중립 겸허한 수용 촉구"

3. 06, # 1,1면, "내일까지 사과 안 하면 노 대통령 탄핵 발의; 민주 강공 -- 한나라 일부 신중론"

3. 09, # 1,1면, "한나라 823억, 노 캠프 113억; 검찰 중간발표 -- 불법모금 '10분의 1' 넘어"

3. 09, # 4,3면, "대선 자금 중간수사 결과 -- 안희정 씨 역할은; 85억 수수 '노 캠프 블랙홀'; 노 캠프 자금 절반 이상 융통 '모금 창구'; '향토 장학금' 발언 등 도덕적 해이 빠져"

3. 10, # 1,1면상 5단, "노 대통령 탄핵안 발의; 한나라-민주의원 159명 서명; 헌정 사상 처음; 내일 표결 시도 -- 우리당 총력 저지 선언; 청와대 '탄핵과정 의연하게 지켜볼 것'"

3. 11, # 5,3면상, "3천만 원 추석선물로 알았다" 노건평 씨 기소 -- 대우건설 사장 연임 청탁받아

〈추가: 다소 부정적(-1) 기사 목록〉

3. 01, # 1,1면, "정치인 2~3명 주중 추가 소환; 검찰 '노-창 처리' 신중 검토"

3. 02, # 2, "돈 받은 지구당 조사 검토; 5대 그룹 중 1곳서 노 캠프에 10억 포착"

3. 03, # 1,1면, "여택수 정 행징관 영장방침; 롯데서 2억 받아; 검 사용처 조사 총선 후로"

3. 03, # 3,3면, "경선 자금 십수억 발언 사실 땐 강 법무 '검찰서 조사' 밝혀; 노, 정자법 위반일 수도"

3. 04, # 2,1면, "안희정 씨 롯데서 6억 받아; 5대 그룹 돈 노측 유입 첫 확인"

3. 04, # 4,2면하, "야 '노 사과하고 선거 손 떼라'; 청 당혹, 우리당 유감; 권력 눈치 보기 선관위도 맹비난"

3. 04, # 5,4면 사설, "측근 비리 끝이 보이지 않는다"

3. 04, # 6,4면상, "노 캠프 불법자금 롯데뿐?; 5대 그룹서 제공 첫 확인 파장; 다른 4대 기업도 '보험금' 제공 의혹; 측근 당선 축하금 수수도 속속 들통"

3. 05, # 4,4면 사설, "노 대통령 선관위 결정 수용해야"

3. 06, # 2,2면, "양날의 칼, 아슬아슬한 탄핵 정국; 갈 데까지 간다, 민주 속전"

3. 08, # 1,4면, "막 가는 탄핵 정국, 긴박한 발의 전야; 사생 결단 기 싸움; 민주 강경 고수 -- 거야에 러브콜"

3. 09, # 3,1면, "건평 씨 전격 소환 조사; 검찰 '민 펀드 사건 무마 청탁 받았는지 추궁; 12시간 조사받고 귀가"

3. 09, # 5,3면, "말문 닫은 청와대"

3. 10, # 2,2면상, "한나라 격론끝 전격 공조 '강수'; 발의-본회의 보고 안팎; 한나라 의결도 가능할 것 자신감; 민주 반색 -- '헌정 수호 행군 시작' "

3. 10, # 7,5면, "대통령은 대의 따라 스스로 판단하길; 노 겨냥한 창 끝; 동반 책임론 거론하며 거센 반격"

3. 10, # 9, "거취 표명 분명히 하라 2야 대선자금 '10분의 1' 발언 노 압박"

3. 12, # 6,4면, "야 불붙는 데 기름 끼얹어"

3. 12, # 7,4면, "그들을 믿는다 -- 제 식구 감싸기; 측근 친인척 비리"

기간 4 (04년 3월 13일자에서 4월 15일자까지)

3. 13, # 1,1면 통단 큰 글씨 제목, "노 대통령 직무 정지; 탄핵 찬 193, 반 2 가결 -- 헌정 사상 초유 사태; 고건 총리 권한 대행 시작; 우리당 의원직 사퇴 결의"

〈추가: 다소 부정적(-1)기사 목록〉

3. 13, # 14,8면, "청 타협 거부 표결 강행 결단; 야 손 들어준 박의장"

3. 13, # 16,10면, "비판 여론 뿌리친 조-홍 찰떡 공조; 초유 사태 성사의 주역"

3. 17, # 1,1면, "2야 탄핵 사유 추가 논란; 총선-재신임 연계 발언, 노사-시위정책 등; 강 법무 발언도 고발 의뢰키로"

3. 25, # 1,1면, " '노 10분의 1 발언 책임져야 ; 한나라 박 대표 단독 인터뷰"

기간 5 (04년 4월 16일자부터 5월 14일자까지)

4. 26, # 1,3면상 칼럼, "여권 왜 이러나; 승리 도취, 개혁 의지 후퇴; '시간은 화살' 할 일 해야"

〈추가: 다소 부정적(-1)기사 목록〉

5. 08, # 2,7면, "6세때 천자문 뗀 노 천재; 김해시 대통령 찬양 만화 5,000부 제작"(-1)

기간 6 (04년 5월 15일자부터 5월 29일자까지)

5. 15, # 6,3면하 3단, "가벼운 노의 입에 따끔한 일침"

5. 25, # 1,1면상 4단, "고 총리 제청 거부 사표; 노 대통령 집권 2기 조기 개각 무산;여권 일부 김혁규 총리 지명 이견도; 향후 정국 운영 구상에 차질 빚을 듯"

5. 25, # 2,3면, "거수기 퇴장 싫다, 반기 들고 떠난 고; 고 총리 각료 제청 고사 배경;명분 유리 판단 노심 외면 정면 돌파; 평소 상식 중시 -- 예상 밖의 강수"

5. 26, # 5,5면상 4단, "개각 자충수, 노도 당도 흔들; 안정적 국정운영 차질 -- 우리당 갈등 불시만 남겨"

5. 26, # 6,13면상 사설, "고 총리의 쓸쓸한 퇴장과 개각"

5. 29, # 2,5면상 3단, "노 대통령 분열적 사고 버려야; 박근혜 대표 '리더십 특강' 강도 높게 비판"

5. 29, # 3,14면 칼럼, "집권 2기 '요란한 빈 수레'"

〈추가: 다소 부정적(-1) 기사 목록〉

5. 18, # 3,5면하 3단, "개혁 빌미 경제위기 애써 외면; 한나라 박대표, 노 대통령 상황 인식 비판"

5. 18, # 4,5면하 2단, "청와대 풀 기자단 취재 차단 '잡음'"

5. 25, # 3,3면, "청와대 -- 이게 아닌데"

5. 25, # 4,3면중, "꼬인 개각 자업자득; 차기 주자 수업용, 자리다툼, 인사원칙 무시; 김혁규 총리 구도도 흔들"

5. 25, # 5,4면상 4단, "야 '청 무리수', 여 '설왕설래' "

5. 27, # 2,4면상 2단, "김혁규 카드 커지는 마찰음; 한나라 청문회 못 견딜 것; 민노당 '개혁 총리 찾아야'; 여 반박 속 일부 반대론도"

5. 29, # 4,5면 사설, "노 대통령 민생현장과 거리 있다"

목록 2: 매우 긍정적 기사(+2) 기사의 제목

기간 1: 03년 2월 26일자에서 3월 25일자까지

2. 26, # 1,1면상 6단, "한반도에 평화 일구자"; 노무현 16대 대통령 취임; 국민통합 도약의 디딤돌로; 민주-균형-평화 3대 국정목표 제시; 동북아 공영 이룩 -- 새 역사 동참 호소

2. 26, # 3,3면상 통단, "노무현 대통령 취임; 반칙, 특권 용납되던 시대는 끝났다"; 국민통합은 이 시대 숙제, 지속 성장 위해 부패 척결; 취임사에 담긴 국정 운영

2. 26, # 5,3면상 기획, "참여정부 출범2; 국정주도 세력의 변화: '뉴스트림' 대부상, 정치 지형 바뀐다"

2. 26, # 6,4면, "노무현 대통령 취임; 여성, 40대 대거 발탁 '파격인사'; 서열-남성 중심 관료사회 물갈이 예고; 교육, 통신, 산자 총리 내정자 입김 작용"

2. 26, # 7,4면, "첫날부터 숨가쁜 4강 외교; 고이즈미에 '적극 역할' 주문; '한-미 이견 대화로 풀 수 있다'; 파월 면담선 양국 입장 조율"

2. 26, # 8,5면, "노무현 대통령 취임; 취임사로 본 경제운용 방향; 지속적 개혁으로 성장동력 창출; '투자하고 싶은 나라' 실현, 동북아 중심국가 발돋움"

2. 26, # 9,5면중 2단, "밤 늦게까지 10여 개 일정 소화 -- 취임 첫날 이모저모"

2. 26, # 10,5면상 2단, "노무현 16대 대통령 취임사(요지); 수많은 도전 극복한

저력으로; 위기를 기회로 만든 지혜로; 마음 합쳐 새 역사를 만들자"

2. 26, # 12,6면하 2단, "퍼스트 레이디 권양숙 여사 -- 친인척 관리에 최우선; 당분간 외부활동 자제, 탁아 등 아동복지 관심" (사진 곁들여)

2. 27, # 1,1면, "북 송금 특검법 국회통과, 총리 임명동의안도 가결; 특검안 민주 불참속 야 단독처리, 고건 총리 찬 163-반 81표로 인준"

2. 27, # 2,1면, "사정 속도 조절 필요 -- 노 대통령 '정권초기 국민 불안감 조성 않는 게 중요'; 첫 수석회의 주재"

2. 27, # 5,4면, 청와대 사정속도 조절론 배경; "혁은 칼 아닌 정책으로" "알아서 긁는 검찰에 경고도"

2. 27, # 6,5면, 노 대통령 공식일정만 16개 -- 취임 이틀째 '바쁘다 바빠'; "집 이 엄청 크더라고요" 첫 수석회의 일성; "북한 핵 해결 잘 도와 달라" 외빈 잇따 라 접견

2. 27, # 7,5면, 참여정부 출범3, 새로운 성장엔진, 과감한 개방경제

2. 28, # 1,1면, "참여정부 첫 내각 출범; 재경 김진표-접무 강금실 -- 교육은 미 정,정 통일 유임 -- 외교 운영관-행자 김두관"

2. 28, # 3,3면, "참여정부 첫 내각 -- 파격 발탁 여럿 -- 공직사회 인사태풍 예 고;힘센 부처 등 여성장관 4명 '성 파괴' -- 평등 실험"

2. 28, # 4,4면, "참여정부 첫 내각 -- 노, '장관 임기 2년 이상 보장' -- 분위기 쇄신용 개각을 않을 것; 교육장관 더 좋은 분 찾고 있다"

2. 28, # 6,4면, "고 총리 2차례 이상 의견 제시 -- 달라진 총리 제정 절차; 노 대통령도 3배수부터 협의; 윤 산자, 최 건교 등 입각시킨 듯"

3. 01, # 1,1면상 4단, "근엄한 장관님? 낡은 틀은 깹시다; 발탁 인사 파격 행보 -- 관료사회 변화 예고"

3. 01, # 2,2면, "인사청탁 용납없다" 노 대동령 형 건평씨 논란 규명 지시, 문 수 석 통해 주의 -- "청탁자 틀림없이 불이익"

3. 01, # 4,4면하 2단, "친인척 관리는 인연 먼 사람에게; 양인석 사정 비서관 인선 화제"

3. 03, # 1,1면, "노, 권력기관 대대적 개혁; 3. 1절 기념사 -- '권력에 아부하는 사람 설 땅 없을 것"

3. 03, # 3,3면, "탈권위 청와대 '국민 곁으로'; 노 입성 1주일 변화의 바람; 백악관 식 '두이(=)' 자 자리 배치; 수석 회의도 토론식 진행; 국정운영 직접 국민에 설명"

3. 03, # 6,5면, "대통령이 여야 중재 팔 걷었다 -- 노, 특검법 중진회담 추진 안팎"

3. 05, # 1,1면하 1단, "노, 언론간섭 않겠다 -- '권력 눈치 보지 말라' 강조"(+1)

3. 05, # 3,3면, "발의-반론-재반론; 3시간 난상토론; 첫 국무회의 안팎; 회의도 중 10분간 휴식도; 최연소 김 행자 인사 깍듯; 실장 등 9명 자리 뒷줄로"

3. 05, # 5,4면하 2단, "노, 중대현안 여야 중진과 직접 대화; 한국 정치 '새 패러다임'; 권위주의 벗고 '상생의 정치' 추진"

3. 07, # 6,5면중 1단, "청남대 '주민 곁으로' -- 노 대통령 지시로 20년 만에"

3. 08, # 1,1면, 노 대통령 "검찰 반발 징계 검토"; 일부 검사 요구 도 넘어 -- 단호 대처 천명

3. 08, # 5, 화난 노 대통령 집단항명에 "NO" -- 검찰 반발에 단호 대처 천명 안팎; "검찰에 신세 지지 않겠다" 취임 후 최고 수위 발언 강 법무엔 '철의 여인' 격려

3. 08, # 6,4면, "참여정부 첫 국정토론회 안팎 -- 각료들에 맡기고 지켜볼 것 -- 국정 이념 공유 위한 '워크숍' -- 38명 참석 -- 노 대통령 '학습 조직 바람직' 노력 당부 -- 진 정통, '국가 발전에 기여하겠다' 의욕"

3. 10, # 2,1면, "검찰 인사 그대로 간다"; 노 대통령 수뇌부 신뢰 못해 -- 총장 인사제청권 거부; 대통령-평검사 40명 헌정사상 첫 공개토론

3. 11, # 2,3면, "검찰총장 내부 승진 '검 신진 대사' -- 노 대통령 개혁 구상 본격화 -- '대폭 물갈이' 의지 굳힌 듯 -- 수뇌부 인사 후 제도 개혁"

3. 13, # 1,1면, "DJ측근까지 철저 조사 -- 노 대통령 '북한 관련 부분은 재협의' -- 특검 조건부 수용 제시 -- 박희태 대행 등 야 지도부와 청와대 회동"

3. 14, # 1,1면, "노-부시 '북핵 평화 해결' -- 첫 전화 회담 -- 이라크 사태 해결 미 노력 지지 -- 노 대통령 이른 시일내 방미 합의"

3. 14, # 4,5면, "노-부시 통화 내용과 담긴 뜻, 대북 공조 틈새 메워, 위기설 진화; 현안 논의 '시의 적절' 평가 -- 이라크전 지원 가시화될 듯"

3. 15, # 1,1면, "북 송금 특검법 공포 -- 노 대통령, 거부권 행사 않고 수사범위 적절히 제한 기대 -- 한 달간 준비 거쳐 내달중순 특검 수사 착수"

3. 15, # 2,2면 사설, "특검 신뢰 바탕 진실 규명을"

3. 15, # 3,3면 해설, "특검법 수용 배경과 정치권 전망 -- '정국 경색 막기' 고난의 선택"

3. 15, # 4,3면, "노 대통령 일문일답 -- 한나라 약속대로 타협안 내놓길"

3. 18, # 1,1면, "양심수 특별 사면 추진 -- 노 대통령, 한총련 등 포함 -- 석가 탄신일 전에; 이적 단체, 노동문제 새로운 접근 필요 -- 장기 수배자, 노동자 등 대거 포함될 듯"

3. 18, # 2,1면, 노 대통령 "언론 지침 부적절"; 문광부 개편안 정부 개입 오해 소지

3. 18, # 7,5면, "청와대 본관 시민에 개방"

3. 19, # 2,5면, "노 대통령 '탈권위' 행보 연일 화제"

3. 20, # 2,4면, "노 대통령 국방위원 14명 불러 만찬 -- '파병하려면 빨리' -- 여도 야도 맞장구 -- 미국식 초청 정치 본격 도입 -- 이라크전 정부 대책 등 대화"

3. 21, # 1,1면, "노 대통령 '국익 고려 미 지지' -- 오늘 임시 각의 소집 파병 동의안 의결" (참고: 미국, 3월 20일, 이라크 공격 개시)

3. 22, # 1,8면, "미 이라크 침공 -- 노, 정치 경제 '밀착 대응 25시'"

3. 22, # 2,8면, "파병-반전 사이 노심 초사 -- 청와대 이라크전 딜레마"

3. 24, # 2,7면, "노 대통령의 역사 바로 세우기 바쁜 행보 -- '정의의 승리 꼭 보여줘야'"

기간 2: 03년 10월 11일자에서 11월 10일자까지

10. 11, # 1,1면 통단제목, "노 대통령 '재신임 묻겠다' -- 문 수석 '국민투표 방법 최우선 검토' -- 내년 총선 전후까지 -- 최도술 씨 의혹 사과"

10. 13, # 8,5면, "재신임 여론 급상승 -- 갈수록 격차 벌어져"

10. 14, # 1,1면, "12월 15일께 재신임 투표 -- 노 대통령 시정 연설 -- 정책과 연계 안 해"

10. 21, # 1,1면, "다자 문서로 북 안전보장 -- 한미 정상회담 -- 미 대북 정책 전환 시사 주목 -- 부시 '미군 감축 결정내린 바 없다' -- 한일 정상 연내 FTA 교섭"

10. 21, # 3,3면, "부시 노 대통령은 미의 친구이자 나의 친구 -- 연설 잘했다고 높이 평가"

10. 24, # 1,1면, "노 재신임 시기 조정 용의 -- 대선 자금도 4당 대표와 논의키로"

11. 05, # 1,5면, "노, 통신-방송사 국장 만찬; 정부-언론 갈등 접고 협력해야"

기간 3: 04년 2월 28일자에서 3월 12일자까지

3. 02, # 1,1면 4단, "한국민 상처주는 발언 말라; 노 대통령 3-1절 기념사; 일 총리 '신사 참배' 경고; 독립 유공자-후손 처우 개선도 다짐"

3. 02, # 3,2면 머리, "거꾸로 가는 일본에 No 일침: 노 대통령 3-1절 기념사 의미- 안팎; 일 총리 직접 겨냥 '노무현식 역사 세우기'; 측근들도 모른 원고 직접 수정, 강한 의지"

3. 08, # 2,4면, "청 '대통령 그만둬도 굴복 없다'; 우리당 '국익에 정면 위배' 불가 홍보전"

3. 11, # 2,1면, "재신임, 총선으로 심판 받겠다; 노 대통령 오늘 회견 –– 탄핵 횡포에 굴복 안해"

기간 4: 04년 3월 13일자에서 4월 15일자까지

3. 13, # 3,2면상, 대형사설: "나라꼴 왜 이 지경 됐나; 다수당의 횡포, 의회의 폭거, 국정 표류 막아야"

3. 13, # 9,5면, "전국 곳곳 '탄핵 불복종' 촛불 행렬; 주부까지 동참 –– 저항운동 거센 불길; 시민단체 '제2의 6월항쟁 나설 터'"

3. 13, # 11,7면, "노 '몇 달 뒤 국민 앞에 다시 서게 되길'; 대통령의 길었던 하루" *매우 친밀한 묘사

3. 13, # 17,12면 전체 화보, "국민은 없었다 –– 허탈, 분노 충격; 통곡, 소리 없는 울분; 국회는 죽었다" *노 대통령을 간접 지지

3. 14, # 1,1면, "탄핵 무효 '국민저항' 확산; 어제 광화문 촛불 집회 7만여 명 참가; 부산 경성대 교수 56명 동참 결의"

3. 14, # 5,3면, 직무 정지 첫날; 노 대통령 "그래도 역사는 앞으로 간다" 정 의장 전화받고 "가슴 아픈 일"; 평소처럼 기상 대처 전기 탐독

3. 14, # 7,5면, "질의 토론 없는 탄핵안 표결 위법; 의장 본회의 개의시간 변경도 잘못; 법조계선 소추의결서상 오류 지적; 국회법상 질의 규정 없다"

3. 14, # 11,9면 2/3 크기 사설 "국민의 분노는 정당하다"

3. 15, # 1,1면, "지지율 급락에 야권 비상; 탄핵 역풍 총선구도 급변 –– 친노 반

노로 재편; 민주 지도부 사퇴 요구 내분 재연; 한나라 일각 총선 연기, 개헌론"

3. 18, # 1,1면, "야 3당 비현역 공천자 '탄핵 잘된 일' 39%뿐"

3. 22, # 5,4면상, 노 대통령 "재신임—우리 입당 난감"; 탄핵국면 운신폭 좁아 —— 대 국민 약속 신의 고민 *인간적 묘사

3. 29, # 1,1면, "촛불을 끄다; 16일 동안 전국 곳곳 150만 참여; '탄핵 무효' 평화 시위 새 장 열여"

4. 12, # 1,1면하 2단, "노 대통령 '총선 후 통합 정치'; 부패—지역 정치 해소 —— 대결서 대화로"

4. 12, # 2,2면하, "탄핵—총선 심판에 춘사불사춘"; 노 대통령 정치 달라질 것 심경변화 시사

기간 5: 04년 4월 16일자부터 5월 14일자까지

4. 16, # 1,1면하, 김종필 조순형 낙선; 홍사덕 박상천 추미애 등 탄핵주도 중진 쓴 잔

4. 16, # 2,2면상 5단, "4-15 선택 '탄핵 역풍'이 만든 여대 야소"

4. 16, # 3,6면상 통단제목, 4-15선택 "거여 업은 노 대통령 상생의 정치 탄력 받아"

4. 16, # 5,9면상, 선거 혁명; 물갈이폭 사상최대 4-15 선택 탄핵 태풍에 현역당선 비율 37%에 불과; 3김세대 안전 퇴장 '젊은정치' 활짝

4. 21, # 1,1면상 5단, "노 총선결과 재신임 간주"

5. 03, # 1,1면상 4단, "이달 하순 6~8개 부처 개각; 정동영, 김근태 동반 입각 가능성; 김혁규 씨 차기 총리 사실상 내성; 동일 국빙 행자부 등 교체 대상"

5. 03, # 2,3면상, "강한 내각 포석, 당 수뇌 '앞으로'; 윤곽 드러나는 내각—비서실 개편; 정—김 동반 입각 '차기' 관리 기회 제공; 청, 사회수석 신설 등 참모 기능 강화"

5. 07, # 1,1면상, "김혁규 씨 총리 지명 불변; 노 대통령 정동영—김근태 씨 동반 입각 정리; 노 대통령 5일 여 지도부와 극비 회동; 내달 20일께 개각 단행 뜻 밝혀"

기간6:04년 5월 15일자부터 5월 29일자까지

5. 15, # 1,1면상 6단, "탄핵 기각 –– 노 대통령 직무 복귀; 헌재 '일부 선거법 위반했으나 파면 중대 사유 안 돼'; 재판관 3명 소수 의견설 –– 공개는 안 해"

5. 15, # 10,5면하, "비서실 직원 박수로 '복귀 세리머니'; 청화대 표정"

5. 15, # 14,8면중 3단, "고향 김해 봉하 마을 –– 태극기 휘날리며 '만세' 환호성"

5. 17, # 1,1면하 3단, "노, 집권 2기 경제 개혁 주력; 오늘 경제 장관 간담회; 고위 당정 부활 –– 여야정 회의 검토"

5. 21, # 1,1면중 2단, "협력적 자주 국방 조기에 구축하라; 노 대통령 안보장관 회의서 지시"

5. 21, # 5,13면 사설 "노 대통령의 입당과 여당의 책임"

PRESIDENTIAL COMMUNICATION AND NEWS MEDIA

How Do News Media Flatter Or Criticize The President?

대통령과 언론, 친구인가 적인가

초판 1쇄 발행 2005년 1월 10일

지은이 설원태
디자인 조희정
편집 윤남희
발행 (주)엔북

(주)엔북

우)110-280 서울 마포구 상수동 341-9 보림빌딩 B동 4층
http://www.nbook.seoul.kr
전화 02-334-6721~2
팩스 02-332-6720
메일 goodbook@nbook.seoul.kr

신고 제300-2003-161
ISBN 89-89683-33-5 03070

값 15,000원